Case, Agreement, and their Interactions

Linguistische Arbeiten

Edited by
Klaus von Heusinger, Agnes Jäger,
Gereon Müller, Ingo Plag,
Elisabeth Stark und Richard Wiese

Volume 572

Case, Agreement, and their Interactions

—

New Perspectives on Differential Argument Marking

Edited by
András Bárány and Laura Kalin

DE GRUYTER

ISBN 978-3-11-099238-0
e-ISBN (PDF) 978-3-11-066613-7
e-ISBN (EPUB) 978-3-11-066623-6
ISSN 0344-6727

Library of Congress Control Number: 2020939064

Bibliographic information published by the Deutsche Nationalbibliothek
The Deutsche Nationalbibliothek lists this publication in the Deutsche Nationalbibliografie;
detailed bibliographic data are available on the Internet at http://dnb.dnb.de.

© 2022 Walter de Gruyter GmbH, Berlin/Boston
This volume is text- and page-identical with the hardback published in 2020.
Printing and binding: CPI books GmbH, Leck

www.degruyter.com

Contents

List of abbreviations —— VII

Preface and acknowledgements —— IX

András Bárány and Laura Kalin
Introduction —— 1

Gereon Müller
Cumulative effects in differential argument encoding and long-distance extraction —— 27

Monica Alexandrina Irimia
Types of structural objects —— 77

Jaklin Kornfilt
DOM and DSM in Turkish —— 127

Vassilios Spyropoulos
Abstract and morphological case in a nominative–accusative system with differential case marking —— 175

M. Rita Manzini, Leonardo Savoia, and Ludovico Franco
DOM and dative in (Italo-)Romance —— 219

Pei-Jung Kuo
Topicality and differential object marking in Mandarin Chinese: Identity and variety in an array of structures —— 269

Elsi Kaiser, Merilin Miljan, and Virve Vihman
Estonian speakers' representation of morphological case —— 301

Index —— 349

List of abbreviations

1	first person	INF	infinitive
2	second person	IO	indirect object
3	third person	IPFV	imperfective
ABL	ablative	L	L-suffix (Senaya)
ABS	absolutive	LE	linguistic expression
ACC	accusative	LFG	Lexical-Functional Grammar
ADE	adessive	LK	linker
ALL	allative	LOC	locative
AN	action nominal	M	masculine
AOR	aorist	MP	middle-passive
ASP	aspect	MS	morphological structure
AUG	augmented	N	neuter
AUX	auxiliary	NEG	negative
CAUS	causative	NFN	non-factive nominalization
CL	clitic	NMLZ	nominalizer, nominalization
CLF	classifier	NOM	nominative
COM	comitative	OBJ	object
DAM	differential argument marking	OT	Optimality Theory
DAT	dative	PART	partitive
DCM	differential case marking	PASS	passive
DEF	definite	PCC	person case constraint
DEM	demonstrative	PF	phonological form
DFLT	default	PFV	perfective
DO	direct object	PL	plural
DOM	differential object marking	PRF	perfect
DSM	differential subject marking	PROG	progressive
EA	external argument	PRON	pronoun
ECM	exceptional case marking	PRS	present
ELA	elative	PST	past
EPP	extended projection principle	PTCL	particle
ERG	ergative	PTCP	participle
EXCL	exclamative	Q	question particle
F	feminine	REFL	reflexive
FN	factive nominalization	S	S-suffix (Senaya)
GEN	genitive	SBJ	subject
GER	gerund	SBJV	subjunctive
HAB	habitual aspect	SC	small clause
ILL	illative	SG	singular
IMP	imperative	TOP	topic
IND	indicative	TR	transitive
INDEF	indefinite	TRANSL	translative
INE	inessive		

Preface and acknowledgements

This edited volume is the result of a productive themed session on Differential Object Marking held at the 2015 Annual Meeting of the Societas Linguistica Europaea at Leiden University in The Netherlands.

The session brought together experts from different fields, including experimental syntax, theoretical syntax, comparative syntax, typology, corpus linguistics, semantics, and pragmatics, and different theoretical frameworks, including Minimalism, Optimality Theory, and Role and Reference Grammar, for an exchange of ideas and proposals across these boundaries. The two-day event also saw an incredible diversity of languages, including novel observations across many language families: Estonian, Finnish, and Hungarian (Uralic), Spanish and Romanian (Romance), Greek (Hellenic), Senaya (Semitic), Turkish (Altaic), Mandarin Chinese (Sinitic), and several Bantu languages. Across these diverse frameworks, subfields, methodologies, and languages, participants presented cutting edge linguistic research, relating to and expanding on recent developments in syntax and morphology.

We are very grateful to all the authors who submitted their work to this volume, as well as to the reviewers, whose time, energy, and thoughtful feedback greatly improved the chapters within. For comments on the introductory chapter in particular, we'd like to thank Stefan Keine and Philipp Weisser, and for careful proofreading of the whole volume, we thank Kelsey Kraus.

András Bárány and Laura Kalin
Introduction

Abstract: Our introduction to this volume provides an empirical overview of the phenomenon of DOM, Section 1, a theoretical overview of approaches to modeling and understanding DOM, Section 2, a deeper look at some of the challenges that the data pose for a unified approach to DOM, Section 3, and finally, a preview of the contributions to this volume, Section 4.

Keywords: Case and agreement, differential object marking, differential subject marking, licensing, dependent case

1 What is differential object marking?

Differential object marking (DOM) is a widespread linguistic phenomenon that (canonically) divides objects into two classes—a class that is overtly marked and a class that is not overtly marked (Comrie 1979, Croft 1988, Bossong 1991, Enç 1991, de Hoop 1996, Torrego 1998, Woolford 1999, Aissen 2003, de Swart 2007, Dalrymple & Nikolaeva 2011, Witzlack-Makarevich & Seržant 2018, *i.a.*).[1] Canonical DOM involves a two-way contrast in case marking on direct objects, as in (1)—the object may be morphologically unmarked, (1a), or bear an overt case marker, (1b).

(1) DOM in Hindi (Bhatt 2007)

    a. *Mina   ek   bacca uṭhaa rahii   hai.*
       Mina.F a/one child lift   PROG.F be.PRS.3SG
       'Mina is picking up a child.'

    b. *Mina   ek   bacce-**ko** uṭhaa rahii   hai.*
       Mina.F a/one child-**DAT** lift   PROG.F be.PRS.3SG
       'Mina is picking up a particular child.'

---

[1] Note that our use of the terms "marked, marking" (etc.) throughout this chapter refers to overt morphological marking, not to "markedness".

András Bárány, Leiden University
Laura Kalin, Princeton University

https://doi.org/10.1515/9783110666137-001

In (1) in Hindi, it is the *specificity* of the object that determines whether it is casemarked or not: non-specific nominals are not marked, (1a), while specific nominals are, (1b).[2]

Another hallmark of DOM, also exemplified by Hindi, is that the "accusative" case marking on marked direct objects is often syncretic with the morphological dative case on indirect objects; this is represented in our gloss of -*ko* as DAT in (1b). It is a matter of debate whether this syncretism is due to a morphological factor or whether marked direct objects are indeed licensed syntactically in the same way as dative indirect objects are (see, e.g., Bossong 1991, Manzini & Franco 2016, Bárány 2018, Kalin 2018)—in the present volume this question is addressed by the contribution of Rita Manzini, Leonardo Savoia, and Ludovico Franco. Finally, there are some instances of DOM where direct objects alternate between two marked forms, rather than a marked and unmarked form; we will see such a case in (7) below.

1.1 Factors triggering DOM

DOM may be triggered by factors relating to definiteness, animacy, affectedness, and information structure, often with more than one factor coming into play. These factors can be modeled in scales, (2):

(2) a. **Animacy/person** (Silverstein 1976, Croft 1988, Comrie 1989, *i.a.*)
   1/2 > 3 Pronoun > Name > Human > Animate > Inanimate

   b. **Specificity/definiteness** (Silverstein 1976, Croft 1988, Comrie 1989, *i.a.*)
   Pronoun > Name > Definite > Specific Indefinite > Non-specific

   c. **Information structure**[3] (Dalrymple & Nikolaeva 2011)
   Topic > Non-topic

   d. **Affectedness** (Næss 2004)
   Affected > Unaffected

---

2 Depending on the particular dialect in question, animacy may also play a role in DOM in Hindi. For a detailed review of the diachrony and synchrony of DOM in Hindi, see Montaut (2018).

It is generally objects on the left side of the scale (the "more prominent" objects) that are overtly marked. But languages differ as to which scale(s) factor into the differentiation of objects, as well as where along the scale(s) the marked/unmarked cut off is made. DOM may also be cumulative, in the sense that only objects that have two (or more) certain characteristics are marked, where these characteristics on their own would not be enough to trigger DOM. Cumulative DOM is addressed in Gereon Müller's chapter in this volume.

1.2 Surface realizations of DOM

While DOM is often taken to be descriptively limited to case marking, a number of other morphological phenomena also target objects and are sensitive to the same factors and scales as differential case marking. For example, DOM based on specificity is found taking the form of (i) case, as in Hindi, (1), and Turkish, (3); (ii) agreement, as in Senaya (Semitic; Iran), (4); (iii) clitic doubling, as in Amharic (Semitic; Ethiopia), (5); and (iv) an adposition, as in Spanish, (6).

(3) DOM as case marking in Turkish (Kornfilt 2008: 81)

    a. *(Ben) bir kitap oku-du-m.*
        I   a   book read-PST-1SG
        'I read a book.' (non-specific)

    b. *(Ben) bir kitab-ı oku-du-m.*
        I   a   book-ACC read-PST-1SG
        'I read a certain book.' (specific)

---

[3] Woolford (1999) reports that focus (rather than topichood) factors into DOM in Ruwund, where DOM is determined by a complex interaction of factors involving animacy, specificity, and theta role, in addition to focus. Since focus seems to be a much rarer factor in DOM, we take the information structure scale in (2c) to be the relevant one for information-structure-related DOM more generally.

(4) DOM as agreement marking in Senaya (Kalin 2018: 119)

    a. *Āna ksūta kasw-an.*
       I   book.F write.IPFV-SBJ.1SG.F
       'I (will) write a/some book.' (non-specific)

    b. *Āna ō ksūta kasw-an-ā.*
       I that book.F write.IPFV-SBJ.1SG.F-**OBJ.3SG.F**
       'I (will) write that book.' (specific)

(5) DOM as case marking and clitic doubling in Amharic (Kramer 2014: 601)

    a. *Almaz doro wät' bäll-atʃtʃ*
       Almaz.F chicken stew eat-SBJ.3SG.F
       'Almaz ate chicken stew.' (non-specific)

    b. *Almaz doro wät'-u-**n** bäll-atʃtʃ-**ɨw***
       Almaz.F chicken stew-DEF.M-**ACC** eat-SBJ.3SG.F-**OBJ.3SG.M**
       'Almaz ate the chicken stew.' (specific)

(6) DOM as an adposition in Spanish (Rodríguez-Mondoñedo 2007: 16)

    a. *Besó una mujer.*
       kiss.PST.3SG a woman
       'He kissed a woman.' (non-specific)

    b. *Besó **a** una mujer.*
       kiss.PST.3SG **DAT** a woman
       'He kissed a (certain) woman.' (specific)

In addition to the marked/unmarked patterns in (3)–(6), DOM can also appear as an alternation of different overt exponents, for example in Kolyma Yukaghir (Samoyedic; Russia), where the exponent of ACC depends on the person of both the subject and the object (Maslova 2003, Keine 2010).

(7) DOM with multiple exponents in Kolyma Yukaghir (Maslova 2003: 95, 93)

    a. *Met-**ul** amde-l-get polde-mek.*
       me-**ACC** die.PFV-AN-ABL save-TR.2SG
       'You have saved me from death.'

    b. *Tet kimnī met-**kele** kudede-m.*
       your whip me-**ACC** kill-TR.3SG
       'Your whip has killed me.'

DOM is extremely common crosslinguistically. In fact, among languages that have object marking of some kind, it is more likely for that marking to be differential than uniform (Sinnemäki 2014).

In sum, DOM is a robustly-attested crosslinguistic phenomenon whereby direct objects with features high on certain scales are differentiated from objects with features low on those scales through the appearance of an overt marker. The main challenge faced by accounts of DOM is, of course, unifying the diverse characteristics of DOM while still allowing for the observed variation.

2 Why are objects marked differentially?

The cross-linguistic prevalence of DOM and its largely uniform behavior is often taken to call out for a deep explanation. Accounts of DOM vary widely, though a number of repeating themes can be found across these diverse analyses:
- DOM is the result of pressure to differentiate two nominals, either because of their structural proximity to each other or their functional proximity
- DOM encodes the (a)typicality of NPs in certain thematic/structural positions
- DOM reflects relative featural prominence and/or relative syntactic height
- DOM exists because some objects need special licensing
- DOM is at least in part a surface morphological phenomenon, not necessarily transparently corresponding to any deep syntactic differences

Many approaches to DOM draw on one or more of the themes above in building a complete analysis. Bárány (2017), for example, approaches differential agreement in Hungarian in the following terms: objects that do not trigger agreement are licensed just like those that do trigger agreement; the agreement is a surface-level phenomenon that results from certain objects carrying more features than others.

In this section, we briefly cover what we take to be the major different approaches to understanding and modeling DOM.

2.1 Functional approaches

In the functional/typological literature, DOM is typically explained in terms of case marking having two interacting functions, both of which favor the overt marking of "prominent" (more animate, more definite) objects (Silverstein 1976, Hopper & Thompson 1980, Bossong 1985, 1991, Croft 1988, Comrie 1989, Croft 2003,

Næss 2004, *i.a.*). These accounts thus rely most heavily on the themes of differentiation and atypicality.

Such functional/typological explanations typically start from the basic assumption that subjects are canonically more prominent than objects. Next, it is proposed that (overt) case marking surfaces for two primary functional reasons. First is the disambiguating/discriminating function: case serves to distinguish the subject from the object. In a "canonical" transitive, there will be an animate/definite subject and an inanimate/indefinite object, such that disambiguation is easy even without overt marking. However, when an object is prominent (e.g., definite, animate), it is more similar to a subject, and so the disambiguating function will drive overt case marking of the object in such instances. The second function of case marking is the identifying/indexing function: case serves to identify certain semantic roles. The way this brings about DOM is that when the object is prominent, it is (typically) semantically more affected than a non-prominent object. The identifying function can thus drive case marking of an affected object. Both functions motivate DOM across languages, though different languages may make the prominent/non-prominent cut-off in different places, may care more about one functional factor, and may place different amounts of weight on the different scales discussed in Section 1.1. Additionally, disambiguation can operate "locally" (taking into account only the object) or "globally" (taking into account the relative prominence of the subject and object).

This kind of functional approach has been formalized in generative frameworks, most notably in Optimality-Theoretic analyses (see Section 2.2), but it has also been argued that the extra-linguistic motivation for a functional analysis of DOM is strong enough to make grammatical or syntactic analyses unnecessary (see Haspelmath 2008, 2009, for example).

2.2 Optimality-based approaches

Optimality-Theoretic (OT) approaches to DOM have surfaced as a tool to investigate and predict DOM patterns based on the disambiguating and identifying functions (both locally and globally). OT is particularly useful on this front because it is able to model variation through constraint re-ranking as well as capture the effects of universal prominence scales. The intuition behind OT (Prince & Smolensky 1993) is that multiple possible surface forms (candidates) compete with each other for realization; this competition is regulated by constraints on well-formed surface forms, which penalize candidates that are not "optimal" in some way. Constraints are ranked: violating high-ranked constraints is worse than violating low-ranked constraints. A particular candidate will "win" (will be the grammatical surface form) just in case every other candidate violates some higher-ranked constraint (or violates a particular constraint more times) than the winner does.

Perhaps the most influential OT account of DOM is that of Aissen (2003). Aissen proposes a hierarchy of markedness constraints that target objects, (8), with the relevant constraints formed by local conjunction of (i) a markedness constraint penalizing the lack of case, $*\emptyset_C$, with (ii) a subhierarchy of markedness constraints penalizing prominent objects, e.g., *Object/Pronoun. The former constraint says (essentially) "don't be a nominal that lacks case", while the latter says "don't be a nominal of type X and be an object"; when conjoined, these constraints say something like "don't be an object of type X and lack case." In accordance with the disambiguating and identifying functions, it is worse to be an object that is high in prominence (e.g., pronominal, definite) and lack case than it is to be an object that is low in prominence and lack case.

(8) a. *Object/Pronoun & $*\emptyset_C$ >>   (= *pronominal object lacking case)
    b. *Object/Name & $*\emptyset_C$ >>   (= *proper name object lacking case)
    c. *Object/Definite & $*\emptyset_C$ >>   (= *definite object lacking case)
    d. *Object/Specific & $*\emptyset_C$ >>   (= *specific object lacking case)
    e. *Object/Non-specific & $*\emptyset_C$ (= *non-specific object lacking case)

If these were the only constraints, then all objects would be case marked, since all of the constraints in (8) penalize objects that *lack* case marking. There is thus also an economy constraint that penalizes the *presence* of case marking, (9) ("don't have case").

(9) *STRUC$_C$ (= *having a case value)

This economy constraint can be ranked in any place within or at the edges of the fixed ordering of the constraints in (8). Note that any given object will necessarily violate one of the constraints in (8) or the constraint in (9), since every object must either have case (violating (9)) or not have case (violating one of the constraints in (8)).

Depending on where *STRUC$_C$ is ranked within (8), different patterns of DOM will emerge. For example, *STRUC$_C$ could be ranked immediately below *Object/Pronoun & $*\emptyset_C$, as in (10).

(10) a. *Object/Pronoun & *Ø$_C$ >>   (= *pronominal object lacking case)
     b. *STRUC$_C$ >>   (= *having a case value)
     c. *Object/Name & *Ø$_C$ >>   (= *proper name object lacking case)
     d. *Object/Definite & *Ø$_C$ >>   (= *definite object lacking case)
     e. *Object/Specific & *Ø$_C$ >>   (= *specific object lacking case)
     f. *Object/Non-specific & *Ø$_C$ (= *non-specific object lacking case)

In this system, only pronominal objects will be case marked. This is because of how the competition will play out. First, imagine two candidates that are both pronominal objects, one of which has case and one of which doesn't. The case-marked pronominal object will violate the constraint *STRUC$_C$, but it will not violate the higher-ranked constraint *Object/Pronoun & *Ø$_C$. The competitor, the non-case-marked pronominal object, will violate the higher-ranked constraint, *Object/Pronoun & *Ø$_C$, but not the lower one, *STRUC$_C$. Since the non-case-marked pronominal object violates the higher-ranked of the two constraints, it will lose out to the case-marked pronominal object; thus, all object pronouns will be case-marked in this system. Next, consider proper names in the same scenario. A case-marked proper name will violate *STRUC$_C$ but not *Object/Name & *Ø$_C$. A proper name without case marking will not violate *STRUC$_C$, but will violate *Object/Name & *Ø$_C$. Since the higher-ranked constraint here is *STRUC$_C$, case-marked proper names lose out against those without case marking.

A number of OT accounts of DOM have followed in the spirit of Aissen (2003), modifying certain aspects of the basic intuition by taking the addressee's expectations into account as well; see, e.g., de Swart (2007), de Hoop & Malchukov (2007).

2.3 Morphological approaches

A different approach to modeling DOM capitalizes on the idea that DOM is principally a surface-level phenomenon. The general idea behind morphological approaches to DOM is that all direct objects have abstract accusative "capital-C Case", but this uniform abstract Case might not be *realized* uniformly (or even overtly). As a starting point, most morphological approaches to DOM model case not as an atomic entity but as a bundle of features, with different exponents (i.e., surface morphological case forms) spelling out different combinations of features. If accusative Case is a certain bundle of features, one could imagine this bundle being altered in some way before an exponent is chosen, e.g., some feature(s) might be "frozen" (Glushan 2010) or deleted (Keine & Müller 2008, Keine 2010).

To take a concrete example, Keine & Müller (2008) and Keine (2010) take DOM to result from the interaction of Case feature bundles with morphological impoverishment (deletion) rules. The application of impoverishment rules is in turn triggered by an interaction of markedness and faithfulness constraints (cf. the discussion in Section 2.2 above). Unlike Aissen-style OT accounts, in which constraint rankings block or allow case assignment/marking, these accounts use a language's constraint ranking to determine when an impoverishment rule does or does not apply.

Let's see this at work for Hindi, in which (as exemplified in (1)) specificity determines whether the DOM-marker -*ko* appears. The verb in Hindi generally assigns accusative Case to all objects and this accusative Case feature bundle—consisting of the (hypothetical) features [F1] and [F2] below, (11a)—is generally spelled out as -*ko*, (12b). But, there is a markedness constraint penalizing one of the features in the accusative feature bundle, and this constraint is ranked above the faithfulness constraint that says that Case features for inanimate and non-specific objects should not be deleted. Thus, if the object is non-specific, an impoverishment rule, (11b), deletes the offending feature in the accusative feature bundle, as illustrated in (11c).[4]

(11) a. $\text{ACC} = \begin{bmatrix} \text{F1} \\ \text{F2} \end{bmatrix}$

　　b. $[\text{F2}] \rightarrow \emptyset / \_\_ [-\text{SPEC}]$

　　c.
$$\underset{\begin{bmatrix} -\text{SPEC} \\ \text{CASE} \begin{bmatrix} \text{F1} \\ \text{F2} \end{bmatrix} \end{bmatrix}}{\text{DP}} \xrightarrow{\text{Impoverishment (10b)}} \underset{\begin{bmatrix} -\text{SPEC} \\ \text{CASE} \begin{bmatrix} \text{F1} \end{bmatrix} \end{bmatrix}}{\text{DP}}$$

The non-specific DP in (11c) thus ends up with a single Case feature, [F1]. The exponents of Case features are then determined by Vocabulary Insertion rules like those in (12). Note that nominative Case in Hindi is null, and so we assume here that the null spell-out of both nominative Case and impoverished accusative Case can be unified as a null spell-out of [F1].

---

4 The rule in (11) is similar to the one in Keine & Müller (2008: 101, (19c)), which also includes reference to a [−HUMAN] feature. There seems to be dialect variation in Hindi with respect to whether human objects must always be marked with -*ko* in or not; cf. (1) above.

(12) a. NOM: $[\text{F1}] \leftrightarrow \text{-}\emptyset$

b. ACC: $\begin{bmatrix} \text{F1} \\ \text{F2} \end{bmatrix} \leftrightarrow \text{-}ko$

The impoverishment rule in (11b) and the spell-out rules in (12) give rise to the correct result: specific noun phrases retain their (canonical) case marker, while non-specific noun phrases appear without case marking, because they no longer fit the description for the insertion of the overt exponent -*ko*.

Note that morphological approaches that manipulate feature bundles can help us model DOM systems where the alternation is not between having an exponent and not having an exponent, but rather between two (or more) exponents, like in the Samoyedic languages Tundra Yukaghir (Matić 2019) and Kolyma Yukaghir (Maslova 2003, Keine 2010), as illustrated in (7) above. Morphological approaches also straightforwardly model syncretism between, for example, dative case and the marked accusative case. In the Hindi account above, if the dative Case feature bundle contains [F1] and [F2] (and there is no relevant vocabulary item more specific than (12b)), then this feature bundle will also receive the -*ko* exponent. (See Vassilios Spyropoulos' contribution to this volume for another impoverishment-based approach to DOM; and see Elsi Kaiser, Merilin Miljan and Virve Vihman's chapter, which argues that morphological case plays quite a different role in the derivation.)

Morphological approaches imply a slightly different perspective from functional approaches to DOM: rather than triggering case marking on atypical objects, the impoverishment approach conspires against case marking while holding that objects typically do have Case. In other words, the default on the impoverishment approach is that objects have Case but markedness results in this Case not being realized on the surface. On most functional approaches, the default assumption is that objects are *not* case-marked, but markedness can lead to the addition of case marking. The results are largely the same for both types of approaches.

2.4 Syntactic approaches

We now turn to a completely different sort of approach to DOM, one that picks up on the themes of (relative) syntactic position and/or syntactic licensing. There are quite a number of different syntactic approaches to DOM, but there are three recurring ingredients: (i) object movement, (ii) object size, and (iii) object licensing. We will discuss each ingredient in turn, though it is important to note that many accounts appeal to more than one of these ingredients to derive DOM.

The first common core ingredient to syntactic approaches to DOM is movement. The idea here is that marked objects raise out of VP, while unmarked objects do not, (13) (Bhatt & Anagnostopoulou 1996, de Hoop 1996, Torrego 1998, Woolford 1999, Bhatt 2007, Baker & Vinokurova 2010, Rodríguez-Mondoñedo 2007, N. Richards 2010, Ormazabal & Romero 2013, Baker 2014, *i.a.*).

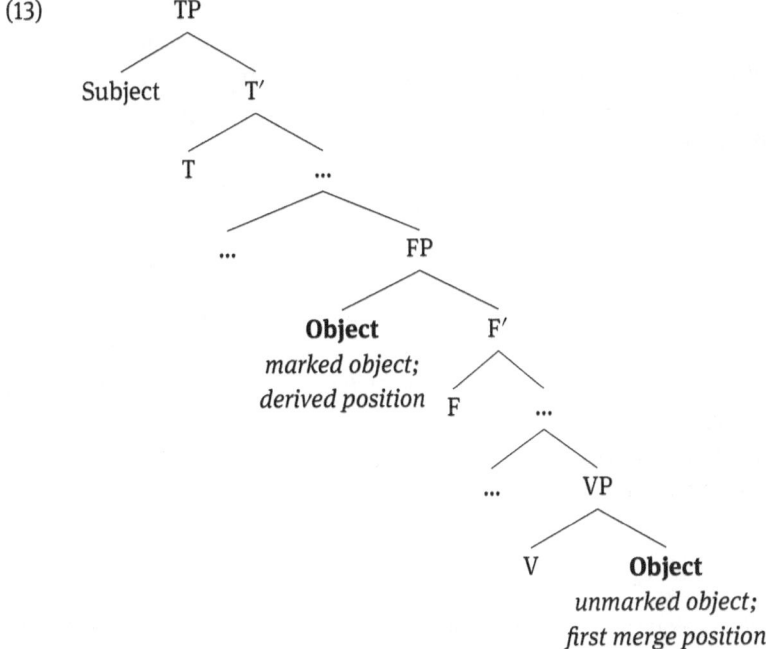

The higher position of the object may result in Case assignment/case marking because of locality with a higher case-assigner (e.g., Woolford 1999, Rodríguez-Mondoñedo 2007, López 2012) or locality with another argument, enabling so-called "dependent" case (e.g., Baker & Vinokurova 2010, Baker 2014, 2015, Levin & Preminger 2015; see also Section 3.3 and Jaklin Kornfilt, this volume) or resulting in the spell-out of the object as a phase in order to remain distinct from the subject (N. Richards 2010).

The second common ingredient in syntactic DOM accounts is a difference in structural size, (14), leading to a *visible-for-case vs. invisible-for-case* distinction between marked and unmarked objects, respectively (Massam 2001, Danon 2006, Lidz 2006, Rodríguez-Mondoñedo 2007, M. Richards 2008, López 2012, Lyutikova & Pereltsvaig 2015, Bárány 2017, *i.a.*).

(14)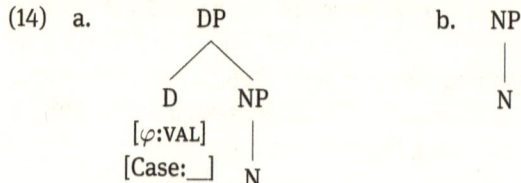

Objects lacking certain features and/or structure, (14b), are not visible to Case or agreement processes, and so remain unmarked, while objects with the relevant features and/or structure, (14a), are visible, and so do participate in Case and agreement processes.

The final ingredient in many syntactic DOM accounts is a difference in licensing between marked and unmarked objects: marked objects need (special) licensing, while unmarked objects do not. (Monica Irimia's contribution to this volume speaks to this point.) Licensing may correlate with an object having a larger structure (and thus bearing a Case feature, (14a)), and/or with an object needing to raise in order to get Case, (13), or even just some objects needing to be semantically licensed outside VP (à la Diesing 1992). Some accounts hold that objects that are unmarked are in fact unlicensed (Massam 2001, Danon 2006, Ormazabal & Romero 2013, Kalin 2018, *i.a.*), while others take unmarked objects to need some sort of licensing apart from normal Case (Baker 1988, de Hoop 1996, Baker & Vinokurova 2010 *i.a.*). Yet others assume there is a Case with a null exponent that suffices to license such objects (Laka 1993, Bhatt 2007, Rodríguez-Mondoñedo 2007, *i.a.*).

Syntactic accounts of DOM thus appeal to an interplay among raising (only marked objects raise), visibility (only marked objects are visible to Case and agreement processes), and licensing (only marked objects need Case licensing).

2.5 Information structure approaches

DOM based on both information structure and affectedness pose a challenge for the aforementioned accounts of DOM, since discourse role and degree of affectedness are not properties of the object in isolation, but rather depend on the discourse and the predicate (respectively; see e.g. von Heusinger 2008 on the influence of the latter). Here, we will focus on the role of information structure; for affectedness, see Næss (2004). For a number of languages, it has been argued that information structure determines differential case marking or differential agreement, at least in part (cf. Leonetti 2004, 2008 on Spanish, Indo-European, Nikolaeva 1999, 2001 on Khanty, Virtanen 2015 on Mansi, both Uralic, and Dalrymple & Nikolaeva 2011 on a range of other languages).

DOM based on information structure differs from the types discussed above in that the discourse context plays an essential role in determining whether an argument is differentially marked or not, in addition to or instead of other syntactic properties of a sentence. Context can thus be the only variable distinguishing minimal pairs from each other,[5] as illustrated with the following examples from Tundra Nenets (Uralic, Samoyedic; ° is the transcription of an extra-short schwa).

(15) Tundra Nenets (Nikolaeva 2014: 206)

Context: *Whom did he hit?*
Wera-m   ladə°   / # ladº°ə-da.
Wera-ACC hit.3SG.SBJ   hit-3SG.SBJ>SG.OBJ
'He hit Wera.'

A felicitous answer to the question in (15) has narrow focus on the direct object. In this scenario, Tundra Nenets allows the verb form *ladə°* 'hit.3SG', which only agrees with the subject. The form *ladə°-da* 'hit-3SG.SBJ>SG.OBJ', which also agrees with the object in number, is infelicitous in this context. Conversely, if a context establishes a topical direct object, object agreement is required:

(16) Tundra Nenets (Dalrymple & Nikolaeva 2011: 128)

Context: *What did a/the man do to the/a reindeer?*
xasawa ti-m   xadaº-da   / # xadaº
man   reindeer-ACC   kill-3SG.SBJ>SG.OBJ   kill.3SG.SBJ
'A/the man killed a/the reindeer.'

There are nevertheless morphosyntactic restrictions on what can participate in DOM. In some varieties of Tundra Nenets, for example, only third person pronouns can trigger agreement, but first and second person pronouns cannot; in other varieties *no* pronouns trigger agreement (Nikolaeva 2014: 202f. cf. also É. Kiss 2017). Further, wh-words, some quantifiers (such as *ŋoka* 'many,

---

[5] It is of course highly plausible that the information structure of a sentence is reflected in the syntactic derivation structurally and/or featurally, but this is not universally assumed. Note that this question is raised also for DOM triggered by specificity, as it is not generally agreed upon whether specificity is a property of a nominal or emergent from context (or some combination).

much'), and indefinite and negative pronouns do not trigger object agreement. At least some of these elements have in common that they are not 'topic-worthy': only referential NPs can be topical, so non-referential NPs can be ruled out. For dialects with restrictions on pronouns, however, a separate factor must constrain agreement.

Dalrymple & Nikolaeva (2011) propose that information-structure-based DOM is in fact the canonical case of DOM. More specifically, they argue that all instances of DOM (taken to include both case marking and agreement) are either historically or synchronically related to topicality, defined as pragmatic saliency within a communicative context; DOM is thus really just a special case of the sort of all-purpose topic-marking found in languages like Quechua and Japanese. DOM serves to signal a similarity between subjects (which are typically topical) and topical objects (taking objects to be equally likely to be topical or nontopical). Over time, topicality-based DOM may be narrowed to a subset of topical objects, or spread to all objects with certain semantic features that are typical of topics (e.g., specificity or animacy). Dalrymple and Nikolaeva's account is formalized within the Lexical-Functional Grammar (LFG) framework, with certain morphological marking requiring that the nominal that the marking is associated with be interpreted with a certain information structure role, namely, that of being a topic.

Cases where information structure directly conditions DOM pose a number of additional challenges for a unified analysis of DOM. First, not all theories of grammar allow modeling the influence of information structure in syntax in a straightforward way. This is related to the fact that the unacceptability of an example like (15b) follows from its use in a certain *context*, not ungrammaticality *per se*. In other words, pragmatics plays a certain role in determining the felicity of utterances with and without DOM. Indeed, Danon (2006) suggests that DOM might follow a grammaticalization path from more pragmatic to more formal in the history of languages. He proposes that this is the case for Modern Hebrew, and the history of Hungarian shows a similar development (Marcantonio 1985, É. Kiss 2013, 2017).

A second challenge relates to identifying a trigger: is it always topics that trigger DOM? In other words, can we identify a consistent topicality hierarchy similar to the scales discussed in Section 1.1 above? Is the topicality hierarchy shown in (2c) empirically as well-supported as animacy and definiteness scales? Woolford (1999) and Klumpp (2012) present evidence from different languages that *focus*, too, can give rise to differential marking, not just topicality. These questions remain a matter for future research, and are addressed in Pei-Jung Kuo's chapter in this volume.

3 What can DOM tell us about case, agreement, and licensing?

One of the reasons that DOM has remained a relevant and productive area of research is that it has many complexities which are hard to capture in a single unified account across languages, and often even within a single language, as attested by the many differing analyses mentioned in Section 2. These are in fact only a small sampling of the existent literature on DOM. In this section, we hone in on a few specific bigger picture questions raised for generative syntactic theory through the study of DOM, as this is a recurring point of interest in the contributions to this volume.

3.1 DOM and licensing

Generative syntactic theory since the late 1970s (Vergnaud 2008 [1977], Chomsky 1980) has typically held that all nominals need the same sort of abstract licensing, namely, Case. On the surface, DOM seems to show us that, in fact, not all nominals need Case (at least insofar as morphological case reflects abstract Case, cf. Section 2.3), therefore posing a major challenge to the longstanding view. A more explicit question in this respect is whether DOM is better analyzed in terms of abstract Case or morphological case—in other words, does the lack of morphological case indicate the lack of abstract Case (i.e., licensing), too? Monica Irimia, Jaklin Kornfilt, Gereon Müller, and Vassilios Spyropoulos all address this and related questions in their respective chapters in this volume.

An analogous question is relevant for differential object *agreement*. In much Minimalist theorising, abstract Case is assigned to an argument by an *Agree* relation between a functional head, a so-called probe, and a nominal, a goal. Chomsky (2000, 2001) suggests that a goal's Case feature and a probe's φ-features are valued simultaneously under Agree relations. Agree is thus argued to be responsible for licensing arguments; if a goal fails to be licensed by an Agree relation, it will lack a value for Case and violate the Case Filter. This approach implies that a language like English, which does not have object agreement, nevertheless has abstract object Agreement. Just like differential case marking raises questions about the relation of abstract and morphological case, so does differential *agreement*. In languages where differential marking is expressed in verbal morphology, does agreement serve to license direct objects or is it simply that some (already licensed) objects trigger agreement, while others do not?

Further, if case marking and/or agreement indicate the licensing of a direct object, we expect differences in syntactic behavior based on whether an object is agreed with/has overt case or not—is this empirically borne out? The crosslinguistic evidence is mixed: the Uralic family, for example, shows both possible patterns—in some Uralic languages, overt marking correlates with differences in syntactic behavior, and in others, it does not. In Hungarian, objects do not show positional differences nor differences in their binding properties whether agreed with or not (É. Kiss 2002, Bárány 2017). In the Ugric language Northern Ostyak, however, agreeing objects are in a higher syntactic position and can bind and control arguments that non-agreeing objects cannot access (Nikolaeva 1999, Dalrymple & Nikolaeva 2011, Smith 2018). Hindi and Spanish have been argued to be similar: case-marked objects are also syntactically more prominent and can enter binding relations that objects without DOM cannot (Bhatt & Anagnostopoulou 1996, Bhatt 2007, López 2012). The question of where DOM objects are represented in the clause is tackled in this volume in the chapters by Jaklin Kornfilt and by Rita Manzini, Leonardo Savoia, and Ludovica Franco.

3.2 Case, agreement, and DOM

In recent years, the traditional tight connection between abstract Case, morphological case, and agreement has been called into question (Zaenen et al. 1985, Marantz 1991, Bhatt 2005, Bobaljik 2008, Baker 2012, 2015). The reason for this is that there are mismatches among overt case, overt agreement, and syntactic behavior. If Agree is a single operation that values both Case and φ-features, both of which can, but do not have to be spelled out, and that performs a licensing function, we expect to observe certain types of mismatches between case marking and agreement but not others.

Hungarian, for example, shows differential object agreement, but no differential case marking. Direct objects are morphologically accusative independently of their referential properties, while definite direct objects generally trigger object agreement (and most indefinite objects do not, cf. É. Kiss 2002, 2013, Coppock & Wechsler 2012, Coppock 2013, Bárány 2015a,b, 2017). If both Case and agreement happen at an abstract level uniformly, and differential marking is a matter of spell-out only, explaining Hungarian object agreement is a matter of determining when agreement is spelled out and when it is not. Crucially, whatever its spell-out, the object case/agreement relation can be modeled as one between the verb and the direct object: the verb assigns accusative and agrees with the direct object, uniformly.

In other languages, abstract agreement relations are not so clear-cut. Baker (2012) discusses Amharic in this context. Amharic displays both differential object case-marking and differential object agreement, but the two are independent. (17a) and (17b) show that a definite object gets accusative case marking, but only optionally triggers agreement. In addition, the verb can agree with the *indirect object* instead of the direct object, and while agreement with the indirect object preempts (replaces) direct object agreement (direct and indirect object agreement come from the same paradigm and seem to occupy the same slot), this does *not* interfere with the direct object getting its accusative/differential case. This is shown in (17c): the verb does not agree with the (masculine) direct object *məs'əhaf-u-n* 'book-DEF-ACC' but rather the (feminine) indirect object *l-Almaz* 'DAT-Almaz'.

(17) Amharic (Baker 2012: 257, 258)

    a. *Ləmma wɪʃʃa-w-ɪn j-aj-al.*
       Lemma dog-DEF-ACC 3.M.SBJ-see-AUX(3.M.SBJ)
       'Lemma sees the dog.'

    b. *Ləmma wɪʃʃa-w-ɪn j-aj-əw-al.*
       Lemma dog-DEF-ACC 3.M.SBJ-see-3.M.OBJ-AUX(3.M.SBJ)
       'Lemma sees the dog.'

    c. *Ləmma l-Almaz məs'əhaf-u-n sət't'-**at**.*
       Lemma DAT-Almaz.F book-DEF-ACC give(3.M.SBJ)-**3.F.OBJ**
       'Lemma gave the book to Almaz.'

Baker argues that such data show that case marking (accusative on the direct object) and agreement (on the verb) cannot have been the result of the same relation and simultaneous valuation of φ-features and Case. Assuming that *v* assigns accusative to the direct object, how can it agree with the indirect object in (17c) if we are dealing with a single operation? In addition, since the spell-out of agreement is the same, independently of whether the verb agrees with the indirect or the direct object, it can be assumed that the same head is involved. But where do the arguments get their case marking from? Baker's (2012, 2015) answer is dependent case, which we turn to next.

3.3 Dependent case and DOM

Mismatches between case and agreement have contributed to a recent revival of Marantz 1991-style *dependent case* approaches to case marking (e.g., McFadden

2004, Bobaljik 2008, Preminger 2014, Baker & Vinokurova 2010, Baker 2015, Yuan 2016, Jenks & Sande 2017, Yuan 2018). Dependent case is the term for a case that is assigned to one nominal of two, when the two nominals occupy the same relevant syntactic domain, e.g., they are in the same phase, and one of the nominals c-commands the other. Ergative languages are characterized by dependent case being assigned to the higher of two nominals (i.e., the subject in a transitive clause), while accusative languages are characterized by dependent case being assigned to the lower of two nominals (i.e., the object in a transitive clause). The single argument of intransitives is typically morphologically unmarked in both ergative and accusative languages: since there is no second nominal in intransitives, there is no dependent case to assign and the argument gets "unmarked" case, which is often phonologically null (or perhaps absent altogether).

Baker (2015) proposes that this approach straightforwardly explains the connection between object movement and DOM, discussed in Section 2.4. If TP and VP are independent domains, and the subject is always in spec-TP, then the subject and object will only be in the *same* domain as each other if the object raises out of VP, as shown in (18).

(18)

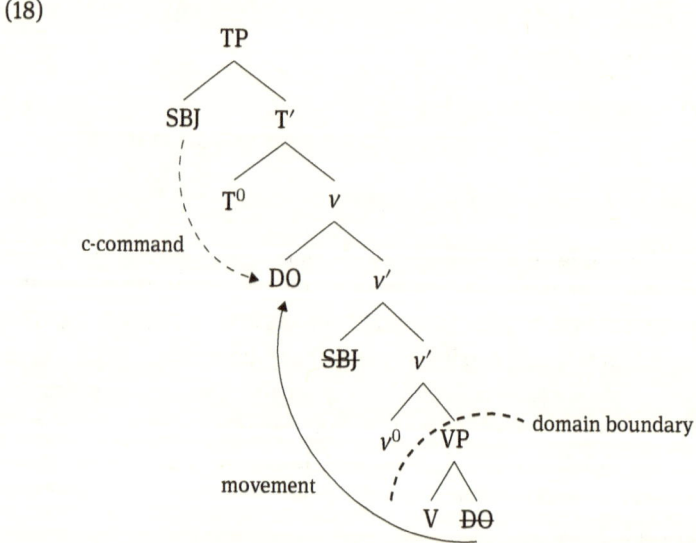

The result of movement in (18) may be dependent ACC assigned to the object, (19), or dependent ERG assigned to the subject, (20). Note that there are independent arguments for movement of the object in the (b) examples but not the (a) examples that we do not review here; see Baker & Vinokurova (2010) and Massam (2001).

(19) Sakha (Vinokurova 2005, cited in Baker & Vinokurova 2010)

    a. *Min saharxaj sibekki ürgee-ti-m.*
       I.NOM yellow flower buy-PST-1SG.SBJ
       'I picked yellow flowers.'

    b. *Min saharxaj sibekki-ni ürgee-ti-m.*
       I.NOM yellow flower-ACC buy-PST-1SG.SBJ
       'I picked the/a certain yellow flower.'

(20) Niuean (Massam 2000, cited in Woolford 2015)

    a. *Ne inu kofe a Sione.*
       PST drink coffee NOM Sione
       'Sione drank coffee.'

    b. *Ne inu **e** Sione e kofe.*
       PST drink ERG Sione NOM coffee
       'Sione drank the coffee.'

Dependent case thus provides an *independent* means of understanding surface case marking apart from Case that is assigned via agreement. This is reflected in Kornfilt's contribution to this volume, in which she puts forth a proposal to extend dependent case to dependent Agree. In addition, incorporating the idea that dependent case is assigned only in a given syntactic domain can provide an explanation of the role of movement in differential case marking. It is relevant to note that it does not seem that a dependent case account is always appropriate, nor is object movement always a plausible step in the derivation: Kalin & Weisser (2019) have recently mounted a challenge to such approaches by showing that DOM can appear on just one conjunct in a coordination in a number of DOM languages; assuming that coordinations are islands (Ross 1967), it cannot be that one conjunct has raised out of the coordination to a higher position.

4 DOM in this volume

This volume comprises papers which introduce new empirical findings about DOM, implement several different approaches to DOM, and discuss a number of issues that DOM raises for linguistic theory. In this section, we briefly summarize the main contributions of each chapter.

In the most theory-centered contribution to the volume, Gereon Müller uses differential marking phenomena as a testing ground for contrasting how two different theoretical models, namely Harmonic Grammar and local conjunction of constraints in Optimality Theory, deal with cumulative effects in grammar. Cumulative effects are found when two factors (e.g. grammatical features) determine a grammatical effect together, but not by themselves. In DOM in Mannheim German, these two factors are an NP's definiteness and animacy features. Müller argues that local conjunction fares better in modeling the sort of cumulativity seen in differential marking in this variety, challenging aspects of the Harmonic Grammar model.

Monica Irimia, discussing Romanian and other Romance languages and taking a very different perspective, regards DOM as a puzzle for licensing: she revisits *Kayne's Generalization* (Jaeggli 1981) and argues that an account based on secondary licensing (cf. Kalin 2018) can explain the distribution of the DOM marker *pe* in Romanian, as well as differential clitic doubling. This DOM marker spells out the additional licensing relation that is made necessary by the presence of a [+PERSON] feature on an object.

Jaklin Kornfilt's contribution focuses on Turkish, and makes a strong theoretical claim. Kornfilt, discussing both DOM and differential subject marking (DSM), takes on dependent case theory and argues that Case can equally well be seen as licensed by functional heads. However, the ability of a functional head to license Case on its argument can depend on whether another argument has already been licensed or not. She thus proposes that a type of dependent Agree licenses Case on an object only if a subject has been licensed by a previous Agree relation.

The chapter by Vassilios Spyropoulos also discusses Turkish, but his main empirical focus is Pontic Greek. Spyropoulos, like Kornfilt, addresses both DOM and DSM and argues against a functional base for these phenomena. He uses a morphological approach to explain the case alternations and discusses microvariation in Asia Minor Greek varieties as well.

In contrast, the chapter by Rita Manzini, Leonardo Savoia, and Ludovica Franco endorses an explicitly syntactic, rather than morphological approach to DOM. The authors discuss a range of varieties of Italian and Romance which have homophonous exponents of DOM and dative case. They argue that this homophony is not morphological, e.g. due to syncretism, but that it has a syntactic source: DOM objects are syntactically dative.

Pei-Jung Kuo discusses DOM in a perhaps surprising language, one that is traditionally seen as lacking both case and agreement (at least overtly), Mandarin Chinese. Kuo identifies several types of differential marking phenomena in Mandarin Chinese which she analyses in terms of information structure. Kuo argues that specific objects undergo internal topicalization which is spelled out in one of three distinct ways, all essentially encoding DOM.

Finally, Elsi Kaiser, Merilin Miljan and Virve Vihman combine recent theoretical approaches to Case with a psycholinguistic perspective and probe the role of case marking in language comprehension. In their paper, they report the results of experiments on case alternations in Estonian and discuss the implications of their results for theories of Case. They argue that morphological case plays a much more active role in syntactic derivations than is usually assumed.

5 Conclusions

DOM illuminates intersections between and among morphology, syntax, semantics, and information structure. As is clear from the literature reviewed in this introduction as well as the contributions to this volume, there remain several open questions in the study of DOM. We still have a long way to go in fully understanding what DOM is telling us about the different components of grammar and about human language more generally, as well as what the right approach to understanding DOM is. Could there possibly be one sort of analysis that is appropriate for all instances of DOM? Or is DOM in fact not a uniform phenomenon at all? The work presented in this volume moves us closer to a robust understanding of DOM and an answer to these questions.

References

Aissen, Judith. 2003. Differential object marking: Iconicity vs. economy. *Natural Language & Linguistic Theory* 21(3). 435–483. https://doi.org/10.1023/A:1024109008573.
Baker, Mark C. 1988. *Incorporation: A theory of grammatical function changing*. Chicago, IL: University of Chicago Press.
Baker, Mark C. 2012. On the relationship of object agreement and accusative case: Evidence from Amharic. *Linguistic Inquiry* 43(2). 255–274. https://doi.org/10.1162/LING_a_00085.
Baker, Mark C. 2014. Types of cross-linguistic variation in case assignment. In M. Carme Picallo (ed.), *Linguistic variation in a minimalist framework*. New York: Oxford University Press.
Baker, Mark C. 2015. *Case: Its principles and its parameters*. Cambridge: Cambridge University Press.
Baker, Mark C. & Nadya Vinokurova. 2010. Two modalities of case assignment. *Natural Language & Linguistic Theory* 28(3). 593–642. https://doi.org/10.1007/s11049-010-9105-1.
Bárány, András. 2015a. *Differential object marking in Hungarian and the morphosyntax of case and agreement*. University of Cambridge PhD dissertation.

Bárány, András. 2015b. Inverse agreement and Hungarian verb paradigms. In Katalin É. Kiss, Balázs Surányi & Éva Dékány (eds.), *Approaches to Hungarian*, 37–64. John Benjamins. https://doi.org/10.1075/atoh.14.02bar.

Bárány, András. 2017. *Person, case, and agreement: The morphosyntax of inverse agreement and global case splits*. Oxford University Press. https://doi.org/10.1093/oso/9780198804185.001.0001.

Bárány, András. 2018. DOM and dative case. *Glossa: a journal of general linguistics* 3(1), 97. https://doi.org/10.5334/gjgl.639.

Bhatt, Rajesh. 2005. Long distance agreement in Hindi-Urdu. *Natural Language & Linguistic Theory* 23(4). 757–807. https://doi.org/10.1007/s11049-004-4136-0.

Bhatt, Rajesh. 2007. Unaccusativity and case licensing. Ms., University of Massachusetts at Amherst.

Bhatt, Rajesh & Elena Anagnostopoulou. 1996. Object shift and specificity: Evidence from *ko*-phrases in Hindi. In Lisa M. Dobrin, Kora Singer & Lisa McNair (eds.), *Papers from the 32nd regional meeting of the Chicago Linguistics Society*, 11–22. Chicago: Chicago Linguistic Society.

Bobaljik, Jonathan David. 2008. Where's phi? Agreement as a postsyntactic operation. In Daniel Harbour, David Adger & Susana Béjar (eds.), *Phi-theory*, 295–328. Oxford: Oxford University Press.

Bossong, Georg. 1985. *Differentielle Objektmarkierung in den Neuiranischen Sprachen*. Gunter Narr.

Bossong, Georg. 1991. Differential object marking in Romance and beyond. In Douglas A. Kibbee & Dieter Wanner (eds.), *New analyses in Romance linguistics*, 143–170. Amsterdam: John Benjamins. https://doi.org/10.1075/cilt.69.14bos.

Chomsky, Noam. 1980. On binding. *Linguistic Inquiry* 11(1). 1–46.

Chomsky, Noam. 2000. Minimalist inquiries: The framework. In Roger Martin, David Michaels & Juan Uriagereka (eds.), *Step by step: Essays on minimalist syntax in honor of Howard Lasnik*, 89–155. Cambridge, MA: MIT Press.

Chomsky, Noam. 2001. Derivation by phase. In Michael Kenstowicz (ed.), *Ken Hale: A life in language*, 1–52. Cambridge, MA: MIT Press.

Comrie, Bernard. 1979. Definite and animate direct objects: A natural class. *Linguistica silesiana* 3. 13–21.

Comrie, Bernard. 1989. *Language universals and linguistic typology*. Chicago, IL: University of Chicago Press.

Coppock, Elizabeth. 2013. A semantic solution to the problem of Hungarian object agreement. *Natural Language Semantics* 21(4). 345–371. https://doi.org/10.1007/s11050-013-9096-7.

Coppock, Elizabeth & Stephen Wechsler. 2012. The objective conjugation in Hungarian. *Natural Language & Linguistic Theory* 30(3). 699–740. https://doi.org/10.1007/s11049-012-9165-5.

Croft, William. 1988. Agreement vs. case marking and direct objects. In Michael Barlow & Charles A. Ferguson (eds.), *Agreement in natural language: Approaches, theories, descriptions*, 159–179. CSLI.

Croft, William. 2003. *Typology and universals*. Cambridge: Cambridge University Press.

Dalrymple, Mary & Irina Nikolaeva. 2011. *Objects and information structure*. Cambridge: Cambridge University Press.

Danon, Gabi. 2006. Caseless nominals and the projection of DP. *Natural Language & Linguistic Theory* 24(4). 977–1008. https://doi.org/10.1007/s11049-006-9005-6.

Diesing, Molly. 1992. *Indefinites*. Cambridge, MA: MIT Press.

É. Kiss, Katalin. 2002. *The syntax of Hungarian*. Cambridge: Cambridge University Press.

É. Kiss, Katalin. 2013. The inverse agreement constraint in Uralic languages. *Finno-Ugric Languages and Linguistics* 2(3). 2–21.

É. Kiss, Katalin. 2017. The person-case constraint and the inverse agreement constraint are manifestations of the same inverse topicality constraint. *The Linguistic Review* 34(2). 365–395. https://doi.org/10.1515/tlr-2017-0004.

Enç, Mürvet. 1991. The semantics of specificity. *Linguistic Inquiry* 22(1). 1–25.

Glushan, Zhanna. 2010. Deriving case syncretism in differential object marking systems. Ms., University of Connecticut.

Haspelmath, Martin. 2008. Parametric versus functional explanations of syntactic universals. In Theresa Biberauer (ed.), *The limits of syntactic variation*, 75–107. John Benjamins. https://doi.org/10.1075/la.132.04has.

Haspelmath, Martin. 2009. The best-supported language universals refer to scalar patterns deriving from processing cost. *Behavioral and Brain Sciences* 32(5). 457–458. https://doi.org/10.1017/S0140525X09990689.

von Heusinger, Klaus. 2008. Verbal semantics and the diachronic development of DOM in Spanish. *Probus* 20(1). 1–31. https://doi.org/10.1515/PROBUS.2008.001.

de Hoop, Helen. 1996. *Case configuration and noun phrase interpretation*. New York: Garland.

de Hoop, Helen & Andrej L. Malchukov. 2007. On fluid differential case marking. *Lingua* 117(9). 1636–1656. https://doi.org/10.1016/j.lingua.2006.06.010.

Hopper, Paul J. & Sandra A. Thompson. 1980. Transitivity in grammar and discourse. *Language* 56(2). 251–299.

Jaeggli, Osvaldo. 1981. *Topics in Romance syntax*. Dordrecht: Foris.

Jenks, Peter & Hannah Sande. 2017. Dependent accusative case and caselessness in Moro. In Andrew Lamont & Katerina A. Tetzloff (eds.), *Proceedings of the forty-seventh annual meeting of the north east linguistic society*, 109–118. Amherst, MA: Graduate Linguistics Student Association.

Kalin, Laura. 2018. Licensing and differential object marking: The view from Neo-Aramaic. *Syntax* 21(2). 112–159. https://doi.org/10.1111/synt.12153.

Kalin, Laura & Philipp Weisser. 2019. Asymmetric DOM in coordination: A problem for movement-based approaches. *Linguistic Inquiry* 50(3). 662–676. https://doi.org/10.1162/ling_a_00298.

Keine, Stefan. 2010. *Case and agreement from fringe to core*. Berlin: De Gruyter.

Keine, Stefan & Gereon Müller. 2008. Differential argument encoding by impoverishment. In Marc Richards & Andrej L. Malchukov (eds.), *Scales* (Linguistische Arbeitsberichte 86), 83–136. Leipzig: Universität Leipzig.

Klumpp, Gerson. 2012. Differential object marking and information structure. *ESUKA - JEFUL [Journal of Estonian and Finno-Ugric Linguistics]* 3(1). 343–372.

Kornfilt, Jaklin. 2008. DOM and two types of DSM in Turkish. In Helen de Hoop & Peter de Swart (eds.), *Differential subject marking* (Studies in Natural Language & Linguistic Theory), 79–111. Dordrecht: Springer. https://doi.org/10.1007/978-1-4020-6497-5.

Kramer, Ruth. 2014. Clitic doubling or object agreement: The view from Amharic. *Natural Language & Linguistic Theory* 32(2). 593–634. https://doi.org/10.1007/s11049-014-9233-0.

Laka, Itziar. 1993. Unergatives that assign ergative, unaccusatives that assign accusative. In Jonathan Bobaljik & Colin Phillips (eds.), *Papers on case and agreement 1*, 149–172. MIT Working Papers in Linguistics 18.

Leonetti, Manuel. 2004. Specificity and differential object marking in Spanish. *Catalan Journal of Linguistics* 3. 75–114. https://doi.org/10.5565/rev/catjl.106.

Leonetti, Manuel. 2008. Specificity in clitic doubling and differential object marking. *Probus* 20(1). 33–66. https://doi.org/10.1515/PROBUS.2008.002.

Levin, Theodore & Omer Preminger. 2015. Case in Sakha: Are two modalities really necessary? *Natural Language & Linguistic Theory* 33. 231–250. https://doi.org/10.1007/s11049-014-9250-z.

Lidz, Jeffrey. 2006. The grammar of accusative case in Kannada. *Language* 82(1). 1–23. https://doi.org/10.1353/lan.2006.0054.

López, Luis. 2012. *Indefinite objects: Scrambling, choice functions, and differential marking*. Cambridge, MA: MIT Press.

Lyutikova, Ekaterina & Asya Pereltsvaig. 2015. The Tatar DP. *Canadian Journal of Linguistics* 60(3). 289–325.

Manzini, M. Rita & Ludovico Franco. 2016. Goal and DOM datives. *Natural Language & Linguistic Theory* 34(1). 197–240. https://doi.org/10.1007/s11049-015-9303-y.

Marantz, Alec. 1991. Case and licensing. In German Westphal, Benjamin Ao & Hee-Rahk Chae (eds.), *Proceedings of the 8th Eastern States Conference on Linguistics (ESCOL 8)*, 234–253. Ithaca, NY: CLC Publications.

Marcantonio, Angela. 1985. On the definite vs. indefinite conjugation in Hungarian: A typological and diachronic analysis. *Acta Linguistica Academiae Scientiarum Hungaricae* 35(3-4). 267–298.

Maslova, Elena. 2003. *A grammar of Kolyma Yukaghir*. Berlin: De Gruyter.

Massam, Diane. 2000. VSO and VOS: Aspects of Niuean word order. In Andrew Carnie & Eithne Guilfoyle (eds.), *The syntax of verb initial languages*, 97–116. Oxford: Oxford University Press.

Massam, Diane. 2001. Pseudo noun incorporation in Niuean. *Natural Language & Linguistic Theory* 19(1). 153–197. https://doi.org/10.1023/A:1006465130442.

Matić, Dejan. 2019. A case for syntactic case: The accusative in Tundra Yukaghir. *Morphology*. https://doi.org/10.1007/s11525-019-09343-4.

McFadden, Thomas. 2004. *The position of morphological case in the derivation*. University of Pennsylvania dissertation.

Montaut, Annie. 2018. The rise of differential object marking in Hindi and related languages. In Ilja Seržant & Alena Witzlack-Makarevich (eds.), *Diachrony of differential argument marking*, 281–313. Berlin: Language Science Press. https://doi.org/10.5281/zenodo.1228261.

Næss, Åshild. 2004. What markedness marks: The markedness problem with direct objects. *Lingua* 114(9–10). 1186–1212. https://doi.org/10.1016/j.lingua.2003.07.005.

Nikolaeva, Irina. 1999. Object agreement, grammatical relations, and information structure. *Studies in Language* 23. 331–376. https://doi.org/10.1075/sl.23.2.05nik.

Nikolaeva, Irina. 2001. Secondary topic as a relation in information structure. *Linguistics* 39(1). 1–49. https://doi.org/10.1515/ling.2001.006.

Nikolaeva, Irina. 2014. *A grammar of Tundra Nenets*. Berlin: De Gruyter.

Ormazabal, Javier & Juan Romero. 2013. Differential object marking, case and agreement. *Borealis*: An International Journal of Hispanic Linguistics 2(2). 221–239. https://doi.org/10.7557/1.2.2.2808.

Preminger, Omer. 2014. *Agreement and its failures*. Cambridge, MA: MIT Press.

Prince, Alan & Paul Smolensky. 1993. Optimality Theory: Constraint interaction in generative grammar. Ms., Rutgers University Center for Cognitive Science.

Richards, Marc. 2008. Defective agree, case alternations, and the prominence of person. In Marc Richards & Andrej L. Malchukov (eds.), *Scales* (Linguistische Arbeits Berichte 86), 137–161. Leipzig: Universität Leipzig.

Richards, Norvin. 2010. *Uttering trees*. Cambridge, MA: MIT Press.

Rodríguez-Mondoñedo, Miguel. 2007. *The syntax of objects: Agree and differential object marking*. University of Connecticut dissertation.

Ross, John. 1967. *Constraints on variables in syntax*. Cambridge, MA: MIT dissertation.

Silverstein, Michael. 1976. Hierarchy of features and ergativity. In R. M. W. Dixon (ed.), *Grammatical categories in Australian languages*, 112–171. Canberra: Australian Institute of Aboriginal Studies.

Sinnemäki, Kaius. 2014. A typological perspective on differential object marking. *Linguistics* 52(2). 281–313. https://doi.org/10.1515/ling-2013-0063.

Smith, Peter W. 2018. Object agreement and grammatical functions: A re-evaluation. Ms., Goethe-Universität Frankfurt.

de Swart, Peter. 2007. *Cross-linguistic variation in object marking*. Utrecht University dissertation.

Torrego, Esther. 1998. *The dependencies of objects*. Cambridge, MA: MIT Press.

Vergnaud, Jean-Roger. 2008 [1977]. Letter to Noam Chomsky and Howard Lasnik on "Filters and Control," April 17, 1977. In Robert Freidin, Carlos P. Otero & Maria Luisa Zubizarreta (eds.), *Foundational issues in linguistic theory. Essays in honor of Jean-Roger Vergnaud*, 3–15. Cambridge, MA: MIT Press.

Vinokurova, Nadezhda. 2005. *Lexical categories and argument structure: A study with reference to Sakha*. Universiteit Utrecht dissertation.

Virtanen, Susanna. 2015. *Transitivity in Eastern Mansi*. University of Helsinki dissertation.

Witzlack-Makarevich, Alena & Ilja A. Seržant. 2018. Differential argument marking: Patterns of variation. In Alena Witzlack-Makarevich & Ilja A. Seržant (eds.), *Diachrony of differential argument marking*, 1–40. Berlin: Language Science Press. https://doi.org/10.5281/zenodo.1228243.

Woolford, Ellen. 1999. Animacy hierarchy effects on object agreement. In Paul Kotey (ed.), *New dimensions in African linguistics and languages*, 203–216. Trenton, NJ: Africa World Press.

Woolford, Ellen. 2015. Ergativity and transitivity. *Linguistic Inquiry* 46(3). 489–531. https://doi.org/10.1162/ling_a_00190.

Yuan, Michelle. 2016. Dependent case is dissimilation: Evidence from Yimas. In Christopher Hammerly & Brandon Prickett (eds.), *Proceedings of the 46th meeting of the North East Linguistics Society*, 299–308. Amherst, MA: GLSA.

Yuan, Michelle. 2018. *Dimensions of ergativity in Inuit: Theory and microvariation*. MIT dissertation.

Zaenen, Annie, Joan Maling & Höskuldur Thráinsson. 1985. Case and grammatical functions: The Icelandic passive. *Natural Language & Linguistic Theory* 3. 441–483. https://doi.org/10.1007/BF00133285.

Gereon Müller

Cumulative effects in differential argument encoding and long-distance extraction

Local conjunction vs. Harmonic Grammar

Abstract: Only few grammatical theories can faithfully incorporate cumulative effects. In Optimality Theory, two different means have been suggested to account for cumulativity of constraint interaction, viz., local constraint conjunction and Harmonic Grammar. The present paper considers cumulative effects in morphology (with differential argument encoding) and syntax (with long-distance extraction) and shows that existing analyses in terms of local constraint conjunction cannot be transferred to Harmonic Grammar analyses. Whereas cumulative constraint interaction can be selectively switched off in local conjunction analyses, this is impossible for principled reasons in Harmonic Grammar analyses. Consequently, even though Harmonic Grammar is explicitly designed to capture cumulative effects, it turns out that this approach is systematically unable to derive a certain kind of cumulativity because it cannot prevent unwanted concurrent cumulative interaction.

Keywords: differential argument encoding, long-distance extraction, cumulativity, local conjunction, Harmonic Grammar, Optimality Theory

1 Introduction

Grammatical building blocks (constraints, operations, rules, schemata) can interact in different ways, essentially along two dimensions. On the one hand, the interaction can be *simultaneous* (the building blocks apply in parallel) or *sequential* (the building blocks apply one after the other). On the other hand, the interaction can be *inhibitory* (one building block precludes the application of the other building block) or *excitatory* (one building block makes the application of the second building block possible). Cumulative effects in grammar qualify as a core instance of excitatory simultaneous interaction. In this kind of scenario, there are two factors F_1, F_2 which by themselves are too weak to determine a given property π of a linguistic expression LE, but if F_1 and F_2 combine their forces (i.e., are both present in some grammatical context), they can successfully ensure that LE has π.

Gereon Müller, Universität Leipzig

https://doi.org/10.1515/9783110666137-002

A basic premise underlying the present paper is that cumulativity shows up in differential argument encoding. For instance, with differential object marking in the substandard variety of German spoken in and around Mannheim (which will figure prominently in the analysis developed in Section 2 below), the absence of a designated accusative marker in masculine DPs is determined by two separate factors which by themselves may not be strong enough to trigger the effect, but may do so if they interact in a cumulative fashion. Low positioning on the *definiteness* scale may have to be combined with low positioning on the *animacy* scale, and there is in fact an option of compensating for a slightly higher position on one scale by a sufficiently low position on the other scale. Thus, e.g., definite DPs with a human referent show differential marking whereas, say, indefinite DPs with a human referent, definite DPs with an animate (non-human) referent, and proper name DPs with an inanimate referent all do not. It is hard to see how one could account for this clearly cumulative effect insightfully by postulating a single abstract feature (like generalized [Person]) that captures the relevant cut-off point (see footnote 14 below). The same reasoning can be given for many other phenomena involving differential argument encoding (one of which I will also address in this paper, viz., three-way systems of argument encoding), and many syntactic phenomena outside the realm of differential marking (like long-distance extraction, which I will also address). For these reasons, I take cumulativity in grammar to be real, and in need of a proper account that does not treat it as an epiphenomenon.

That said, there are few grammatical theories which can faithfully (i.e., without attributing it to an accidental conspiracy) model simultaneous excitatory interaction and thereby account for cumulativity. Among these, the best-developed and most widely pursued approach would seem to be Optimality Theory (Prince & Smolensky 1993, 2004). However, even here, integrating cumulativity is not straightforward: Given *strict domination*, no number of violations of lower-ranked constraints can ever outweigh even a single violation of a higher-ranked constraint. Against this background, cumulativity has been approached in Optimality Theory by postulating the concept of *local conjunction* of constraints (see Smolensky 1995, 2006).

(1) *Local conjunction*:
   a. Local conjunction of two constraints Con_1, Con_2 with respect to a local domain D yields a new constraint $Con_1 \&_D Con_2$ that is violated iff there are two separate violations of Con_1 and Con_2 in a single domain D.
   b. Universal ranking: $Con_1 \&_D Con_2 \gg \{Con_1, Con_2\}$
   c. Local conjunction can be reflexive (with $Con_1 = Con_2$).

Thus, suppose that there are three constraints A, B, and C, with A dominating B and C in an optimality-theoretic ranking. Given strict domination, no individual violations of B and C can outweigh a violation of higher-ranked A; see (2a), where output O_1 must emerge as the winning candidate even though it incurs more violations than output O_2. However, suppose now that B and C are locally conjoined: $B\&_DC$. From (1b), it follows that $B\&_DC$ outranks both B and C; it can then also be ranked higher than A, as shown in (2b). Thus, given that output O_1 violates both B and C in the local domain D, it will also fatally violate $B\&_DC$, and the excitatory interaction of B and C can thus bring about property π (which implies a violation of A) in the optimal output: O_2 emerges as the optimal candidate.

(2) a. *No cumulativity under strict domination*

	A	B	C
☞ O_1		★	★
O_2	★		

b. *Cumulativity under local conjunction*

	$B\&_DC$	A	B	C
O_1	★!		★	★
☞ O_2		★		

In phonology, phenomena like Obligatory Countour Principle effects, sonority effects, vowel harmony, derived environment effects, and chain shifts have all successfully been addressed in terms of local conjunction; see Alderete (1997), Itô & Mester (1998), Kager (1999: 392–400), and Łubowicz (2005), among many others. In syntax, local conjunction has been invoked in accounts of several phenomena suggesting cumulativity, such as locality constraints on movement (see Legendre et al. 1998, Legendre et al. 2006b) and assignment of quantifier scope (see Fischer 2001). Aissen (1999, 2003) has proposed that restrictions on differential argument encoding in the world's languages can to a substantial part be predicted by combining local conjunction with *harmonic alignment* of prominence scales. It is argued in Keine & Müller (2011, 2014) that Aissen's account of differential argument encoding should be reanalyzed as a morphological approach (based on allomorphic variation in realization of a single syntactic case rather than presence or absence of case in the syntax). In Müller & Thomas (2017), such a morphological approach is extended to putative three-way systems that have often been taken to imply the co-existence of ergative, absolutive and accusative in a single language; again, local conjunction of prominence scales is shown to play a crucial role.

More recently (but actually based on pre-optimality theory work by Paul Smolensky and others), *Harmonic Grammar* has been developed as a version of Optimality Theory that assigns weights to constraints and thereby abandons the tenet of strict domination; see Pater (2009, 2016). On this view, weight differences between constraints replace the traditional constraint rankings. The core concept of harmony is defined as in (3) (where w_k is a numerical value and s_k collects the number of constraint violations).

(3)　*Harmony* (Pater 2009: 1006):
$$H = \sum_{k=1}^{K} s_k w_k$$
w_k = weight of a constraint
s_k = violation score of a candidate

Thus, every constraint C_k ($k = 1, ..., K$) is associated with a weight w_k (e.g., –2); the violation score s_k captures the number of violations of C_k of a candidate (e.g., 3 if the candidate violates C_k three times); and the two values are then multiplied (= –6, in the case at hand). For each candidate output, the results of the multiplication of s_k and w_k for all constraints C_k of the grammar are then summed. This determines H, the harmony value of a candidate. If, for instance, there are only three constraints A, B, C in the grammar, with associated weights –2, –1, and –4, respectively, and an output O_1 violates A three times (yielding –6, via multiplication of –2 and 3), B twice (yielding –2), and C not at all (yielding 0), the Harmony score H of O_1 will be –8. Another output O_2 may violate A only once, B once, and C also once; this candidate will then have a Harmony score H of –7.

On this basis, the concept of optimality can be understood as in (4) (see Pater 2009: 1006). An output qualifies as optimal if it is the candidate with maximal harmony in its candidate set.

(4)　*Optimality*:
When constraints assign negative scores, and weights are nonnegative, the optimum has the value closest to zero, that is, the lowest penalty.

So, in the abstract example just presented, if O_1 (H: –8) and O_2 (H: –7) were the only outputs in the candidate set, O_2 would be optimal.

Harmonic Grammar systematically envisages cumulativity in natural language: Combined violations of constraints B, C with lower weights can easily "gang up" and outweigh the violation of another constraint A with a higher weight than both B and C individually.

For applications of Harmonic Grammar in phonology, see the contributions to McCarthy & Pater (2016) (and references cited there). In morphology, the approach has been pursued by Englisch (2015) for Czech verb inflection, by Kushnir (2019) for case-marking in Latvian PPs, and by Georgi (2019) for hierarchical agreement in Hayu and Haya. In syntax, Harmonic Grammar has been invoked by Murphy (2017) for phenomena such as the excitatory interaction of factors regulating left-branch extraction and superiority in Slavic languages, quantifier stranding and multiple scrambling in Korean, multiple correlative displacement in Hindi, and several other constructions instantiating gang effects.[1]

There are thus two principled approaches to simultaneous excitatory interaction of building blocks on the market. Assuming that only one of these should be needed in grammatical theory (though cf. Smolensky & Legendre 2006, Smolensky 2017 for a somewhat different view), the question arises which one is to be preferred. One can approach the issue from a conceptual perspective, or from an empirical perspective. In what follows, I will do the latter. For concreteness, in Section 2, I will consider the morphological analyses of differential argument encoding developed in Keine & Müller (2014) and Müller & Thomas (2017), and see whether the original accounts in terms of local conjunction can be transferred to Harmonic Grammar. After that, in Section 3, I will consider the syntactic analysis of constraints on long-distance extraction developed in Legendre et al. (1998, 2006b), and determine whether it can be transferred from a local conjunction approach to one based on Harmonic Grammar. In both cases, the result will be negative, and it will turn out that there is a single underlying reason (Section 4): With local conjunction, excitatory interaction can sometimes be selectively switched off for some combinations of constraints. With Harmonic Grammar, excitatory interaction can never be selectively switched off for some combinations of constraints. However, the cumulative effects observable in differential argument encoding and long-distance extraction imply that excitatory interaction must be switched off for some combinations of constraints. The last two points together form what I take to be a fundamental problem: Harmonic Grammar cannot prevent unwanted cumulative interaction of constraints.

---

[1] Other syntactic analyses that share essential properties with Harmonic Grammar as regards the postulation of an excitatory interaction of building blocks as a means to capture cumulative effects include Dietrich (1999), Uszkoreit (1986), Jacobs (1988), Pafel (1998), and Featherston (2005); also see Müller (2000: Ch. 4&6) for discussion of how such approaches relate to Optimality Theory.

2 Differential argument encoding

2.1 Local conjunction and differential argument encoding in syntax

Differential argument encoding refers to scenarios where there is systematic variation in case marker exponence on an external or internal argument DP (DP_{ext}, DP_{int}) (or systematic variation in argument encoding of DP_{ext}, DP_{int} by agreement in head-marking systems) in a language depending on the DP's placement on some prominence scale(s), with the syntactic context otherwise being identical. Among these prominence scales are the following hierarchies (see Hale 1972 and Silverstein 1976):

(5) a. *Person scale*:
Local Pers. (1,2) > 3. Pers.

b. *Animacy scale*:
Hum(an) > Anim(ate) > Inan(imate)

c. *Definiteness scale*:
Pro(noun) > Name (PN) > Def(inite) > Indefinite Specific (Spec) > NonSpecific (NSpec)

As regards differential argument encoding of DP_{int} in transitive contexts in an accusative system (i.e., differential object marking), a cross-linguistically valid conclusion seems to be that the higher DP_{int} is on one of these scales, the more likely it is that it is overtly case-marked. Aissen (1999, 2003) proposes to account for these implicational generalizations by adopting the constraint-generating mechanism of *harmonic alignment* introduced in Prince & Smolensky (1993, 2004).[2] On this

---

2 Harmonic alignment is defined as in (i).

(i) *Harmonic alignment* (Prince & Smolensky 2004: 161):
Suppose given a binary dimension D_1 with a scale X > Y on its elements {X,Y}, and another dimension D_2 with a scale a > b >...> z on its elements {a,b,...,z}. The *harmonic alignment* of D_1 and D_2 is the pair of Harmony scales H_X, H_Y:
H_X: X/a ≻ X/b ≻ ...≻ X/z
H_Y: Y/z ≻ ...≻ Y/b ≻ Y/a
The *constraint alignment* is the pair of constraint hierarchies C_X, C_Y:
C_X: *X/z ≫ ...≫ *X/b ≫ *X/a
C_Y: *Y/a ≫ *Y/b ≫ ...≫ *Y/z

view, the scales in (5) can be harmonically aligned with a basic, binary scale for grammatical functions (DP$_{ext}$, DP$_{int}$); for a DP$_{int}$ of a transitive verb, this produces the constraint hierarchies in (6), with a fixed order among the constraints thus derived in all three cases.

(6) a. *DP$_{int}$/Loc ≫ *DP$_{int}$/3
   b. *DP$_{int}$/Hum ≫ *DP$_{int}$/Anim ≫ *DP$_{int}$/Inan
   c. *DP$_{int}$/Pro ≫ *DP$_{int}$/PN ≫ *DP$_{int}$/Def ≫ *DP$_{int}$/Spec ≫ *DP$_{int}$/NSpec

The constraints in (6) uniformly preclude the very existence of the respective objects. Since the DP$_{int}$s do regularly show up in the cases which are relevant in the present contexts, Aissen (2003) takes all these constraints to be so low-ranked as to be per se ineffective in differential argument encoding systems. However, the constraints in (6) are assumed to be locally conjoined with the constraint in (7).[3]

(7) *Ø$_C$ (Star-Zero(Case)):
   A DP must have a value for the feature CASE.

Given that local conjunction of *Ø$_C$ with the individual constraints in (6) must preserve the original order, this derives the constraint system in (8); for present purposes, we can assume that the domain of local conjunction is the minimal XP (i.e., DP in the case at hand).

According to H$_X$, it is least marked for an X to be an a, more marked for an X to be a b, and most marked for an X to be a z; in the same way, it follows that it is least marked for a Y to be a z, and most marked for a Y to be an a. By prefixing the configurations derived in the first step and systematically reversing their order, constraint hierarchies (C$_X$, C$_Y$) are automatically derived which have an internal order that must be respected by all possible rankings (i.e., harmonic alignment provides a way of introducing fixed rankings into a system that otherwise envisages full rerankability of the constraints (*factorial typology*)). Crucially, an internally fixed ranking like *X/z ≫ ... ≫ *X/b ≫ *X/a (= C$_X$) predicts that the prohibition against an X being an a will always be lower-ranked (and thus violable more easily) than the ban on an X being a z; consequently, X/a scenarios correspond to the unmarked case, whereas X/z scenarios are predicted to be highly marked, and not easily attainable in grammars.

3 Here and in what follows, CASE is supposed to cover both regular case marking and argument encoding by agreement. Note that this does not imply that the two operations are mirror images of one another; see Bobaljik (2015) and references cited there.

(8) a. $*DP_{int}/Loc\ \&_{XP}\ *\emptyset_C \gg *DP_{int}/3\ \&_{XP}\ *\emptyset_C$
b. $*DP_{int}/Hum\ \&_{XP}\ *\emptyset_C \gg *DP_{int}/Anim\ \&_{XP}\ *\emptyset_C \gg *DP_{int}/Inan\ \&_{XP}\ *\emptyset_C$
c. $*DP_{int}/Pro\ \&_{XP}\ *\emptyset_C \gg *DP_{int}/PN\ \&_{XP}\ *\emptyset_C \gg *DP_{int}/Def\ \&_{XP}\ *\emptyset_C$
$\gg *DP_{int}/Spec\ \&_{XP}\ *\emptyset_C \gg *DP_{int}/NSpec\ \&_{XP}\ *\emptyset_C$

A constraint like $*DP_{int}/Loc\ \&_{XP}\ *\emptyset_C$ is violated if there are separate violations of (i) $*DP_{int}/Loc$ (because there is a DP_{int} which is first or second person) and (ii) $*\emptyset_C$ (because there is no CASE present); and similar considerations apply with all the other constraints in (8).[4] Each individual constraint in (8a,b,c) thus instantiates a cumulative interaction: The constraint is violated if absence of CASE marking and a certain DP status are combined. Clearly, to give rise to *differential* argument encoding, there must be a conflicting markedness constraint that is violated when a DP has a CASE feature; see (9).

(9) $*STRUC_C$ (Star-Structure(Case)):
A DP must not have a value for the feature CASE.

The ranking of $*STRUC_C$ relative to the constraints of the three internally fixed orders in (8a,b,c) will then determine the presence and degree of differential argument encoding of objects (by case or agreement). As an illustration, consider the hierarchy of constraints in (8c). If $*STRUC_C$ outranks all these constraints demanding CASE on DPs of varying degrees of definiteness, there will be no CASE marking of DP_{int} whatsoever in the language; Aissen mentions Kalkatungu as a case in point. If $*STRUC_C$ is outranked by all these constraints, CASE marking of DP_{int} is predicted to be ubiquitous, as in (written) Japanese. More interestingly, if $*STRUC_C$ is interspersed with the constraints of the hierarchy, differential argument encoding will arise. If $*STRUC_C$ intervenes between $*DP_{int}/Pro\ \&_{XP}\ *\emptyset_C$ and $*DP_{int}/PN\ \&_{XP}\ *\emptyset_C$, only pronominal objects will be CASE-marked; this corresponds to the situation in Catalan. If $*STRUC_C$ is ranked below $*DP_{int}/PN\ \&_{XP}\ *\emptyset_C$ but above $*DP_{int}/Def\ \&_{XP}\ *\emptyset_C$, only pronominal and proper name objects will be CASE-marked; Aissen assumes that this scenario obtains in Pitjantjatjara (but cf. Section 2.4 below, which would require a qualification of this claim). A placement of $*STRUC_C$ between $*DP_{int}/Def\ \&_{XP}\ *\emptyset_C$ and $*DP_{int}/Spec\ \&_{XP}\ *\emptyset_C$ predicts that only

---

[4] If the phase (see Chomsky 2001) rather than the minimal XP is the relevant locality domain for local conjunction, one might expect that $*DP_{int}/Loc\ \&_{XP}\ *\emptyset_C$ could in fact also be violated if there is a first or second person DP_{int} and *some other* DP within the same phase remains without CASE. This potential problem can be solved by adopting cyclic phase-based spellout (see Müller & Thomas 2017: 289), and we will later see independent evidence for phases as the domains for local conjunction; but assuming XP to be the domain for local conjunction will do for now.

pronominal, proper name, and definite objects are CASE-marked (as in Hebrew). Finally, a ranking of *STRUC$_C$ below *DP$_{int}$/Spec &$_{XP}$ *Ø$_C$ but above *DP$_{int}$/NSpec &$_{XP}$ *Ø$_C$ gives rise to the Turkish pattern, where only nonspecific indefinite objects fail to be CASE-marked.

Essentially the same kinds of considerations apply in the cases of differential argument encoding based on other constraint subhierarchies with fixed internal orders, such as those in (8a,b). Three further remarks are in order, though. First, as shown by Aissen (2003) (on the basis of differential object marking in El Cid Spanish, Hindi, and Persian), differential argument encoding can be a *two-dimensional* phenomenon in a language. For instance, the place of a DP$_{int}$ on both the animacy *and* the definiteness scale may be relevant for determining whether the argument is differentially encoded by CASE or not. This is accounted for by assuming that the constraints of the subhierarchies in (8b) and (8c) are all locally conjoined with one another, and the resulting constraints are then locally conjoined with *Ø$_C$, thereby giving rise to partially fixed and partially variable orders of constraints. I will address this issue in the next subsection.

Second, in some cases there may be optionality with differential argument encoding. Aissen (2003) accounts for this by invoking stochastic Optimality Theory (Boersma & Hayes 2001, Bresnan et al. 2001), which replaces fixed rankings with discrete domains on numerical scales and arbitrarily selected evaluation points in these domains for each optimization. Since this issue is orthogonal to the question of how cumulative excitatory interaction can be derived, I will generally abstract away from it in the remainder of this paper (but cf. footnote 9 below).

Finally, and perhaps most importantly in the present context, a core assumption required for the approach to work is that unlike the constraint that requires a CASE marker – viz., *Ø$_C$ –, the constraint that brings about absence of a CASE marker – viz., *STRUC$_C$ – cannot be locally conjoined with constraints derived from harmonic alignment of prominence scales like those in (6). If such local conjunction were (also) possible, it would completely undermine the account of implicational universals. For instance, local conjunction of *STRUC$_C$ with the fixed hierarchy resulting from harmonic alignment of the grammatical function scale with the definiteness scale in (6c) would yield the prediction that there are triggers for CASE marker omission that are sensitive to the position of a DP$_{int}$ on the definiteness scale, and that the constraints demanding omission with objects higher up on the scale actually outrank the constraints demanding CASE marker omission with objects lower on the scale; see (10).

(10)   *DP$_{int}$/Pro &$_{XP}$ *STRUC$_C$ ≫ *DP$_{int}$/PN &$_{XP}$ *STRUC$_C$ ≫
       *DP$_{int}$/Def &$_{XP}$ *STRUC$_C$ ≫ *DP$_{int}$/Spec &$_{XP}$ *STRUC$_C$ ≫
                                          *DP$_{int}$/NSpec &$_{XP}$ *STRUC$_C$

The predictions made by (10) are the opposite of what can be observed cross-linguistically: Whereas it follows from (10) that the *higher* the position of an object is on the definiteness scale, the more likely it should be that it is not encoded by CASE, in actual fact the generalization holds that the *lower* the position of an object is on the definiteness scale, the more likely it is that it is not encoded by CASE. Thus, local conjunction of the constraints in (6) with *STRUC$_C$ must not be an option in the world's languages. This systematic unavailability can be *stated* in a local conjunction approach; but of course, the question arises of whether it can also be *derived* from more general assumptions. To this end, Aissen (1999, 2003) advances a functional motivation: "From the functional perspective, it is pointless to locally conjoin the same subhierarchies with *STRUC, since the result would favour overt marking where it is least needed, and penalize it where it is most needed" (Aissen 1999: 703). However, such a functional motivation for possible constraint rankings is at variance with standard assumptions about constraint ranking in Optimality Theory. Moreover, it is not quite clear why the approach in terms of harmonic alignment and local conjunction would then be needed in the first place, given that the literature abounds with functional motivations of differential argument encoding. It is the great merit of the approach in terms of harmonic alignment and local conjunction that it offers a way to account for both individual patterns and typological generalizations with differential argument encoding without invoking functional motivations, and adding such motivations to close the gap in the analysis created by the non-availability of (10) would threaten to undercut the whole approach. For present purposes, I will therefore take the unavailability of local conjunction in (10) as given, and leave open the question of whether it can be derived from some principled assumptions relating to the nature of the constraints involved.

These considerations notwithstanding, it seems that Aissen's system of cumulative constraint interaction based on local conjunction and harmonic alignment emerges as both flexible enough to cover cross-linguistic variation, and sufficiently restrictive to derive implicational universals (e.g., it predicts that there should not be languages where indefinite objects are systematically CASE-marked whereas object pronouns or definite objects are not).

2.2 Local conjunction and differential argument encoding in morphology

2.2.1 From syntax to morphology

In Keine & Müller (2011, 2014), we argue that Aissen's approach, while basically on the right track, should not be viewed as a syntactic analysis, but should be reconsidered as a morphological analysis. The main evidence for this comes from the observation that some languages employ non-zero/non-zero alternations in differential argument encoding, and not just non-zero/zero alternations of the type that Aissen was exclusively concerned with.[5]

Still, these non-zero/non-zero alternations can be shown to be subject to exactly the same kinds of prominence scale-effects as the standard non-zero/zero alternations. This shows that it is not the syntactic presence or absence of CASE per se that underlies the phenomenon, but rather CASE marker *allomorphy* in the morphological component. Relevant instances of non-zero/non-zero alternations discussed in Keine & Müller (2011, 2014) include differential object marking in Cavineña (with two case allomorphs *-kwe* and *-ja*, whose choice is determined by person and number scales), differential object marking in Trumai (with three object case allomorphs *-(V)tl*, *-ki* and *-(V)s*, whose choice is determined by individuation and discourse prominence scales), and differential object marking in Finnish (with four case allomorphs *-t*, *-n*, *-a*, and Ø, whose choice is determined by definiteness and boundedness scales).[6]

Given this state of affairs, the proposal is to conceive of *$\emptyset_C$ as a faithfulness constraint MAX-C that prohibits deletion of syntactic case features in a post-syntactic morphological component prior to morphological realization via vocabulary insertion; to leave constraint subhierarchies derived by harmonic alignment of scales (as in (6)) fully intact; and to postulate order-preserving local conjunc-

---

[5] In line with this, it can be observed that approaches that view differential argument encoding as a purely syntactic phenomenon are typically exclusively concerned with languages instantiating non-zero/zero patterns; in the present volume, see, e.g., Manzini, Savoia and Franco on varieties of Italian, and Kornfilt on Turkish. On the other hand, Spyropoulos develops a morphological account of differential subject marking in Pontic Greek (which involves non-zero/non-zero alternations) that centers around the concept of impoverishment rules. I will return to this issue below, in the context of discussing an impoverishment approach as a potential alternative to cumulative constraint interaction (see (21), and (i) in footnote 20).

[6] This latter case shows that differential object marking can also depend on the semantic properties of the verb. Also see Kaiser, Miljan and Vihman (this volume) for related facts from Estonian; and von Heusinger (2008), von Heusinger & Kaiser (2011) for evidence from Spanish and further references.

tion of MAX-C with these constraints, exactly as in (8). An important additional assumption, independently motivated by purely morphological considerations related to syncretism, is that CASE features are decomposed into combinations of more primitive binary features (see Jakobson 1962, Bierwisch 1967). For instance, the syntactic feature [accusative] is actually composed of two more primitive features: [–obl(ique),+gov(erned)]; and morphological exponents may be underspecified with respect to these features. Finally, instead of a single general constraint like *STRUC$_C$, there are individual markedness constraints acting against the more primitive CASE features — *[+gov] and *[–obl], in the case at hand. Differential argument encoding then emerges as a morphological phenomenon where post-syntactic deletion of primitive case features as a consequence of optimization leads to impoverished feature structures that then form the input for morphological realization, with the consequence that a less specific (more underspecified) morphological exponent will be inserted into a given functional head. All of this is more or less exactly as in standard Distributed Morphology approaches (cf. Halle & Marantz 1993), except that the retreat to the general case with morphological realization is not brought about by designed impoverishment rules, but rather by optimization procedures which resolve conflicts between special kinds of faithfulness constraints (based on harmonic alignment of scales and local conjunction with MAX-C) and markedness constraints (demanding deletion of primitive case features).

2.2.2 Two-Dimensional differential object marking in Mannheim German

For concreteness, let us look at one particular empirical phenomenon in a bit more detail, viz., the case of differential object marking in Mannheim German. In all varieties of German, feminine, neuter and plural DPs are morphologically indistinguishable in nominative and accusative environments (plural DPs never show gender contrasts in German). In the substandard variety of German spoken in and around Mannheim (and elsewhere in Palatine and Rhine areas), the same holds generally for masculine DPs, in contrast to what is the case in Standard German (see below).[7] This is shown for some types of masculine DP$_{int}$ arguments by the sentences in (11). In all these examples, the morphological exponents glossed as ACC are identical to the ones used in nominative contexts in both Mannheim Ger-

---

[7] This phenomenon is also known as "Rheinischer Akkusativ"; see, e.g., Behaghel (1911), Bräutigam (1934), Karch (1975a,b), Post (1990), Müller (2003), and Keine (2010).

man and Standard German; and Standard German would have a morphological exponent -*n* instead of the -*r* exponent in all these cases.[8]

(11) a. Ich   wünsch Ihnen   [_DP_ ein-Ø schön-er Tag] noch
          I   wish   you.DAT   a-ACC   nice-ACC day   PTCL

      b. Wir haben [_DP_ pädagogisch-er Planungstag]
          we   have   pedagocial-ACC planning day

      c. Ich hab   auch [_DP_ ein-Ø schön-er Ball], meinst du,   bloß du
          I   have also   a-ACC nice-ACC ball,   think   you, just you
          hast   [_DP_ ein-er] ?
          have   a-ACC

      d. Man müsste mal wieder so   richtig [_DP_ ein-er   ] drauf machen
          one should PTCL again   PTCL really   one-ACC   on it make
          'We should really have a night on the town again.'

      e. Hol   mir mal   [_DP_ d-er   Eimer]
          fetch me   PTCL   the-ACC   bucket

However, there are two contexts where this pattern of nominative/accusative syncretism fails to show up with masculine DPs in Mannheim German. First, as noted in Keine & Müller (2011, 2014), use of -*r* instead of -*n* is systematically not extended to *pronouns*. As shown in (12), masculine personal pronouns are marked differently in nominative and accusative contexts.

(12) Hol   [_DP_ en   / *er   ] mir   mal   her
      fetch   him-ACC   he-ACC   me-DAT   PTCL PTCL

Second, Kalin (2016) claims (based on data provided by Philipp Weisser (p.c.)) that use of -*r* instead of -*n* does not occur with *human* referents; see (13a). In contrast,

---

[8] The *ə* preceding -*r* is presumably not inherently part of the exponent but inserted in the phonological component. Also note that writing is normalized as much as possible, here and in what follows, even though the literature often renders these kinds of examples in a writing that is closer to Palatine pronunciation (with IPA-based notation as in Karch (1975a) as an extreme case). One reason for this is to simplify exposition; another one is that the morphosyntactic phenomenon at hand is actually not inherently tied to typical pronunciation of any Palatine *dialect* in the strict sense but may co-occur with a pronunciation that is close to that of Standard German, or may, in fact, be confined to written contexts (as is the case, e.g., with (11b), which I found printed on a sheet pinned to a notice board in a Mannheim nursery school in 2002).

it is observed in Müller (2003: 353–354) that *-r* rather than *-n* does in fact occur with human referents; see (13b).

(13) a. Du hast [_DP_ d-*en* / *d-*er* Mann] gesehen
you have   the-ACC / the-ACC man seen

b. Die find' [_DP_ kein-Ø ander-*er* Mann]
she.DEM finds   no-ACC other-ACC man

It would seem that for at least some version of the Mannheim German variety, both assessments are correct, with definiteness as the relevant factor discriminating between the two cases: A DP$_{int}$ with a *definite human* referent does not permit assimilation of nominative and accusative, whereas a DP$_{int}$ with an *indefinite human* referent does.[9]

---

[9] It should be pointed out that there is substantial variation with respect to differential object marking in Mannheim German. Evidence from spoken language corpora suggests that speakers who employ Rheinischer Akkusativ also regularly employ the Standard German forms; e.g., Karch (1975a) documents two cases where a single speaker switches between the two options within a single recording. Cf., for instance, (i a) vs. (i b) (from Karch's speaker Sp$_1$) and (i c) vs. (i d) (from Karch's speaker Sp$_4$).

(i) a. Dann mach ich [_DP_ mein-Ø Spaziergang]
then make I   my-ACC walk

b. Nachher hat man ja [_DP_ d-*en* Parkring]
afterwards has one PTCL   the-ACC park ring road

c. [_DP_ Ein-Ø großer Raum in unserer Versorgung] spielt die Jugendarbeit
a-ACC great-ACC room in our logistics plays the streetwork

d. Er muss [_DP_ d-*en* Aufbau der Photographie] erlernen
he must   the-ACC structure of the photography learn

Only (i a) and (i c) correspond to what is assumed in the text about Mannheim German (with *-Ø* instead of *-r* as the exponent that is otherwise confined to nominative contexts in the case of determiners triggering a "mixed" (weak/strong) inflection like *ein* or *mein*.) I will leave open the question of whether such variation should be assumed to reveal underlying optionality (and might then be addressed in terms of stochastic optimality; see above), or whether it should perhaps be taken to indicate code-switching between standard and substandard varieties of German. From a broader perspective, these qualifications may suggest that the generalizations made about differential object marking in Mannheim German in the main text involve some idealization — but the general pattern of Rheinischer Akkusativ and its selective absence in highly atypical environments for DP$_{int}$ arguments cannot be called into question.

In contrast to what is the case in Mannheim German, masculine DPs in Standard German uniformly exhibit designated object markers -*n* on pre-nominal material, irrespectively of definiteness and animacy status of the DP; compare, e.g., the Standard German versions of (11a), (11e), and (13b), which are given in (14).

(14) a. *Ich wünsche Ihnen* [$_{DP}$ *ein-en schön-en Tag*] *noch*
I wish you.DAT a-ACC nice-ACC day PTCL

b. *Hol mir mal* [$_{DP}$ *d-en Eimer*]
fetch me PTCL the-ACC bucket

c. *Die findet* [$_{DP}$ *kein-en ander-en Mann*]
she.DEM finds no-ACC other-ACC man

Thus, Mannheim German does, and Standard German does not, make use of differential object marking. Clearly, Hale/Silverstein scales are at work in the former variety: Pronouns outrank nouns on the definiteness scale (see (5c)), human referents outrank inanimates on the animacy scale (see (5b)), and differential object marking (with a special exponent -*n* instead of the more general, non-accusative specific -*r*) occurs in contexts regulated by these two factors, i.e., with non-prototypical DP$_{int}$ arguments. This suggests an application of Aissen's approach to this phenomenon. Extending the analysis in Keine & Müller (2011, 2014) that is solely concerned with the definiteness scale by the evidence from Kalin (2016) and Müller (2003) on animacy, the first thing to note is that differential object marking in Mannheim German needs to be treated as a two-dimensional phenomenon: As we have just seen, both the animacy scale and the definiteness scale play a role. Harmonic alignment with the basic, binary grammatical function scale gives rise to (15a,b) (= (6b), (6c)).

(15) a. *DP$_{int}$/Hum ≫ *DP$_{int}$/Anim ≫ *DP$_{int}$/Inan

b. *DP$_{int}$/Pro ≫ *DP$_{int}$/PN ≫ *DP$_{int}$/Def ≫ *DP$_{int}$/Spec ≫ *DP$_{int}$/NSpec

Next, the two hierarchies with fixed internal rankings thus derived are locally conjoined with one another, giving rise to two-dimensional local conjunction. Here, each constraint of one hierarchy is locally conjoined with each constraint of the other hierarchy, preserving original orders, as before. The new hierarchies that result are given in (16a,b).[10]

---

[10] Following Aissen (2003), I adopt a simplified notation where, e.g., "*DP$_{int}$/Hum/Pro" stands for "*DP$_{int}$/Hum &$_{XP}$ *DP$_{int}$/Pro" (where linear order of the two conjuncts is irrelevant).

(16) a. (i) $*DP_{int}$/Pro/Hum $\gg$ $*DP_{int}$/PN/Hum $\gg$ $*DP_{int}$/Def/Hum $\gg$ $*DP_{int}$/Spec/Hum $\gg$ $*DP_{int}$/NSpec/Hum
     (ii) $*DP_{int}$/Pro/Anim $\gg$ $*DP_{int}$/PN/Anim $\gg$ $*DP_{int}$/Def/Anim $\gg$ $*DP_{int}$/Spec/Anim $\gg$ $*DP_{int}$/NSpec/Anim
     (iii) $*DP_{int}$/Pro/Inan $\gg$ $*DP_{int}$/PN/Inan $\gg$ $*DP_{int}$/Def/Inan $\gg$ $*DP_{int}$/Spec/Inan $\gg$ $*DP_{int}$/NSpec/Inan
   b. (i) $*DP_{int}$/Pro/Hum $\gg$ $*DP_{int}$/Pro/Anim $\gg$ $*DP_{int}$/Pro/Inan
     (ii) $*DP_{int}$/PN/Hum $\gg$ $*DP_{int}$/PN/Anim $\gg$ $*DP_{int}$/PN/Inan
     (iii) $*DP_{int}$/Def/Hum $\gg$ $*DP_{int}$/Def/Anim $\gg$ $*DP_{int}$/Def/Inan
     (iv) $*DP_{int}$/Spec/Hum $\gg$ $*DP_{int}$/Spec/Anim $\gg$ $*DP_{int}$/Spec/Inan
     (v) $*DP_{int}$/NSpec/Hum $\gg$ $*DP_{int}$/NSpec/Anim $\gg$ $*DP_{int}$/NSpec/Inan

Finally, the hierarchies in (16) are locally conjoined with MAX-C, again preserving original orders. As a consequence, a two-dimensional system of differential object marking arises where some constraint pairs exhibit a fixed ranking, and others do not (such that languages simply can choose how they rank the constraints with respect to one another). Following Aissen (2003), fixed and variable rankings among the constraints generated by local conjunction of members of fixed hierarchies with one another and with MAX-C can be represented as in (17). In this graph, constraints that stand in a domination relation invariantly have a fixed ranking, whereas constraints that do not stand in a domination relation are freely ordered with respect to each other.

(17) *Two-dimensional differential object marking in Mannheim German*

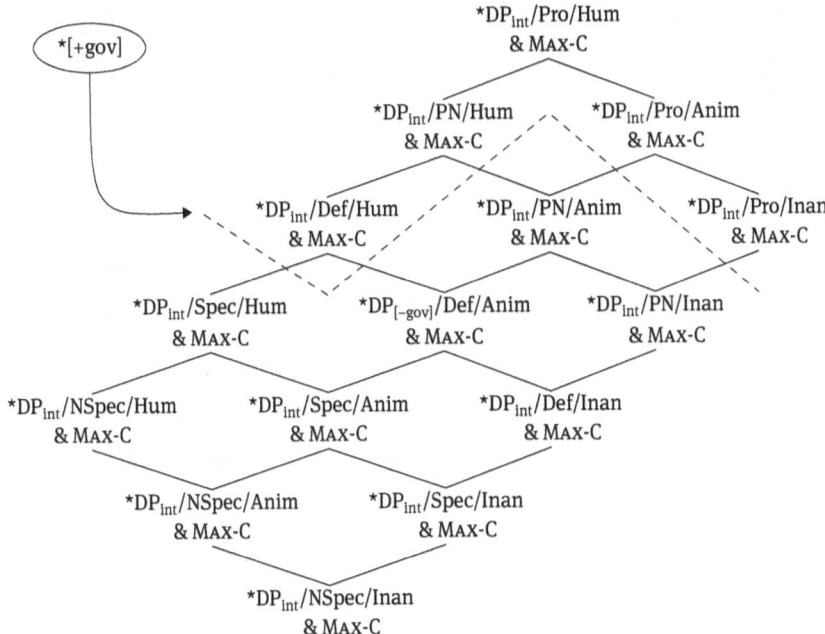

All the constraints in (17) derived by (repeated) local conjunction demand preservation of syntactic case features for morphological realization. These constraints are counteracted by the markedness constraint *[+gov], which brings about case feature deletion. The combined evidence from Müller (2003), Keine & Müller (2011, 2014) and Kalin (2016) suggests that *[+gov] is ranked with respect to the complex faithfulness constraints as indicated in (17). It thus brings about deletion of [+gov] in environments that are (insufficiently) protected by lower-ranked constraints. The sample optimizations in (18) and (19) illustrate the outcoume of the competition in two minimally different scenarios. In (18), the syntax has delivered an object DP with a complex accusative case feature ([−obl,+gov]) which is masculine, has a human referent, and qualifies as indefinite specific. This forms the input to post-syntactic optimization, from which the output O_1 in which [+gov] is deleted emerges as optimal: *[+gov] (which demands deletion of [+gov]) outranks *DP_{int}/Spec/Hum & Max-C (which demands preservation of [+gov] for this input), and this blocks O_2.

(18) *Local conjunction sample optimization I: deletion of [+gov]:*

I: DP$_{int}$:[+masc,−def, +hum,+gov,−obl]	*DP$_{int}$/Def/Hum & Max-C	*[+gov]	*DP$_{int}$/Spec/Hum & Max-C	*DP$_{int}$/Def/Anim & Max-C
☞O$_1$: DP$_{int}$[−obl]			*	
O$_2$: DP$_{int}$[+gov,−obl]		*!		

In (19), there is again an object DP bearing accusative ([−obl,+gov]) which is masculine and has a human referent. However, this time, DP$_{int}$ qualifies as definite (rather than indefinite, as in (18)). Now O$_2$, which retains the case feature [+gov], emerges as optimal: *DP$_{int}$/Def/Hum & Max-C outranks *[+gov], and O$_1$'s violation of the former constraint becomes fatal.

(19) *Local conjunction sample optimization II: preservation of [+gov]:*

I: DP$_{int}$:[+masc,+def, +hum,+gov,−obl]	*DP$_{int}$/Def/Hum & Max-C	*[+gov]	*DP$_{int}$/Spec/Hum & Max-C	*DP$_{int}$/Def/Anim & Max-C
O$_1$: DP$_{int}$[−obl]	*!			
☞O$_2$: DP$_{int}$[+gov,−obl]		*		

The outputs of these interface optimization procedures then form the input to morphological realization. Suppose that the (underspecified) feature specifications associated with the two masculine case exponents under consideration look as in (20) (in both Standard and Mannheim German), with *-n* being the more specific masculine accusative exponent, and *-r* a general masculine marker of structural case.[11] Then, given that morphological exponence ("vocabulary insertion") requires both compatibility and maximal specificity (see, e.g., Halle's (1997) Subset Principle), deletion of [+gov] in contexts covered by complex faithfulness constraints dominated by *[+gov] in the ranking is correctly predicted to result in *-r* as the accusative marker, and preservation of [+gov] in contexts covered by complex faithfulness constraints dominating *[+gov] in the ranking is correctly predicted to result in *-n* as the accusative marker.[12]

---

[11] This alternation shows up in *strong* declension contexts. Completely analogous considerations to what is said about this in the main text will apply in the case of *weak* declension contexts, where Ø alternates with *-n*.

[12] Of course, it is perfectly conceivable that post-syntactic morphological realization is also handled in an optimality-theoretic way (which incorporates the compatibility and specificity requirements); see Trommer (2001), among others.

(20) *Masculine exponents for structural case in German*:
  a. -n → [+masc,+gov,−obl]
  b. -r → [+masc,−obl]

A side remark: This approach views differential argument encoding as a consequence of post-syntactic feature deletion.[13] One might therefore think that the postulation of genuine impoverishment rules might be a viable alternative. However, this is not the case. First, as can be seen in (17), the contexts in which case feature deletion takes place in Mannheim German do not form a natural class that can be referred to by a single impoverishment rule; therefore two separate impoverishment rules would have to be stipulated, as in (21). Second, an impoverishment approach cannot derive the implicational generalizations that hold with differential argument encoding.

(21) a. [+gov] → Ø / DP$_{[+hum,-def]}$__
     b. [+gov] → Ø / DP$_{[-hum,-pro]}$__

The contexts in which deletion occurs do form a natural class in the optimality-theoretic approach to deletion, though, which is defined by the property of being dominated by the markedness constraint *[+gov].[14]

Returning to the main plot, it can be concluded that cumulativity plays an important role in this analysis. Focussing just on the two scenarios at hand (see (18) and (19)), here is how constraints must be ranked with respect to *[+gov]: First, *DP$_{int}$/Def must be ranked below *[+gov] (definite object DPs can occur in principle, as in (11b), (11e), (13a), and (i a,b,d) of footnote 9).[15] Second, MAX-C must be ranked below *[+gov] ([+gov] is often deleted in optimal outputs; cf. the examples in (11), (13a), and (i a,c) of footnote 9). Third, the constraint *DP$_{int}$/Def &$_{XP}$ MAX-C

---

13 Such feature deletion effects a retreat to the general case, which will then often involve a zero exponent given that there is a general tendency of iconicity in these systems, with morphological exponents characterized by fewer phonological segments typically being associated with more underspecification with respect to morphosyntactic features, and zero exponents often emerging as maximally underspecified; see Halle & Marantz (1993), Wiese (1996, 2004).

14 A similar issue can arise in syntactic approaches that strive to make do with a single syntactic feature (like (generalized) [Person]) for differential object marking in a given language where the empirical evidence may suggest cumulative interaction of various factors; see Richards (2014), Bárány (2015), among others.

15 See Aissen (1999) for the possibility that marked configurations may not only come at the price of special argument encoding, but may in fact also be prohibited completely in a language, thereby triggering non-trivial grammatical function-changing.

resulting from local conjunction must be ranked below *[+gov] (there are definite object DPs with their [+gov] feature deleted, as in (11b), (11e), and (i a) of footnote 9). Fourth, *DP_{int}/Hum must be ranked below *[+gov] (there are object DPs with a human referent, as in (13a) and (13b)). Fifth, the constraint *DP_{int}/Hum &$_{XP}$ MAX-C that is generated via local conjunction must be ranked below *[+gov] (there are object DPs with a human referent where [+gov] is deleted; see (13b)). Sixth, the constraint *DP_{int}/Def &$_{XP}$ *DP_{int}/Hum is ranked below *[+gov] (there are object DPs that are definite and have a human referent, as in (13a)). However, seventh and finally, when the three individual constraints *DP_{int}/Def, *DP_{int}/Hum, and MAX-C combine their efforts by local conjunction, resulting in *DP_{int}/Def &$_{XP}$ *DP_{int}/Hum &$_{XP}$ MAX-C, this complex constraint is finally ranked *above* *[+gov]. There are no accusative object DPs in Mannheim German which (i) are definite, (ii) have a human referent, and (iii) have their case feature deleted. Thus, the cumulative interaction of *DP_{int}/Def, *DP_{int}/Hum and MAX-C can outweigh high-ranked *[+gov] and thereby suppress case feature deletion. On the other hand, by assumption, there is no such cumulative interaction of *[+gov] and *DP_{int}/Def, *DP_{int}/Hum: *[+gov] simply does not undergo local conjunction with these other constraints.

2.3 Harmonic Grammar and differential argument encoding in morphology

Let us now try to transfer the gist of this analysis of Mannheim German object marking into a Harmonic Grammar account. Here are some prerequisites, focussing on the same scenarios as before (cf. (18), (19)). First, recall that harmonic alignment of scales produces a fixed ranking among the constraints thus generated; harmonic alignment is independently needed in Harmonic Grammar as well, and what used to be a fixed ranking will now translate into invariant weight differences among the individual constraints. For instance, if *DP_{int}/Spec (for indefinite specific object DPs) is assumed to have a weight of 1.0, *DP_{int}/Def (for definite object DPs) will have to have a greater weight like, e.g., 2.0.[16] Second, cumulative interaction of *DP_{int}/Def and MAX-C does not per se outweigh *[+gov] (this is so because *[+gov] triggers case feature deletion in [–hum] contexts); so the weight of *[+gov] must be greater than the combined weights of *DP_{int}/Def and MAX-C. Third, cumulative interaction of *DP_{int}/Hum and MAX-C does not

---

[16] A basic characteristic of Harmonic Grammar is that the specific assignment of weights to constraints (e.g., 1.0 and 2.0) does not actually matter; the only thing that is crucial is the relative distance between weights. So, in the case at hand, the two constraints under consideration could in principle also have been assigned weights like 2.0 vs. 4.0, respectively.

per se outweigh *[+gov] either (given that *[+gov] triggers case feature deletion in [−def] contexts); so the weight of *[+gov] must be greater than the combined weights of *DP$_{int}$/Hum and MAX-C. Fourth, cumulative interaction of *DP$_{int}$/Spec, *DP$_{int}$/Hum and MAX-C still does not outweigh *[+gov] (*[+gov] triggers case feature deletion in [−def,+hum] contexts); so the weight of *[+gov] must be greater than the weights of *DP$_{int}$/Spec, *DP$_{int}$/Hum and MAX-C taken together. Fifth, cumulative interaction of *DP$_{int}$/Def, *DP$_{int}$/Hum and MAX-C finally manages to outweigh *[+gov] (*[+gov] does not trigger case feature deletion in [+def,+hum] contexts). One might think that all of this can be accomplished by assigning the relevant constraints the weights in (22): Only if *DP$_{int}$/Def (with a weight of 2.0), *DP$_{int}$/Hum (2.0), and MAX-C (1.0) gang up can they ensure that *[+gov] (4.5) can be violated by an optimal candidate, and case feature deletion is suppressed.

(22) *Constraints and weights*:

    a.   *DP$_{int}$/Def $w = 2.0$

    b.   *DP$_{int}$/Hum $w = 2.0$

    c.   *DP$_{int}$/Spec $w = 1.0$

    d.   MAX-C $w = 1.0$

    e.   *[+gov] $w = 4.5$

However, it turns out that this is not the case: Neither based on the weights in (22), nor based on any other conceivable weight assignment can the interacting constraints in (22) yield the intended effects. Consider first case feature deletion in environments where the accusative object DP has a human referent but is indefinite specific. The competition is illustrated in (23) (cf. (18)).

(23) *Harmonic Grammar sample optimization I: deletion of [+gov]*:

I: DP$_{int}$:[+masc,−def, +hum,+gov,−obl]	*DP$_{int}$/Def $w = 2.0$	*DP$_{int}$/Hum $w = 2.0$	*DP$_{int}$/Spec $w = 1.0$	MAX-C $w = 1.0$	*[+gov] $w = 4.5$	H
☞ O$_1$: DP$_{int}$[−obl]		−1	−1	−1		−4
O$_2$: DP$_{int}$[+gov,−obl]		−1	−1		−1	−7.5

At first sight, this might look like the right result. The joint efforts of *DP$_{int}$/Hum, *DP$_{int}$/Spec and MAX-C are not enough to ensure case feature preservation against *[+gov], which demands case feature deletion. As shown by the column labelled H (where H stands for Harmony as defined in (3)), O$_1$ (with deletion of [+gov]) is assigned a harmony score of −4, whereas O$_2$ (with preservation of [+gov]) has a harmony score of −7.5. However, (23) already illustrates the fundamental problem:

Candidate O_2 does not only violate *[+gov] (as intended); it automatically and invariably also violates *DP_{int}/Hum and *DP_{int}/Spec. The reason for this is that whether or not DP_{int} has its [+gov] feature deleted, it always qualifies as having a human referent (thereby violating *DP_{int}/Hum) and as being indefinite specific (thereby violating *DP_{int}/Spec). Thus, to ensure that O_1 is optimal in (23), it would actually suffice to assume that *[+gov] has a weight that is minimally greater than that of Max-C (e.g., 1.5); it is these two constraints alone that determine the optimal output since the candidates do not differ with respect to all the other constraints. The additional, unintended violations of *DP_{int}/Hum and *DP_{int}/Spec by O_2 (which are signalled by boxes here), though harmless in (23), will then become fatal in competitions where the output with case feature preservation is supposed to win; cf. (24).

(24) *Harmonic Grammar sample optimization II: failure of preservation of [+gov]:*

I: DP_{int}:[+masc,+def, +hum,+gov,−obl]	*DP_{int}/Def $w = 2.0$	*DP_{int}/Hum $w = 2.0$	*DP_{int}/Spec $w = 1.0$	Max-C $w = 1.0$	*[+gov] $w = 4.5$	H
☞O_1: DP_{int}[−obl]	−1	−1		−1		−5
O_2: DP_{int}[+gov,−obl]	−1	−1			−1	−8.5

Here the added weights of *DP_{int}/Def (2.0), *DP_{int}/Hum (2.0) and Max-C (1.0) are indeed greater than the individual weight of *[+gov] (4.5). However, as shown in (24), O_1 (with case feature deletion) will still be the optimal candidate since O_2 (with case feature preservation) not only violates *[+gov], but also *DP_{int}/Def and *DP_{int}/Hum. Thus, again it turns out that the actual weight assigned to *[+gov] is irrelevant (as long as is is greater than that of Max-C to ensure the possibility of case feature deletion in the first place). The underlying rationale here is that constraints can never be switched off in Harmonic Grammar, and this implies that there will be an unwanted excitatory interaction of *[+gov], *DP_{int}/Def, and *DP_{int}/Hum in a candidate that preserves [+gov] on a human, definite object DP.

One can ask whether there might be a way to salvage the Harmonic Grammar account after all. Three possibilities come to mind. First, either *[+gov] or both *DP_{int}/Def and *DP_{int}/Hum might be modified in such a way that *[+gov] does not interact with the other constraints anymore. However, an appropriate reformulation seems impossible: If, e.g., *[+gov] would be conceived of as stating that [+gov] must be absent in an output DP_{int}, and that this absence then implies the absence of information about the definiteness and animacy status of DP_{int}, this would be (i) utterly *ad hoc*, (ii) contradicted by factual observation (after all, the definiteness and animacy information is still accessible), (iii) at variance with basic optimality-theoretic views as to what complexity primitive constraints can have in morphosyntax (see Grimshaw 1998), and (iv) actually extremely difficult to formulate properly. Second, one might try to modify the domain for constraint evaluation. Reducing the domain for constraint evaluation might remove an unwanted gang effect if the constraints apply in different local domains. The problem here is that the local domain for case evaluation would have to be smaller than the minimal XP; but then, the cumulative interaction with MAX-C could not be modelled anymore either. The problem here is that MAX-C and *[+gov] talk about the same feature. Third, one might adopt an approach that combines Harmonic Grammar with Harmonic Serialism (see McCarthy & Pater 2016). Harmonic serialism removes many potential cumulative interactions of constraints because of the tenet that (a) optimization proceeds serially, and (b) outputs may differ from inputs only by the application of at most one operation. However, this does not hold for the case at hand. The two relevant outputs O_1 and O_2 in (23) and (24) are generated on the basis of an input in accordance with the basic tenets of Harmonic Serialism already (viz., application of at most one operation; see McCarthy 2010, 2016, Heck & Müller 2007, 2016).

In view of these considerations, I think it is safe to conclude that the problem of unwanted cumulative interaction of constraints in Harmonic Grammar poses an insurmountable obstacle to a faithful transfer of the analysis of cumulative effects with differential object marking in Mannheim German along the lines of Aissen (2003) from an optimality-theoretic approach based on local conjunction to an approach in terms of Harmonic Grammar. What is more, it turns out that this consequence is not merely an accidental property of the specific pattern and analysis of differential argument encoding in Mannheim German; it does in fact hold much more generally. In the next subsection, this is illustrated on the basis of a morphological reanalysis of argument encoding in three-way systems.

2.4 Three-way systems

In some languages (among them Antekerrepenhe, Kham, Warrangu, Djapu, Nez Perce, Arabana, Pitjantjatjara, Dyirbal, Warlpiri, and Upriver Halkomelem), argument encoding proceeds in a way that has been described as involving a syntactic three-way system, such that there is an ergative case for DP_{ext} of a transitive V, an accusative case for DP_{int} of a transitive V, and an absolutive case for DP_{ext} or DP_{int} of an intransitive V. In Müller & Thomas (2017) it is argued that apparent three-way systems do not exist, and that these patterns should be viewed as regular ergative or (less often) accusative encoding systems exhibiting allomorphy of case markers (typically of the non-zero/zero type). Against the background of Keine & Müller (2014), direct evidence for this is provided by the observation that virtually all instances of putative three-way systems also exhibit differential argument encoding governed by prominence scales, i.e., the distribution of "ergative" and "accusative" case markers never seems to be purely based on the DP_{ext} vs. DP_{int} status in a transitive environment.[17] Furthermore, closer inspection reveals independent syntactic evidence for postulating standard two-way systems of argument encoding rather than three-way systems (based on phenomena like case-matching in topic chaining constructions, concord in complex DPs, and coordination of different types of DPs, all of which suggest that differences in case exponence are purely morphological and do not indicate the presence of two different syntactic cases here).[18]

As an example, consider the argument encoding system in the Tibeto-Burman language Kham (see Watters 2002: 66f.). As shown in (25), there are three different morphological case exponents. This has been taken to instantiate a three-way system of syntactic case assignment involving ergative, absolutive, and accusative case.

(25) *Distribution of case markers in Kham*

	1st	2nd	3rd, definite	3rd, indefinite
DP_{ext}-V_{trans}	-Ø	-Ø	-e/-ye	-e/-ye
$DP_{ext/int}$-$V_{intrans}$	-Ø	-Ø	-Ø	-Ø
DP_{int}-V_{trans}	-lai	-lai	-lai	-Ø

In contrast, in Müller & Thomas (2017) it is argued that Kham actually employs a canonical ergative case system in the syntax, with differential encoding of syntactically ergative arguments along the person scale (see (5a)), and two-dimensional differential encoding of syntactically absolutive arguments along (i) the definiteness scale (see (5c)) and (ii) a further transitivity scale that takes the form of (26).

---

[17] As described by Bittner & Hale (1996), the Central Australian language Antekerrepenhe might perhaps be an exception in this regard; however, the scarcity of the available empirical evidence makes it difficult to draw firm conclusions here.

[18] See Legate (2008), Kalin & Weisser (2019), and Weisser (2017) for further evidence that variation in morphological case exponence often does not indicate variation in syntactic case assignment. Also see Müller & Thomas (2017) and Thomas (2015: Sect. 3) for morphology-based accounts of the few cases where it may initially look like there is in fact independent syntactic evidence after all for postulating three separate syntactic cases underlying languages with three-way systems, as argued by Legate (2008) on the basis of zero-marked DPs in non-finite contexts in Warlpiri, and by Deal (2014) for DP-internal modifiers and coordination in Nez Perce.

(26) *Transitivity scale:*

$V_{t(rans)} > V_{i(ntrans)}$

On this view, *-e/-ye* is the canonical ergative exponent and *-lai* is the canonical absolutive exponent; *-Ø* is an elsewhere marker that is inserted after case feature deletion at the syntax/morphology interface (affecting both syntactic ergative and syntactic absolutive). Thus, the simple person-based split in ergative contexts, and the more complex transitivity-/definiteness-based split in absolutive contexts, are instances of allomorphic variation reducible to scale-driven optimization. Relevant examples from Kham are given in (27) (see Watters 2002: 66–67, Thomas 2015: 6); the glosses reflect the view that the language does not instantiate a three-way system but is a based on an ergative encoding pattern, with allomorphic variation in both the ergative (*-e/-ye* in (27b,c) vs. *-Ø* in (27d,e)) and the absolutive (*-lai* in (27b) vs. *-Ø* in (27a,c,d,e)).

(27) a. *laː-Ø   si-ke*
leopard-ABS die-PRF
'The leopard died.'

b. *gẽːh-ye ŋa-lai duhp-na-ke-o*
OX-ERG I-ABS butt-1SG-PRF-3SG
'The ox butted me.'

c. *tipəlkya-e   laː-Ø   səih-ke-o*
Tipalkya-ERG leopard-ABS kill-PRF-3SG
'Tipalkya killed a leopard.'

d. *ŋaː-Ø laː-Ø   ŋa-səih-ke*
I-ERG leopard-ABS 1SG-kill-PRF
'I killed a leopard.'

e. *ŋaː-Ø noː-lai ŋa-r̃ɨːh-ke*
I-ERG he-ABS 1SG-see-PRF
'I saw him.'

One additional assumption needs to be made for an analysis based on harmonic alignment and local conjunction. Here the basic binary scale required for harmonic alignment cannot simply be a hierarchy of grammatical functions (DP_{ext}, DP_{int}). Rather it must be a hierarchy of cases assigned in the syntax (DP_{erg}, DP_{abs}; where ergative is assumed to be characterized by the case feature [+gov], and absolutive by the case feature [−gov]).

Focussing exclusively on differential absolute marking here and in what follows, harmonic alignment of the binary case scale with the transitivity scale and the definiteness scale yields the two constraint hierarchies for absolutive ([–gov]) DPs in (28).

(28) a. $*DP_{[-gov]}/v_t \gg *DP_{[-gov]}/v_i$

b. $*DP_{[-gov]}/Pro \gg *DP_{[-gov]}/PN \gg *DP_{[-gov]}/Def \gg *DP_{[-gov]}/Spec \gg *DP_{[-gov]}/NSpec$

Note that this presupposes that the information about predicate type is locally accessible on a DP. As argued in Müller & Thomas (2017), this follows if the *phase* is the relevant domain for local conjunction, rather than the minimal XP, as assumed so far (see Section 2.1 and footnote 4).

Next, the two hierarchies with fixed internal rankings thus derived are locally conjoined with one another, giving rise to two-dimensional local conjunction, as before; see (29).

(29) a. $*DP_{[-gov]}/Pro/v_t \gg *DP_{[-gov]}/PN/v_t \gg *DP_{[-gov]}/Def/v_t \gg *DP_{[-gov]}/Spec/v_t \gg *DP_{[-gov]}/NSpec/v_t$

b. $*DP_{[-gov]}/Pro/v_i \gg *DP_{[-gov]}/PN/v_i \gg *DP_{[-gov]}/Def/v_i \gg *DP_{[-gov]}/Spec/v_i \gg *DP_{[-gov]}/NSpec/v_i$

c. $*DP_{[-gov]}/Pro/v_t \gg *DP_{[-gov]}/Pro/v_i$

d. $*DP_{[-gov]}/PN/v_t \gg *DP_{[-gov]}/PN/v_i$

e. $*DP_{[-gov]}/Def/v_t \gg *DP_{[-gov]}/Def/v_i$

f. $*DP_{[-gov]}/Spec/v_t \gg *DP_{[-gov]}/Spec/v_i$

g. $*DP_{[-gov]}/NSpec/v_t \gg *DP_{[-gov]}/NSpec/v_i$

Finally, the hierarchies in (29) are locally conjoined with Max-C, again preserving original orders. As a consequence, a two-dimensional system of argument encoding arises where some constraint pairs exhibit a fixed ranking, and others do not; see (30).

(30) *Two-dimensional differential absolutive marking in Kham*

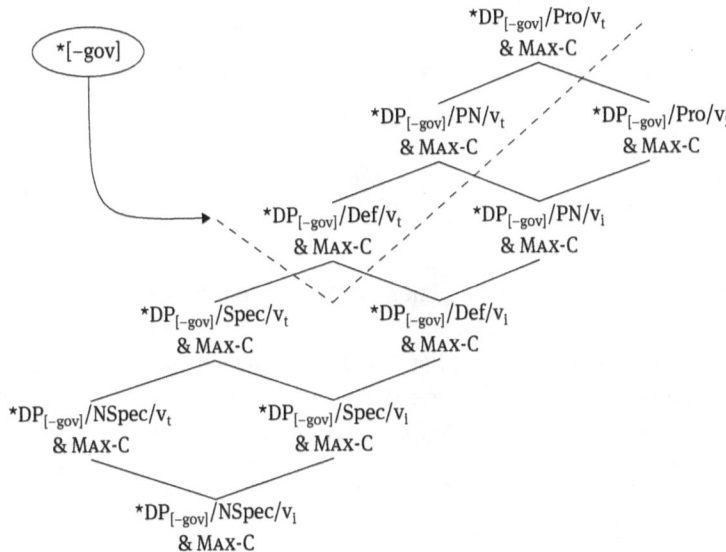

Suppose, again following Aissen (1999, 2003), that *[–gov] cannot be locally conjoined with the constraints in (29); and suppose further that that *[–gov] is interspersed with the constraints derived by multiple local conjunction in the way shown here. It can then be derived that absolutive case ([–gov]) is deleted in the environments protected by constraints that are outranked by *[–gov] in (30) (ultimately yielding -Ø as the morphological exponent), whereas [–gov] is retained in environments protected by constraints that outrank *[–gov] in (30) (ultimately yielding the non-zero absolutive marker -*lai*).[19]

Let us again consider two sample optimizations. In (31), the input to optimization at the syntax/morphology interface is an absolutive-marked DP that is interpreted as indefinite specific and occurs with a transitive verb. Since *[–gov] is ranked higher than *$DP_{[-gov]}$/Spec/v_t & Max-C in (31), the optimal candidate O_1

---

[19] Two further remarks. First, in this analysis, [–gov] plays a dual role. On the one hand, [–gov] in "*$DP_{[-gov]}$/v_t" refers to the input (i.e., the syntactic representation where feature deletion is not yet an issue). Thus, constraints like *$DP_{[-gov]}$/v_t & Max-C are not only output-sensitive, but also input-sensitive (see Trommer 2006). On the other hand, [–gov] in "Max-C" refers to the output (i.e., the post-syntactic representation in which feature deletion may or may not have applied). Second, this analysis evidently presupposes that the absolutive can indeed be a non-zero case, even if there is a cross-linguistic tendency for it to be less (or not) marked segmentally. See Handschuh (2014) for evidence and discussion.

has deletion of the case feature (and subsequent morphological realization by -∅).

(31) *Local conjunction sample optimization III: deletion of [–gov]:*

I: DP:[–def,–gov]	*DP$_{[-gov]}$/Def/v$_t$ & Max-C	*[–gov]	*DP$_{[-gov]}$/Spec/v$_t$ & Max-C	*DP$_{[-gov]}$/Def/v$_i$ & Max-C
☞ O$_1$: DP:[–]			*	
O$_2$: DP:[–gov]		*!		

In (32), the input is minimally different in that the absolutive DP in a transitive environment qualifies as definite. Since *DP$_{[-gov]}$/Def/v$_t$ & Max-C dominates *[–gov], the case feature [–gov] is preserved on the DP, and subsequent morphological realiziation will involve -*lai* (characterized by [–gov]) rather than -∅ (characterized by [–]) because of the specificity/compatibility requirements of morphological insertion.[20]

(32) *Local conjunction sample optimization IV: preservation of [–gov]:*

I: DP:[+def,–gov]	*DP$_{[-gov]}$/Def/v$_t$ & Max-C	*[–gov]	*DP$_{[-gov]}$/Spec/v$_t$ & Max-C	*DP$_{[-gov]}$/Def/v$_i$ & Max-C
O$_1$: DP:[–]	*!			
☞ O$_2$: DP:[–gov]		*		

Note that this analysis again crucially relies on cumulativity. Focussing again on just the two contexts currently under consideration, it can first be noted that neither *DP$_{[-gov]}$/Def nor *DP$_{[-gov]}$/v$_t$ can bring about a violation of *[–gov] in an optimal candidate; these constraints must be ranked below *[–gov]. Similarly, Max-C alone must also be ranked below *[–gov] (otherwise, deletion would never occur). Next, the excitatory interaction of *DP$_{[-gov]}$/Def and Max-C (via local conjunction, yielding *DP$_{[-gov]}$/Def & Max-C) is not sufficient to prevent deletion of

---

20 As before (see (21)), deriving [–gov] deletion by impoverishment rules does not look like a viable alternative: First, there would have to be two separate rules (see (i a,b)) since the deletion contexts (viz., intransitive clause and indefinite interpretation of DP) do not form a natural class.

(i) a. [–gov] → ∅ / DP__[v$_i$]
    b. [–gov] → ∅ / DP$_{[-def]}$__

Second, the contexts in which deletion applies would have to be stipulated rather than be derived from prominence scales. And third, (i a,b) would give rise to redundancies with indefinite (specific or non-specific) DPs in intransitive contexts.

[–gov] by making *[–gov] violable in an optimal output (case feature deletion as required by *[–gov] takes place in intransitive contexts). The same goes for the interaction of *DP$_{[-gov]}$/v$_t$ and MAX-C: *DP$_{[-gov]}$/v$_t$ & MAX-C must be ranked below *[–gov] because there are transitive environments where deletion of [–gov] occurs (viz., with indefinites). However, the cumulative interaction of *DP$_{[-gov]}$/v$_t$, *DP$_{[-gov]}$/Def, and MAX-C (yielding *DP$_{[-gov]}$/Def/v$_t$ & MAX-C) finally suffices to outweigh the effects of *[–gov] and ensure case feature preservation in an optimal output, in violation of *[–gov].

As in the case of differential argument encoding in Mannheim German, it turns out that a faithful transfer of the analysis to a Harmonic Grammar approach is impossible. The sample optimizations in (33) and (34) mirror those in (23) and (24), respectively. As shown in (33), effecting deletion of [–gov] in the appropriate contexts is unproblematic; the only assumption that is required is that MAX-C has a lower weight than *[–gov]. (Here I have given *[–gov] a weight of 4.5, so as to express the assumption that it alone yields a worse harmony score than the combination of *DP$_{[-gov]}$/Def, *DP$_{[-gov]}$/v$_i$, and MAX-C; as shown in the tableau, because of spurious violations of two of these constraints by O$_2$, a minimally greater weight than that of MAX-C would have sufficed.)

(33) *Harmonic Grammar sample optimization III: deletion of [–gov]:*

I: DP:[–def,–gov]	*DP$_{[-gov]}$/v$_t$ w = 2.0	*DP$_{[-gov]}$/Def w = 2.0	*DP$_{[-gov]}$/v$_i$ w = 1.0	MAX-C w = 1.0	*[–gov] w = 4.5	H
☞O$_1$: DP:[–]		–1	–1	–1		–4
O$_2$: DP:[–gov]		–1		–1		–1	–7.5

However, as shown in (34), the cumulative interaction of *DP$_{[-gov]}$/v$_t$, *DP$_{[-gov]}$/Def, and MAX-C that should lead to an optimal violation of *[–gov] (i.e., to case feature preservation) cannot be modelled in the Harmonic Grammar approach because constraints can never be switched off, and as soon as *[–gov] is violated with a definite absolutive DP in a transitive context (because its case feature is not deleted), *DP$_{[-gov]}$/v$_t$ and *DP$_{[-gov]}$/Def will invariably also be violated (because we are still dealing with a transitive context, and because the DP is still definite).[21]

---

[21] It is interesting to note that Thomas (2015: 29ff.) develops a Harmonic Grammar reanalysis of the local conjunction approach to apparent three-way systems in Müller & Thomas (2017) that can derive all the relevant contrasts. However, I would like to contend that this analysis is Harmonic Grammar in name only — the crucial cumulative interactions of constraints are not derived via gang effects of simple constraints but rather by postulating a new kind of harmonic alignment that produces contextual faithfulness constraints in much the same way that these constraints are generated under the local conjunction approach.

(34) *Harmonic Grammar sample optimization IV: failure of preservation of [−gov]:*

I: DP:[+def,−gov]	$*DP_{[-gov]}/v_t$ $w = 2.0$	$*DP_{[-gov]}/Def$ $w = 2.0$	$*DP_{[-gov]}/v_i$ $w = 1.0$	MAX-C $w = 1.0$	$*[-gov]$ $w = 4.5$	H
☞ O_1: DP:[−]	−1	−1		−1		−5
O_2: DP:[−gov]	−1	−1			−1	−8.5

To sum up so far, we arrive at a negative result for Harmonic Grammar: Harmonic Grammar as such can account for various kinds of cumulative effects, but it cannot account for the cumulative effects that show up with differential argument encoding. In the following section, I will show that exactly the same conclusion can be drawn from looking at the domain of extraction restrictions in syntax. Again, there is a cumulative effect, and its abstract pattern emerges as exactly the same as with differential argument encoding. And again, an approach in terms of local conjunction succeeds whereas an approach in terms of Harmonic Grammar fails. This, in turn, shows that the failure of Harmonic Grammar to account for cumulativity in differential argument encoding is not just an accidental, minor problem for Harmonic Grammar, but rather indicates a deep, principled shortcoming of the approach.

3 Long-distance extraction

3.1 Some restrictions on movement

In Legendre et al. (1998, 2006b), an optimality-theoretic approach to locality restrictions on movement is developed that is designed to be both flexible enough to cover the observable cross-linguistic variation, and restrictive enough to derive some implicational generalizations that seem to hold more generally. As for the latter, the authors identify two tendencies. First, the more barriers intervene in a single movement step, the more likely it is that extraction is blocked. And second, adverbials (or, more properly, non-referential items) are more restricted in their extraction options than arguments (or referential items). To account for this, Legendre et al. (1998, 2006b) rely on the assumption that cumulativity is a relevant concept, and that this concept can be implemented by invoking local conjunction.

The core data to be derived in a language like English are given in (35)–(37). In (35a,b) it is shown that both adjuncts and arguments can undergo extraction from declarative complement clauses.

(35) a. How$_1$ do [$_{TP}$ you [$_{VP}$ think [$_{CP}$ t'$_1$ that [$_{TP}$ she [$_{VP}$ did it] t$_1$]]]] ?

   b. What$_1$ do [$_{TP}$ you [$_{VP}$ think [$_{CP}$ t'$_1$ that [$_{TP}$ she [$_{VP}$ did t$_1$]]]]] ?

(36a) illustrates that wh-complement clauses are islands for extraction (see the *Wh-Island Condition* from Chomsky 1973) in the case of an adjunct. However, at least with non-finite complements (Chomsky 1986, Frampton 1990), arguments can avoid this kind of effect; see (36b).

(36) a. *How$_1$ do [$_{TP}$ you [$_{VP}$ wonder [$_{CP}$ t'$_1$ what [$_{TP}$ PRO to fix t t$_1$]]]]?

   b. What$_1$ do [$_{TP}$ you [$_{VP}$ wonder [$_{CP}$ t'$_1$ when [$_{TP}$ PRO [$_{VP}$ to fix t$_1$]]]]]?

Finally, (37a,b) shows that adjunct clauses are invariably islands for extraction, irrespective of the status of the moved item as an argument or adjunct.

(37) a. *How$_1$ was [$_{TP}$ he [$_{VP}$ fired [$_{CP}$ after behaving t$_1$]]]?

   b. *What$_1$ was [$_{TP}$ he [$_{VP}$ fired [$_{CP}$ after reading t$_1$]]]?

In view of this evidence, Legendre et al.'s (1998, 2006) hypothesis is that cumulativity plays a crucial role. On this view, extraction in (37a,b) involves too many violations of a locality constraint on movement, and extraction in (36a) involves a fatal combination of violations of this locality constraint and a separate constraint on movement of adjuncts (or non–referential items) that (35a) manages to avoid.

3.2 Local conjunction and restrictions on long-distance extraction

First, it needs to be clarified how the candidate set is defined which defines the set of competing syntactic outputs. It is assumed in Legendre et al. (1998: 257) and Legendre et al. (2006b: 225) that the concept of syntactic competition is to be understood as in (38).

(38) *Candidate sets*:
   Two candidates O$_i$, O$_j$ are part of the same candidate set iff (a) and (b) hold:
   a. O$_i$ and O$_j$ realize identical predicate/argument structure.
   b. O$_i$ and O$_j$ target identical LFs.

According to (38), syntactic competition is defined exclusively via input identity (in contrast to what is the case in most other versions of OT syntax; cf. Müller 2000 and Heck et al. 2002): The input contains predicate/argument structures with an associated LF representation. These abstract LF representations include target positions for movement that differ from base positions and are indicated by abstract scope markers in the input. More generally, this special version of the input is referred to by Legendre et al. (1998, 2006b) as the *Index*.[22]

Presupposing the basic validity of Chomsky's (1986) analysis of locality restrictions on movement in terms of barriers, Legendre et al. (1998) observe that an optimality-theoretic approach offers the possibility to adopt a simple concept of barrier based on L-marking that does not have to be accompanied by category-specific modifications and exceptions in order to ensure that VP and TP do in fact normally not block extraction even though they should qualify as barriers according to the definitions of barrier in (39), and of L-marking in (40).

(39) *Barrier* (Chomsky 1986):
An XP is a barrier iff it is not L-marked.

(40) *L-Marking* (Chomsky 1986):

α L-marks β iff (a)–(c) hold:

a. α is a lexical X^0 category.

b. α θ-marks β.

c. β is a sister of α.

Since both VP and TP are not L-marked (neither is a sister of a lexical category that might θ-mark it), these projections will qualify as barriers; however, given that constraints are violable in Optimality Theory, this does not necessarily imply that movement of some XP across either one or both of these categories (e.g., movement of an object wh-phrase to SpecC) is impossible. The central locality constraint adopted by Legendre et al. (1998, 2006b) is BAR.

---

[22] There are various non-trivial questions raised by this concept of an Index. For instance, it is not quite clear where the structure that is present in an Index comes from, given that an Index is a pre-syntactic object that forms the input to the GEN component of an optimality-theoretic grammar. However, these questions are largely orthogonal to the issue of cumulativity, and I will not dwell on them here but simply presuppose that the information about the intended scope of a scope-bearing element (such as a wh-phrase) can be represented in a syntactic input in some way, even if that input cannot yet be the result of syntactic structure-building. (Alternatively, one could assume D-structures in the sense of Chomsky (1981) to be the inputs, enriched by abstract scope markers that signal target positions for syntactic movement in S-structures. The D-Structures themselves would then arise via an earlier optimization procedure; see Heck (2001) for such a model.)

(41) BAR:
A single link of a movement chain must not cross a barrier.

By assumption, the only intermediate positions that can be targetted by movement are SpecC positions.[23] Next, a non-categorical, gradient conception of BAR (where multiple violations of this constraint simply add up) does not suffice to force intermediate movement steps via SpecC. The reason is that on such a view, it would be wrongly predicted that O_1 (with an intermediate movement step to SpecC and, consequently, two chain links) and O_2 (with movement in one fell swoop) have the same status with respect to BAR; see (42).

(42) *A wrong prediction under BAR:*

	BAR
☞ O_1: α_1 ... β ... β ... t'_1 ... β ... t_1	** *
☛ O_2: α_1 ... β ... β ... β ... t_1	***

In view of this, Legendre et al. (1998, 2006b) postulate reflexive local conjunction (see (1c)) of BAR, yielding a subhierarchy of BAR constraints, as in (43).

(43) BAR subhierarchy (derived by reflexive local conjunction):

a. BAR&$_D$BAR = BAR^2:
   A single link of a chain must not cross two barriers.

b. BAR^2&$_D$BAR = BAR^3:
   A single link of a chain must not cross three barriers.

c. BARn:
   A single link of chain must not cross n barriers.

Given that a complex constraint derived by local conjunction always outranks the constraint(s) that it is composed of (see (1b)), BAR^3 must dominate BAR^2, which in turn must dominate BAR^1. Hence, the problem of distinguishing between the two outputs O_1 and O_2 in (42) is now solved. As shown by the competition in (44), O_2 violates BAR^3 (its sole chain link crosses three barriers) whereas O_1 does not (none of the two chain links crosses more than two barriers).[24]

---

[23] This is incompatible with Chomsky's (2001) view that vP is a phase, and that movement must take place via Specv (because of the Phase Impenetrability Condition). See, however, Keine (2016) for recent arguments supporting Legendre et al.'s view.

[24] Two remarks are in order here. First, O_2 in (44) of course also violates BAR^2 and BAR^1 here. However, since these violations can never play a role, they can be ignored in tableaux.

(44) *A correct prediction derivable from the BAR subhierarchy*

	BAR³	BAR²	BAR¹
☞ O_1: $α_1$ ... β ... β ... t'_1 ... β ... t_1		*	*
O_2: $α_1$ ... β ... β ... β ... t_1	*!		

Counteracting the BAR constraints is a constraint that triggers movement. The faithfulness constraint PARSEWH in (45) takes over this role.

(45) PARSEWH:
A wh-feature contained in an Index must be realized by an operator-variable chain in the output.

Suppose now a ranking BAR³ ≫ PARSEWH ≫ BAR². Independently of whether adjunct clauses have an accessible SpecC position, this will block movement in (37a) and (37b): An adjunct CP is not L-marked, and neither are matrix VP and TP. Thus, movement fatally crosses three barriers here, and PARSEWH is violated by the optimal output.[25] Movement from complement clauses in (35a) and (35b) is uniformly predicted to be possible, with matrix VP and TP crossed by the second chain link in both cases, and embedded TP (in the case of adjunct movement) or embedded VP and TP (in the case of object movement) crossed by the first chain link. Finally, depending on whether or not an intermediate trace can be established with embedded wh-clauses, (36a) and (36b) are uniformly predicted to be possible or

---

Second, the question arises of what the domain D for local reflexive conjunction applying to BAR is. If the relevant domain is, e.g., the clause (as a unit that contains a chain link), the scenario has to be blocked where some completely different movement operation applying to some item β adds to the overall number of barriers crossed by the operation applying to the item α that we are interested in. Essentially, it looks as though the relevant domain should be the chain link. However, it is not fully clear how this can be made to work, given that the chain link is not a discrete phrase-structural unit. I will leave this question unresolved here since it does not directly affect the main issue of how to determine cumulative constraint interaction as such in Optimality Theory.

25 What does the optimal candidate look like that blocks the output with movement as suboptimal? This is part of a more general question of how ineffability (i.e., absolute ungrammaticality) is derived in optimality-theoretic syntax. Legendre et al. (1998, 2006b) assume that the optimal candidate that violates PARSEWH here simply does not create a wh-chain; it could then, e.g., reinterpret the wh-phrase as an indefinite phrase, or give rise to an uninterpretable candidate with wh-in situ throughout the derivation. An alternative to this would be to replace PARSEWH with the Empty Output Condition (EOC; a constraint also known as "Avoid Null Parse"); see Ackema & Neeleman (1998) and Heck & Müller (2003), among others. More generally, both PARSEWH and EOC introduce a threshold into constraint rankings, such that no optimal output can ever violate a constraint that dominates them. See Müller (2015) for discussion.

impossible; thus, the difference in grammaticality in (36) is not yet accounted for. To do so, it seems clear that a constraint has to be introduced that distinguishes between arguments and adjuncts. Following Cinque (1990) and others, Legendre et al. (1998, 2006b) take the real difference here to be one between referential and non-referential items, where the former include most arguments and some adjuncts, and the latter include most adjuncts and some arguments.[26] The constraint in question is (46), where a non-trivial chain is a chain consisting of more than one member (i.e., simplifying a bit, a chain based on movement).

(46) REF:
A non-trivial chain is referential.

The assumption now is that not only can BAR constraints undergo *reflexive* local conjunction (see (43)); the BAR subhierarchy can also be locally conjoined with REF. The resulting complex constraints look as in (47).

(47) BARn&$_D$REF = BARn[–ref]:
A single link of a non-referential chain must not cross n barriers.

Thus, a constraint like BAR^2[–ref] is violated if a single chain link crosses a first barrier, and the same chain link crosses a second barrier, and the chain to which the chain link belongs is not referential. Local conjunction with REF preserves the original order of BAR constraints in exactly the same way that we have seen with local conjunction with MAX-C in the previous section; so BAR^3[–ref] invariably dominates BAR^2[–ref], which in turn must outrank BAR^1[–ref]. It also follows from the system of local conjunction that BARn[–ref] must dominate BARn; and this fact makes it possible to accomodate the evidence that adjunct movement is generally more restricted than argument movement in the world's languages.

It might seem that one could now simply postulate that BAR^2[–ref] dominates PARSEWH whereas BAR^2 is dominated by PARSEWH. Returning to the question of

---

[26] Some data in support of this view based on wh-islands are given in (i). (i a) shows that non-referential argument DPs cannot be extracted from wh-clauses, like prototypical adjuncts; in contrast, (i b) shows that referential adjuncts can do so, like protoypical arguments. See Aoun (1986), Cinque (1990).

(i) a. *How many kilos do you wonder whether he weighs?
 b. ?Where do you wonder whether to go?

whether there can be intermediate traces in SpecC in wh-island contexts as in (36a) and (36b), assuming that there cannot be such traces would incorrectly block both argument movement and adjunct movement (since three or four barriers would be crossed by a single chain link, depending on the exact base position of the moved item). In contrast, if intermediate traces can be generated in SpecC, the ranking will make correct predictions for wh-islands as in (36), but it will make wrong predictions for regular extraction of adjuncts from declarative clauses, as in (35a). Legendre et al. conclude from this that an intermediate trace can indeed be generated in SpecC in wh-island contexts (note that this assumption is fully in accordance with more recent minimalist approaches where multiple specifiers cannot be excluded, especially so with intermediate steps to phase edges; cf. Chomsky 2001, 2008, 2013); and they point out that there must then be another faithfulness constraint in addition to PARSEWH that plays a role, and that can be violated in (36a) but cannot be legitimately violated in (35a). This constraint is PARSESCOPE in (48).

(48) PARSESCOPE:
The scope of a wh-chain contained in an Index must be realized by syntactic chain formation in the output.

An output may violate PARSESCOPE without simultaneously violating PARSEWH: This situation occurs when chain formation (via movement) applies to a wh-phrase (so PARSEWH is respected), but the first member of the wh-chain is not in the scope position that is specified for it in the Index (so PARSESCOPE is violated).

The resulting system of ranked constraints in shown in (49). PARSESCOPE intervenes between BAR²[–ref] and BAR² in the ranking; in contrast, PARSEWH outranks BAR²[–ref] and BAR².[27]

---

[27] As before, because of the laws governing local conjunction, some of the rankings among the BAR-based constraints in (49) are fixed (like BAR²[–ref] ≫ BAR², or BAR³ ≫ BAR²), whereas others are variable. As for the latter, Legendre et al. suggest that (i ab) provides direct evidence for a language-specific ranking BAR² ≫ BAR¹[–ref] in English.

(i) a. How$_1$ did [$_{TP}$ he [$_{VP}$ fix what$_2$] t$_1$] ?
    b. *What$_2$ did [$_{TP}$ he [$_{VP}$ fix t$_2$] how$_1$] ?
    c. How$_1$ did [$_{TP}$ she [$_{VP}$ do it] t$_1$] ?
    d. What$_1$ did [$_{TP}$ she [$_{VP}$ do t$_1$]] ?

Given that the multiple questions in (i a) and (i b) qualify as competing outputs, (i a) (with the wh-adjunct *how* crossing one TP barrier, in violation of BAR¹[–ref]) will block (i b) (with the wh-

(49)   *Two-dimensional restrictions on long-distance extraction:*

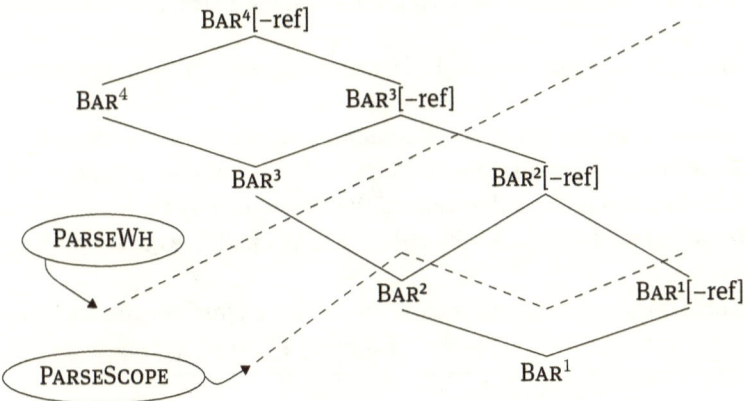

Now adjunct (more specifically, non–referential XP) extraction from a wh-clause will be blocked in favour of a candidate that carries out movement (thereby satisfying higher-ranked PARSEWH) but reduces the scope to the embedded clause; argument (or referential XP) extraction can proceed from a wh-clause without scope reduction because the BAR² constraint that is then violated is ranked below PARSE-SCOPE. At this point, the remaining question is what saves adjunct extraction from a declarative clause, as in (35a). Again, a ranking BAR²[–ref] ≫ PARSESCOPE would, other things being equal, seem to predict that short (clause-bound) movement is optimal in the same way that it turned out as optimal with embedded wh-clauses. However, it is in fact not the case that the two scenarios are completely analogous: Legendre et al. point out that reducing the Index-encoded scope of a wh-phrase with embedded wh-clauses is unproblematic from the point of view of selection; but reducing the Index-encoded scope of a wh-phrase with embedded declarative clauses will violate the selection requirement in (50) because a matrix verb that selects a [–wh] complement will now end up with a [+wh] complement, due to the presence of the wh-phrase in the specifier (and, by assumption, the scope-taking of that wh-phrase).

---

object crossing a VP barrier and a TP barrier, in fatal violation of higher-ranked BAR²). Still, the crossing of two barriers with wh-movement of an object is entirely unproblematic as such (i.e., if there is no competing output with a better constraint profile) in the single constituent question in (i d) – here, (i c) does not go back to the same Index as (i d).

(50) SELECTION (SEL):
Lexically marked selection requirements must be respected in the output.

If SEL outranks BAR²[–ref] (or is, in fact, undominated in (49)), the asymmetry with adjunct movement documented in (35a) vs. (36a) is accounted for. (51) shows how the ban against wh-extraction of an adjunct from a wh-clause (see (36a)) is derived. In wh-island contexts, long-distance movement of a wh-adjunct is blocked by a candidate that reduces the scope of the wh-adjunct by applying short movement in the embedded clause (which then acts as a multiple question).[28]

(51) *Local conjunction optimization V: Wh-extraction from wh-clauses, adjuncts*

	SEL	BAR²[–ref]	PARSESCOPE	BAR²
O_1: [$_{Q_1}$ how$_1$] ... $V_{[+wh]}$ [$_{CP}$ t′$_1$ ... t$_1$ ...]		*!		
☞O_2: [$_{Q_1}$ –] ... $V_{[+wh]}$ [$_{CP}$ how$_1$ ... t$_1$ ...]			*	

(52) exemplifies a minimally different competition in which the wh-phrase that needs to undergo extraction from a wh-clause is a (referential) argument, as in (36b). Here a violation of PARSESCOPE will be fatal since long-distance movement via SpecC violates only the lower-ranked constraint BAR².

(52) *Local conjunction optimization VI: Wh-extraction from wh-clauses, arguments*

	SEL	BAR²[–ref]	PARSESCOPE	BAR²
☞O_1: [$_{Q_1}$ what$_1$] ... $V_{[+wh]}$ [$_{CP}$ t′$_1$ ... t$_1$ ...]				*
O_2: [$_{Q_1}$ –] ... $V_{[+wh]}$ [$_{CP}$ what$_1$ ... t$_1$ ...]			*!	

Finally, consider adjunct movement from declarative clauses, as in (35a). (53) shows that from a purely locality-based perspective, O_2, which reduces wide wh-scope in the Index to narrow wh-scope in the output, would also be the best option with embedded declaratives. However, O_2 will then fatally violate the higher-ranked SEL requirement; hence, the same violation of BAR²[–ref] (incurred

---

[28] Here and in the following tableaux, Q_i stands for the scope position for a wh-XP$_i$ that is given as part of the Index. Outputs that fatally violate higher-ranked PARSEWH are not included here. The winning candidate O_2 in (51) also emerges as optimal in another competition that goes back to an Index in which the wh-adjunct takes embedded scope to begin with. This is a standard instance of *neutralization* in Optimality Theory (see Prince & Smolensky 1993, 2004), which gives rise to well-known questions concerning the concept of input optimization (or lexicon optimization in phonology). These questions are of no relevance in the present context, though.

by long-distance movement) that proves fatal for O_1 with embedded wh-clauses (cf. (51)) is tolerable for O_1 with embedded declarative clauses.

(53) *Local conjunction optimization VII: Wh-extraction from that-clauses, adjuncts*

	SEL	BAR²[−ref]	PARSESCOPE	BAR²
☞ O_1: [$_{Q_1}$ how$_1$] ... V$_{[-wh]}$ [$_{CP}$ t′$_1$ ... t$_1$ ...]		*		
O_2: [$_{Q_1}$ −] ... V$_{[-wh]}$ [$_{CP}$ how$_1$ ... t$_1$ ...]	*!		*	

So, somewhat surprisingly, what *rules out* wh-island constructions (with adjunct extraction) is the fact that a violation of locality *can be avoided* by relocating the wh-scope to the embedded clause; and what *permits* extraction from declarative complements is the fact that a violation of locality *cannot be avoided* here without even greater damage. To sum up, this account of wh-islands effects does not rely on the idea of an intervention effect triggered by another wh-phrase in the embedded SpecC.[29] Nevertheless, it manages to avoid negative consequences for extraction from declarative complements, and it does so in a way that would seem to be unique to an optimality-theoretic approach. Importantly, the analysis relies on two types of cumulative excitatory interaction: First, BAR can (recursively) undergo reflexive local conjunction; and second, the resulting BARn constraints are locally conjoined with REF. However, it is imperative that not all constraints can be locally conjoined with one another. As was the case with the constraint *[+gov] and the prominence scale-derived constraints in the study of differential argument encoding in Mannheim German, and with the constraint *[−gov] and the prominence scale-derived constraints in the study of three-way systems, it turns out that local conjunction involving PARSESCOPE and REF must be excluded. As we will see in the next subsection, the impossibility to avoid such cumulative interaction in an Harmonic Grammar approach implies that the elegant, highly original analysis of restrictions on long-distance extraction in Legendre et al. (1998, 2006b) cannot be maintained in Harmonic Grammar.

---

29 As such, it is fundamentally different from nearly all other approaches in the tradition of Rizzi (1990, 2004), which are strictly intervention-based.

3.3 Harmonic Grammar and restrictions on long-distance extraction

To begin with, let us ignore SEL, PARSESCOPE, and their joint effects underlying the asymmetry between wh-adjunct movement from declarative clauses and wh-clauses, and focus solely on the interaction of PARSEWH, BAR, and REF. For the time being, suppose counterfactually that wh-adjuncts can never cross more than two barriers (i.e., that (35a) is ungrammatical), whereas everything else is as described in the previous subsection. The empirical evidence presented so far then follows if the three constraints currently under consideration have the weights specified in (54).[30]

(54) *Constraints and their weights*:
  a. PARSEWH: 7.0
  b. BAR: 3.0
  c. REF: 2.0

According to (54), wh-movement of an argument across two barriers, as in extractions from wh-clauses (cf. (36b)), is possible since the combined BAR violations are less severe than a single violation of PARSEWH that is triggered by a failure to carry out movement; see (55).[31]

(55) *Harmonic Grammar optimization V: Wh-extraction from wh-clauses, arguments*

	PARSEWH $w = 7.0$	BAR $w = 3.0$	REF $w = 2.0$	H
☞ O_1: [$_{Q_1}$ what$_1$] ... V$_{[+wh]}$ [$_{CP}$ t'$_1$ ... t$_1$ ...]		−2		−6
O_2: [$_{Q_1}$ −] ... V$_{[+wh]}$ [$_{CP}$ ... what$_1$ ...]	−1			−7

In the same way, wh-movement of an adjunct across one barrier is legitimate since the combined violations of BAR and REF are less severe than a violation of PARSEWH; see (56).

---

[30] Constraint weightings in this subsection have been checked by using the software *OT-Help*; see Staubs et al. (2010).
[31] Throughout, optimal candidates that violate PARSEWH derive ineffability. As remarked in footnote 25, these candidates could just as well be conceived of as empty outputs Ø, with the Empty Output Condition the sole constraint that they violate.

(56) *Harmonic Grammar optimization VI: Clause-bound wh-extraction, adjuncts*

	ParseWh w = 7.0	Bar w = 3.0	Ref w = 2.0	H
☞ O_1: [$_{Q_1}$ how$_1$] C [$_{TP}$ ... t$_1$ ...]		–1	–1	–5
O_2: [$_{Q_1}$ –] C [$_{TP}$ ... how$_1$ ...]	–1			–7

In contrast, wh-extraction of an adjunct from a wh-clause is excluded; as shown in (57), the in-situ candidate encoding ineffability wins in this case.

(57) *Harmonic Grammar optimization VII: Wh-extraction from wh-clauses, adjuncts*

	ParseWh w = 7.0	Bar w = 3.0	Ref w = 2.0	H
O_1: [$_{Q_1}$ how$_1$] ... V$_{[+wh]}$ [$_{CP}$ t$'_1$ ... t$_1$ ...]		–2	–1	–8
☞ O_2: [$_{Q_1}$ –] ... V$_{[+wh]}$ [$_{CP}$ ... how$_1$ ...]	–1			–7

Next, wh-movement of an argument from an adjunct clause (as in (37b)) is ruled out as shown in (58).

(58) *Harmonic Grammar optimization VIII: Wh-extraction from adjunct clauses, arguments*

	ParseWh w = 7.0	Bar w = 3.0	Ref w = 2.0	H
O_1: [$_{Q_1}$ what$_1$] ... [$_{TP}$ ... [$_{VP}$ ... [$_{CP}$ t$'_1$ ...]]]		–3		–9
☞ O_2: [$_{Q_1}$ –] ... [$_{TP}$ ... [$_{VP}$ ... [$_{CP}$ ... what$_1$ ...]]]	–1			–7

Needless to say, the same reasoning applies with wh-movement of an adjunct (as in (37a)) in this environment. The superiority-like effect with clause-bound wh-movement in multiple questions reported in footnote 27 can also be straightforwardly be derived: A single violation of Bar (–3) that is combined with a violation of Ref (–2) yields a harmony score of –5, which is outweighed by a double violation of Bar, which yields a harmony score of –6. Therefore adjunct movement blocks object movement in a multiple question. And so on. Crucially, the system works so far because a violation of ParseWh does not trigger a concurrent violation of Ref — recall that (46) only demands referential status of *moved* items. It can be easily verified that if ParseWh violations in scenarios involving wh-adjuncts in situ were accompanied by Ref violations, optimality of candidates such as O_2 in (57) (i.e., ineffability) could not be derived anymore.

So far, so good. However, as it stands, the analysis still predicts wh-adjunct extraction from declarative clauses, as in (35a), to be ungrammatical in the same way that wh-adjunct extraction from wh-clauses is. It was this problem that motivated the postulation of PARSESCOPE (and SEL) in Legendre et al. (1998). Unfortunately, adding PARSESCOPE will fail to work in the Harmonic Grammar approach, for principled reasons. Here is why.

Suppose first the weight of PARSEWH is changed from 7.0 to 8.5. This ensures that only 3 violations of BAR (with a harmony score of −9) can render a violation of it optimal; two violations of BAR and one violation of REF (with a harmony score of −8) cannot outweigh it. Recall that this corresponds to the assumptions of Legendre et al. (1998) (see (49)). Empirically, what is needed now is that a joint violation of BAR and REF (−5) yields a better harmony score than a violation of PARSESCOPE, as does a double violation of BAR (−6), and that a double violation of BAR plus a violation of REF (−8) yields a worse harmony score than a violation of PARSESCOPE (so that the latter may become optimal). The weights in (59) may at first sight seem to achieve this.[32]

(59) *Constraints and their weights* (revised):

    a. PARSEWH: 8.5

    b. PARSESCOPE: 7.0

    c. BAR: 3.0

    d. REF: 2.0

On this basis, consider now the revised competition underlying adjunct movement from wh-clauses in (60) (cf. (57)). O_2, with clause-bound movement and reduced scope, is the intended winner (that could then be blocked via SEL in favour of the long-distance movement candidate in declarative contexts). However, as (60) illustrates, O_2 has a lower harmony score than O_1.

---

[32] We do not have to worry about the weight attachted to SEL at this point since it can only become relevant in adjunct extraction from declarative clauses; but recall that this account presupposes that adjunct extraction from wh-clauses can be blocked via an optimal PARSESCOPE violation; as will become clear momentarily, this is not the case.

(60) *Harmonic Grammar optimization IX: Wh-extraction from wh-clauses, adjuncts* (revised)

	Parse Wh $w = 8.5$	Parse Scope $w = 7.0$	Bar $w = 3.0$	Ref $w = 2.0$	H
☛ O_1: $[_{Q_1}$ how$_1$] ... V$_{[+wh]}$ $[_{CP}$ t'$_1$ ... t$_1$ ...]			−2	−1	−8
O_2: $[_{Q_1}$ −] ... V$_{[+wh]}$ $[_{CP}$ how$_1$ ... t$_1$ ...]		−1		−1	−9
O_3: $[_{Q_1}$ −] ... V$_{[+wh]}$ $[_{CP}$ ... how$_1$ ...]	−1				−8.5

The problem with (60) is that a violation of PARSESCOPE will automatically trigger an unintended violation of REF (indicated here by the box around the violation): A shorter movement operation still qualifies as a movement operation, and the resulting chain is clearly not referential. This problem exactly parallels the problems with unwanted cumulative constraint interaction in the case of differential argument encoding discussed above (see (24), (34)). This unwanted cumulative interaction of constraints can be circumvented in the local conjunction approach by simple stipulation. In contrast, in Harmonic Grammar, the effects one gets from local conjunction will always be present for two constraints; the excitatory interaction of PARSESCOPE and REF cannot be switched off. And if the weight of PARSESCOPE is decreased so that O_2 can become optimal in (60), it will invariably, and fatally, also become optimal with wh-argument extraction from wh-clauses (see (55)) — the violations of REF just cancel each other out.

As with the case of differential argument encoding, one may ask oneself whether there is a way to save the Harmonic Grammar reconstruction of Legendre et al.'s (1998) account of cumulative effects with long-distance extraction; and as before, the answer is no. First, an appropriate modification of either PARSESCOPE or REF does not seem possible. It would have to be assumed that a violation of PARSESCOPE by reduced chains does not automatically trigger a violation of REF. This would then strangely predict that optimal candidates ensuring ineffability can violate more islands than other candidates. More importantly, though, such a move would be totally *ad hoc*: As noted, a reduced, clause-bound chain is still a non-trivial chain whose referentiality status can be detected. Second, one might try to change the domain for constraint evaluation, such that an unwanted gang effect (of PARSESCOPE and REF) could be avoided. The problem with this strategy is that a chain link that violates PARSESCOPE already involves a *smaller* domain than a chain involving faithful scope-taking. Third and finally, and again as before, it is hard to see how adopting Harmonic Serialism could help in the case at hand.

4 Conclusion

To sum up, there is evidence for cumulative effects in morphology (differential argument encoding) and syntax (long-distance extraction). The excitatory interaction of grammatical building blocks involved here has been successfully addressed in terms of local constraint conjunction (against the background of an optimality-theoretic approach to grammar). However, these analyses cannot be transferred to Harmonic Grammar, and this result holds for principled reasons: In Harmonic Grammar, cumulative interaction of two constraints Con_1 and Con_2 that is predicted given the semantics of Con_1 and Con_2 can simply never be switched off, which leads to unwanted excitatory interactions. Since the two case studies addressed in the present paper (based on Aissen 2003 and Legendre et al. 1998) are arguably among the most insightful and best-established applications of cumulativity in morphosyntax so far, this result can be taken to shed doubt on the viability of Harmonic Grammar more generally, in particular since one of the primary justifications of Harmonic Grammar is that it can offer a convincing account of cumulative effects.

That said, it should be clear from the references cited in Section 1 that Harmonic Grammar does in fact provide elegant analyses of many other cumulative effects – not only in phonology, but also in morphology and syntax.[33] To end this paper, I would therefore like to briefly address the question of what it is about the cumulative interactions observed with differential argument encoding and long-distance extraction that makes them resist an account in terms of Harmonic Grammar. Closer inspection reveals that the problem of unwanted cumulative interaction shows up with constraints that are in what I will call an *actual stringency* relation. The concept of stringency as such is well understood in Optimality Theory; a standard definition is given in (61).

(61) *Stringency* (Baković 1995, McCarthy 2002):
Two constraints Con_1 and Con_2 are in a stringency relation if for every input in which Con_1 applies non-vacuously, a violation of Con_1 in an output implies a violation of Con_2.

However, this concept cannot be adopted for present purposes in exactly this form: *[+gov] may be violated by some input even though a violation of, say, *DP_{int}/Def

---

[33] Also see Legendre et al. (2006a: 343–345) for an argument against Harmonic Grammar based on based on unbounded trade-offs (where Harmonic Grammar predicts apparently non-existing patterns of stress assignment that rely on counting syllables), and Pater (2016: 30ff.) for an empirically based refutation of this argument.

can be avoided (e.g., because DP is a direct object that is not definite, or because it is an indirect or oblique object); and PARSESCOPE may be violated by some input without a simultaneous violation of REF (because the reduced chain is referential). It is the co-occurrences of violations of these constraints, though, that pose the problem for Harmonic Grammar. Thus, what is needed is a concept of *actual stringency*, as in (62).

(62) *Actual stringency*:
Two constraints Con_1 and Con_2 are in an actual stringency relation for a given input I if a violation of Con_1 implies a violation of Con_2 in outputs going back to I.

The problematic scenario then is the following: Harmonic Grammar cannot prevent unwanted cumulative interaction of constraints that are in an actual stringency relation. This restriction has also been referred to as an *asymmetric trade-off* requirement in the phonological literature (see Pater 2009, 2016); in actual stringency environments, there is a *symmetric trade-off*, and modelling cumulative interaction in Harmonic Grammar becomes impossible. In all existing successful applications of Harmonic Grammar to cumulative effects, this problem does not arise (also see Murphy 2017: ch. 3 for an explicit discussion of asymmetric trade-off with certain cumulative effects in syntax, based on phase theory); with the analyses of differential argument encoding and long-distance extraction discussed in the present paper, it does.[34]

---

[34] As a matter of fact, a similar kind of argument to the one given for morphology and syntax in the present study is developed in Smolensky (2006) for phonology. Smolensky argues that final devoicing in a language like Polish should be viewed as a cumulative effect going back to the excitatory interaction of two constraints *VOICEOBS (banning voiced obstruents) and NOCODA (banning coda consonants), which are individually violable in optimal outputs, but whose combined violation in a faithful output O_1 lets another output O_2 become optimal in which devoicing has taken place in violation of higher-ranked IDENTVOICE; thus, *VOICEOBS and NOCODA successfully gang up against IDENTVOICE. This interaction can easily be implemented by means of local conjunction: *VOICEOBS&NOCODA outranks IDENT-VOICE (which outranks *VOICEOBS and NOCODA). In contrast, the cumulative interaction of *VOICEOBS and NOCODA cannot be captured in Harmonic Grammar because of a lack of asymmetric trade-off: A consonant in a coda violates NOCODA irrespectively of whether it has remained voiced (thereby violating *VOICEOBS) or has undergone devoicing (thereby violating *IDENTVOICE) — NOCODA and *IDENTVOICE are in an actual stringency relation in O_2. In view of this situation, it is observed in Pater et al. (2007) and Pater (2016) that the analysis based on local conjunction would also predict non-existing patterns if the domain for local conjunction is sufficiently large (e.g., simultaneous onset devoicing if the domain is the prosodic word). The conclusion in Pater (2016) then is that the cumulative nature

Acknowledgements

For helpful comments and discussion, I am grateful to Doreen Georgi, Fabian Heck, Johannes Hein, Klaus von Heusinger, Yurij Kushnir, Géraldine Legendre, Andrew Murphy, Paul Smolensky, Philipp Weisser, Eva Zimmermann, two anonymous reviewers, the editors of this volume, and audiences at Universeit Leiden (SLE-Conference 48, Workshop on Differential Marking) and Universität Leipzig. Research for this article was supported by the DFG graduate programme 2011 IGRA (*Interaction of Grammatical Building Blocks*).

References

Ackema, Peter & Ad Neeleman. 1998. Optimal questions. *Natural Language & Linguistic Theory* 16(3). 443–490. https://doi.org/10.1023/A:1006020702441.
Aissen, Judith. 1999. Markedness and subject choice in Optimality Theory. *Natural Language & Linguistic Theory* 17(4). 673–711. https://doi.org/10.1023/A:1006335629372.
Aissen, Judith. 2003. Differential object marking: Iconicity vs. economy. *Natural Language & Linguistic Theory* 21(3). 435–483. https://doi.org/10.1023/A:1024109008573.
Alderete, John. 1997. Dissimilation as local conjunction. In Kiyomi Kusumoto (ed.), *Proceedings of the twenty-seventh annual meeting of the North East Linguistic Society*, 17–32. Amherst, MA: GLSA Publications.
Aoun, Joseph. 1986. *Generalized binding*. Dordrecht: Foris.
Baković, Eric. 1995. A markedness subhierarchy in syntax. Ms., Rutgers University.
Bárány, András. 2015. *Differential object marking in Hungarian and the morphosyntax of case and agreement*. University of Cambridge PhD dissertation.
Behaghel, Otto. 1911. *Geschichte der deutschen Sprache*. Straßburg: Trübner.
Bierwisch, Manfred. 1967. Syntactic features in morphology: General problems of so-called pronominal inflection in German. In *To honor Roman Jakobson*, vol. 1, 239–270. The Hague: Mouton.
Bittner, Maria & Ken Hale. 1996. Ergativity: Toward a theory of a heterogeneous class. *Linguistic Inquiry* 27(4). 531–604.
Bobaljik, Jonathan. 2015. Some differences between case and agreement. Ms., Unversity of Connecticut.
Boersma, Paul & Bruce Hayes. 2001. Empirical tests of the Gradual Learning Algorithm. *Linguistic Inquiry* 32(1). 45–86. https://doi.org/10.1162/002438901554586.
Bräutigam, Kurt. 1934. *Die Mannheimer Mundart*. Universität Heidelberg dissertation.
Bresnan, Joan, Shipra Dingare & Christopher Manning. 2001. Soft constraints mirror hard constraints: Voice and person in English and Lummi. In *Proceedings of the LFG01 confer-*

---

of final devoicing must be denied; on this view, there is a single primitive constraint *CODAVOICE that is responsible for the phenomenon.

ence, University of Hong Kong. On-line, CSLI Publications: http://csli-publications.stanford.edu/LFG/6/lfg01.html.

Chomsky, Noam. 1973. Conditions on transformations. In Stephen Anderson & Paul Kiparsky (eds.), *A Festschrift for Morris Halle*, 232–286. New York: Academic Press.

Chomsky, Noam. 1981. *Lectures on government and binding*. Dordrecht: Foris.

Chomsky, Noam. 1986. *Barriers*. Cambridge, MA: MIT Press.

Chomsky, Noam. 2001. Derivation by phase. In Michael Kenstowicz (ed.), *Ken Hale: A life in language*, 1–52. Cambridge, MA: MIT Press.

Chomsky, Noam. 2008. On phases. In Robert Freidin, Carlos P. Otero & Maria Luisa Zubizarreta (eds.), *Foundational issues in linguistic theory: Essays in honor of Jean-Roger Vergnaud*, 133–166. Cambridge, MA: MIT Press.

Chomsky, Noam. 2013. Problems of projection. *Lingua* 130. 33–49. https://doi.org/10.1016/j.lingua.2012.12.003.

Cinque, Guglielmo. 1990. *Types of A-bar dependencies*. Cambridge, MA: MIT Press.

Deal, Amy Rose. 2014. Person-based split ergativity in Nez Perce is syntactic. Ms., University of California, Santa Cruz.

Dietrich, Rainer. 1999. On the production of of word order and the origin of incrementality. In Ralf Klabunde & Christiane von Stutterheim (eds.), *Representations and processes in language production*. Wiesbaden: Deutscher Universitätsverlag. https://doi.org/10.1007/978-3-322-99290-1_3.

Englisch, Johannes. 2015. *An underspecification-free approach to syncretism*. Universität Leipzig MA thesis.

Featherston, Sam. 2005. The decathlon model of empirical syntax. In Stephan Kepser & Marga Reis (eds.), *Linguistic evidence*, 187–208. Berlin: De Gruyter.

Fischer, Silke. 2001. On the integration of cumulative effects into Optimality Theory. In Gereon Müller & Wolfgang Sternefeld (eds.), *Competition in syntax*, 151–173. Berlin: Mouton/de Gruyter.

Frampton, John. 1990. Parasitic gaps and the theory of wh-chains. *Linguistic Inquiry* 21(1). 49–77.

Georgi, Doreen. 2019. On prominence scale interactions in Hayu: A Harmonic Grammar account. *Nordlyd* 43(1). 1–13. https://doi.org/10.7557/12.4206.

Grimshaw, Jane. 1998. Constraints on constraints in Optimality Theoretic syntax. Ms., Rutgers University, New Brunswick, New Jersey.

Hale, Ken. 1972. A new perspective on American Indian linguistics. In Alfonso Ortiz (ed.), *New perspectives on the pueblos*, 87–103. Albuquerque: University of New Mexico Press.

Halle, Morris. 1997. Distributed morphology: Impoverishment and fission. In Benjamin Bruening, Yoonjung Kang & Martha McGinnis (eds.), *Papers at the interface*, vol. 30 (MIT Working Papers in Linguistics), 425–449. Cambridge, MA: MIT Press.

Halle, Morris & Alec Marantz. 1993. Distributed Morphology and the pieces of inflection. In Ken Hale & Samuel Jay Keyser (eds.), *The view from building 20*, 111–176. Cambridge, MA: MIT Press.

Handschuh, Corinna. 2014. *A typology of marked-S languages*. Berlin: Language Science Press.

Heck, Fabian. 2001. Quantifier scope in German and cyclic optimization. In Gereon Müller & Wolfgang Sternefeld (eds.), *Competition in syntax*, 175–209. Berlin: De Gruyter.

Heck, Fabian & Gereon Müller. 2003. Derivational optimization of wh-movement. *Linguistic Analysis* 33. (Volume appeared 2007), 97–148.

Heck, Fabian & Gereon Müller. 2007. Extremely local optimization. Proceedings of WECOL 2006. California State University, Fresno.

Heck, Fabian & Gereon Müller. 2016. On accelerating and decelarating movement: From minimalist preference principles to harmonic serialism. In Géraldine Legendre, Michael Putnam, Henriette de Swart & Erin Zaroukian (eds.), *Optimality-theoretic syntax, semantics, and pragmatics*, 78–110. Universität Leipzig: Oxford University Press.

Heck, Fabian, Gereon Müller, Ralf Vogel, Silke Fischer, Sten Vikner & Tanja Schmid. 2002. On the nature of the input in Optimality Theory. *The Linguistic Review* 19(4). 345–376. https://doi.org/10.1515/tlir.2002.003.

von Heusinger, Klaus. 2008. Verbal semantics and the diachronic development of DOM in Spanish. *Probus* 20(1). 1–31. https://doi.org/10.1515/PROBUS.2008.001.

von Heusinger, Klaus & Georg A. Kaiser. 2011. Affectedness and differential object marking in Spanish. *Morphology* 21(3-4). 593–617. https://doi.org/10.1007/s11525-010-9177-y.

Itô, Junko & Armin Mester. 1998. Markedness and word structure: OCP effects in Japanese. Ms., UC Santa Cruz. (ROA 255).

Jacobs, Joachim. 1988. Probleme der freien Wortstellung im Deutschen. *Sprache und Pragmatik* 5. 8–37.

Jakobson, Roman. 1962. Morfologičeskije nabljudenija. In *Selected writings*, vol. 2, 154–181. The Hague & Paris: Mouton.

Kager, René. 1999. *Optimality theory*. Cambridge: Cambridge University Press.

Kalin, Laura. 2016. Phi-features as derivational time bombs: a new model of nominal licensing. Ms., Princeton University.

Kalin, Laura & Philipp Weisser. 2019. Asymmetric DOM in coordination: A problem for movement-based approaches. *Linguistic Inquiry* 50(3). 662–676. https://doi.org/10.1162/ling_a_00298.

Karch, Dieter. 1975a. *Mannheim: Umgangssprache* (Phonai Monographien 8). Tübingen: Niemeyer.

Karch, Dieter. 1975b. *Zur Morphologie vorderpfälzischer Dialekte*. Niemeyer.

Keine, Stefan. 2010. *Case and agreement from fringe to core: Impoverishment effects on Agree* (Linguistische Arbeiten). Berlin: De Gruyter.

Keine, Stefan. 2016. *Probes and their horizons*. University of Massachusetts, Amherst dissertation.

Keine, Stefan & Gereon Müller. 2011. Non-zero/non-zero alternations in differential object marking. In Suzi Lima, Kevin Mullin & Brian Smith (eds.), *NELS 39: Proceedings of the thirty-ninth annual meeting of the North East Linguistics Society*, 441–454. Amherst, MA: GLSA Publications.

Keine, Stefan & Gereon Müller. 2014. Differential argument encoding by impoverishment. In Ina Bornkessel-Schlesewsky, Andrej Malchukov & Marc Richards (eds.), *Scales and hierarchies* (Trends in Linguistics), 75–130. Berlin: De Gruyter.

Kushnir, Yuriy. 2019. Deceptive datives: Prepositional case in Latvian. *Glossa: a journal of general linguistics* 4(1), 71. https://doi.org/10.5334/gjgl.518.

Legate, Julie Anne. 2008. Morphological and abstract case. *Linguistic Inquiry* 39(1). 55–101. https://doi.org/10.1162/ling.2008.39.1.55.

Legendre, Géraldine, Paul Smolensky & Colin Wilson. 1998. When is less more? Faithfulness and minimal links in wh-chains. In Pilar Barbosa, Danny Fox, Paul Hagstrom, Martha McGinnis & David Pesetsky (eds.), *Is the best good enough? Optimality and competition in syntax*, 249–289. Cambridge, MA: MIT Press & MITWPL.

Legendre, Géraldine, Antonella Sorace & Paul Smolensky. 2006a. The optimality theory–harmonic grammar connection. In Paul Smolensky & Géraldine Legendre (eds.), *The harmonic mind*, vol. II, 339–402. Cambridge, MA: MIT Press.
Legendre, Géraldine, Colin Wilson, Paul Smolensky, Kristin Homer & William Raymond. 2006b. Optimality in syntax II: Wh-questions. In Paul Smolensky & Géraldine Legendre (eds.), *The harmonic mind*, vol. II, 183–230. Cambridge, MA: MIT Press.
Łubowicz, Anna. 2005. Locality of conjunction. In John Alderete, Chung-hye Han & Alexei Kochetov (eds.), *Proceedings of the 24th West Coast Conference on Formal Linguistics*, 254–262. Somerville, MA: Cascadilla Press.
McCarthy, John. 2002. *A thematic guide to Optimality Theory*. Cambridge: Cambridge University Press.
McCarthy, John. 2010. An introduction to Harmonic Serialism. *Language and Linguistics Compass* 4(10). 1001–1018. https://doi.org/10.1111/j.1749-818X.2010.00240.x.
McCarthy, John. 2016. The theory and practice of harmonic serialism. In John McCarthy & Joe Pater (eds.), *Harmonic grammar and harmonic serialism*, 47–87. Sheffield: Equinox.
McCarthy, John & Joe Pater (eds.). 2016. *Harmonic grammar and harmonic serialism*. Sheffield: Equinox.
Müller, Gereon. 2000. *Elemente der optimalitätstheoretischen Syntax*. Tübingen: Stauffenburg.
Müller, Gereon. 2003. Zwei Theorien der pronominalen Flexion im Deutschen (Versionen Standard und Mannheim). *Deutsche Sprache* 30. 328–363.
Müller, Gereon. 2015. Optimality-theoretic syntax. In Tibor Kiss & Artemis Alexiadou (eds.), *Syntax. an international handbook*, vol. 2, 875–936. Berlin: De Gruyter.
Müller, Gereon & Daniela Thomas. 2017. Three-way systems do not exist. In Jessica Coon, Lisa Travis & Diane Massam (eds.), *The Oxford handbook of ergativity*, 279–307. Oxford: Oxford University Press.
Murphy, Andrew. 2017. *Cumulativity in syntactic derivations*. Universität Leipzig dissertation.
Pafel, Jürgen. 1998. Skopus und logische Struktur: Studien zum Quantorenskopus im Deutschen. Habilitation thesis, Universität Tübingen.
Pater, Joe. 2009. Weighted constraints in generative linguistics. *Cognitive Science* 33(6). 999–1035. https://doi.org/10.1111/j.1551-6709.2009.01047.x.
Pater, Joe. 2016. Universal grammar with weighted constraints. In John McCarthy & Joe Pater (eds.), *Harmonic grammar and harmonic serialism*, 1–46. Sheffield: Equinox.
Pater, Joe, Rajesh Bhatt & Christopher Potts. 2007. Linguistic optimization. Ms., University of Massachusetts, Amherst.
Post, Rudolf. 1990. *Pfälzisch*. Landau: Pfälzische Verlagsanstalt.
Prince, Alan & Paul Smolensky. 1993. Optimality theory: Constraint interaction in generative grammar. Book ms., Rutgers University.
Prince, Alan & Paul Smolensky. 2004. *Optimality theory: Constraint interaction in generative grammar*. Oxford: Blackwell.
Richards, Marc. 2014. Defective agree, case alternations, and the prominence of person. In Ina Bornkessel-Schlesewsky, Andrej Malchukov & Marc Richards (eds.), *Scales and hierarchies* (Trends in Linguistics), 173–196. Berlin: De Gruyter.
Rizzi, Luigi. 1990. *Relativized minimality*. Cambridge, MA: MIT Press.
Rizzi, Luigi. 2004. Locality and left periphery. In Luigi Rizzi (ed.), *The structure of CP and IP*, vol. 2 (The Cartography of Syntactic Structures), 223–251. Oxford University Press.

Silverstein, Michael. 1976. Hierarchy of features and ergativity. In R.M.W. Dixon (ed.), *Grammatical categories in Australian languages*, 112–171. Canberra: Australian Institute of Aboriginal Studies.

Smolensky, Paul. 1995. On the internal structure of Con, the constraint component of UG. Ms., Johns Hopkins University.

Smolensky, Paul. 2006. Harmonic completeness, local constraint conjunction, and feature domain markedness. In Paul Smolensky & Géraldine Legendre (eds.), *The harmonic mind*, vol. II, 27–160. Cambridge, MA: MIT Press.

Smolensky, Paul. 2017. Gradient representations. Tutorial, Universität Leipzig; November 10-12, 2017.

Smolensky, Paul & Geraldine Legendre. 2006. *The harmonic mind*. Cambridge, MA: MIT Press.

Staubs, Robert, Michael Becker, Christopher Potts, Patrick Pratt, John McCarthy & Joe Pater. 2010. Ot-help 2.0. software package. University of Massachusetts, Amherst.

Thomas, Daniela. 2015. *Deriving scale effects in argument encoding in Harmonic Grammar*. Universität Leipzig MA thesis.

Trommer, Jochen. 2001. *Distributed optimality*. Universität Potsdam dissertation.

Trommer, Jochen. 2006. Person and number agreement in Dumi. *Linguistics* 44(5). 1011–1057. https://doi.org/10.1515/LING.2006.033.

Uszkoreit, Hans Jürgen. 1986. Constraints on order. *Linguistics* 24(5). 883–906. https://doi.org/10.1515/ling.1986.24.5.883.

Watters, David E. 2002. *A grammar of Kham*. Cambridge: Cambridge University Press.

Weisser, Philipp. 2017. Why is there no such thing as closest conjunct case? In Andrew Lamont & Katerina Tetzloff (eds.), *Proceedings of the forty-seventh annual meeting of the North East Linguistic Society*, vol. 3, 219–232. University of Massachusetts, Amhherst: GLSA Publications.

Wiese, Bernd. 1996. Iconicity and syncretism: On pronominal inflection in Modern German. In Robin Sackmann & Monika Budde (eds.), *Theoretical linguistics and grammatical description*, 323–344. Amsterdam: John Benjamins. https://doi.org/10.1075/cilt.138.25wie.

Wiese, Bernd. 2004. Categories and paradigms: On underspecification in Russian declension. In Gereon Müller, Lutz Gunkel & Gisela Zifonun (eds.), *Explorations in nominal inflection*, 321–372. Berlin: De Gruyter.

Monica Alexandrina Irimia
Types of structural objects
Some remarks on differential object marking in Romanian

Abstract: This paper examines differential object marking in Romanian, also focusing on less-discussed configurations where 'canonical' features such as animacy or specificity are missing. The analysis builds on an adaptation of classical *secondary licensing* accounts stemming from *Kayne's Generalization* (Kayne 1975, Jaeggli 1982, 1986, a.o.). More specifically, under the current proposal the differential marker does not result from (Case) licensing competition between the (accusative) clitic and its correferential DP (as in *Kayne's Generalization*). It is rather the need to license more than one piece of structure in a given nominal when the initial/primary licenser is subject to a (φ-/δ-)*Uniqueness Constraint*. An implementation along these lines avoids the counterarguments brought to *Kayne's Generalization*, while still preserving a useful *secondary licensing* intuition. It also straightforwardly explains the extension of differential marking to classes (such as inanimates) that have generally resisted explanation.

Keywords: differential object marking, Romanian, licensing

1 Introduction

Romanian exhibits one of the most complex patterns of *differential object marking* (DOM). Some direct objects are preceded by a preposition, while still functioning as true arguments and even requiring (ACC) clitic doubling in some contexts (Farkaş 1978, Dobrovie-Sorin 1994, Cornilescu 2000, von Heusinger & Onea 2008, Tigău 2010, 2011, Hill 2013, Mardale 2009, 2015, Avram & Zafiu 2017, a.o.). Prima facie, the relevant classes seem to follow the hierarchical implications of so-called *scales* (Aissen 2003, a.o.) in a DOM system based on animacy:

(1) *Animacy scale*
    1/2 > proper name > 3 > human > animate > inanimate

   Specificity/Definiteness scale
   pronoun > name > definite > specific indefinite > non-specific

---
Monica Alexandrina Irimia, University of Modena and Reggio Emilia

https://doi.org/10.1515/9783110666137-003

We see in (2a) that tonic pronouns must be preceded by the preposition *pe*,[1] which will be glossed as DOM. The animate noun in (2b) can also be differentially marked, while the inanimate in (2c) cannot take DOM:[2]

(2) a. *Elena *(m)-a văzut *(pe) mine.*
 Elena CL.1SG.ACC-has seen DOM 1SG.ACC
 'Elena saw me.'

 b. *(L-)au lăudat pe studentul inteligent.*
 CL.3SG.M.ACC-have praised DOM student.DEF.M.SG intelligent.M.SG
 'They have praised the intelligent student.'

 c. *(*L-)au lăudat (*pe) romanul clasic.*
 CL.3SG.M.ACC-have praised DOM novel.DEF.N.SG classical.N.SG
 'They have praised the classical novel.'

The data are however not without challenges. One puzzle is that examples like (2b) are *grammatical* without DOM. Thus, the sentence in (3) is also possible. This is different from other (related) languages (for example Spanish, see Ormazabal & Romero 2007, 2013, a.o.), where referential definite animates must show differential marking.

---

1 This preposition also has locative uses, meaning 'on', as illustrated below:

(i) *A pus cartea pe masă.*
 has put book.DEF.F.SG on table
 'S/he has put the book on the table.'

The recruitment of a locative preposition to signal types of differentially marked objects is not uncommon cross-linguistically. See Comrie (1989), Bossong (1991), Lazard (2001), a.o., as well as the typological remarks in the introduction to this volume.

2 Note that, besides DOM, the tonic form of the pronoun must show non-nominative morphology for first and second person in Modern Romanian. Nominative inflection is ungrammatical, (i). Nouns have lost the accusative inflection in Romanian, and preserve only the dative case marking. Overt pronouns in object position also require obligatory accusative clitic doubling.

(i) *Elena *(m)-a văzut pe *eu / mine.*
 Elena CL.1SG.ACC-has seen DOM 1SG.NOM 1SG.ACC
 intended: 'Elena saw me.'

(3) Au   lăudat studentul   inteligent.
    have praised student.DEF.M.SG intelligent.M.SG
    'They have praised the intelligent student.'

Yet, one cannot conclude that animacy is only *optionally* marked in Romanian. Leaving aside pronouns, other *animacy* configurations such as those containing the negative quantifier are ungrammatical without DOM. See the contrast between (4a) and (4b):

(4) Negative quantifiers

   a. *Nu am   văzut *(pe) nimeni.*
      not have.1SG seen   DOM   nobody
      'I didn't see anybody.'

   b. *Nu am   văzut (*pe) nimic.*
      not have.1SG seen   DOM   nothing
      'I didn't see anything.'

A second puzzle is that there are contexts where DOM is *obligatory* irrespective of animacy (Cornilescu 2000, Pană-Dindelegan 2013, Avram & Zafiu 2017, Irimia 2018). These include nominal ellipsis (5a), some types of partitives (5b), D-linked pronouns (5c), as well as some types of equality comparatives (5d). The latter have been rarely discussed, some remarks being provided by Pană-Dindelegan (2013) or Irimia (2018):

(5) a. *L-am   cumpărat *(pe) acest-a.*
       CL.3SG.N.ACC-have bought   DOM   this-AUG
       'I have bought this (one).' (animate or inanimate)

   b. *Am   citit-o   numai *(pe) una   dintre*
      have.1SG read-CL.3SG.F.ACC only   DOM   one.F.SG from
      cărţile   recomandate.
      books.DEF.F.PL recommended.F.PL
      'I have read only one of the recommended books.' (Avram & Zafiu 2017: (13))

   c. **(Pe) care   l-ai   cumpărat?*
      DOM   which CL.3SG.N.ACC-have.2 bought
      'Which one have you bought?' (animate or inanimate)

d. *L-am   păstrat   ca   *(pe)   un   dar.*
   CL.3SG.N.ACC-have kept   as   DOM   a.N.SG   gift
   'I have kept it as (one would keep) a gift.'

Generally, Modern Romanian DOM can be split into three patterns: (i) obligatory (as in (5) or (4a)); (ii) ungrammatical (as in (2c), (4b)) and other examples discussed in Section 5; and (iii) apparently optional (the definite animate in (3)). The non-trivial question is how to unify all these contexts, and also capture the non-systematic behavior of inanimates.

The novel account developed here builds on the intuition of *additonal licensing*, adapting some classical insights from *Kayne's Generalization* to recent frameworks where (C/case) licensing operations may apply to nominals more than once (Baker & Vinokurova 2010, N. Richards 2013, Pesetsky 2014, Levin & Preminger 2015, Levin 2016, Preminger 2019, Chen 2018, a.o.). In a nutshell, the differential marker signals the application of an additional licensing operation on a DP in the same *local domain* (below VoiceP), as illustrated below. The problem with the nominal in (6) is that, besides a Case feature, it also contains a [PERSON] specification; as the two features need licensing, an additional licenser must be recruited, whose contribution at spell-out is the differential marking preposition.

(6)   DOM licensing

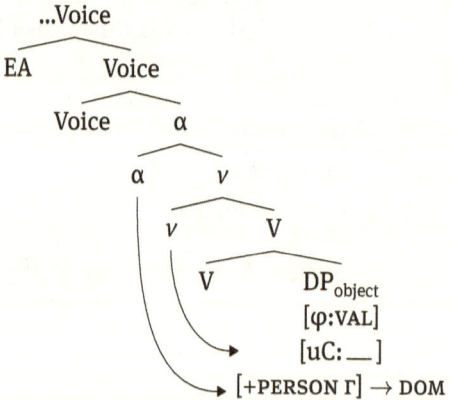

Thus, in Romanian, prepositional DOM does not (necessarily) signal the difference between unlicensed/Caseless nominals (those that are treated as predicates or are lexically marked) and licensed/Case-checked nominals (those that are overtly signaled by DOM), as recently proposed for differential objects in other languages (Ormazabal & Romero 2013, Kalin 2018, Levin 2019, a.o.).

The difference between examples such as (3) and (2b) resides rather in the distinct featural composition of the DP, which leads to differences in licensing. As we further show in the next sections, the D⁰ of referential definites in (3) is associated with a [uC] feature (Giusti 1993, a.o.). Following Bernstein (2008), Longobardi (2008), a.o., [uC] can be seen as the reflex of a [PERSON] feature. As recent research has shown (Zubizarreta & Pancheva 2017, Preminger 2011, 2014, Wiltschko 2014, Bárány 2015, 2017, a.o.), [PERSON] appears to be one of the (interpretable) features which require valuation in narrow syntax by entering into a relationship with a functional head (broadly, the *probe* in minimalist terms) in the clausal spine (a type of argument *licensing*). However, [PERSON] can have other reflexes in Romanian. For example, when merged on a gender (γ)-defining head, [PERSON γ] is interpreted as *semantic gender*, outputting the difference between animates and inanimates (following Cornilescu 2000, Adger & Harbour 2007, M. Richards 2008, Kučerová 2018, a.o.).

As observed elsewhere, Romanian licensers are subject to a *Uniqueness Licensing Constraint*. This allows them to check just one feature type at a time. Thus, configurations that contain two [PERSON] features will need an *additional* licenser. The locative *preposition* signalling DOM spells-out exactly the presence of the supplementary licenser. Yet besides animacy and D⁰, other pieces of structure can have as an effect the introduction of extra features that require licensing. For example, nominal ellipsis is decomposed in narrow syntax into complex clusters of features, among which *definiteness* (see Elbourne 2013, or Cornilescu & Nicolae 2012 for Romanian). Various contexts of nominal ellipsis as well as some partitives (among which those illustrated in (5a) or (5b)) will end up containing two definiteness ([PERSON]) features, which must be licensed. The need of an additional licenser is predicted here too.

More generally, Romanian provides evidence that (i) the nominal phase head D⁰ can undergo licensing; (ii) a [PERSON] feature can be merged at various points inside a nominal (such as D, *n*, K, etc.). When merged in K, it will be spelled-out by the (accusative) clitic double. Various diagnostics show that clitics are licensed above VoiceP. The data show evidence that a given domain (e.g. *v*P) can have *only one* additional licenser (besides the regular licenser, see also Vainikka & Brattico 2014, a.o.). If features are left unvalued after the recruitment of the secondary licenser, they will need to be valued in a different domain. Based on these observations, Romanian prepositional DOM contexts can be unified as in (7):

(7) *Differential (object) licensing in Romanian*
   If a DP contains more than one feature of the same type that requires valuation (licensing) in the same domain, an additional licenser must be made available.

The structure of the paper is as follows. Section 2 introduces the background on *Kayne's Generalization* (Kayne 1975, Jaeggli 1982, 1986, see also Anagnostopoulou 1994, 2003, 2006, a.o.), how the idea of *secondary licensing* is adapted here, as well as differences from other accounts in terms of (secondary) licensing (more specifically, Kalin 2018). Section 3 further motivates the additional licensing analysis. Section 4 derives the obligatory DOM contexts. Section 5 discusses optional and ungrammatical DOM. Section 6 contains a brief comparison with other accounts proposed for the Romanian differential marker (especially Cornilescu 2000), and presents empirical arguments that Romanian DOM is not syntactically dative/oblique. Section 7 contains the conclusions.

2 DOM as secondary licensing: Kayne's generalization

One of the earliest formal accounts of prepositional DOM in Romance is in terms of the so-called *Kayne's Generalization*. Under this constraint, the prepositional differential marker is seen as a Case convergence mechanism in contexts where direct objects interact with clitic doubling. A canonical formulation of *Kayne's Generalization* is given below from Jaeggli (1982):

(8) *Kayne's Generalization* (Jaeggli 1982: 20)
An object NP may be doubled by a clitic only if the NP is preceded by a preposition

This requirement was attributed to a Case competition strategy. The clitic 'absorbs' the case from V, leaving the DP correlate without the possibility to get case. This leads to a violation of the *Case Filter* (Chomsky 1981) which causes ungrammaticality. What is spelled out as a preposition functions like a *secondary, last resort* mechanism which assigns Case to the correlate DP. As is well known, there are at least two possible syntactic representations for the structure of clitics, the so-called *Big DP Hypothesis* (illustrated in (9), Uriagereka 1995, a.o.) or the *Clitics as Agreement* markers (illustrated in (10), see also Preminger 2019 for a recent overview). Leaving aside the non-trivial differences between these two representations (see Sportiche 1996 for extensive discussion), what matters for the current discussion is that the clitic and its associate stand in a local relation, at least at some point in the derivation. Under *Kayne's Generalization* in (8), this connection creates competition in terms of Case licensing.

(9) *Big DP structure for clitics*   (10) *Clitics as agreement*

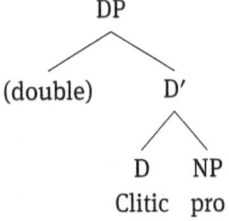
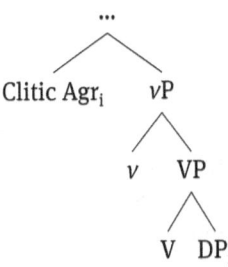

An early analysis of Romanian prepositional DOM in terms of *Kayne's Generalization* is to be found in Dobrovie-Sorin (1994). It captures the observation that there is a correlation between clitic doubling and the presence of the DOM preposition, as seen in examples like (2a). Indeed, such sentences are ungrammatical if either the clitic or DOM is missing.[3] However, numerous counterexamples have also been put forward, demonstrating that the Generalization is incorrect under its formulation in (8). On the one hand, there are numerous contexts where the clitic appears to be 'optional', as the readers could already see in (2b), for example. More importantly, there are also sentences where DOM is obligatory while clitic doubling is ungrammatical (see also Suñer 1988 for discussion). For Romanian, one example is the animate negative quantifier, seen in (11). Another context is provided by the *wh-* animate *cine* ('who'), where DOM is equally obligatory but clitic doubling results in severe ungrammaticality (see the extensive discussion in Dobrovie-Sorin 1990):

(11)   Nu   (*l-)am   văzut *(*pe*)   nimeni.
       not CL.3SG.M.ACC-have.1SG seen   DOM   nobody
       'I didn't see anybody.'

---

[3] This restriction also appears to hold elsewhere in Romance, for example, with Standard Spanish pronouns, or in Porteño (examples from Leonetti 2008, ex. (2a) and (3c)):

(i) Standard Spanish   (ii) Porteño
     *(*Lo*)   vimos *(*a*) él.   *(*Lo*)   vimos *(*a*) Guille.
     CL.3SG.M.ACC saw   DOM   he   CL.3SG.M.ACC saw   DOM   Willy
     'We saw him.'   'We saw Willy.'

(12) *(Pe) cine (*l-)ai   văzut?
     DOM who   CL.3SG.M.ACC-have.2SG seen
     'Who did you see?'

On the other hand, clitic doubling is possible with non-DOM objects. Older stages of Romanian exhibited such patterns (see Mardale 2015, a.o.), often co-occurring with a separate prepositional DOM strategy. Modern varieties, such as Megleno-Romanian or Aromanian, the latter illustrated in (13) also show clitic doubled objects without prepositional DOM.[4]

(13) Aromanian (Mišeska Tomić 2006: (272b))
      Lu   *vidzu*   *Belgrad(lu)*.
      CL.3SG.M.ACC see.AOR.3SG   Belgrade(DEF.M.SG)
      'S/he saw Belgrade.'

Clitic doubling is moreover seen in many other languages that do not have (prepositional) differential marking, from Indo-European or beyond. Extensive discussion can be found in Anagnostopoulou (1994, 1999, 2006), Kallulli (2008), or Wiltschko (2014), to cite just a few authors. More generally, as Cornilescu (2000) also points out, although clitic doubling and prepositional DOM might have similar semantic/pragmatic outputs, the two phenomena are completely separate when it comes to their nature, diachrony, and distribution.

Counterexamples of this type convincingly prove that the source of DOM cannot be Case competition triggered by a clitic (found in the same Case domain regulated by a single licenser). Thus, the generalization in (8) must be abandoned, leaving the nature of prepositional DOM open. Two insights in the original generalization have however been shown to be correct and have been extended to various other phenomena besides DOM: (i) the presence of a [PERSON] component interferes with the licensing of a DP (possibly in distinct ways, as argued for recently by Preminger 2019); (ii) in certain domains more than one piece of structure might require licensing, but only one primary licenser is available (Anagnostopoulou 2003, a.o.).

The proposal put forward in this paper is that an adaptation of *Kayne's Generalization* is able to derive the prepositional DOM patterns (starting from Romanian). The prepositional marker is a *supplementary* licenser, as in *Kayne's Generalization*. However the licensing competition is not triggered by a clitic, but by the

---

[4] Other Romance varieties (such as Neapolitan, etc.) similarly demonstrate that clitic doubling is not dependent on a preposition introducing the DP associate.

presence of *more than one feature that requires licensing* in the same DP, irrespective of the clitic. While it is uncontroversial that the clitic double spells out the result of a licensing operation, this appears to be independent of DOM itself. The assumption that the differential preposition is connected to licensing is also necessary, as discussed throughout the paper. However, we will also demonstrate in the next section that there is yet another category that requires licensing in Romanian, namely the referential D⁰. Romanian, similarly to other Romance languages, provides evidence that the prepositional marker operates on nominals with a certain type of structure, namely DPs as opposed to NPs, and excludes predicates. As in Romanian (as opposed to Spanish), there is a D⁰ head independently containing a [PERSON] feature, it is D⁰ itself that undergoes an initial licensing operation. Thus, if [PERSON γ] (interpreted as animacy) is also merged, it can get licensed, but an additional licenser must be made available, as the initial one has been used up by the referential D⁰.

Before proceeding with the formal details, the next two subsections contain a brief discussion about two recent DOM accounts which also use the idea of *supplementary licensing*, as well as some further remarks about the problem of licensing multiple accusatives.

2.1 Secondary and last resort licensing: Differences from other accounts

A recent account where DOM revolves around the idea of *(supplementary) licensing* has been proposed by Kalin (2018). The primary data come from the Neo-Aramaic language Senaya which has various so-called *partial agreement reversal* patterns. Relevant for the present discussion is that objects with a specific interpretation are only possible in the imperfective and use agreement morphology which is otherwise seen with subjects in the perfective. In (14), the specific object has the L-suffix, the same as the subject in the perfective (15):

(14) Senaya imperfectives (Kalin 2018: 119, (10a))
 Objects agree if specific; morphological form = L-suffix
 Āna (xa) ksūta xazy-an-ā.
 I a book.F see.IPFV-S.1SG.F-**L.3SG.F**
 'I see **a (specific) book** (e.g., on the table).'

(15) Senaya perfectives (Kalin 2018: 118, (9b))
Subjects agree obligatorily; morphological form = L-suffix
*Āyet ksū-wā-**lox**.*
You write.PFV-PST-**L.2SG.M**
'**You** wrote (a long time ago).'

Kalin (2018) explains these patterns starting from two assumptions: (i) certain types of DP needs obligatory licensing, as they carry an uninterpretable Case ([uC]) feature; (ii) clauses normally contain one obligatory licenser. When needed for convergence, secondary licensers can be merged.[5] In the Senaya imperfectives, the structure is large enough as to permit the merge of a secondary licenser which will check the ([uC]) on the primary object. The primary licenser, namely Asp, licenses instead the closest argument in its domain, the subject.

The idea that DOM results from merging a secondary licenser in a configuration where the primary licenser is not active (anymore) rests on the same reasoning as *Kayne's Generalization*. However, although Kalin (2018) elegantly captures the Senaya facts, secondary licensing along the lines of *Kayne's Generalization* fares better when applied to Romance.[6] In Kalin's typology (as seen in Kalin 2018: 159, Table 51) the primary licenser can either be T, Asp or v. v can be an obligatory licenser only if T (or Asp) is the primary obligatory licenser. Configurations where v is an obligatory licenser are predicted to either lack DOM or have only an unique ACC marker.

What the Romanian data show instead is that the prepositional DOM 'licensing competition' must be relativized in other terms. In Jaeggli's (1986) classic discussion it was the (accusative) clitic, and not the subject, that 'absorbed Case' from the primary licenser, leaving the object DP caseless (and thus violating the *Case Filter*). *Kayne's Generalization* starts from the correct intuition that, with respect to Romanian DOM, the licensing competition is between *categories that need structural accusative*, and not just any type of Case licensing. Translating this into Kalin's (2018) implementation would imply having v as a primary licenser, and a preposition as a secondary licenser. This precise configuration is however (among the ones that are) not included in Kalin's Table 51.

---

5 *Licensing Economy Principle*: A secondary licenser is activated iff the derivation will otherwise not converge. (Kalin: 139, (36)).
6 When relativized to domains, it can also easily derive other types of DOM languages. A detailed comparison between the two accounts cannot be included here for lack of space.

2.2 More than one structural accusative

More generally, the puzzle Romanian poses is that the same nominal can enter into multiple structural dependencies. This is in fact an issue at the core of differential object marking. Languages that show more than one structural accusative (or more than one type of accusative that requires licensing) are not rare, as also discussed in the contributions by Müller, as well as Spyropoulos and Kuo in this volume. Besides Romance, we see a similar picture in Indo-Aryan, Basque varieties that exhibit DOM, (varieties of) Chinese, Finnish, to cite just a few examples.

There are at least two main possibilities to model patterns of this type. One way out could be that adpositional DOM does not have the syntax of a true ACC but that of DAT or obliques. A recent analysis along these lines is in Manzini & Franco (2016) or the two authors' contribution to this volume. As shown in Section 6 this solution proves, at least prima facie, problematic for Romanian. DOM and datives/obliques appear to be subject to distinct syntactic diagnostics.

Other recent accounts assume instead that a theoretical answer to this problem has to comprehensively address a multitude of variables. For example, this is the conclusion Vainikka & Brattico (2014) or Brattico (2012) support for the issue of 'multiple accusatives' in Finnish, illustrated below:[7]

(16) Finnish accusative (Vainikka & Brattico 2014: 75, (1a–c))

  a. … *näin häne-t.*
      saw he-ACC(t)
      '(I) saw him.'

---

[7] Note that the problem is *not* the well-known split partitive–accusative ((i) and (ii), from Kiparsky (1998: (1a,b))). The accusative is normally analyzed as having a structural nature. The partitive, on the other hand, rather signals a type of inherent Case, and behaves more like a predicate undergoing incorporation. From the vast literature on the topic, see Vainikka & Maling (1996), de Hoop (1996), Kiparsky (1998), Ramchand (2008), a.o.

(i) Finnish partitive
    ammu-i-n   karhu-a.
    shot-PST-1.SG bear-PART
    'I shot at the bear.'

(ii) Finnish accusative
    ammu-i-n   karhu-n.
    shot-PST-1SG bear-ACC
    'I shot the bear.'

b. ... *näin auto-n.*
   saw car-ACC(n)
   '(I) saw the car.'

c. ... *täytyy nähdä auto.*
   must see   car.ACC(Ø)
   '(I) must see the car.'

As the descriptive literature has noticed, and as also argued by Kiparsky (2001), as well as by Brattico (2012), or Vainikka & Brattico (2014), the three forms are not conditioned *morphologically*, but *syntactically*. Moreover, out of the three variants, (i) *-t* is only possible with pronouns; (ii) *-n* shows homophony with the genitive, and (iii) the Ø form is syncretic with the nominative. Syncretism with other structural cases is not surprising for 'accusatives', due to its cross-linguistic pervasiveness. However, Vainikka & Brattico (2014) provide crucial diagnostics demonstrating that the latter two forms do not have the syntax of true genitives (possessors, etc.) or nominatives (subjects, etc.).

Vainikka & Brattico (2014) show that deriving the difference between the three forms requires a formal model where several parameters need to be taken into account: (i) the general idea of last-resort licensing: under certain conditions, heads higher in the clause such as C or Agr can check the case of a direct object in order to avoid crash of the derivation; (ii) the agreement features of the DP itself; (iii) c-command; (iv) agreement higher in the structure.

Another insight from Vainikka & Brattico (2014) is that a language can contain *more than one* last-resort licenser. Various last-resort licensers can license direct objects under various conditions. *Kayne's Generalization*, on the other hand, builds on the crucial observation that a DP can contain *more than one* feature that requires licensing. This assumption also matches recent accounts where (C/case) licensing operations may apply to nominals more than once (Baker & Vinokurova 2010, N. Richards 2013, Pesetsky 2014, Wiltschko 2014, Levin & Preminger 2015, Levin 2016, Preminger 2019, Chen 2018, a.o.). Combining these observations is a starting point for a formal discussion of the Romanian differential marker.

3 Modeling multiple structural objects

As extensively discussed in the other contributions to this volume, differential object marking has been associated to the idea of licensing in many recent formal analyses. Under several accounts (Ormazabal & Romero 2007, 2013, López 2012,

Wiltschko 2014, Bárány 2015, Kalin 2018, Levin 2019, a.o.), what unifies the special marking on certain classes of objects is their requirement to enter into a (φ-) relationship with functions heads (*v*, T, C, etc.) in the clausal spine (see also Béjar & Rezac 2009). This is, in a nutshell, one instantiation of the general mechanics of *licensing* nominal categories can be subject to. The advantages of this line of investigation are important for languages where *overt movement* of special objects cannot be motivated unstipulatively. As we will see shortly, there is evidence that (some) Romance differential objects do not raise above VoiceP (López 2012), and in fact, in languages like Romanian *any type of movement* is difficult to motivate. Licensing requirements are introduced by the presence of a certain piece of structure in the composition of special objects. Normally, unlicensed objects are seen as NPs, that is, as nominals lacking the D⁰ projection (Danon 2006, 2011, a.o.). Objects that must undergo licensing are more complex; they contain the DP layer, where D⁰ introduces an uninterpretable Case [uC] feature, as illustrated below:

(17) *Unlicensed objects*   (18) *Objects undergoing licensing*

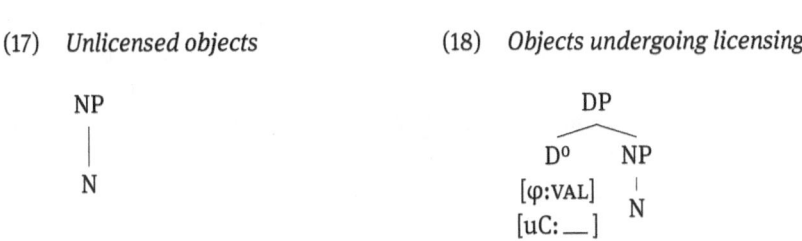

Following strict minimalist conditions on narrow syntax derivations as well as legibility conditions imposed by interfaces where uninterpretable (Case)features cannot be read, the latter must be eliminated under checking by appropriate heads in the sentential domain (Chomsky 2001 et subseq.). The challenge posed by Romance languages is that their rich nominal morphology makes it harder to precisely detect the categories that undergo licensing. As we have seen, across Romance there is D⁰ morphology, but also differential marking.

One licensing solution has been proposed based on Spanish, a close relative of Romanian, which also exhibits robust differential marking. The conclusion Ormazabal & Romero (2007), Alcaraz (2018), as well as Rodríguez-Mondoñedo (2007), a.o. arrive at with respect to standard Spanish is that non-*DOM definites* (and any other nominals that do not show differential marking) do not need licensing, despite possibly being DPs (Ormazabal & Romero, Ormazabal & Romero 2013, Alcaraz, as well as Rodríguez-Mondoñedo 2007, a.o.). Differentially marked objects, on the other hand, are KPs (Bittner & Hale 1996, a.o.). They contain a KP layer, merged above the DP and housing an [uC] feature on K⁰, as shown schematically in (20). [uC] forces the DOM animate in (19) to undergo checking/valuation in the syntax:

(19) Spanish
    *He   visto *(a)   la   niña.*
    have.1SG seen   DOM DEF.F.SG girl
    'I have seen the girl.'

(20)   KP
          /   \
      K⁰   DP
    [φ:VAL]   la niña
    [uC:__]

The split between lack of licensing/licensing finds a clear correlate in Spanish. On the one hand, differential marking is *obligatory* on animate referential definites. On the other hand, in restricted contexts where the differential marker can be dropped with definite animates, a change in the interpretation of the DP object is observed. The readings seem to be similar to non-referential definites.

(21) Spanish
    He   encontrado la   niña (que buscas).
    have.1SG found   DEF.F.SG girl   that search.2SG
    'I have found the type of girl (you are looking for).'
    #'I have found the specific girl (you are looking for).'

Similarly, those definites that are obligatorily interpreted non-specific will not require the differential marker, irrespectively of animacy. A relevant example is provided below from the so-called Quine definites (see Espinal & Cyrino 2017 for a recent discussion about non-specific definites in Romance).

(22) Spanish
    Juan busca   la   mujer   perfecta.
    Juan search.2SG DEF.F.SG woman perfect.F.SG
    'Juan is looking for the perfect woman.'

Another canonical way to detect obligatory nominal licensing is through an examination of contexts where special (Case) morphology is necessary *irrespective of the interpretation* the nominal receives (see also Wiltschko 2014). As López (2012) correctly observes, small clauses (SCs) provide an excellent testing ground for differential marking in Spanish. One of the puzzles with examples similar to (23) is that the differential marker is necessary on the animate indefinite, even on a non-specific, narrow scope reading. A modal adjective like *necessary* normally triggers narrow scope on a nominal, and thus the preferred interpretation of (23) is that I do not have in mind a specific student to be necessary for a project, and any student would do. The indefinite takes narrow scope with respect to both the intensional predicate *consider*, as well as the modal adjective *necessary*.

(23) Spanish
Considero   *(a)   un   estudiante necessario   por   un
consider.1SG DOM   a.M.SG student   necessary.M.SG for   a.M.SG
projeto.
project
'I consider a student necessary for a project.'
consider > necessary > a student

DOM obligatoriness irrespective of specificity, however, poses a challenge. In Spanish run-of-the-mill extensional contexts, the prepositional marker tends to be regulated by *specificity* if the nominal is indefinite. Non-specific readings of indefinite inanimates are *not* constructed with differential marking, as seen in the examples below. What the sentence (24b) shows is that the DOM-less animate indefinite is only possible with the subjunctive mood, that is, restricted to non-specificity, by default. The subjunctive mood, which is a hallmark of non-specificity (Rivero 1979), *does not* require a differentially marked object. We see in (24a) that the differential marker surfaces with the indicative (the subjunctive also being possible). The dilemma is why the differential marker is *needed* (for many speakers) in examples like (23), where the context also triggers non-specificity.

(24) Spanish (López 2012: 18, (38a,b))

a. *María buscó   **a**   una   gestora   que habla   alemán.*
María searched DOM a.F.SG manager that speaks.IND German
'Maria looked for a manager that speaks German.'

b. *María buscó   una   gestora   que *habla   /✓hable*
María searched a.F.SG manager that speaks.IND speaks.SBJV
alemán.
German
'Maria looked for a manager that could speak German.'

According to López (2012), the answer resides in the observation that SCs force licensing on the shared objects, due to a particular syntactic configuration. As the predicate *consider* merges with a SC, its complement position is occupied, (25). Thus, incorporation of the DP into *consider* is blocked. The DP cannot incorporate into the AP either, as it is not merged as a complement (among other reasons). Thus, the DP has to undergo some type of licensing, for well-formedness. Leaving aside the specific mechanism under which incorporated objects are derived, what is relevant to the present discussion is that they will be found under the scope of an existential (∃) quantifier at some point in the derivation and are akin to predicates. *Differentially-marked objects* signal an anti-incorporation mechanism. The presence of [uC] does not permit the nominal to incorporate, as the feature cannot be licitly checked, leading to a crash in the derivation.

(25) [consider [DP AP]]

We have examined above two licensing diagnostics: (i) obligatoriness of DOM with referential definites; (ii) obligatoriness of DOM with animates in SCs. Turning now to Romanian, we notice some important distinctions. First, as we have mentioned in the introduction, the prepositional marker is *not* obligatory on referential definites. The animate definite in (26), repeated here from (3), *can* be interpreted referentially:

(26) Au lăudat studentul inteligent.
 have praised student.DEF.M.SG intelligent.M.SG
 'They have praised the (specific) intelligent student.'

Second, the differential marker is not obligatory with animates in SCs either. The example in (27) is grammatical in Romanian, even without the prepositional marker:

(27) *Consideră* (***pe***) *studenţii români foarte*
 considers DOM student.M.PL.DEF.M.PL Romanian.M.PL very
  inteligenţi.
  intelligent.M.PL
 'S/he considers the Romanian students very intelligent.'

A possible solution according to which the prepositional objects do not need licensing would be problematic. We have seen that there are non-trivial contexts where the special morphology is *necessary* irrespective of animacy and specificity (the contexts in (5)). A second solution that would take Romanian SCs not to require licensing is also difficult to maintain. The crucial point is that, although the differential marker is not obligatory in SCs, nominals cannot be used bare. Thus, the sentence in (28a), where the definite has been removed and the nominal only shows plural morphology, is strictly ungrammatical under a SCs construal (the example is grammatical under an attributive reading of the adjective, irrelevant here). Note that a bare plural is otherwise possible as an object in Romanian (28b):

(28) a. *Consideră studenți români foarte inteligenți.
considers student.M.PL Romanian.M.PL very intelligent.M.PL
intended: 'S/he considers Romanian students very intelligent.'

b. Consideră studenți români pentru proiect.
considers student.M.PL Romanian.M.PL for project
'S/he considers Romanian students for the project.'

The same point is strengthened by other types of nominals, which require *obligatory* definiteness when used in SCs. We illustrate with mass nouns, which in Romanian can be used bare even in the singular, as seen in (29). However, when the same nominal is used in a SC, definiteness morphology is obligatory (see also Belletti 1988).

(29) Consideră / vinde / vede miere.
considers sells sees honey
'S/he considers/sells/sees honey.'

(30) Consideră miere-*(a) sănătoasă.
considers honey-DEF.F.SG healthy-F.SG
'S/he considers honey healthy.'

The puzzle is that the DP does not have to be interpreted definite in (30b).[8] It must however have at least a generic reading. Both Belletti (1988) and more recently

---

8 Note that an explanation which attributes the obligatory presence of the definite to a putative subject position inside a small clause *cannot* be the answer. This hypothesis is based on the observation that subjects cannot normally be bare in Romance. However, *bare subjects* are possible in Romanian, especially with unaccusatives. Given that adjectives have an unaccusative behavior, it's not clear what would block the absence of the bare forms. Second, a SC analysis for these constructions is not accepted unanimously. To solve some non-trivial challenges of these constructions, contributions by Chomsky (1975) or Williams (1983) rather propose a V-Adj complex predicate structure to which the argument is compositionally merged. And third, even under (re-

Irimia (2016) have independently supported López's (2012) conclusion, namely that the problem is one of nominal *licensing* in this context. These patterns can be straightforwardly derived under the assumption that D⁰ contains an uninterpretable Case feature [uC] in Romanian. This is different from Spanish, where D⁰ is not associated with a [uC] feature by default.

We further assume a decomposition of the low functional verbal domain, into v and Voice, the latter being the structural layer where the external argument (EA) is introduced (see also Legate (2014)). [uC] on D⁰ is licensed by a low licenser (v, below Voice, (31)) or configurational case assignment (Marantz 1991). Additionally, a [PERSON] feature can be merged on a DP *argument*. If found on a gender (γ)-related projection, [PERSON] will be interpreted as *semantic gender* ([PERSON γ] in (32)), giving the split between animates and inanimates. As we mentioned, we build on a rich line of research which connects animacy to a [PERSON] feature (also Cornilescu 2000, Ormazabal & Romero 2007, Adger & Harbour 2007, M. Richards 2008, a.o.). At the end of Section 6, we see in fact some examples which could further support a link between animacy and [PERSON], based on P(erson)C(ase)C(onstraint)-like effects DOM triggers in the presence of another [PERSON] (contributed by a third person clitic) in the same local domain. Although we do not discuss clitic doubling in detail here, argument DPs can show yet another [PERSON], merged higher in the DP, as a clitic. This latter [PERSON$_{clitic}$], when licensed, outputs clitic doubling; it has distinct interpretive effects from [+PERSON γ] and independent contexts of use from DOM. What unifies both [PERSON γ] and [PERSON$_{clitic}$] is that their licensing *cannot* fail when merged and they are dependent on a previous licensing operation, as they act on *arguments* (see also Preminger 2019 for similar remarks about [PERSON]).

---

cent) SC accounts, this type of embedded domain is not a domain of quantification, thus the D⁰ head (containing definiteness) could not have been merged inside the SC anyway (see especially Moulton (2013)).

(31) D⁰ licensing

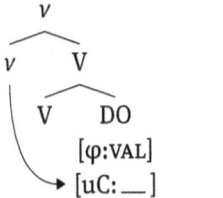

argumenthood, individuation, etc.

(32) DOM licensing

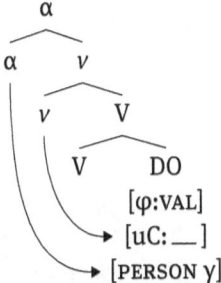

animacy, prominence, low topicalization ⇒ **ADPOSITION**

(33) Clitic licensing

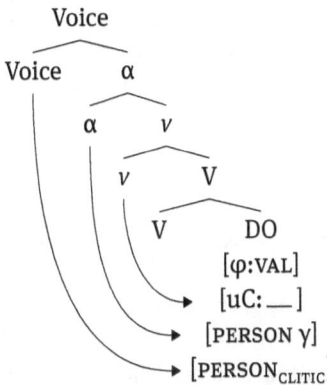

wide scope specificity, D-linking, partitives/generics, etc.

However, [PERSON$_{clitic}$] is distinct in that it requires *raising* for licensing. In Romanian, ACC clitic doubled arguments take wide scope with respect to EAs, indicating that they are interpreted above vP. At least two pieces of evidence support this conclusion. First, clitics are overtly placed above elements that mark the Voice edge, for example polarity sensitive particle *mai* 'anymore' (see also Dobrovie-Sorin 1994). Second, a simple binding test goes through from a clitic-doubled argument into the EA, as illustrated in the example below:

(34) Părinț-i-i   lor$_{i/j}$ nu i-au   mai   lăudat
    parent-M.PL-DEF.M.PL   their   not CL.M.PL.ACC-have.3.PL anymore   praised
    pe   copi-i$_i$.[9]
    DOM   child-N.PL

'Their$_i$ parents have not praised the children$_i$ anymore.'

DOM (with [PERSON γ]), on the other hand, is licensed *in-situ* and cannot take scope over the EA, when the same binding test is applied. In fact, in Romanian, DOM DPs have the same position as referential definites and are not interpreted above EAs. The two examples in (35) prove that coreferentiality from a non-clitic doubled object into the EA gives rise to ungrammaticality, irrespective of the presence of DOM:

(35) a. Părinț-i-i   lor$_{*i/j}$ au   lăudat   **pe**   copi-i$_i$
        parent-M.PL-DEF.M.PL their   have.3.PL   praised   DOM   child-N.PL
        'Their$_{*i}$ parents have praised the children$_i$.'

    b. Părinț-i-i   lor$_{*i/j}$ au   lăudat   copi-i-i$_i$.
        parent-M.PL-DEF.M.PL their   have.3.PL   praised   child-N.PL-DEF.N.PL
        'Their$_{*i}$ parents have praised the children$_i$.'

This similarity between DOM arguments and referential definites can be best captured if the former undergo an *additional licensing operation in the same local licensing domain*.

To conclude, in this section we have motivated the assumption that DOM involves an additional licensing operation on a nominal. This operation applies in the same licensing domain as the initial operation, and thus differentially marked objects are not distinguished from other licensed objects in terms of a higher overt position above the EA. In the next section we show how the various cases of differential marking are unified under the additional licensing hypothesis.

---

[9] Note that in Romanian non-modified DPs cannot show overt definiteness after a preposition (compare (34) with (2b)). However, the DP is interpreted as definite. The problem of the deleted definite is independent of DOM.

4 The differential marker

In the previous two subsections we have presented several conclusions regarding the nature of differential object marking. Similarly to López (2012), as well as Ormazabal & Romero (2013), we assume that the distinction between lack of a [uC] feature, thus lack of licensing by a clausal functional head vs. feature valuation and licensing (on DPs that carry a [uC] case feature) is at the core of differential marking. Where the present analysis diverges is in further specifying the type of *sentential licensing* involved in differential object marking. We have motivated the assumption that differential marking signals an *additional licensing* operation in the same local domain.

Following Bernstein (2008), Longobardi (2008), a.o., referential definiteness in D⁰ spells out a PERSON feature. Other types of morphology found in D⁰, such as certain types of referential indefinites, can also be connected to PERSON in D⁰ (strong D⁰ in Longobardi's terms), but are not discussed here as they introduce various complications which are orthogonal to DOM. On the other hand, researchers such as M. Richards (2008), Cornilescu (2000), or Adger & Harbour (2007), a.o. have linked a [PERSON] feature to animacy. We have proposed that the two views can be reconciled by connecting the multi-faceted behavior of PERSON to the position in which it merges. Some demonstratives (the so-called *augmented* forms, as discussed in this section) also require obligatory definiteness marking in Romanian, motivating the assumption that a [PERSON] also merges with this category.

The Romanian data further show that licensing is relativized to features and to domains (Baker & Vinokurova 2010, Baker 2015, a.o.). Both the referential definite as well as the differential object need licensing below the VoiceP domain. Also, a DP can contain more than one feature that requires licensing (see the case stacking literature, and also d'Alessandro 2017, or Oxford 2014, a.o.). The result is that a DP can enter into multiple licensing operations such that all the relevant features can get licensed (see also Béjar & Rezac 2009). We combine Vainikka & Brattico (2014) with an adaptation of *Kayne's Generalization*. A given domain has just one primary licenser available. As in *Kayne's Generalization* or more recently Vainikka & Brattico (2014), an additional licenser is recruited to value additional features which would otherwise trigger crash if left unlicensed. If any features are still left unlicensed after the application of the secondary licenser, they will need to be licensed in a different domain.

The intuitive idea that a DP feature must enter into a relationship with a functional head in the clausal spine can be implemented in a variety of framework, thus no particular mechanics is specified here. The basic terminology from minimalist implementations (Chomsky 2001, a.o.) assumed is: *probe* (component on a functional category in the clausal spine licensing a DP), and *goal* (DP undergoing licensing).

We can now proceed with the differential marker. We have seen that its distribution follows three patterns: (a) contexts in which the preposition is obligatory; (b) contexts where the preposition is optional; (c) contexts where the preposition leads to ungrammaticality. Let's start with the most canonical cases, namely those of pronouns (example (2a), repeated here in (36a)) and proper names, seen in (36b)). These are strictly ungrammatical without the differential marker.

(36) a. *Elena m-a   văzut *(pe) *eu   / mine.*
        Elena CL.1SG.ACC-has seen   DOM 1SG.NOM   1SG.ACC
        intended: 'Elena saw me.'

    b. *Elena a   chemat-(o)   *(pe) Maria.*
        Elena has called-CL.3SG.F.ACC DOM   Maria
        'Elena has called Maria.'

As just mentioned, we connect grammaticalized humanness/animacy to the presence of a [PERSON γ] feature (M. Richards 2008, Adger & Harbour 2007, a.o.) merged on gender (γ)-introducing functional projection (see especially Cornilescu 2000, a.o.). [PERSON γ] is interpreted as *semantic gender*, that is as signaling animacy (or humaness). Building on feature geometries proposed for pronouns, we assume that third person/animate DPs contain a [PERSON γ]. A simplified geometry from Harley & Ritter (2002) is included in Table 1 below. Third person *inanimates* lack the [PERSON γ] feature, and thus do not require an additional licensing operation.

Tab. 1: Person and Animacy (building on Harley & Ritter 2002)

Person/animacy	Features	
1st person	[PERSON]	[+PARTICIPANT] (speaker)
2nd person	[PERSON]	[+PARTICIPANT] (addressee)
3nd person, +human, +animate	[PERSON]	

Both pronouns, as well as proper names, are classes that contain a referential D⁰ in Romanian (in Longobardi's 1994 terms they require obligatory raising to D⁰). Supplementary, they also obligatorily grammaticalize *animacy*, and thus have

[PERSON γ].[10] Thus, these classes contain two [PERSON] features. Given that the probe the on *v* licenses the referential material in D (a [PERSON] feature), the extra [PERSON] feature on *n* needs an *additional* licenser. The preposition spells out the presence of this additional licenser, as shown below:

(37) DOM licensing

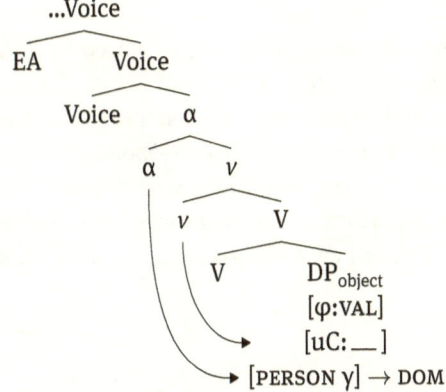

Other classes that contain an obligatory [PERSON γ] feature are the *wh*-element *cine* ('who'), as well as the negative quantifier *nimeni* ('nobody'), due to their obligatory restriction to animacy. As we noticed in (11) and (12), repeated here as (38) and (39), these categories require the obligatory differential preposition, but are ungrammatical with clitic-doubling.

---

10 In modern Romanian, third person pronouns (as well as first and second person ones) are restricted to animates:

(i) *(L)-am văzut *(pe) el.
 CL.3SG.ACC.M-have.1 seen DOM he
 'I saw him.', # 'I saw it.'

An inanimate third person object only requires the overt clitic. Similarly, proper names, if not referring to animate entities do not easily accept the adpositional marker.

(ii) Am cumpărat-o ??(pe) Toyota.
 have.1SG bought-CL.3SG.ACC.F DOM Toyota
  intended: 'I bought the Toyota.' (when referring to the car; example is ok with the prepositional marker if the entity intended is animate, for example a cat called Toyota.)

(38) a. *Nu (*l-)am văzut *(pe) nimeni.*
   not   CL.3SG.M.ACC-have.1SG seen DOM nobody
   'I didn't see anybody.'

b. **(Pe) cine (*l-)ai văzut?*
   DOM who CL.3SG.M.ACC-have.2SG seen
   'Who did you see?'

An account for the clitic doubling restriction is the one proposed by Dobrovie-Sorin (1990) in terms of *Kayne's Generalization*. The gist of her analysis is that, in examples like (38), *wh-* is a quantifier and thus must bind a variable (given the ban against vacuous quantification). But the structure corresponding to (38) contains no available variable. A variable must be Case-marked;[11] however, in the representation in (39), corresponding to (38), the clitic absorbs the available Case, and thus the empty category *e* will be left caseless, and thus does not qualify as the right variable:

(39) wh_i cl_i e_i

We have seen however that Kayne's Generalization is problematic in its classical form. The configuration in (39) could nevertheless be adequate for quantifier-variable links. In more minimalist terms it might indicate an *intervention* effect caused by the clitic. Given that the clitic (under discussion here) is an unambiguously D⁰ category, it must the case that both the *wh-* quantifier, as well as the negative quantifier project at least up to D⁰ (even if a negative quantifier like *nimeni* cannot be referential). Thus, they will require licensing. Moreover, the animate quantifiers *obligatorily* grammaticalize *animacy* which, following Cornilescu (2000, p.3) is *an in-built restriction on their domain of quantification*. Thus, an extra probe is needed in these contexts to value the second [PERSON]. The same analysis applies to the quantifiers *cineva* 'somebody' and *oricine* 'anybody' (built from *cine*, as their morphology overtly shows). Unsurprisingly, when used as objects, they are ungrammatical without the prepositional marker. DOM signals the presence of an additional probe that licenses an extra-feature in the same domain as the first feature having undergone licensing:

---

[11] Following Chomsky's (1981) definition of variables: α is a variable if and only if α is an empty category that (a) occupies an A-position, (b) is bound by a quantifier, and (c) is Case-marked (Chomsky 1981: 69, 102; Dobrovie-Sorin 1990: (10)).

(40) *Prepostional differential (object) licensing in Romanian*
If a DP contains more than one feature of the same type that requires valuation in the same domain, an additional licenser must be made available.

4.1 The prepositional marker in 'non-canonical' configurations

By far, the most problematic aspects of the prepositional accusative concern its obligatoriness in contexts where animacy/specificity or both are missing. These instances have been rarely discussed from a more formal perspective, one exception being Cornilescu (2000). At least prima facie, these instances indicate that the preposition itself is *not* an animacy or specificity marker. Under the *additional licensing* account proposed here, they can however be derived straightforwardly.

As mentioned in the introduction (5a)–(5d), DOM without animacy/specificity groups together the following contexts: (i) nominal ellipsis, (ii) D-linking and partitives; (iii) some types of comparatives. The first context will be discussed here, and partitives and the comparative in the next subsections. The facts with nominal ellipsis are best illustrated by the contrast in (41):

(41) a. Ai cumpărat (*pe*) paltonul acela?
 have.2SG bought DOM coat.DEF.N.SG that.N.SG.AUG
 'Did you buy that coat?'

 b. L-am cumpărat *(pe*) acesta.
 CL.3SG.M/N.ACC-have bought DOM this.N.SG.AUG
 'I have bought this one.' (*referring to the coat*)

In (41a), the demonstrative is used as an adjective, modifying the DP *paltonul*. As the head noun is inanimate, the prepositional DOM is *not* possible. In (41b), which repeats example (5a), the demonstrative is used as a pronoun in a nominal ellipsis construction, which contains a null *pro* head. It also tracks an inanimate antecedent. Note that nominal ellipsis of this type requires *obligatory* prepositional ACC, irrespective of animacy. Two other definite determiners in the language show the same behavior as the demonstratives. These are the so-called adjectival demonstrative CEL,[12] and the the genitive linker *a* which contains a suf-

---

[12] CEL is a form that developed from the endophoric distal demonstrative *acel/acela*, the latter descending from the Latin complex demonstrative *ecce/eccum* (an adverbial reinforcer) + *illum* (distal demonstrative).

fixed definite determiner under nominal ellipsis (see especially Cornilescu & Nicolae 2012 for a detailed discussion of these categories). The examples in (42) and (43) illustrate the similarity with the elliptical demonstratives:[13]

(42) a. Vrei (*pe) paltonul roşu?
   want.2SG DOM coat.DEF.N.SG red.N.SG
   'Do you want the red coat?'

b. Nu, îl vreau *(pe) cel albastru.
   No, CL.M.SG.ACC want.1SG DOM CEL.N.SG blue.N.SG
   'No, I want the blue one.' (referring to the coat)

(43) a. Ai citit (*pe) lucrările lui Hegel?
   have.2SG read DOM work.F.PL.DEF.F.PL GEN.M.SG Hegel
   'Have you read Hegel's works?'

b. Nu, le-am citit *(pe) a-le lui Chomsky.
   No, CL.F.PL-have.1 read DOM LK-DEF.F.PL GEN.M.SG Chomsky
   'No, I have read Chomsky's.' (referring to the works)

In examples of this type, if the head noun is present, the differential marker will behave according to animacy. In (42)[a] and (43a) the head noun is inanimate, and the DOM preposition is not tolerated. In (42)[b] and (43b), where CEL and the genitive linker are used under ellipsis, the ACC preposition becomes obligatory irrespective of animacy. An explanation for these patterns has to obviously be tied to the internal structure of nominal ellipsis.

Another observation made by Cornilescu (2000) is following: when ellipsis affects *propositional content*, PE is normally absent with the demonstrative, as in the example below (adapted from Cornilescu 2000):

(44) Eu am spus (*pe) asta: să mergem la cinema.
   I have.1SG said DOM this.DFLT.AUG SBJV go.SBJV.1PL at cinema
   'I said this: Let's go to the cinema.'

Ellipsis of propositional content is signaled by a morphologically default demonstrative form, in this case one that looks like the augmented feminine (*asta*).

---

[13] The universal quantifier *toţi/toate* 'all$_{M/F.Pl}$' also requires the obligatory prepositional marker under ellipsis. It will be discussed in the next section where other quantifiers are examined.

Under the *additional licensing* proposal put forward in this paper, these patters are accounted as follows. Based on the extensive discussion in Cornilescu & Nicolae (2012), nominal ellipsis is decomposed in the syntax into several components: a) a contrastive focus position at the left periphery of the DP (where the remnant moves); b) *ellipsis sites function as definite descriptions* (see also Elbourne 2013). Thus, in the case of nominal ellipsis, a nominal structure contains a definite determiner. As a result, it may be marked with the feature *anaphoric* ([+a]), and deleted at PF. Robust evidence for the decomposition of ellipsis into definiteness comes from the presence of overt definite morphology in elliptical contexts in Romanian. As discussed by Cornilescu & Nicolae (2012), the overt counterpart of a definite ellipsis DP is marked by a double definite construction.[14] See the examples in (45) (their (25), p. 1084):

(45) acestea   de pe   masă.
     these.AUG.F.PL of from table
     'these on the table'

(46) cărț**ile**   acestea   de pe masă.
     books.F.PL these.AUG.F.PL of on table
     'these books from the table'

Also note that pronominal demonstratives always take the augmented form (the *-a* ending), which is assumed to be related to definiteness (the definite demonstrative).[15]

Let's examine first a non-elided demonstrative structure, namely that in (41a), repeated here in (47). What we see here is a definite noun followed by the demon-

---

[14] Another piece of evidence comes from indefinites which show an obligatory definite suffix under ellipsis:

(i) Am   scris   unu-l.
     have.1SG written INDEF.M/N.SG-DEF.M/N.SG
     'I wrote one.' (closest translation to English, but note that examples of this type do not necessarily involve numerals.)

[15] Based on their position and morphology, adjectival demonstratives come in two classes in Romanian: a) those that follow a definite noun and must take the augmented form (i); b) those that precede an indefinite noun and cannot take the augmented form (ii). Adjectival demonstratives which do not follow a definite noun cannot take the augmented form. See especially Giusti (1993) or Giurgea (2008):

strative adjective in its augmented form. As already mentioned, these configurations are characterized by so-called *double definiteness*. The adjectival demonstrative contains a definiteness feature which is however valued via concord with the definiteness in D (in the same way as the gender and number features on the demonstrative). The possibility of concord *precludes the need of an additional licenser*, as concord licenses the PERSON feature in D⁰:

(47) Ai   cumpărat (*pe)   paltonul   acela?
     have.2 bought   DOM   coat.DEF.N.SG that.N.SG.AUG
     'Did you buy that coat?'

Under all canonical accounts about the structure of N-Def demonstratives (see references cited in footnote 15, as well as Cornilescu 1992, or Nicolae 2015), N-Def demonstratives must contain a DP layer. Moreover, the augmented demonstrative (also called *strong*) in (47) is diagnosed as phrasal under various tests (see especially Cornilescu 2005). Assuming the standard set of functional projections in the upper part of the Romanian DP (footnote 15, Brugè 2002, Nicolae 2013, Nicolae 2015, a.o.): DP > Dem P > QP >...., and given that definiteness starts out low, the post nominal position of the adjectival demonstrative is obtained as a result of head movement of N to D across Dem (see also Nicolae 2015, a.o.):

(48) paltonu-*(l)   acest-a   (albastru).
     coat-DEF.N.SG   this.N.SG-AUG   blue.N.SG

   a. [DemP acesta [NP paltonul]]
   b. [DP [N+D paltonul [DemP acesta] [NP paltonul]]

Turning now to nominal (non-sentential) ellipsis, as in (49) (repeated from 41b) we obtain the structure in (50), modeled on elliptical configurations proposed in Cornilescu & Nicolae (2012). The ellipsis site is marked with an E.

(i) copilu-*(l)   acest-a   (ii) acest(*-a)   copil
     child-DEF.M.SG this.M.SG-AUG   this.M.SG(-AUG)   child
     'this child'   'this child'

(49) L-am   cumpărat *(pe) acest-a.
    CL.3SG.M.ACC-have bought   DOM   this-N.SG.AUG
    'I have bought this (one).'

(50)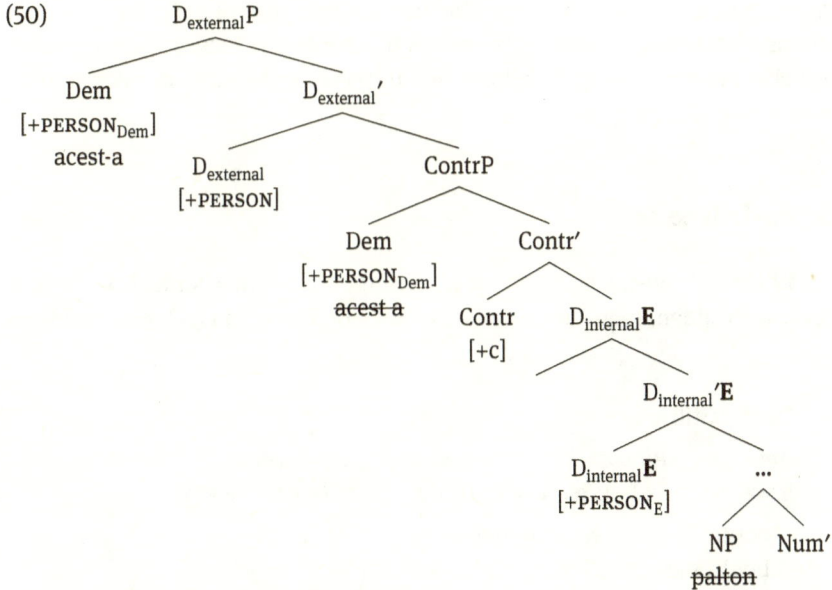

A reminder that Cornilescu & Nicolae (2012) assume the presence of a contrastive focus position (notated Contr) in elliptical structures, as well as a split-DP hypothesis. For convenience, we follow these details here.[16] The structure in (50) contains two [PERSON] features, one merged with Dem and the other attached to the ellipsis site. As there is no lexical N that could raise to D, the [PERSON] feature on Dem cannot be valued via concord. Thus, *an additional licenser* will be needed for the extra [PERSON] feature, resulting in the recruitment of PE.[17] The same reasoning applies to the other two *cel* and *al* in (42b) and (43b). Cornilescu & Nicolae (2012) show that *cel* (which is a determiner originating from reduced demonstrative form, see footnote 12) obligatorily merges in D in ellptical structures (their ex. (50)). As a definite determiner that can only attach high (above the predication layer inside the DP) it also contains a [+PERSON] feature. Given that elliptical structures

---

[16] Structural implementations that do not contain a split DP configuration are also possible. What is important for us is that ellipsis involves a definite description.

[17] Alternatively, the *pro-form a* (seen in the LK genitive) merges in D⁰. As it also has a [+PERSON] feature that requires licensing, the additional licenser is recruited to value its feature. Subsequently, it licenses the [+PERSON] on the augmented demonstrative via concord.

already have [+PERSON], and both these features require licensing, a secondary licenser is needed here too. As already indicated, *al* is composed from the linker *-a* and morphology that is identical to the definite determiner. Both Giurgea (2008), as well as Irimia et al. (2018) have shown that *-a* is a type of *pronoun*, which always merges in D⁰ (and is only possible under elliptical configurations). Thus, it contains a [PERSON] feature, which needs licensing. The [PERSON] feature of ellipsis also needs licensing. It follows that in these configurations an additional licenser is obligatory.

4.2 Partitives

The additional licensing account can also be applied to other contexts where *animacy* is overridden, more specifically partitives of the type in (51), resumed from (5b):

(51) DOM partitive
Am citit-o numai *(pe) un-a dintre
have.1SG read-CL.3SG.F.ACC only DOM a-DEF.F.SG from
cărţile recomandate.
books.DEF.F.PL recommended.F.PL
'I have read only one of the recommended books.' (Avram & Zafiu 2017: (13))

A complication with these examples is that they might not necessarily be analyzed as involving ellipsis. We have seen above that, when N was present, its non-animacy could not have been overridden (the contrast between the examples in (41), (42), and (43a) involving ellipsis). As inanimate Ns need to be specified as lacking [PERSON] in order to correctly derive DOM under ellipsis, an analysis that ties the prepositional marker to semantic gender will predict examples like (51) to be ungrammatical, contrary to what the data show. These types of sentences, in fact, although mentioned in descriptive studies, have not been addressed formally.

Adapting the analysis of partitivity proposed by Enç (1991), we show that *secondary licensing* can derive these patterns. For Enç (1991) the types of partitives we are concerned with here contain two referential indices, as in (52), which following Heim (1982) correspond to discourse referents. All DPs (NPs in Enç's 1991 terminology) are specified with a pair of indices, which themselves have a *definiteness* feature. The first index is responsible for the definiteness of the DP. We adapt Enç's analysis by proposing the second index accounts for its relation to other members of a set, and not necessarily specificity. More precisely, the second index can constrain in what way the referent of the DP is related to other discourse referents. As can be seen in (51), in Romanian the differentially-marked partitives carry overt *definiteness* morphology suffixed to an indefinite stem.[18]

(52) Partitives (Enç 1991: (22))
Every $[_{NP}\ \alpha]_{<ij>}$ is interpreted as $\alpha\ (x_i)$ and
$(x_i) \subseteq (x_j)$ if $NP_{<ij>}$ is plural,
$\{x_i\} \subseteq (x_j)$ if $NP_{<ij>}$ is singular.

In the case of indefinites, the index j must obey the Novelty Condition (the context cannot already have a referent (x_j)). The new referent that is introduced into the domain will have '(x_i), the referent of the NP, as its subset' (Enç 1991). Given that the index responsible for the subset relation of indefinites is interpreted above D (where definiteness is), it results that in this configuration there are *two* features that require licensing. Thus, an additional licenser must be made available. More clearly put, the problem is that there is another feature above D⁰, which requires linking to the context. As D⁰ is a phase head, anything merged above it requires licensing. Thus, the D⁰ itself will require licensing. The same structure is seen with the so-called D-linked *wh-* elements, which are interpreted as specific partitives. Unsurprisingly, they exhibit obligatory DOM, irrespective of animacy, as they too contain more than one feature that requires licensing. Example (5c) is resumed here:

(53) *__(Pe)__ care l-ai cumpărat?
 DOM which CL.3SG.M.ACC-have.2 bought
 'Which one have you bought?'

A similar analysis can be extended to cases like the following, where differential marking together with clitic doubling are also obligatory on an inanimate (see also Avram & Zafiu 2017):

(54) a. *(L)-ai uitat *(pe) i.
 CL.3SG.M.ACC-have.2SG forgotten DOM i
 'You have omitted the i.' (*in a text*)

---

18 Thus, these examples are morphologically similar to the elliptical 'definite' indefinites illustrated in footnote 14.

b. Trebuie să   *(îl)   adaugi   și   *(pe)   7.
   must   SBJV CL.3SG.M.ACC add.2SG   and   DOM   7

   'You also need to add (the) 7.'

4.3 Comparatives with obligatory prepositional DOM

There is yet another context where animacy is obligatorily overridden in differential marking contexts, namely on the standard of comparatives of the type seen in (55a), repeated from (5d). Another example is in (55b). In both these sentences the inanimate indefinites are also interpreted non-specific:

(55) a. L-am   păstrat ca   *(pe)   un   dar.
        CL.3SG.M.ACC-have kept   as/like DOM   a.N.SG   gift

        'I have kept it as (one would keep) a gift.'

   b. L-a   aruncat ca   *(pe)   o   minge
      CL.3SG.ACC.M-have.3SG thrown as/like DOM   a.F.SG   ball

      'S/he has thrown it as (one would throw) a ball.'

These examples are strictly ungrammatical without PE. As expected, if the inanimate is found in the corresponding non-comparative context, PE is ill-formed. Compare (55b) with (56):

(56) A   aruncat (*pe) o   minge
     have-3SG thrown DOM   a.F.SG   ball

     'S/he has thrown a ball.'

Although very frequent in colloquial speech, these comparatives are basically novel to formal accounts.[19] Here we will build on the only formal analysis proposed for these constructions, namely Irimia (2018). One important observation is that the differential marking preposition is not a *lexical* marker introducing the standard. These comparatives are not *phrasal* in Romanian. Unambiguous evidence comes from obligatory grammatical function tracking. For example, if

---

[19] Also note that they are not just a quirk of Romanian. They seem to be present in many unrelated languages that have (adpositional) differential marking (see Irimia 2018, to appear for remarks from other Romance varieties, as well as from Indo-Aryan).

the associate is an indirect object, the standard must show obligatory dative Case, as seen below. The dative case is not homophonous with the prepositional DOM in Romanian:

(57) *I-au dăruit cadouri ca* **unui** *rege* / *un rege
CL.3SG.DAT.M-have given gift.PL as like a.DAT.SG king a.NOM.SG
/ ***pe** *un rege.*
king DOM a
'They have given gifts to him as (one would give gifts) a king.'

Grammatical function tracking is sufficient to demonstrate both the structural nature of DOM as well as the clausal (non-phrasal) status of the equative in Romanian. Moreover, this type of Case identity restriction is seen in other VP ellipsis contexts. Some authors propose that Case Identity is in fact one of the conditions of the licensing of ellipsis (see Chung & Ladusaw 2004, and more recently Takita 2015). The condition Takita (2015) introduces is the following:

(58) *Case-oriented syntactic identity* (Takita 2015: (24))
If a DP is extracted from an ellipsis site, and if the head that Case-licenses the DP is contained in the ellipsis site, the Case-licensing head in the ellipsis site must have an identical head in the antecedent that Case-licenses the correlating DP.

Another observation Irimia (2018) makes is that these comparatives have reduced clausal structure. The interpretations provided by native speakers signal the use of so-called *evasion* strategies.[20] The two evasion strategies seen in the Romanian comparative are: (i) reduced syntactic structure (absence of C, T projections) in the comparative which forces obligatory mismatched temporal/aspectual interpretations (i.e. readings of the type 'as one would throw a ball'); (ii) copular clause ('as if it were a ball'). Thus, the comparative in (55a) and (55b) is based on one of the structures below:

(59) *Evasion strategies for DOM comparative structures* (Irimia 2018: (18))
  a. [... as [$_{TOP}$ Obj Top$_{[CaseAcc]}$ [$_{vP}$ V <Obj>]]]
  b. [... as [$_{TOP}$ DP Top$_{[CaseAcc]}$ [$_{SC}$ be <DP>]]]

---

20 *Evasion strategies* are necessary when strict syntactic and semantic parallelism cannot be obtained between the antecedent and the constituent undergoing ellipsis, as it would violate other principles of grammar. For more details, see especially Thoms (2013).

As the Case-licensing head is contained in the ellipsis site, the object will have to undergo extra-licensing so its Case licensing head is similar to that of the antecedent. An additional head is recruited which will license the object as a last-resort strategy (confirming the last-resort nature of the differential preposition in *Kayne's Generalization*). The structure of reduced comparatives makes plausible the assumption that the additional licenser is a low Topic head (see Belletti 2004 for the low information-structure periphery). A low information structure specified head (e.g., topic) is otherwise needed to generate elliptical structures and to link them to their discourse antecedent (see Merchant 2001, a.o.). Thus, a secondary licensing account also explains these puzzling data.

5 Other differential marking contexts

As mentioned in the introduction, there are also contexts where the prepositional marker appears to be *optional* or ungrammatical. We will briefly address them here starting with optional configurations. Typical representatives of the so-called 'optional DOM' are DOM definite animates as in (60), repeated from (3):

(60)   *Au*   *lăudat*   *studentul*   *inteligent*.
       have   praised   student.DEF.M.SG   intelligent.M.SG
       'They have praised the intelligent student.'

As Cornilescu (2000) also notices, this class also contains weak determiners like the negative *nici un/nici o* 'no$_{F/M}$', the polarity indefinite *vreun/vreo* 'some/any$_{F/M}$', weak plural quantifiers *mulți/multe* 'many$_{F/M}$', *puțini/puține* 'few$_{F/M}$', as well as cardinals. When used adjectivally, PE is sensitive to the animacy of the head noun, inanimates being ill-formed:

(61)   a.   *Am*   *citit*   **(*pe)**   *multe*   *cărți*.
             have.1SG   read   DOM   many.F.PL   book.F.PL
             'I read many books.'

       b.   *Am*   *văzut*   *doar*   **(*pe)**   *două*   *filme*.
             have.1SG   seen   only   DOM   two.N   movie.N.PL
             'I only saw two movies.'

       c.   *Nu*   *a*   *găsit*   **(*pe)**   *vreo*   *greșeală*.
             not   have.3SG   found   DOM   some/any.F.SG   error
             'S/he hasn't found any error.'

If the head noun is animate, the prepositional marker can be absent without giving rise to ungrammaticality. With prepositional DOM the quantified DP is normally interpreted as 'specific'. When the marker is absent, a weak, non-specific interpretation arises. The alternation between a 'specific' (also called 'strong') and a non-specific ('weak' reading) is typical of weak quantifiers (see Milsark 1979, de Hoop 1996, a.o.). The alternation is illustrated in (62) and (63):

(62) a. *Am văzut multe fete.*
   have.1SG seen many.F.PL girl.F.PL
   'I saw many girls.'

   b. *Am văzut doar două fete.*
   have.1SG seen only two.F girl.F.PL
   'I only saw two girls.'

   c. *Nu (și)-a găsit vreun prieten.*
   not (REFL.DAT)-have.3SG found some/any.M.SG friend
   'S/he hasn't found any friend (for herself/himself).'

(63) a. *(Le-)am văzut **pe** multe fete.*
   CL.F.PL.ACC-have.1SG seen DOM many.F.PL girl.F.PL
   'I saw many (specific) girls.'

   b. *(Le-)am văzut doar **pe** două fete.*
   CL.F.PL.ACC-have.1SG seen only DOM two.F girl.F.PL
   'I only saw two (specific) girls.'

   c. *Nu (l-)a găsit **pe** vreun prieten acasă.*
   not CL.M.SG.ACC-have.3SG found DOM some/any.M.SG friend home
   'S/he hasn't found any (specific) friend home.'

Under nominal ellipsis, PE is only possible if the understood antecedent is animate. We illustrate the contrast between animates and inanimates with the weak quantifier *many*:

(64) a. *A cumpărat zece cărți și....*
   have.3SG bought ten books and
   'S/he bought ten books and ...'

b. *(*Le-)a   citit   (*pe)   multe   (dintre ele).*
   CL.F.PL.ACC-have.3SG seen   DOM   many.F.PL   among they
   'S/he read many (of them).'

(65) a. *Studenții   au   examen astăzi.*
        students.DEF.M.PL   have.3PL   exam   today.
        'The students have an exam today.'

   b. Animate understood antecedent
      (I)-am   văzut pe   mulți   dintre ei   afară.
      CL.M.PL.ACC-have   seen DOM many.M.PL   among they outside.
      'I saw many of them outside.'

   c. *Știu   mulți   care   pot   trece.*
      know.1SG   many.M.PL   who   can.3PL   pass.INF
      'I know many (of them) who can pass the exam.'

At least prima facie, these types of 'alternations' provide support for Cornilescu's (2000) observation that [PERSON] is not just a binary feature, with a ± value. It can also come as *unspecified* [αPERSON]. When merged into a gender-defining category, it will indicate that the semantic gender is *not inanimate*. However, [αPERSON] does not require licensing in the syntax. It differs thus from [+PERSON]. An obvious question is whether this solution is a simple mechanical trick or has a deeper significance with respect to the taxonomy of features, and their role in the grammar. A more detailed discussion is obviously needed to systematically address this issue. For now, we can mention that the need of [αPERSON] (besides the binary ± specification) has also been argued for in Kučerová (2018) for a separate class of phenomena (from outside Romanian).

Assuming that we can derive the example in (60) along these lines, we still need to say something about the weak quantifiers. In Cornilescu (2000) the restriction to animacy is modeled on the types of interpretation grammatical gender obtains in certain contexts (see the discussion in the previous section). But, as we saw that PE goes beyond the presence of specified grammatical gender, an alternative explanation is also needed for the weak quantifiers. We propose that the answer to the restriction to animacy for quantifiers resides in the way in which [PERSON] is interpreted when merged with a D head that contains a quantifier structure. We already mentioned that weak quantifiers alternate between a weak and a strong reading (Milsark 1979, de Hoop 1996, a.o.). This alternation is connected to the position in which these elements can be found. Assuming once again, the functional hierarchy: QP > DemP > DP (Nicolae 2015, Cornilescu 1992, Giusti 1997,

2002, a.o.), when the quantifier is found in Q it is interpreted as *weak*. When it is found in D instead, and a [+PERSON] feature is merged in D, the latter cannot be interpreted as *specific*, given that the semantics of quantifiers clashes with specificity. We propose that a [+PERSON] is interpreted instead as *a restriction on the domain of quantification* of Q, resulting in an *animacy restriction* (see also Cornilescu 2000). As the DP will end up containing two features, an additional licenser will be employed. A similar type of explanation can also be attempted for the relative pronoun *care* 'who/which'. In normative grammars its use is banned without PE irrespective of animacy. However, in colloquial speech, the prepositional accusative marker is easily omitted:

(66) cartea   *(pe)*   care   am   citit-o.
book.DEF.F.SG DOM which have.1SG read-CL.F.SG.ACC
'the book I read'

Another prediction the current account makes is the following: given that the structural projection D⁰ requires licensing (as the edge of the nominal phase), any elements that have to merge above D will undergo licensing *irrespective* of its animacy. If the structure contains yet another feature that must be valued, an additional licenser will have to be selected. This prediction goes through in the case of the universal quantifier (just like with the D-linked *wh-* elements we discussed in the previous section). When used pronominally, under ellipsis, the universal quantifier gives rise to ungrammaticality without PE, irrespective of animacy. This is seen in (67):

(67) Le-am   văzut *(pe)   toate.
CL.F/N.PL-have.1 seen   DOM all.F/N.PL
'I saw them all.' (animate or inanimate)

We have evidence that this quantifier merges above D⁰, as it can only take a definite noun, when used adjectivally:

(68) toate   fete-*(le)
all.F.PL girls-DEF.F.PL
'All the girls.'

Thus, in (67) the feature contributed by ellipsis will count as an additional feature and will trigger the presence of the secondary licenser.

Given that this analysis connects the presence of the prepositional accusative marker to the need of more than one feature to be valued in the same domain, types of nominals that do not undergo licensing via a relation with functional heads in the clause are predicted to be ungrammatical with DOM. This is borne out by the data. Nominals found in existential contexts, bare singular nouns, and in general all classes of nominals that are interpreted as predicates reject the prepositional marker. An example is in (69):

(69) Ion   are   *(pe) copii.
     John   have.3SG   DOM   children
     'John has children.'

This example is ungrammatical with DOM under an existential interpretation. If the prepositional accusative is maintained, only a specific reading becomes possible, e.g., John has in his care the specific children previously mentioned in the discourse.[21]

6 Other accounts

In this section we discuss some alternative accounts that have been proposed for or can be extended to Romanian DOM. We show where they differ from the current proposal and where the current analysis in terms of secondary licensing makes better predictions.

6.1 Cornilescu (2000)

A few remarks are especially in order about Cornilescu's (2000) alternative account, which also attributes an important role to [PERSON] in prepositional DOM. Although different in both the mechanics as well as the analysis, the discussion in

---

[21] Some generics seem to pattern like the bare plurals in (69) in that they reject DOM under certain interpretations, but allow it in others, such as (i) (see also Cornilescu 2000, Mardale 2009, Tigău 2011). These classes can be understood along the same lines.

(i) Îi   ştiu   eu pe   politicieni.
    CL.M.PL.ACC   know.1SG   I   DOM   politicians.
    'I know the politicians.' (I know what the politicians are like)

this paper is indebted to some crucial intuitions in Cornilescu (2000). The gist of Cornilescu's (2000) proposal is that differential object marking is connected to *semantic gender* in Romanian. Besides categories that obligatorily contain a semantic gender specification (the *wh- cine* 'who', the negative Q *nimeni* 'nobody'), there are also instances where *grammatical* gender features are interpreted as *semantic* gender. For Cornilescu (2000), animacy as a reflex of semantic gender equals to featural specification as [–Neuter]. Thus, the preposition *pe* is viewed as a functional head specified with the feature [–Neuter], according to the criterion in (70):

(70) The preposition PE is not selected in the Accusative if a DP is specified for semantic gender as [–Person], that is, [+NEUTER] or [α PERSON]. PE is obligatory otherwise. (Cornilescu 2000: 4′)

Most of the data discussed up to now cannot disambiguate between the present account and Cornilescu's (2000). However, once propositional ellipsis is examined in yet more detail, it appears that DOM is not necessarily sensitive to the absence of a [NEUTER] feature. Let us look specifically at the ellipsis contexts, where we have seen that animacy can be overriden. Given the connection between semantic gender and *grammatical gender*, Cornilescu (2000) assumes that the grammatical gender on *pro* heading non-sentential ellipsis can either be [+Masculine] or [+Feminine]. The gender specification on *pro* results from an agreement relation with the relevant nominal head. But, as the elided N always contains a specified gender feature, non-sentential *pro* cannot be [+Neuter]. Following Iatridou & Embick (1997), only the clausal pronominal substitute *pro* is [+Neuter]. This builds on the observation that demonstratives tend to show agreement in gender, number and case with their nominal heads (be they lexical or *pro*), as noticed in the examples in Section 4. Propositional ellipsis on the other hand uses a *default* form of the demonstrative, which is set to feminine. Cornilescu (2000) thus predicts that propositional ellipsis cannot show up with the prepositional ACC. This is confirmed by data similar to (44), repeated here in (71):

(71) *Eu am spus (*pe) asta: să mergem la cinema.*
 I have.1 said DOM this.DFLT.AUG SBJV go.SBJV.1PL at cinema
 'I said this: Let's go to the cinema.'

However, it does not seem to always be the case that propositional ellipsis blocks the prepositional ACC. The example below, obtained from ordinary speech, has the uninflected form *asta* referring to propositional ellipsis, but also the differential marker:[22]

(72) a. *Au   evadat   iar   criminalii.*
       have.3PL escaped again murderers.DEF.M.PL
       'The murderers have escaped from the prison yet again.'

   b. *Ei, n-o   mai   cred   **pe**-asta.*
       wow, not-CL.F.SG more believe DEF.M.PL-this.DFLT
       'Wow, I don't believe this.'

Given that propositional ellipsis is connected to [+Neuter], it must be the case that the prepositional differential marker is sensitive to some other specification. The secondary licensing reasoning can derive these facts. One explanation could be the following. Despite being [+Neuter], the propositional elliptical demonstrative *asta* can behave like the definite demonstratives, which contain a [PERSON] feature. Examples like (72) have the feeling of *prominence* or *specificity*, although more detailed investigation is needed. It could be that in some contexts where the propositional content needs to be signaled more prominently, an extra feature is added to the demonstrative. As elliptical structures (of the type discussed here) project (at least) up to D^0, this additional feature, besides the [PERSON] feature in ellipsis will need an additional licenser.

6.2 DOM and raising

Formal work on differential object marking in Romance has also explored other options. One canonical analysis is to assume that structural objects introduced by the preposition are found in a higher position than other accusatives. The recent discussion in López (2012) identifies an α position between V and *v*, entailing that

---

[22] The additive operator *mai* seems to have a contribution to the presence of PE. This is even clearer in contexts which also have an additional additive operator, spelled-out by *și* 'and':

(i) *Am   mai   auzit-o   și   **pe** asta.*
    have more heard-CL.F.SG.ACC   and DOM   this.DFLT.AUG
    'Now I've heard even this.'

In fact, a preliminary investigation shows that native speakers tend to prefer PE marking on the demonstrative in this context.

other objects are probably interpreted lower. An overt raising analysis is however hard to independently prove for the Romanian prepositional objects.[23] The diagnostics are extremely volatile (see also Hill 2017), and even if they can apply they will also target specific definites which do not have the prepositional marker. The only valid conclusions that can be drawn for Romanian is that the prepositional accusatives that are also clitic doubled are interpreted/licensed higher than prepositional DOM without clitics. As we have showed in the previous sections, clitics appear to trigger raising above VoiceP. The binding options contrast between (73a) and (73b) demonstrates that clitics go at least above the EA (see also Anagnostopoulou 2003 for cross-linguistic observations in the same direction):

(73) a. *Părinț-i-i   lor*$_{*i/j}$ *au   lăudat   pe   copi-i*$_i$.
       parent-M.PL-DEF.M.PL their   have.3PL praised DOM child-N.PL
       'Their$_{*i}$ parents have praised the children$_i$.'

   b. *Părinț-i-i   lor*$_{i/j}$ *i-au   lăudat   pe*
       parent-M.PL-DEF.M.PL their   CL.M.PL.ACC-have.3PL praised DOM
       copi-i$_i$.
       child-N.PL
       'Their$_i$ parents have praised the children$_i$.'

The same variability is seen with respect to López's (2012) coordination test. For some speakers, objects that are differentially marked can be coordinated with regular definites/indefinites, but not with bare nouns. This is unsurprising, as specific definites and prepositional objects have the same semantic type (they are both of type $\langle e \rangle$), while bare singulars have a different semantic type ($\langle e,t \rangle$). However, the coordination data are not crystal clear and no firm conclusions can be drawn at this point. Some speakers strictly reject coordinating prepositional accusatives with non-prepositional accusatives. Moreover, most speakers allow co-

---

23 Note however that the ungrammaticality of differential marking in a preverbal position *cannot* be used to conclude that such objects do not raise. Verb movement targets a very high position in Romanian, at least above TP. Even if prepositional DOM raised, it would be highly unexpected for it to target a position in the C domain.

(i) **Pe   copii   văd.*
      DOM children see.1SG
    Intended: 'I see the children.'

ordination of clitic doubled prepositional DOM with non-clitic doubled prepositional DOM. We have seen that the clitic is licensed above vP, while prepositional DOM appears to stay inside vP. Thus, coordination tests might not tell us anything about the position of such objects.

6.3 DOM as syntactically oblique

Another solution proposed in the literature is to group the prepositionally-marked objects together with datives/obliques in the syntax. As already mentioned, this is the strategy Manzini & Franco (2016) endorse (see also their discussion in this volume). The two authors agree with the observation that referential definites also undergo licensing. In their view, this licensing puzzle can be solved if prepositional DOM is seen as an instantiation of a broader syntactic category *dative/oblique* that also encompasses the goal dative. More precisely, prepositional DOM is the *definiteness/animacy dative/oblique*. Although the authors motivate this connection on a cross-linguistic picture, in Romanian, however, this unification proves harder to maintain. Objects that have the differential preposition fail to pattern like datives/obliques under a variety of non-trivial syntactic tests tests, such as passivization, hosting reduced relative clauses, etc. A comprehensive presentation of all the diagnostics can be found in Irimia (2020).

6.4 DOM in morphology?

Yet another very prominent hypothesis about the nature of differential object marking is the morphological one. As the extensive presentation in the introduction to this volume, as well as the paper by Spyropoulos show, several accounts take DOM to simply be a reflection of a morphological process, with no significant correlates in the syntax. In other words, some classes of nominals receive a special marker on the basis of certain features, such as animacy. Otherwise, the differential objects have the same syntax as other structural objects (see also the discussion in López 2012).

The data from Romanian indicate that the morphological explanation faces several non-trivial problems. More specifically, an account under which differential objects are just like other accusatives with the only exception that they are additionally signaled on the morphology side cannot explain some crucial properties and interactions they are involved in and which are purely syntactic. We have seen in Section 3 that some contexts of differential marking are ungrammatical with clitic doubling. A clear case is the animate *wh-* element *cine* 'who' which requires differential marking but is ungrammatical with clitic doubling, as seen in (12). It is not clear how a purely morphological analysis can derive this fact.

Another counterargument to morphology-based explanations comes from interactions between DOM and dative clitics. In Romanian, differential marking gives rise to ungrammaticality when a dative possessor is also present in the structure (74a), or when a dative clitic is used (74b). These restrictions remind better studied person case constraint (PCC) configurations, although they have yet to receive a fully fledged analysis for Romanian (see however Onea & Hole 2017 or Irimia 2020 for recent discussion). Note that the restriction is only seen with third person dative clitics, but not with first/second dative clitics (74c). In other words, some third person clitic co-occurrences are barred. A principled answer to this problem requires a syntactic analysis. What needs to be understood is the precise structure of first/second person clitics (their 'speaker' and 'addressee' specifications), as opposed to third person, and the consequences this has on licensing.

(74) a. *Ion (*și)   l-a   văzut **pe** prieten.*
       Ion REFL.DAT.SG CL.3SG.ACC.M-have.3SG seen DOM friend
       intended: 'Ion has seen his friend.'

   b. ***Le**-am   trimis (*pe) copii.*
       CL.3SG.ACC.M-have.1 sent   DOM children
       intended: 'We have sent children to them.'

   c. ***Mi**   i-a   trimis **pe** copii.*
       CL.1SG.DAT CL.3PL.ACC-have.3SG sent   DOM children
       'S/he has sent the children to me.'

A complex problem is also the heterogeneous nature of differential marking in Romanian. As we have seen, the marker overrides animacy as well as specificity in numerous configurations. A morphological explanation will simply have to list all the environments where the preposition is needed; this procedure will clearly not permit any insight into what differential marking signals in the language. The secondary licensing account proposed in this paper can straightforwardly derive all the differential contexts. It can also predict instances of cumulativity (see also Müller's contribution to this volume), i.e., instances where more than one feature appears to be necessary for the presence of the differential marker.

A last note about syntactic accounts concerns the traditional linking of the differential marker to the need to disambiguate between the subject and the object when both are overt (see Mardale 2015 for the relevant references). What we can briefly mention here is that this assumption is weakened by many types of counterexamples. Just one illustrative point, in structures like (75), there is *only one overt argument* in the reduced non-finite clause, which however takes the prepositional DOM. The secondary licensing analysis discussed in this paper correctly predicts that differential marking is not necessarily the need to disambiguate between subjects and objects.

(75)   Spălând   **pe**   copii,   am   realizat că   ...
         wash.GER DOM children have.1 realized that
         'Washing the children, I have realized that ...' ('While I was washing the children, ...')

7 Conclusions

The gist of the analysis proposed in this paper is that differential marking in Romanian signals classes of objects which undergo an additional licensing operation in the same domain (*v*P). An account along these lines can unify the various instantiations of a class which otherwise escapes description in terms of features like *animacy, specificity*, or processes like overt raising. The present discussion also opens the path to formalizing principled differences between Romanian and related languages like Spanish, where referential definite animates are not possible without the prepositional differential marker. A plausible answer could reside in a distinct taxonomy of categories that undergo licensing in the two languages, as well as in the various interactions clusters of more than one feature are subject to inside a DP.

The steps taken here towards a more comprehensive examination of the differential contexts make possible a better understanding of the Romanian-type prepositional DOM in the typology of *Multiple Agree* systems (Béjar & Rezac 2009, Oxford 2014, Wiltschko 2014, a.o.), as well as with respect to other DOM languages where a *(secondary) licensing* account has also been claimed to better capture the data, but under different mechanics (Vainikka & Brattico 2014, Kalin 2018, a.o.).

Some of the questions the current analysis raises are related to the differences between the morpho-syntactic behavior of objects, as opposed to subjects. In Romanian, subjects do not show a differential preposition. Given that featural configurations inside the DP should not vary according to objecthood or subjecthood status, the question is how *additional licensing* proceeds in the case of subjects.

Another question concerns the nature and distribution of the [αPERSON], if a system similar to Cornilescu (2000) is adopted in order to better explain the optionality contexts. Is this merely a notational device? Does the need for [αPERSON] silently indicate that the licensing of [αPERSON] *can* fail in certain configurations and under certain conditions? If that were the case, in what sense are the contexts where lack of prepositional differential marking results in ungrammaticality distinct from contexts of apparent optionality? A clear answer to this question can only be provided after a careful examination of other domains where animacy and specificity are grammaticalized in Romanian or cross-linguistically.

Finally, although it has been shown here that *Kayne's Generalization* fails in its classical form, some of the configurations that have motivated it demonstrate that in some contexts there is a tight connection between the clitic and the prepositional marker. My current work (Irimia 2020) investigates exactly these conditions and their effect on additional licensing.

Acknowledgements

I would like to express my gratitude to many people who have provided invaluable feedback and discussion on various parts of this work, among which Virginia Hill, Alexandra Cornilescu, Ion Giurgea, Julie Goncharov, Alexandru Mardale, Cristina Guardiano, Giuseppe Longobardi, András Bárány, Laura Kalin, Jaklin Kornfilt, Klaus von Heusinger, Adam Ledgeway, Rita Manzini, two anonymous reviewers, as well as the audiences at SLE 2015 and Going Romance 31 (2017). I am also very thankful to András Bárány and Laura Kalin for their kindness and understanding, as well as to Julie Goncharov for her help with LaTeX. All errors are my own.

References

Adger, David & Daniel Harbour. 2007. Syntax and syncretisms of the person case constraint. *Syntax* 10(1). 2–37. https://doi.org/10.1111/j.1467-9612.2007.00095.x.

Aissen, Judith. 2003. Differential object marking: Iconicity vs. economy. *Natural Language & Linguistic Theory* 21(3). 435–483. https://doi.org/10.1023/A:1024109008573.

Alcaraz, Alejo. 2018. Deep and surface clitics in Northern Castilian Spanish. Handout of paper presented at GLOW 41 in Budapest, Hungary.

Anagnostopoulou, Elena. 1994. *Clitic dependencies in Modern Greek*. University of Salzburg dissertation.

Anagnostopoulou, Elena. 1999. Conditions on clitic doubling in Greek. In Henk van Riemsdjik (ed.), *Clitics in the languages of Europe*, vol. 3, 761–798. Berlin: De Gruyter. https://doi.org/10.1515/9783110804010.761.

Anagnostopoulou, Elena. 2003. *The syntax of ditransitives: Evidence from clitics*. Berlin: De Gruyter.

Anagnostopoulou, Elena. 2006. Clitic doubling. In Martin Everaert & Henk van Riemsdijk (eds.), *The Blackwell companion to syntax*. Vol. 1, chap. 14, 519–581. Oxford: Blackwell.

Avram, Larisa & Rodica Zafiu. 2017. Semantic hierarchies in the evolution of the differential object marking in Romanian. In Adina Dragomirescu, Alexandru Nicolae, Camelia Stan & Rodica Zafiu (eds.), *Sintaxa ca mod de a fi. Omagiu Gabrielei Pană-Dindelegan, la aniversare*, 29–42. București: Editura Universității din București.

Baker, Mark C. 2015. *Case: Its principles and its parameters*. Cambridge: Cambridge University Press.

Baker, Mark C. & Nadya Vinokurova. 2010. Two modalities of case assignment. *Natural Language & Linguistic Theory* 28(3). 593–642. https://doi.org/10.1007/s11049-010-9105-1.

Bárány, András. 2015. *Differential object marking in Hungarian and the morphosyntax of case and agreement*. University of Cambridge PhD dissertation.

Bárány, András. 2017. *Person, case, and agreement: The morphosyntax of inverse agreement and global case splits*. Oxford University Press. https://doi.org/10.1093/oso/9780198804185.001.0001.

Béjar, Susana & Milan Rezac. 2009. Cyclic Agree. *Linguistic Inquiry* 40(1). 35–73. https://doi.org/10.1162/ling.2009.40.1.35.

Belletti, Adriana. 1988. The case of unaccusatives. *Linguistic Inquiry* 19(1). 1–34.

Belletti, Adriana. 2004. Aspects of the low IP area. In Luigi Rizzi (ed.), *The structure of CP and IP*, vol. 2 (The cartography of syntactic structures), 16–51. Oxford: Oxford University Press.

Bernstein, Judy B. 2008. English *th-* forms. In Henrik Høeg Müller & Alex Klinge (eds.), *Essays on nominal determination: From morphology to discourse management*, 213–232. Amsterdam: John Benjamins. https://doi.org/10.1075/slcs.99.12ber.

Bittner, Maria & Ken Hale. 1996. The structural determination of case and agreement. *Linguistic Inquiry* 27(1). 1–68.

Bossong, Georg. 1991. Differential object marking in Romance and beyond. In Douglas A. Kibbee & Dieter Wanner (eds.), *New analyses in Romance linguistics*, 143–170. Amsterdam: John Benjamins. https://doi.org/10.1075/cilt.69.14bos.

Brattico, Pauli. 2012. Long distance case assignment in Finnish. *Studia Linguistica* 66(33). 245–285.

Brugè, Laura. 2002. The position of demonstratives in the extended nominal projection. In Guglielmo Cinque (ed.), *Functional structure in DP and IP*, vol. 1 (The cartography of syntactic structures), 15–54. Oxford: Oxford University Press.

Chen, Tingchun. 2018. Multiple case assignment in Amis: Evidence from case-stacking. In Sherry Hucklebridge & Max Nelson (eds.), *NELS 49: Proceedings of the Forty-Eighth Annual Meeting of the North East Linguistic Society*, vol. 1, 111–124. Amherst, MA: GLSA Publications.

Chomsky, Noam. 1975. *The logical structure of linguistic theory*. New York: Plenum.

Chomsky, Noam. 1981. *Lectures on government and binding*. Dordrecht: Foris.

Chomsky, Noam. 2001. Derivation by phase. In Michael Kenstowicz (ed.), *Ken Hale: A life in language*, 1–52. Cambridge, MA: MIT Press.

Chung, Sandra & William A. Ladusaw. 2004. *Restriction and saturation*. Cambridge, MA: MIT Press.
Comrie, Bernard. 1989. *Language universals and linguistic typology*. Chicago, IL: University of Chicago Press.
Cornilescu, Alexandra. 1992. Remarks on the determiner system of Rumanian: The demonstratives *al* and *cel*. *Probus* 4(3). https://doi.org/10.1515/prbs.1992.4.3.189.
Cornilescu, Alexandra. 2000. On the interpretation of the prepositional accusative in Romanian. *Bucharest Working Papers in Linguistics* 2. 91–106.
Cornilescu, Alexandra. 2005. Demonstratives and minimality. *Bucharest Working Wapers in Linguistics* 7(1). 102–117.
Cornilescu, Alexandra & Alexandru Nicolae. 2012. Nominal ellipsis as definiteness and anaphoricity: The case of Romanian. *Lingua* 122. 1070–1111. https://doi.org/10.1016/j.lingua.2012.05.001.
d'Alessandro, Roberta. 2017. When you have too many features: Auxiliaries, agreement and clitics in Italian varieties. *Glossa: a journal of general linguistics* 2(1), 50. https://doi.org/10.5334/gjgl.102.
Danon, Gabi. 2006. Caseless nominals and the projection of DP. *Natural Language & Linguistic Theory* 24(4). 977–1008. https://doi.org/10.1007/s11049-006-9005-6.
Danon, Gabi. 2011. Agreement and DP-internal feature distribution. *Syntax* 14(4). 297–317. https://doi.org/10.1111/j.1467-9612.2011.00154.x.
Dobrovie-Sorin, Carmen. 1990. Clitic doubling, wh-movement and quantification in Romanian. *Linguistic Inquiry* 21(3). 351–397.
Dobrovie-Sorin, Carmen. 1994. *The syntax of Romanian*. Berlin: De Gruyter.
Elbourne, Paul. 2013. *Definite descriptions*. Oxford: Oxford University Press.
Enç, Mürvet. 1991. The semantics of specificity. *Linguistic Inquiry* 22(1). 1–25.
Espinal, M. Teresa & Sonia Cyrino. 2017. The definite article in Romance expletives and long weak definites. *Glossa: a journal of general linguistics* 2(1), 23. https://doi.org/10.5334/gjgl.160.
Farkaş, Donka. 1978. Direct and indirect object reduplication in Romanian. In Donka Farkas, Wesley M. Jacobsen & Karol W. Todrys (eds.), *Papers from the 14th Regional Meeting of the Chicago Linguistic Society*, 88–97. Chicago: Chicago Linguistic Society.
Giurgea, Ion T. 2008. *Recherches sur la structure interne des pronoms et des expressions nominales sans nom exprimé*. Université Paris 7 Denis Diderot dissertation.
Giusti, Giuliana. 1993. *La sintassi dei determinanti*. Padua: Unipress.
Giusti, Giuliana. 1997. The categorial status of determiners. In Liliane Haegeman (ed.), *The new comparative syntax*, 95–124. London: Longman.
Giusti, Giuliana. 2002. The functional structure of noun phrases: A bare phrase structure approach. In Guglielmo Cinque (ed.), *Functional structure in DP and IP*, vol. 1 (The cartography of syntactic structures), 54–90. Oxford: Oxford University Press.
Harley, Heidi & Elizabeth Ritter. 2002. Person and number in pronouns: A feature-geometric analysis. *Language* 78(3). 482–526. https://doi.org/10.1353/lan.2002.0158.
Heim, Irene. 1982. *The semantics of definite and indefinite noun phrases*. University of Massachusetts, Amherst dissertation.
von Heusinger, Klaus & Edgar Onea. 2008. Triggering and blocking effects in the diachronic development of DOM in Romanian. *Probus* 20(1). https://doi.org/10.1515/probus.2008.003.

Hill, Virginia. 2013. The direct object marker in Romanian: A historical perspective. *Australian Journal of Linguistics* 33(2). 140–151. https://doi.org/10.1080/07268602.2013.814527.

Hill, Virginia. 2017. Diachronic fluctuations for romanian DOM: The [animate] feature. Ms.

de Hoop, Helen. 1996. *Case configuration and noun phrase interpretation*. New York: Garland.

Iatridou, Sabine & David Embick. 1997. Apropos *pro*. *Language* 73(1). 58. https://doi.org/10.2307/416593.

Irimia, Monica Alexandrina. 2016. How small are small clauses? Embedded adjectives and restructuring. In Kyeong-min Kim, Pocholo Umbal, Trevor Block, Queenie Chan, Tanie Cheng, Kelli Finney, Mara Katz, Sophie Nickel-Thompson & Lisa Shorten (eds.), *Proceedings of the 33rd West Coast Conference on Formal Linguistics*, 207–216. Somerville, MA: Cascadilla Proceedings Project.

Irimia, Monica Alexandrina. 2018. When differential object marking is obligatory: Some remarks on the role of case in ellipsis and comparatives. *University of Pennsylvania Working Papers in Linguistics* 24(1), 13. 105–114.

Irimia, Monica Alexandrina. To appear. Exceptional differential object marking in equatives: Some observations from Nepali. *Journal of South Asian Linguistics*.

Irimia, Monica Alexandrina. 2020. Prepositional accusatives and datives are not a homogeneous class in Romanian. Ms.

Irimia, Monica Alexandrina, Giuseppe Longobardi, Dimitris Michelioudakis & Nina Radkevich. 2018. *Romanian genitives and Universal Grammar*. Ms.

Jaeggli, Osvaldo. 1982. *Topics in Romance syntax*. Dordrecht: Foris.

Jaeggli, Osvaldo. 1986. Three issues in the theory of clitics: Case, doubled NPs and extraction. In Hagit Borer (ed.), *The syntax of pronominal clitics*, vol. 19 (Syntax and Semantics), 15–42. Orlando, FL: Academic Press.

Kalin, Laura. 2018. Licensing and differential object marking: The view from Neo-Aramaic. *Syntax* 21(2). 112–159. https://doi.org/10.1111/synt.12153.

Kallulli, Dalina. 2008. Clitic doubling, agreement and information structure. In Dalina Kallulli & Liliane Tasmowski (eds.), *Clitic doubling in the Balkan languages*, 227–255. Amsterdam: John Benjamins. https://doi.org/10.1075/la.130.14kal.

Kayne, Richard S. 1975. *French syntax: The transformational cycle*. Cambridge, MA: MIT Press.

Kiparsky, Paul. 1998. Partitive case and aspect. In William Greuder & Miriam Butt (eds.), *The projection of arguments*, 265–307. Stanford, CA: Centre for the Study of Language & Information.

Kiparsky, Paul. 2001. Structural case in Finnish. *Lingua* 111(4–7). 315–376. https://doi.org/10.1016/S0024-3841(00)00035-8.

Kučerová, Ivona. 2018. Φ-features at the syntax-semantics interface: Evidence from nominal inflection. *Linguistic Inquiry* 49(4). 813–845. https://doi.org/10.1162/ling_a_00290.

Lazard, Gilbert. 2001. Le marquage différentiel de l'objet. In Martin Haspelmath, Ekkehard König, Wulf Oesterreicher & Wolfgang Raible (eds.), *Language typology and language universals: An international handbook*, vol. 2, 873–886. Berlin: De Gruyter.

Legate, Julie Anne. 2014. *Voice and v: Lessons from Acehnese*. Cambridge, MA: MIT Press.

Leonetti, Manuel. 2008. Specificity in clitic doubling and differential object marking. *Probus* 20(1). 33–66. https://doi.org/10.1515/PROBUS.2008.002.

Levin, Theodore. 2016. Successive-cyclic case assignment: Korean nominative-nominative case-stacking. *Natural Language & Linguistic Theory* 35(2). 447–498. https://doi.org/10.1007/s11049-016-9342-z.

Levin, Theodore. 2019. On the nature of differential object marking: Insights from Palauan. *Natural Language & Linguistic Theory* 37(1). 167–213. https://doi.org/10.1007/s11049-018-9412-5.

Levin, Theodore & Omer Preminger. 2015. Case in Sakha: Are two modalities really necessary? *Natural Language & Linguistic Theory* 33. 231–250. https://doi.org/10.1007/s11049-014-9250-z.

Longobardi, Giuseppe. 1994. Reference and proper names: A theory of n-movement in syntax and logical form. *Linguistic Inquiry* 25(4). 609–665.

Longobardi, Giuseppe. 2008. Reference to individuals, person, and the variety of mapping parameters. In Henrik Høeg Müller & Alex Klinge (eds.), *Essays on nominal determination: From morphology to discourse management*, 189–211. Amsterdam: John Benjamins. https://doi.org/10.1075/slcs.99.11lon.

López, Luis. 2012. *Indefinite objects: Scrambling, choice functions, and differential marking*. Cambridge, MA: MIT Press.

Manzini, M. Rita & Ludovico Franco. 2016. Goal and DOM datives. *Natural Language & Linguistic Theory* 34(1). 197–240. https://doi.org/10.1007/s11049-015-9303-y.

Marantz, Alec. 1991. Case and licensing. In *ESCOL '91: Proceedings of the eighth Eastern states conference on linguistics*, 234–253. Ohio State University.

Mardale, Alexandru. 2009. Un regard diachronique sur le marquage différentiel de l'objet en roumain. *Revue Roumaine de Linguistique* LIV (1-2). 65–93.

Mardale, Alexandru. 2015. Differential object marking in the first original Romanian texts. In Virginia Hill (ed.), *Formal approaches to DPs in Old Romanian*, 200–245. Leiden: Brill.

Merchant, Jason. 2001. *The syntax of silence: Sluicing, islands and the theory of ellipsis*. Oxford: Oxford University Press.

Milsark, Gary Lee. 1979. *Existential sentences in English*. New York, NY: Routledge.

Mišeska Tomić, Olga. 2006. *Balkan Sprachbund morpho-syntactic features*. Dordrecht: Springer.

Moulton, Keir. 2013. Raising from the dead. *Linguistic Inquiry* 44(1). 157–167. https://doi.org/10.1162/ling_a_00123.

Nicolae, Alexandru. 2013. Demonstratives. In Gabriela Pană-Dindelegan (ed.), *The grammar of Romanian*, 294–300. Oxford: Oxford University Press.

Nicolae, Alexandru. 2015. On the syntactic specialization of the Romanian demonstratives and the grammaticalization of the article *cel*. *Revue Roumaine de Linguistique* LX. 47–70.

Onea, Edgar & Daniel Hole. 2017. Differential object marking of human definite direct objects in Romanian. *Revue Roumaine de Linguistique* LXII(4). 1–16.

Ormazabal, Javier & Juan Romero. 2007. The object agreement constraint. *Natural Language & Linguistic Theory* 25. 315–347. https://doi.org/10.1007/s11049-006-9010-9.

Ormazabal, Javier & Juan Romero. 2013. Differential object marking, case and agreement. *Borealis*: An International Journal of Hispanic Linguistics 2(2). 221–239. https://doi.org/10.7557/1.2.2.2808.

Oxford, Will. 2014. Multiple instances of agreement in the clausal spine: Evidence from Algonquian. In Robert E. Santana-LaBarge (ed.), *Proceedings of the 31st West Cast Conference in Formal Linguistics*, 335–343. Somerville, MA: Cascadilla Proceedings Project.

Pană-Dindelegan, Gabriela. 2013. The direct objects. In Gabriela Pană-Dindelegan (ed.), *The Grammar of Romanian*, 125–144. Oxford: Oxford University Press.

Pesetsky, David. 2014. *Russian case morphology and the syntactic categories*. Cambridge, MA: MIT Press.

Preminger, Omer. 2011. *Agreement as a fallible operation*. MIT dissertation.
Preminger, Omer. 2014. *Agreement and its failures*. Cambridge, MA: MIT Press.
Preminger, Omer. 2019. What the PCC tells us about "abstract" agreement, head movement, and locality. *Glossa: a journal of general linguistics* 4(1), 13. https://doi.org/10.5334/gjgl.315.
Ramchand, Gillian. 2008. *Verb meaning and the lexicon*. Cambridge: Cambridge University Press. https://doi.org/10.1017/CBO9780511486319.
Richards, Marc. 2008. Defective agree, case alternations, and the prominence of person. In Marc Richards & Andrej L. Malchukov (eds.), *Scales* (Linguistische Arbeits Berichte 86), 137–161. Leipzig: Universität Leipzig.
Richards, Norvin. 2013. Lardil "case stacking" and the timing of case assignment. *Syntax* 16(1). 42–76. https://doi.org/10.1111/j.1467-9612.2012.00169.x.
Rivero, María Luisa. 1979. Referencia y especificidad. In María Luisa Rivero (ed.), *Estudios de gramática generativa del español)*, 123–161. Madrid: Catédra.
Rodríguez-Mondoñedo, Miguel. 2007. *The syntax of objects: Agree and differential object marking*. University of Connecticut dissertation.
Sportiche, Dominique. 1996. Clitic constructions. In Johan Rooryck & Laurie Zaring (eds.), *Phrase structure and the lexicon*, 213–276. Dordrecht: Kluwer.
Suñer, Margarita. 1988. The role of agreement in clitic-doubled constructions. *Natural Language & Linguistic Theory* 6(3). 391–434. https://doi.org/10.1007/BF00133904.
Takita, Kensuke. 2015. Strengthening the role of case in ellipsis. *Nanzan linguistics* 10. 75–106.
Thoms, Gary. 2013. What kind of syntactic identity condition? Paper presented at the Identity in Ellipsis Conference, Leiden University, 20–21 September 2013.
Tigău, Alina M. 2010. Towards an account of differential object marking in Romanian. *Bucharest Working Papers in Linguistics* 12(1). 137–158.
Tigău, Alina M. 2011. *Syntax and interpretation of the direct object in Romance and Germanic languages*. București: Editura Universității din București.
Uriagereka, Juan. 1995. Aspects of the syntax of clitic placement in Western Romance. *Linguistic Inquiry* 26(1). 79–123.
Vainikka, Anne & Pauli Brattico. 2014. The Finnish accusative: Long-distance case assignment under agreement. *Linguistics* 52(1). 73–124. https://doi.org/10.1515/ling-2013-0057.
Vainikka, Anne & Joan Maling. 1996. Is partitive case inherent or structural?: Studies on the meaning and distribution of partitive structures. In Jacob Hoeksema (ed.), *Partitives*, 179–208. Berlin: De Gruyter.
Williams, Edwin. 1983. Against small clauses. *Linguistic Inquiry* 14(2). 287–308.
Wiltschko, Martina. 2014. *The universal structure of categories: Towards a formal typology*. Cambridge: Cambridge University Press.
Zubizarreta, Maria Luisa & Roumyana Pancheva. 2017. A formal characterization of person-based alignment. *Natural Language & Linguistic Theory* 35(4). 1161–1204. https://doi.org/10.1007/s11049-016-9357-5.

Jaklin Kornfilt
DOM and DSM in Turkish
Not only dependent case, but also dependent Agree

Abstract: Current formal studies of Case center on one or both of two main approaches: Case assignment via Agree or dependent case, whereby the case features of a given NP/DP are valued in a particular structural configuration within a particular local domain, unless another NP/DP is assigned Case first (Marantz 1991, Baker & Vinokurova 2010). Some have suggested a mixed approach: Case licensing via Agree for subjects, but via dependent case for direct objects (DOs), for example Baker & Vinokurova (2010).

This paper proposes a novel conciliatory approach to Case. In all instances of structural Case, i.e. for subjects as well as direct objects, Agree with a functional head is necessary. This addresses the conceptual issue of one unique type of licensing mechanism, rather than two. However, the functional licenser of the Case on DOs has to be itself licensed in this capacity. This is possible only when the subject has first been licensed via Agree. This results in the appearance of dependent case, which is an indirect symptom of dependent Agree. This approach is then extended to structural datives.

Keywords: differential object marking, differential subject marking, Turkish dependent case, dependent Agree

1 Introduction

Current formal studies of Case assignment/licensing center on either one, or both of two main approaches: 1. Case assignment/valuation via Agree, or 2. dependent Case, whereby the case features of a given NP_1/DP_1 are valued in a particular structural configuration (e.g. for nominative-accusative languages, being c-commanded by NP_2/DP_2) within a particular local domain (e.g. a phase), unless NP_2/DP_2 is assigned Case first (first proposed by Marantz 1991, later applied by others, e.g. Baker & Vinokurova (B&V) 2010). Some studies have suggested a mixed approach: Case licensing via Agree for subjects, but via dependent Case for direct objects (DOs), and other elements, e.g. indirect objects (IOs). One example for such a mixed approach is Baker & Vinokurova (2010), where non-subject Case

Jaklin Kornfilt, Syracuse University

https://doi.org/10.1515/9783110666137-004

(dative and accusative) in Sakha is treated as dependent (=configurational) Case, under the configurational rules in (1):

(1) Baker & Vinokurova (2010: 595, (4a,b))
   a. If there are two distinct argumental NPs in the same VP-phase such that NP1 c-commands NP2, then value the case feature of NP1 as dative unless NP2 has already been marked for case.
   b. If there are two distinct argumental NPs in the same phase such that NP1 c-commands NP2, then value the case feature of NP2 as accusative unless NP1 has already been marked for case.

In contrast, Baker & Vinokurova's (2010) treatment of subject Case (e.g. nominative and genitive) is the "traditional", Chomskyan one, with the NP/DP in question placed in the specifier position of a functional projection and getting its Case licensed via Agree with the functional head, e.g. T/I, or D (for nominative versus genitive, respectively).

However, more recent work has suggested that a single approach is preferable to a mixed approach on conceptual grounds, proposing to re-analyze subject Case via a configurational Case approach, thus bringing subject Case into the fold of configurational Case as the only valid Case licensing mechanism in general (for structural Cases); one example for such recent work is Levin & Preminger (2015; L&P). It should be noted that lexical Case remains as a phenomenon tightly linked to the assignment of theta roles and selected for by certain heads, such as verbs and adpositions. Thus, in this paper, "Case" will refer to structural Case, unless lexical Case is explicitly referred to.

This paper proposes a new version of a conciliatory approach to Case, which is mixed homogeneously: In all instances of structural Case, i.e. for subjects as well as direct objects (as well as in some instances of objects with structural dative), Agree with a functional head is necessary. (Other recent work is emerging which argues in favor of keeping the importance of agreement for Case licensing, as well, such as Bárány & Sheehan 2019.) This addresses the conceptual issue of one unique type of licensing mechanism, rather than two. However, the functional licenser of the Case on DOs has to be itself licensed in this capacity (i.e. be activated). This is possible only when the subject (Case) has first been licensed via Agree. This results in the appearance of dependent Case, which is, this paper claims, an *indirect symptom* of dependent *Agree*. This approach is then extended to those instances of dative which are structural.

In this paper, I will not compare these two types of approaches (e.g. Levin & Preminger's 2015, versus the one proposed here), each one of which is unified;

the main point here is to take a first step towards showing that the "traditional", Chomskyan approach is at least viable as a basis of a unified approach towards Case. Each instance of the configurational/dependent Case approach would need to be re-analyzed individually to see whether it can be understood within the rival unified approach.

A few words of conceptual nature are in order here. Is the unification of Case licensing necessarily our aim and the best solution cross-linguistically? Even if it is, does it have a price? If so, might it be overpriced?

Everything else being equal, it is clear that a unified, homogeneous account of *any* phenomenon should be valued more highly than a hybrid account, if everything else is equal. Case licensing should not be any different. On the other hand, not "everything else" might be equal. As a specific and relevant example, consider subject Case, i.e. nominative and genitive as subject Cases in fully tensed/verbal versus nominalized clauses, respectively. In many languages, these realizations of subject Case correlate and co-occur with subject agreement morphology, and especially in Turkish and many other Turkic languages, that morphology matches the phi-features (person and number, usually without gender in these languages) of the subject as well as of the particular realization of Case: a "verbal" agreement paradigm when the subject Case is nominative, and a "nominal", or "possessive" agreement paradigm when the subject Case is genitive. Usually, when certain elements co-occur, and especially when their co-occurrence is obligatory, a causal relationship is posited. Thus, the particular type of co-occurrence between subject Case and its realization on the one hand, and the type of agreement with the subject on the other hand seems to call for a statement based on causation, in either one of the two logically possible directions. This is what the "traditional, Chomskyan" approach to structural Case, and in particular to subject Case, is based on.

In order to arrive at a homogeneous approach to structural Case, based solely on configurational statements, one has to give up positing a causal relationship between (overt) subject Case and subject agreement (despite their obligatory co-occurrence), as well as between a particular type of subject Case and a particular type of subject agreement. Indeed, this is what Levin & Preminger (2015) do. While the authors do recognize the obligatory nature of the subject and subject agreement correlation, they do not recognize a causal relationship between subject Case and subject agreement, positing instead a search process, initiated by overtly Case-marked subjects: "... agreement scans the landscape of already case-marked nominals in search of an appropriate target. This move allows nominative and genitive—the two cases argued by Baker & Vinokurova to be assigned by functional heads—and their co-occurrence patterns with overt φ-agreement, to be modeled in a fully configurational manner (as the unmarked case in the domain of TP and DP, respectively)." (L&P 2015: 16)

In my view, depending on how this statement is read, one would either lose a genuine understanding of the co-occurrence between subject Case and subject agreement if one adopts this proposal, in effect claiming that the observed strong correlation is a coincidence, or else there is no loss of insight, but then there is no real difference between this proposal and the "traditional, Chomskyan" approach to subject Case. (Structural object Case might be more debatable.) With the latter remark, I mean the following: It makes sense to view "verbal agreement" as marking the TP and occupying the head position (together with T), and it makes similar sense to view the "nominal/possessive agreement" as occupying the head position of the DP which dominates nominalized clauses.[1] Under such an analysis, the difference between the "traditional, Chomskyan" view of subject Case and the approach of L&P becomes rather minimal. It is true that a difference remains in terms of directionality: In the traditional approach, a Case-*assigning* head fulfills its function via the Agree relation with the nominal phrase in its specifier position. In contrast, as stated above, in L&P's approach, the nominal phrases are already case-marked, and the respective agreement types search for matching nominal phrases with "unmarked" (i.e. nominative or genitive) subject Case.

However, under a "traditional" view, nominal phrases can still owe their subject Case to different types of agreement: not via assignment, but rather via licensing: Subject nominals can be already case marked, just like in L&P's approach, but their positioning and type (i.e. nominative versus genitive, or perhaps zero marking) can be licensed by local agreement of a nominal or verbal type. This would still posit a causal relationship which would explain the obligatoriness of co-occurring agreement and subject Case types.

It is this latter approach which I shall adopt in this paper, and I shall attempt to extend a treatment based on Case licensing (rather than Case assignment) by agreement, from subject Case to other structural Cases (i.e. accusative and structural dative).

So far, I have said nothing about configurationality, nor about Case competition. Note that for the unified approach in L&P, configurationality as well as competition (the latter via the rules in (1)) is relevant for accusative and structural dative, while only configurationality is of relevance for the "unmarked" subject Case, i.e. nominative and genitive. This is fair enough, as it reflects the acknowl-

---

[1] For detailed discussion of subject agreement and its different types, realizations of subject Case, and the functional categories of TP and DP that dominate clauses, see Borsley & Kornfilt (2000) and Kornfilt & Whitman (2011).

edgment that subject Case has a different status within the set of structural Cases. This acknowledgment has motivated me, in turn, to look for an alternative way of approaching the licensing of structural Case. In the approach of L&P, unification starts with establishing configurationality and competition for dative and accusative, and then extending configurationality to nominative and genitive. Here, I want to address a similar task, but start with nominative and genitive, i.e. with subject Case, while attributing a licensing function to agreement, and then extend structural Case licensing via agreement to the licensing of accusative and structural dative, also via agreement; in this extension, configurationality plays a role, too, because subject agreement is higher than object agreement (whether overt or covert), and the former activates the latter.

2 Facts of Turkish with respect to differential case (marking)

The approach I propose in this paper is illustrated here via DOM and DSM in Turkish. (Please note that another contribution in this volume which addresses both phenomena, rather than just DOM, is the chapter by Spyropoulos.)

The basic facts of DOM in Turkish are well known: Non-specific DOs cannot be marked with the Accusative, specific DOs must be so marked.[2] While Turkish has a productive system of agreement with the subject of TP/IP (and with the possessor in possessive DPs), it has no morphological agreement marking on the predicate with the DO; thus, Case and Agree appear to be dissociated for non-subject structural Case—at least for the overt morphological marking of such Case. Here, I will argue that against appearances, they are associated; this becomes clear when DSM is taken into account, as well.

Let us first look at some examples for DOM in Turkish.

2.1 DOM in Turkish

Turkish, as a nominative-accusative language, typically marks its direct objects with accusative morphology. However, this morphology does not always show up:

---

[2] There is a good deal of literature on this issue; Enç (1991) is probably the best known study, but there are also other sources which are quite well-known, e.g. Dede (1981, 1986), von Heusinger & Kornfilt (2005), Kornfilt (2008), Öztürk (2005), among others.

(2) a. definite DO

　　(Ben) kitab-**ı**　　oku-du-m.
　　　I　　book-ACC　read-PST-1SG
　　'I read **the** book.'

b. indefinite non-specific DO

　　(Ben) **bir** kitap oku-du-m.
　　　I　　 **a**　book read-PST-1SG
　　'I read **a** book.'

c. indefinite specific DO

　　(Ben) **bir** kitab-**ı**　　oku-du-m.
　　　I　　 **a**　book-ACC　read-PST-1SG
　　'I read **a certain** book.'

d. generic "(pseudo-)incorporated" DO[3]

　　(Ben) dün　　　bütün gün kitap oku-du-m.
　　　I　　yesterday all　　day　book read-PST-1SG
　　'Yesterday, I read books all day long.', literally: 'I was book-reading all day yesterday.'

Turkish has no definite article, but does have an indefinite article; the numeral *bir* 'one' serves also as the indefinite article.[4] The accusative morphology is thus (in

---

[3] The DO in examples of this kind (i.e. (2d) and (3d), where the DO is totally bare and is not preceded by the indefinite determiner *bir* 'a', is usually assumed to be incorporated or pseudo-incorporated into the verb; the controversy about which of these options (i.e. head-incorporation versus pseudo-incorporation) is correct for Turkish is tangential to the concerns of this paper and will not be addressed here. Whether the DO in examples such as (2b), also bare morphologically, but with an indefinite article, might also be (pseudo-) incorporated into the verb might be of more interest. In this paper, I shall assume that it is not; in prior work, I did propose head incorporation for such examples (e.g. Kornfilt 2003a). Aydemir (2004) claims that the two types of bare NP/DPs differ: for her, the completely bare DO is part of a complex verb (and thus not an argument), while the bare DO with an indefinite article is an argument of the verb. While I believe that a simpler analysis, treating the two types of bare nominals in a similar way, is possible, addressing and critiquing Aydemir's arguments for this distinction would take us too far afield.

[4] The status of the morpheme *bir* 'one; a' is controversial. Some grammars take the same point of view as I do here, by describing this morpheme as an indefinite article (e.g. Kornfilt 1997, Lewis 1967, Underhill 1976), while some more recent work attempts to defend an analysis of the Turkish nominal phrase as lacking any type of determiner. The latter work therefore analyzes *bir* as only a numeral. Examples of such work are Bošković & Şener (2014) and Öztürk (2005); see, however, Kornfilt (2007) for a critique of this view, with counterarguments.

most instances) not just a structural case marker, but (descriptively speaking) also a specificity marker (but not a definiteness marker), as the contrast between (2b) and (2c) shows. It is therefore appropriate to view the presence versus absence of the accusative morphology as an instance of DOM, which is, in Turkish, a reflection of specificity (rather than, for example, of the feature [human], or of other features as in some other languages).[5]

Turkish is a rather word order free language; while its basic word order is SOV, the direct object can scramble around, as long as it bears accusative marking; DOs without such marking must remain (in general, barring some discourse-marked instances where, I would argue, they are base-generated in a Left-Dislocated position—see Kornfilt 2018a) in their position left of the verb:

(2′) a. definite DO

　　　kitab-ı　　BEN　oku-du-m.
　　　book-ACC　I　　read-PST-1SG

　　　'I read **the** book.'

　　　(Here and the next examples, the subject is focalized in its surface, sequential position preceding the verb, so as to make the DO preceding the subject more natural.)

b. indefinite non-specific DO

　　　****bir*** kitap　BEN　oku-du-m.
　　　a　book　I　　read-PST-1SG

　　　intended: 'I read **a** book.'

c. indefinite specific DO

　　　bir kitab-ı　　BEN　oku-du-m.
　　　a　book-ACC　I　　read-PST-1SG

　　　'I read **a certain** book.'

---

[5] One caveat is in order here: There are instances where the overt accusative marking is necessitated for formal morpho-syntactic reasons; for example, a nominal agreement marker on a possessive DP which is a direct object imposes the presence of accusative marking in certain contexts, even if that DP is non-specific; for discussion, see von Heusinger & Kornfilt (2005).

d. generic "(pseudo-)incorporated" DO (cf. footnote 3)

*kitap dün   bütün gün BEN oku-du-m.
book yesterday all   day I   read-PST-1SG

intended: 'Yesterday, I read books all day long.', literally: 'I was book-reading all day yesterday.'

(Under certain discourse conditions, this example is acceptable with the bare DO as a Left-Dislocated, base-generated constituent; again, see Kornfilt 2018a.)

Stress on the subject is marked with capital letters; the *sequential* (not necessarily hierarchically higher) position left of the verb, in addition to obligatorily hosting bare DOs, is also a position for stress. (This is true for DOs in their base position, as well: all DOs, i.e. also those with accusative marking, bear stress in their verb-adjacent position, when they are focused.) Thus, the examples above with a scrambled word order are best when the subject left-adjacent to the verb is stressed. However, even with such stress, (2'b) and (2'd), with the bare DO scrambled away from the verb, are ill-formed (with a special caveat about (2'd), as expressed after that example), while (2'a) and (2'c), where the scrambled DO that precedes the subject is fine, because it bears overt accusative morphology (and the stress on the subject contributes to the well-formedness, while the same stress is not sufficient to offset the ill-formedness of the scrambled *bare* DO in (2'b) and (2'd)).

Before turning to a discussion of DSM, I should mention that the facts of DOM are the same, whether we are dealing with a root clause or an embedded clause, even if the latter is nominalized; I shall give examples corresponding to those in (2) to illustrate this statement, by simply embedding those examples and nominalizing them; the interpretations of the direct objects in the embedded clauses are exactly the same as those of the corresponding direct objects in (2):

(3) a. *Herkes*   [*(ben-im)* kitab-ı   oku-duğ-um-u   ] duy-du.
       everybody   I-GEN   book-ACC read-FN-1.SG-ACC   hear-PST
       'Everybody heard that I read **the** book.'

   b. *Herkes*   [*(ben-im)* **bir** kitap oku-duğ-um-u   ] duy-du.
       everybody   I-GEN   a   book read-FN-1.SG-ACC hear-PST
       'Everybody heard that I read **a** book (non-specific).'

   c. *Herkes*   [*(ben-im)* **bir** kitab-ı   oku-duğ-um-u   ] duy-du.
       everybody   I-GEN   a   book-ACC read-FN-1SG-ACC hear-PST
       'Everybody heard that I read **a certain** book (specific).'

d. *Herkes* [*(ben-im) bütün gün kitap oku-duğ-um-u*] *duy-du.*
   everybody I-GEN all day book read-FN-1SG-ACC hear-PST
   'Everybody heard that I read books all day long.', literally: 'Everybody heard that I was book-reading all day.'

Just as in root clauses, bare DOs cannot be scrambled away from their verb-adjacent positions. I shall not illustrate this separately, due to space considerations.

2.2 Some examples of DSM in Turkish

The DSM facts in Turkish are less well known, although there does exist some literature on this topic, as well (e.g. Cagri 2009, Kennelly 1997, Kornfilt 2008, Öztürk 2009, among others). To introduce this phenomenon, I start with root sentences. Those have nominative subjects which Agree with their local predicates in terms of phi-features, i.e. in terms of person and number. This is illustrated in (4a) and (4b):

(4) a. **(Biz)**   *geçen gün komşu   köy-ü   bas-tı-k.*
       we.NOM past day neighbor village-ACC raid-PST-**1PL**
       'We raided the neighboring village the other day.'

   b. **Haydut-lar**   *geçen gün komşu   köy-ü   bas-tı(-lar).*[6]
      robber-PL.NOM past day neighbor village-ACC raid-PST-**3PL**
      'The robbers raided the neighboring village the other day.'

In both of these examples, the subject is specific and shows up clause-initially, as is typical for subjects in Turkish. When the subject is non-specific, it has to be left-adjacent to the verb, similarly to non-specific direct objects in a DOM-context:

---

[6] Specific third person plural subjects, irrespective of whether they are the nominative subject of a fully tensed root clause or whether they are the genitive subject of a nominalized clause (the latter will be discussed shortly) can co-exist with either the third person singular or the third person plural agreement form; (4b) and (4c) illustrate these options for nominative third person plural subjects; (6b) and (6c) illustrate the same options for nominalized predicates, agreeing with genitive third person plural subjects. For some discussion and for further literature on this phenomenon, the reader is referred to Kornfilt (1991).

(4) c. Geçen gün komşu   köy-ü   **haydut-lar**   bas-tı**(-lar)**.
       past day neighbor village-ACC **robber-PL.NOM**   raid-PST-**3PL**
       'The robbers raided the neighboring village the other day.'

(4c), in its version with *full* agreement with the third person plural subject, corresponds to (4b), in the sense that the subject is specific; in addition, the subject is focalized. In its version with *partial* agreement, i.e. with third person *singular* subject agreement, (4c) is ambiguous between the same reading, i.e. between having a focalized specific subject, and having a non-specific subject. We see that just like with direct objects, the position immediately to the left of the verb appears to host either a focalized DP (in this instance, a focalized subject), or a non-specific nominal phrase—again, in this instance, a subject. I shall return to this issue later. For the time being, there are two points about the third person plural subject agreement marking to take note of: 1. Full agreement is associated only with a specific third person plural subject; 2. Partial agreement is an additional option for a specific third person plural subject (and, for such specific plural subjects, it is a stylistic option which is a variant of the strong agreement); 3. If a third person plural is non-specific, the agreement morphology cannot be the full version; instead, the only option is partial, default, third person singular agreement. This latter agreement is null in the verbal paradigm. In these instances, the agreement is truly defective, rather than being a variant of strong agreement. Because defective agreement is overt in the nominal, "possessive" paradigm, the property of non-specific third person plural subject being associated with partial/defective (rather than altogether null) agreement can be better appreciated in nominalized embedded clauses, as we shall see very soon; before turning to those, let us look at one more option in root sentences.

There is an additional possibility for a non-specific subject as in (4d), namely to omit the plural marking on the subject itself:

(4) d. Geçen gün komşu   köy-ü   **haydut**   bas-tı.
       past day neighbor village-ACC **robber.NOM**   raid-PST
       'Robbers (non-specific) raided the neighboring village the other day (the neighboring village was "robber-raided" the other day.'

Here, the action is understood as an "incorporated" one, i.e. "robber-raiding" happened to the village.

I now turn to embedded clauses which are nominalized, i.e. which have a gerund-like predicate.

Embedded nominalized clauses have genitive subjects, which are specific, and which Agree with their local predicates in terms of phi-features, i.e. in terms of person and number; in other words, they are similar to root clauses in this respect. However, the morphological agreement paradigm for nominalized clauses is different from the fully verbal paradigm, and is the same as the paradigm for nominal possessives. This is illustrated in (5a) through (5d) for possessive phrases, and in (6a), (6b), and (6c) for embedded nominalized clauses:

(5) a. *biz-im film-**imiz***
we-**GEN** film-**1PL**
'our film'

b. *onlar-ın film-i*
they-**GEN** film-**3**
'their film'[7]

c. *onlar-ın film-ler-i*
they-**GEN** film-**PL-3**
'their films'

d. pro *film-ler-i*
film-**PL-3**
'their film / their films'

(6) a. [*Biz-im köy-ü bas-tığ–ımız-ı*] *bil-miyor-lar.*
we-**GEN** village-ACC raid-FN-**1PL**-ACC know-NEG-**3PL**
'They don't know that we raided the village.'

b. [*Haydut-lar-ın köy-ü bas-tığ-ın-ı*] *duy-du-m.*
robber-**PL-GEN** village-ACC raid-FN-**3SG**-ACC hear-PST-1SG
'I heard that robbers (specific for all speakers) raided the village.'

---

[7] The details of the nominal agreement morphology (also sometimes referred to as "possessive" morphology in the literature) are complicated for third persons. For our purposes, the basics will suffice: When the possessor is "dropped", i.e. is *pro*, both the plural and the person components of the nominal morphology have to show up; when the possessor is overt, the plural subpart is dropped. Also, the plural part of the nominal third person morphology is identical to the general plural morpheme for nouns. Given that these two plural morphemes (i.e. one for the general plural, the other part of agreement) cannot be linearized side by side, one of them is dropped. Thus, (5d) is ambiguous between 'their film' and 'their films', when the possessor is *pro* and the agreement is therefore complete.

c. [*Haydut-lar-ın   köy-ü   bas-tık-ların-ı*] *duy-du-m.*
   robber-**PL-GEN** village-ACC raid-FN-**3PL**-ACC hear-PST-1SG
   'I heard that the robbers (specific for all speakers) raided the village.'

Compare the agreement morphology on the nominalized predicates of the embedded clauses with the agreement morphology on the fully verbal predicates of the root clauses in the examples of (4). It is clear that the respective shapes are different; e.g. *-k* for first person plural in the verbal agreement form in (4a), but *-ımız* for the first person plural in the nominalized predicate agreement form in (6a); *-lar* for the full form of third person plural agreement in the verbal agreement form in (4b), but *-ların* for the third person plural in the nominalized predicate agreement form in (6c). On the other hand, the agreement forms on the embedded clauses in the examples in (6) are the same ones as those seen on the possessive nominal phrases in the examples in (5)—up to phonologically conditioned allomorphy, due, for example, to vowel harmony. Note also that (6b) and (6c) illustrate the optional, stylistic variation between full nominal agreement in (6c) and its optional variant in (6b), where the latter does not overtly show plurality—an optional variation we had seen in (4) for verbal agreement, too, insofar as specific subjects are concerned.

We have now seen that despite the fact that the shapes of the agreement morphemes are different on nominalized versus fully verbal clauses, the syntax of nominalized and fully verbal clauses is the same with respect to the phenomena we are interested in, i.e. with respect to DOM and DSM: 1. Focalized as well as non-specific direct objects as well as subjects show up to the immediate left of the verb, and 2. Non-specific direct objects as well as non-specific subjects lack their respective overt structural case morphology (accusative and genitive, respectively). This is a point which is worth making, because it might not be obvious that nominalized clauses have a phrasal architecture of sufficient height and detail to exhibit DOM and DSM effects; the parallels illustrated here establish that they do.

In the examples so far, only (4c), in one of its readings, and (4d) involved a non-specific subject. Given that the nominative morpheme is null, we cannot tell if, in those examples, the non-specific subject is bare of morphological case or not (whereby the null nominative morpheme would count as a morphologically (but not phonologically) present morpheme). We have to look at embedded nominalized clauses to see if the genitive, which is phonologically overt, shows up on non-specific subjects or not.

It turns out that non-specific subjects of nominalized clauses don't bear genitive marking, and typically show up left-adjacent to the verb, as illustrated for transitive predicates in (7a) and by the ungrammatical (7b), where adjacency of the subject to the verb is not observed; this is further illustrated for unaccusative predicates in (8a) with its bare, non-specific subject versus the ungrammaticality of (8b); note that the agreement on the nominalized predicate has to be the defective singular; there is no option for the plural agreement—a point whose importance will become clearer as the paper progresses; with a specific, third person plural subject, the agreement on the predicate has the option of expressing the plurality or not; this is a stylistic issue; but when a third person plural subject is non-specific, the agreement on the predicate is truly defective rather than leaving out plurality as a stylistic choice, i.e. the option of expressing plurality disappears:[8]

(7) Transitive predicate

    a. only non-specific or generic reading, no specific reading

       [*Köy-ü*   (*beş*) **haydut** *bas-tığ-ın-ı*   ] *duy-du-m.*
       village-ACC five **robber** raid-FN-**3SG**-ACC hear-PST-1SG

       'I heard that (five) robbers raided the village.'

    b. non-specific or generic

      *[(*Beş*) **haydut** *köy-ü*   *bas-tığ-ın-ı*   ] *duy-du-m.*
       five **robber** village-ACC raid-FN-**3SG**-ACC hear-PST-1SG

       intended: 'I heard that (five) robbers (non-specific or generic) raided the village.'

(8) Unaccusative (existential) predicate

    a. [*Garaj-da*   **beş araba** *ol-duğ-un-u*   ] *bil-iyor-um.*
       garage-LOC **five car** be-FN-**3SG**-ACC know-PRS.PROG-1SG

       'I know that there are five cars in the garage.'

    b. *[**Beş araba** *garaj-da*   *ol-duğ-un-u*   ] *bil-iyor-um.*
       five car   garage-LOC be-FN-**3SG**-ACC know-PRS.PROG-1SG

       intended: 'I know that there are five cars in the garage.'

I summarize the correlations these two sets of examples illustrate:
- Non-specific subjects cannot bear overt Case; they have to be linearized to the immediate left of the verb; the subject agreement they are associated with is

---

[8] If these non-specific subjects are marked with the genitive, the non-specific interpretation is lost for the examples in (7). The example in (8b) would become ill-formed altogether for a purely existential meaning. This is not surprising, given the Definiteness Effect, familiar from English and related languages. However, also like in English, examples with specific (and thus genitive) subjects and existential predicates are OK with definite/specific subjects under a list reading.

defective/incomplete/weak. (As mentioned earlier, in the text preceding the examples in (7), the importance of this last fact will become even clearer later in the chapter.)
- The predicate of the embedded clauses in (8) is unaccusative.[9] One might therefore be tempted to treat their non-specific (and non-genitive marked) verb-adjacent subjects in exactly the same way as the morphologically bare direct objects, e.g. claim that an abstract "object Case" is licensed on them by a functional head in the verbal domain, by virtue of such subjects being base-generated as the verbs' complement. (A proposal essentially along those lines is found in Kennelly 1997).

However, the existence of well-formed examples such as those in (7a), with bare subjects of transitive predicates, show that this claim is untenable.

Instead, I would like to claim that an essentially "traditional", Chomskyan view is viable: bare direct objects get their structural Case feature checked by AgrO, while bare subjects get their structural case feature checked by small v, which gets the necessary licensing ability from INFL (=Tense and/or agreement as a bundle of φ-features—in these instances, an incomplete, defective bundle), i.e. the agreement component of the clause's head. Thus, non-specific subjects have a weak Case (i.e. a not overtly realized Case) and get it licensed in-situ, i.e. in their base-generated vP-internal position. Specific subjects get their strong subject Case in the specifier position of the "INFLP", i.e. of TP, a position to which they raise from their base position, to have their strong subject Case licensed.

Similar facts hold for tensed clauses with their nominative subjects; I have concentrated here on the genitive subjects of nominalized clauses, because of the clear distinction between the overt genitive morphology and the bare, case-morpheme-less subjects of nominalized clauses. The nominative in Turkish is a zero morpheme, and thus there is no visible, morphological difference between specific nominative subjects and non-specific "bare" ones. But if we are willing to distinguish between a zero morpheme (which is present syntactically as well as morphologically, but which has no phonological features) and total lack of morphological Case, then we can use nominative subjects to make similar points as we have done using genitive subjects: specific subjects would bear nominative Case, expressed morphologically via a zero morpheme (as in (4a) and (4b)), and non-specific subjects would lack morphological case, i.e. those NP/DPs would be

---

[9] I take it to be uncontroversial that existential predicates as in (8) are unaccusatives.

"bare", just as their non-genitive counterparts in nominalized clauses; for root clauses, this is illustrated in (4c), in its version with defective agreement.[10]

How would an approach based uniquely on configurational considerations deal with these facts?

This is somewhat unclear, given that there are not many treatments of differential subject marking in the literature based on a configurational approach. For both B&V (2010) and L&P (2015), non-specific noun phrases in Sakha, which have to be left-adjacent to V, undergo (pseudo-)incorporation into the verb, which would explain their obligatory position. However, the assumption (or claim) in these works is that in all of these "subject (pseudo-)incorporation" instances, the subject is the sole argument of an unaccusative verb. This may be true for Sakha, which is the language studied in these works. However, this cannot be true for Turkish as we saw in this section: DSM can take place even if the verb is not unaccusative.[11]

Note also that the well-formedness of DSM-examples with transitive verbs is problematic for a configurational approach: The accusative marking on the direct object is supposed to be licensed via competition with a (c-commanding) subject, via (1b) (i.e. B&V's (4b)). But in examples exhibiting DSM, the subject is lower than the accusative-marked direct object; thus, some other mechanism would be needed to account for such accusative marking.

2.2.1 Focusing on transitive predicates: How far do DOM and DSM interact?

In the previous section, facts of DSM in Turkish were discussed—facts that are less familiar than DOM, as I mentioned when introducing them. Even less well-known are the facts concerning co-occurrence of non-specific subjects and non-

---

10 One of the anonymous reviewers raises a question of learnability, i.e. how children would learn to distinguish no Case from zero morphological case. Indeed, children have problems learning this distinction and pick it up relatively late. While there are, to my knowledge, no experimental studies that have established the age at which Turkish children have learned to distinguish bare, non-specific direct objects from nominative specific subjects, there is at least one study (Slobin & Bever 1982) which shows that Turkish children have difficulties distinguishing between these two types of nominal phrases at an age where they have learned morphological case markers and have no problems interpreting phrases with such markers correctly. For detailed discussion, the reader is referred to Slobin & Bever (1982) as well as to Kornfilt (1994). Obviously, there are surface clues in addition to morphological case markers for interpreting nominal phrases, such as word order, intonation, and pauses after topics; it appears that such clues are learned by children later than morphological case markers.
11 This observation is made in Öztürk (2009), as well.

specific DOs in nominalized embedded clauses: At the current stage of Turkish, the non-specific subject must bear genitive when it co-occurs with a non-specific DO, whereby the non-specific reading of such a subject becomes secondary (and, for some speakers, non-existent, as we shall see later); the specific reading is always primary for genitive subjects. A genitive subject (no matter what its interpretation) must precede a non-specific DO, as we have seen earlier, e.g. in (3b) and (3d) (although, also as mentioned earlier, word order is free in general, and *specific* subjects and DOs can be scrambled). There is only default subject agreement on the predicate when the subject is non-specific, as we saw in the examples illustrating DSM. The same is true for examples where both subject and object are non-specific, as in (9) and (10).

To summarize the contents of the previous paragraph: It is possible to have combinations of non-specific subject and non-specific direct object (at least for some speakers), as long as the non-specific subject precedes the non-specific direct object, and as long as the subject agreement is defective/weak rather than complete/strong. To illustrate this, let us first look at examples in tensed clauses, with nominative subjects:

(9) *Haydut(-lar) köy bas-ar.*
 robber(-PL) village raid-AOR
 'Robbers raid villages.'

(10) *Çoban(-lar) kaval çal-ar.*
 shepherd(-PL) flute play-AOR
 'Shepherds play flute.'

(11) **Köy haydut(-lar) basar.*
 village robber(-PL) raid-AOR
 intended: 'Robbers raid villages; as for villages, robbers raid them.'

(12) **Kaval çoban(-lar) çal-ar.*
 flute shepherd(-PL) play-AOR
 intended: 'Shepherds play (the) flute; as for (the) flute, shepherds play (it).'

In other words, the DO without morphological case must be V-adjacent. But the non-specific, non-referential subject in tensed clauses can be non-adjacent to the verb, especially when the tense is the *aorist*, i.e. aspectually habitual. Thus, the well-formed examples above are *ambiguous between a specific and non-specific reading for the subject*. Note further that the verbal predicate has no full subject agreement; instead, it has no phonologically realized agreement at all, which I interpret as weak agreement: the third person singular agreement is null in the verbal paradigm, as noted earlier, and this is what I take the agreement to be in these examples.

This ambiguity between a specific and non-specific reading for the subject disappears when the DO is specific, and thus bears overt, i.e. morphological, accusative, and is verb-adjacent, i.e. is preceded by the subject:

(13) Çoban(-lar) kaval-ı çal-ar.
shepherd(-PL) flute-ACC play-AOR
'The (specific) shepherd/the (specific) shepherds play(s) the (definite, specific) flute.'

(14) Haydut(-lar) köy-ü bas-ar.
robber(-PL) village-ACC raid-AOR
'The (specific) robber/the (specific) robbers raid(s) the (definite, specific) village.'

(15) Arı(-lar) çocuğ-u sok-ar.
bee(-PL) child-ACC sting-AOR
'(The) (specific) bee(s) sting(s) (the) (specific) child.'

Here, the subject cannot be non-specific; it has to be specific, referential; this is the only reading available, even when the agreement is defective, because (as I shall state more explicitly later) the specific accusative direct object has moved out of the VP and its functional projection, raising to a higher position. I attribute this to what I call the Diesing Effect (cf. Diesing 1992), which reserves the lower vP-domain for non-specific (in some languages, indefinite) constituents. If the direct object is outside of vP, then the subject, which precedes it, cannot be in Spec,vP and is thus analyzed as occupying its higher, canonical position of Spec,TP. (For some speakers, the non-specific reading for the subject in such word orders is possible, but nonetheless only a weak possibility. I think that this secondary reading is not truly grammatical, but a pragmatic epiphenomenon, born out of the lack of a truly grammatical structure for topicalizing a non-specific subject when the direct object is specific.)

When the subject is singular, the effect is even stronger, i.e. the singular subject preceding the overtly case-marked DO cannot be non-specific; it has to be specific/referential. Here are examples (13) through (15), in their respective versions for the singular subject, which I repeat for the reader's convenience:

(13′) *Çoban kaval-ı çal-ar.*
shepherd flute-ACC play-AOR
'(The) (specific) shepherd (the) (specific) flute.'

(14′) *Haydut köy-ü bas-ar.*
robber village-ACC raid-AOR
'(The) (specific) robber raids (the) (specific) village.'

(15′) *Arı çocuğ-u sok-ar.*
bee child-ACC sting-AOR
'(The) (specific) bee stings (the) (specific) child.'

In addition to the explanation I gave for examples (13) through (15), there is an additional factor in the examples involving a singular subject: the agreement cannot be interpreted as weak or defective, given that its shape (which is null in the verbal paradigm, as mentioned earlier) is that for third person singular subjects. With a full, strong agreement, the associated subject is interpreted as specific, and analyzed as occupying the specifier position of the associated clausal head, i.e. of T(+Agr)P.

On the other hand, when the DO is specific and bears morphological accusative, and has scrambled to the left of the subject, the verb-adjacent subject is, once again, ambiguous between a specific and non-specific reading, with the non-specific reading being the primary interpretation, especially if the subject is plural (while the verbal agreement is defective, i.e. weak):

(16) *Kaval-ı çoban(-lar) çal-ar.*
flute-ACC shepherd(-PL) play-AOR
'(The) shepherd/shepherds (specific, possibly non-spec.) play the flute.'

(17) *Köy-ü haydut(-lar) bas-ar.*
village-ACC robber(-PL) raid-AOR
'(The) robber/robbers (specific, possibly non-specific) raid the village.'

(18) *Çocuğ-u arı(-lar) sok-ar.*
child-ACC bee(-PL) sting-AOR
'(The) bee/bees (specific, possibly non-specific) sting the child.'

My view of this is that in (16) through (18), unless there are adverbs which might mark the left edge of the verbal projection domain, the subject can be analyzed as still being in its basic position, i.e. in Spec,*v*P—at least as an alternative to the higher position reserved for specific subjects, i.e. Spec,TP. Together with the defective/weak subject agreement, which is null in the fully verbal agreement paradigm, this makes the non-specific reading possible. Of course, the other, specific reading is possible as well: there is nothing to preclude an analysis under which the subject is in the higher, canonical subject position of Spec,TP.

We now turn to embedded, nominalized clauses. We have seen some examples of those earlier: the examples in (7) showed that when transitive clauses are embedded and are nominalized, we find DSM effects with respect to the genitive marking on the subject—i.e. the *specific* subject is genitive-marked and can be either before or after the DO, while the *non-specific* subject is bare and can show up only after the DO, adjacent to the verb:

(19) [*Köy-ü   (beş) haydut bas-tığ-ın-ı   ] duy-du-m.*
     village-ACC   five robber raid-FN-3SG-ACC hear-PST-1SG
     'I heard that (five) robbers (non-specific, no genitive) raided the village.'

(20) *[*(Beş) haydut köy-ü   bas-tığ-ın-ı   ] duy-du-m.*
     five robber village-ACC raid-FN-3SG-ACC hear-PST-1SG
     intended: 'I heard that (five) robbers (non-specific, no genitive) raided the village.'

(21) [*Köy-ü   (beş) haydut-un bas-tığ-ın-ı   ] duy-du-m.*
     village-ACC   five robber-GEN raid-FN-3SG-ACC hear-PST-1SG
     'I heard that (the) (specific) robber/five (specific) robbers raided the village.'

(22) [*(beş) haydut-un köy-ü   bas-tığ-ın-ı   ] duy-du-m.*
     five robber-GEN village-ACC raid-FN-3SG-ACC hear-PST-1SG
     'I heard that (the) (specific) robber/five (specific) robbers raided the village.'

When the DO is non-specific and thus is morphologically bare, the only possible well-formed combination is for the subject to precede the DO and to be marked with the genitive, as in (26)—a fact to which I shall return later in the paper:

(23) *[*Köy   haydut bas-tığ-ın-ı   ] duy-du-m.*
     village robber raid-FN-3SG-ACC hear-PST-1SG
     intended: 'I heard that some unspecified robber/robbers raided some unspecified village/villages.'

(24) *[*Haydut köy   bas-tığ-ın-ı*   ] *duy-du-m.*
       robber village raid-FN-3SG-ACC hear-PST-1SG
   intended: same as in (23)

(25) *[*Köy   haydut-un   bas-tığ-ın-ı*   ] *duy-du-m.*
       village robber-GEN raid-FN-3SG-ACC hear-PST-1SG
   intended: 'I heard that (the) (specific) robber raided some unspecified village/villages.'

(26) [*Haydut-un   köy   bas-tığ-ın-ı*   ] *duy-du-m.*
       robber-GEN village raid-FN-3SG-ACC hear-PST-1SG
   'I heard that (the) (specific) robber raided (a) (non-specific) village/villages.'

In well-formed examples such as (26), the genitive subject is specific and even definite.[12] I shall return to such examples in the next section, when I shall discuss details of my proposal and go through the main types of examples illustrating DOM, DSM, and (insofar as it is possible) their combination.

3 Proposal for a unified, but conciliatory approach to Case

3.1 Introduction to the proposal

I propose that it is possible to offer an account of these facts that treats DSM and DOM in parallel fashion: not only DSM, but also DOM depends on a *Case–Agreement correlation*. Only when the subject bears Case (nominative or genitive) and, most importantly, Agrees with the local predicate, can agreement with the

---

[12] However, there are speakers who report a weak, secondary, but nonetheless existing reading of generic, and thus non-specific, interpretation of the subject. (This non-specific reading seems to be easier to get, when the subject is plural, i.e. similar to what was mentioned in passing for tensed root clauses with their nominative subject.) This is interesting, as it makes it possible to have both a subject and a DO be non-specific—a possibility which is simply missing for the speakers who reject examples such as (26) under the non-specific reading for the subject. Interestingly, too, examples such as (24) (i.e. where the subject is non-specific and morphologically bare, i.e. where the genitive is not realized morphologically, and where the subject precedes the bare DO) were possible until fairly recently and are still found in some early 20th century texts, under a non-specific reading for the subject.

DO be "activated" by that higher agreement and can thus license objective case (accusative as the strong realization of object Case, and null as the weak realization of that Case) on the DO.[13] This results in the *appearance* of dependent Case, which is, this paper claims, an *indirect symptom* of dependent *Agree*.

3.2 Older work which has motivated the current proposal

3.2.1 Accusative "assigned" by borrowed (verbal) nouns

The proposal I just made owes its existence to two prior proposals: One is the "jumpstart" mechanism proposed by Keskin (2009), originally motived for rather different phenomena (having to do with verbal nouns which assign Case, crucially accusative as a structural Case, but also lexical Cases such as dative and ablative) but only when there is a "higher", genitive-marked NP/DP, which agrees with the verbal noun. Keskin then expands his proposal to object Case in general, but in somewhat different ways than I do, as we shall see presently.

A brief discussion of structural Case (apparently) assigned by verbal nouns follows.

There are nouns in Turkish mostly borrowed from Arabic, which appear to license accusative Case:

(27)   Keskin (2009: 53, (52))
    [*Siz-in*   *Anadolu-yu*   *mahv-ınız*   ] *herkes-i*   *üz-dü.*
      you.PL-GEN Anatolia-ACC devastation-2PL everyone-ACC upset-PST
    'Your devastation of Anatolia upset everyone.'

It is highly unusual cross-linguistically for nouns to be able to assign/license accusative; in Turkish too, this is impossible in general; only a relatively short list

---

[13] Intuitively speaking, the effects of this proposal should correspond to those of (1b), i.e. B&V's (4b), yet the proposal is not identical to it: there, the DO would receive accusative only if the DP that it is c-commanded by, i.e. the subject, does not bear case yet. Here, the DO would receive Case only if the subject does bear subject Case. It may be possible to arrive at a greater similarity between the proposal I am making here on the one hand, and the one in (1b), if the current proposal does not ask for the subject to actually *bear* subject Case, but only to *Agree* with the local predicate, so as to activate object Case on the DO. The actual subject Case (i.e. nominative or genitive) could then be realized later, after the realization of object Case. I leave it to future research to decide whether this alternative is workable (as well as fitting the empirical work of B&V and of L&P better; it would fit the proposal in Kornfilt & Preminger 2015 perfectly). See also footnote 32, where this issue of "nominative as no-case-at-all" is addressed, as well.

of such borrowed nouns are able to do so. In literature prior to Keskin's work (e.g. Sezer 1991), as well as in some discussions contemporaneous with Keskin's work (e.g. Öztürk 2009), it is assumed that there is an abstract light verb that assigns accusative. However, Keskin advances rather convincing arguments against that assumption. While it would take us too far afield to discuss those arguments, at least one of them should be mentioned: While some of these borrowed nouns (which are actually verbal nouns in their language of origin) appear to assign accusative, some others assign lexical Cases, such as the dative and ablative. If it is an abstract light verb which assigns the structural accusative in examples such as (27), why don't we find the accusative on the complement of *all* such borrowed verbal nouns?

An additional argument against the "light verb hypothesis" leads Keskin to his "jumpstart" proposal:

While the borrowed verbal noun *mahv* 'devastation' appears to assign the accusative to its complement in (27), it apparently cannot do so in all contexts; note, for instance, the following example:

(28) Keskin (2009: 53, (51d))
 *[*Anadolu-yu   mahv*   ] *Moğol-lar-ı*   *tatmin   et-me-di.*
   Anatolia-ACC devastation   Mongolian-PL-ACC satisfaction do-NEG-PST
 intended: 'The devastation (of) Anatolia did not satisfy the Mongolians.'

Keskin focuses on one difference between (27) and (28): while in the well-formed (27), the accusative co-occurs with agreement morphology on the borrowed verbal noun *mahv*, there is no such agreement morphology in the ill-formed (28). Keskin thus posits a causal relationship between the well-formed occurrence of the accusative and the agreement morphology on the verbal noun; he further proposes that actually, there is a (phonologically unrealized) lower functional projection in these complex nominal phrases; that projection's head has the potential to assign accusative to the verbal noun's complement. However, that potential has to be activated by the higher functional projection's head, i.e. the overt agreement.

This proposal would then easily predict well-formedness contrasts such as the contrast we just saw between (27) and (28).

3.2.2 Subject Case alternations between the subject of a nominalized adjunct clause versus the subject of a nominalized argument clause

The second prior proposal which motivated my proposal in this paper is one of my own (cf. Kornfilt 2003b and subsequent work), also for rather different phenomena, namely for nominalized adjunct (adverbial) versus argument clauses. The specific proposal there was intended to differentiate non-genitive subjects in nominalized *adjunct* clauses from genitive subjects in nominalized *argument* clauses; in the latter, the agreement morphology on the argument clause's predicate was claimed to get activated by the (agreement of) the root clause's predicate, while no such activation is possible in adjunct clauses. As a consequence, the subject of a nominalized adjunct clause gets default Case, which is nominative in Turkish.

Note the contrast between the genitive subject in the nominalized argument clause versus the nominative subject in the nominalized adjunct clause in the following pair of examples:

(29) Genitive subject in nominalized argument clause
Herkes [*sen*(-in)* *ödül-ü* *kazan-dığ-ın-ı*] *duy-du*.
everyone you.SG-GEN prize-ACC win-FN-2.SG-ACC hear-PST
'Everyone heard that you won the award.'

(30) Nominative subject in nominalized adjunct clause
Herkes [[*sen(*-in)* *ödül-ü* *kazan-dığ-ın*] *için*] *sevin-di*.
everyone you.SG-GEN prize-ACC win-FN-2SG because rejoice-PST
'Everyone was happy because you won the award.'

This shows that T-heads need to be activated, too: along with Kornfilt & Whitman (2011), I assume that in such gerundive clauses, there is a T-head, which is defective (due to the fact that the nominalized T in "factive nominalizations" can only differentiate between future and non-future). In order to be activated, the argument clause's inflectional head, i.e. the defective T, needs to be c-commanded by the matrix T, which would be true for argument clauses, but not for the head of adjunct clauses. (The actual situation is more complex than can be sketched here; details are offered in Kornfilt 2003b.)

An anonymous reviewer suggests that "category theory", i.e. the distinction between nouns and adjectives, can explain these facts, too: let's assume that gerund-like mixed categories (e.g. *-ing* gerunds in English, and gerundives in Turkish with impoverished tense) are categorially ambiguous between being nominal or adjectival. When the gerundive is nominal, it can head a clause in an argument position and can have a genitive subject; when it is adjectival, it can be in a non-argument position, but cannot have a genitive subject; its subject must have a default nominative case. A nominal constituent cannot be in a non-argument position (unless there is a P-head) by the Theta-Criterion.

While this may be a viable approach to English gerundives, it is unclear to me at this point whether it would work for Turkish/Turkic, and, more generally, whether one can find convincing, independent evidence for the adjectival nature of gerundives that head adjunct clauses. As a matter of fact, if not nominal, shouldn't such a gerundive be adverbial rather than adjectival, given that these adjunct clauses modify the predicate of the higher clause? It is further unclear to me whether the Theta Criterion rules out all nominal constituents in non-argument positions; languages such as Turkish do have nominals in such positions, and one would need to posit empty Ps to explain this aspect of their distribution, thus weakening the explanatory force of this alternative proposal. Thus, I continue to follow the proposal in Kornfilt (2003b), under which the agreement on a predicate must be activated so that it can fulfill its role as licenser of subject Case on the subject, i.e. on the specifier of the TP with that agreement.

4 Further discussion of the proposal and its application to subject and object Case, including DSM and DOM contexts

4.1 Details of the "activation" proposal

As we have seen, Keskin's proposal was motivated by the mystery of apparently case-assigning nouns; it resolved that mystery by attributing the relevant structural case-assigning (or structural case-licensing) to the agreement on the head of the nominal phrase. What is unusual and surprising about that proposal is not the correlation between the structural Case which is thus licensed on the *specifier* of the phrase; this is what I have been referring to here as the traditional Chomskyan approach to structural subject Case, an approach based, at least in part, on proposals in George & Kornfilt (1981) and Kornfilt (1984). The surprising aspect of Keskin's proposal is that the structural case on the head's *complement* is licensed, albeit indirectly, by the agreement with the *specifier*, in an apparently non-local, long-distance fashion. The locality problem is only apparent, because the actual licenser of the case on the complement is a local functional (e.g. AgrO) or lexical (e.g. the N-head of the nominal phrase) head. For theoretical consistency, one could assume that structural Case licensers are all functional (thus staying in the framework of Chomsky 1995 and later work); if so, we would assume that the local head responsible for structural Case in such instances, i.e. in the nominal phrases studied by Keskin, is a functional head, such as AgrO in verbal contexts, and small *n* in nominal ones. For my purposes in this paper, it does not matter whether the head in those nominal phrases is functional or lexical, e.g. for nominal phrases, whether it is an AgrO-type functional head or the N-head. For clauses and their VP-related domain (i.e. vP), I shall assume that the head which is responsible for object Case licensing is indeed the functional head AgrO. What I am mainly interested in for the purposes of this paper is the idea that a local licenser needs to be licensed itself in order to license structural case to the head's complement, i.e. that its local licensing potential gets activated by structurally higher agreement, namely the agreement with the specifier. The fact that there is no overt realization of AgrO in Turkish VPs and NPs should not be a deterrent in this approach, given that in a number of languages, such an element is observable and documented.[14]

---

[14] While Keskin does assume that it is a functional head (abstract in Turkish, overt in some other languages) which is responsible for the accusative case on a complement DP (whether the complement of a verbal noun or of a verb, the latter as a direct object), he also assumes that this functional head, at least for direct objects, is small v rather than AgrO—a head which does not show up in his structures. But if the base position of the subject is the specifier of vP, and if this is the position where the subject gets its theta-role, we have a problem: the subject would not receive Case in that position (under most assumptions in the literature), and would thus be forced to raise to the position of specifier of TP. Keskin makes this assumption, as well. However, at the same time, the small v in a transitive construction would get activated by subject agreement and would thus assign structural Case, i.e. the accusative, to the direct object. In other words, small v would assign the subject theta-role, but the object Case; it crucially would be unable to assign a subject Case. I find this a problematic assumption, although for Keskin, this appears to be an advantage of his approach, because it could be viewed as the "seat" of Burzio's generalizaton: accusative is assigned when an "external" theta role is assigned, and accusative is not assigned when no external theta role can be assigned, e.g. as in passives. If one single element, i.e. small v, is responsible for both the external theta role and the case on the complement, Burzio's correlation would fall out automatically. (In parallel, a small n would need to be assumed in constructions with verbal nouns, with similar separated functions.) Nonetheless, I find this "separation of labor" in the properties of small v counter-intuitive; there are other ways to capture Burzio's generalization. Also, it would need to be stipulated that small v can assign "object Case", i.e. accusative, but no "subject case", i.e. not nominative or genitive. Furthermore, it would differ from inherent/lexical case assigners/licensers in not assigning a theta-role and a case to one and the same element, while also differing from subject agreement, which would assign subject Case, but no theta-role. I assume that the "activated", accusative-assigning functional head is AgrO, while the functional head which assigns a theta-role to the subject in its base position (namely in Spec,vP), is v. This approach most closely parallels what we find for subject Case: For both subject case (nominative and genitive) and object case (accusative), we have a functional head as a licenser, i.e. agreement: subject agreement and object agreement, respectively; neither one assigns a theta-role. This is also the reason for adopting the "old-fashioned" AgrO, rather than a "substantive" head, such as Aspect (thus addressing a comment by one of the anonymous reviewers); in addition, it does not seem to be the case that Aspect is involved in these Case phenomena in any fashion. I return to the issue of agreement as a licenser in the main body of the text.

4.2 Schematic discussion of logical possibilities: Specific/non-specific subjects, and specific/non-specific objects

In what follows, I will give a schematic summary of logically possible linearizations of specific and non-specific subjects and direct objects with and without case marking, and I will discuss how my proposals address the well-formed sequences as well as the ill-formed ones. While doing so, I will distinguish full, or strong, agreement morphology from incomplete, or weak, morphology. One aspect of my proposal will be that non-specific subjects and objects, i.e. nominal phrases that exhibit DSM and DOM effects, need weak Case, and that agreement is involved in the licensing of weak Case as well as of strong (overt) Case; this licensing is also the result of the activation of AgrO by subject agreement. Note that this is an aspect of my proposal which is different from Keskin's, for whom bare DPs (or NPs) don't need and don't have Case; only overtly realized structural Case is what counts and is accounted for; in this respect, his approach is similar to the one in B&V (2010) and L&P (2015).[15]

A Specific subject, specific direct object

(31) [$_{TP,NMLZ}$ *Haydut-lar-ın$_i$* [$_{vP}$ *köy-ü$_j$*   [$_{vP}$ t$_i$ [$_{AgrOP}$ t$_j$ [$_{vP}$ t$_j$
       robber-PL-GEN   village-ACC

   bas-tığ-ın-ı   / *bas-tık-ların-ı*   ]]]]] *duy-du-m.*
   raid-FN-3SG-ACC   raid-FN-3PL-ACC   hear-PST-1SG

   'I heard that the robbers raided the village.'

The overt genitive case on the subject of the embedded clause correlates with full, strong third person plural agreement on the local nominalized predicate; I assume that the genitive, as a strong case here, is licensed by the full, i.e. strong, local agreement. I further assume that here, the form with the singular variant

---

[15] Here, it might be more correct for me to refer to non-specific subjects and direct objects which either have the indefinite marker *bir* 'a, one', or which are in the plural. These are the nominal phrases which I would claim need weak Case (rather than being (pseudo-)incorporated. The completely generic nominal phrases that are completely bare might indeed be (pseudo-)incorporated into the verb. For the purposes of this paper, this is immaterial; limitation to quantified or pluralized subjects and direct objects would be sufficient. (Again, as in footnote 3, the interested reader is directed towards Aydemir (2004), where completely generic bare DOs are distinguished from non-case-marked indefinite DOs).

of the agreement morphology is not a truly weak form, but rather a morphophonologically optional variant of strong agreement, as mentioned earlier in conjunction with the examples in (4) and (6); in other words, where the weak agreement is not obligatory, but is an optional variant, I take it to be not truly weak, but just a stylistic option of full agreement.

The strong subject agreement which licenses the genitive also activates the AgrO of the embedded clause, and thus overt, strong accusative is licensed. The direct object is base-generated as the complement of the transitive verb and moves to the specifier position of AgrO, to get its Case licensed.

Note that I assume that neither the subject nor the object are in their base positions in (31). Following Diesing (1992) and the previous brief mention of the "Diesing Effect" (in conjunction with the examples in (13) through (15)), I assume that non-specific[16] nominal phrases must remain in the vP domain, while specific nominal phrases move out of that domain and either land in Spec,TP (for subjects) or to a vP-adjoined position (for direct objects). This adjunction, creating a higher vP, counts as having escaped the "Diesing domain", i.e. the lower vP for non-specific elements.

One piece of evidence is the placement of the direct object with respect to a morphologically simple adverb; such adverbs are typically used as marking the boundary of VP or vP (see also Keskin 2009; I will assume that the relevant boundary is VP (see also footnote 17):

(32) [$_{TP,NMLZ}$ haydut-lar-ın$_i$ [$_{vP}$ köy-ü$_j$ [$_{vP}$ **çabuk** t$_i$ [$_{AgrO}$ t$_j$ [$_{VP}$ t$_j$
robber-PL-GEN village-ACC **fast**

bas-tığ–ın-ı / bas-tık-ların-ı]]]]] duy-du-m.
raid-FN-3SG-ACC raid-FN-3PL-ACC hear-PST-1SG

'I heard that the robbers raided the village fast.'

If the order between the adverb and the accusative DO is reversed, ill-formedness results for most speakers:

(33) ??/*[haydut-lar-ın **çabuk** köy-ü bas-tığ-ın-ı /
robber-PL-GEN **fast** village-ACC raid-FN-3SG-ACC

bas-tık-ların-ı] duy-du-m.
raid-FN-3PL-ACC hear-PST-1SG

'I heard that the robbers raided the village fast.'

---

[16] For Diesing, the relevant factor is "indefinite"—however, for Turkish the relevant notion must be based on specificity instead.

Even those speakers who accept this order say that they have to stress the direct object, so that the reading which obtains is something like this: 'As for fast (raiding), I heard that the robbers raided THE VILLAGE.' I thus conclude that the specific, accusative direct object has moved out of the "Diesing-domain" of non-specific interpretation. Also, note that here, the specific subject precedes the specific direct object. The subject must therefore be even higher than the specific direct object (in an unmarked order); this falls into place nicely with the assumptions made before, i.e. that the specific direct object is adjoined to *v*P, and that the subject is in *Spec,TP*.

We will contrast these observations with those to be made when the direct object is non-specific, and has to follow the simple adverb:

B Specific subject, non-specific direct object

(34) [$_{TP.NMLZ}$ *haydut-lar-ın$_i$* [$_{vP}$ **çabuk** t$_i$ [$_{AgrOP}$ *köy$_j$* [$_{VP}$ t$_j$ *bas-tığ-ın-ı*
robber-PL-GEN   **fast**   village   raid-FN-3SG-ACC

/ *bas-tık-ların-ı*]]]] *duy-du-m.*
raid-FN-3PL-ACC   hear-PST-1SG

'I heard that the robbers raided a village/villages (=village-raided) fast.'

The reverse order, which was fine in A, becomes unavailable:

(35) *[*haydut-lar-ın   köy   çabuk bas-tığ-ın-ı   / bas-tık-ların-ı*]
robber-PL-GEN village **fast** raid-FN-3SG-ACC raid-FN-3PL-ACC
duy-du-m.
hear-PST-1SG

intended: 'I heard that as for a village/villages (=village-raiding), the robbers raided the village FAST.'

This shows that the non-specific direct object cannot leave the VP-domain and is presumably in its position derived after its first movement, i.e. in the specifier position of AgrOP, where it moved to have its (weak) Case licensed. I make the simplest assumptions concerning the cause of the ill-formedness: the non-specific direct object's being trapped in the VP is due to the "Diesing Effect". We don't have to assume (pseudo-)incorporation into the verb (e.g. Baker & Vinokurova 2010),[17]

---

[17] An anonymous reviewer asks whether in examples involving non-specific, bare nominals, separation from the verb by an adverb is permissible. (The question addresses bare subjects,

or that non-specific nominal phrases do not need Case (e.g. Keskin 2009, Öztürk 2005). The strong subject agreement on the TP activates the AgrO, which licenses Case on the direct object; the direct object, in turn, cannot select the strong version of the object Case, i.e. the accusative, because its non-specific semantics require the weak version of the accusative, which is morphologically zero. In addition, being non-specific, the direct object remains in the position of Spec,AgrOP.

C *Non-specific subject, specific direct object

(36) *[Haydut[18] köy-ü   bas-tığ-ın-ı   ] duy-du-m.
         robber   village-ACC raid-FN-3SG-ACC   hear-PST-1SG
    intended: 'I heard that robbers raided the village.'

---

but it can carry over to DOs, as well.) The reviewer then suggests that if adjacency is required, (pseudo-)incorporation of the nominal into the verb would be a more adequate analysis than the Diesing Effect, which does not necessarily predict such adjacency. The adjacency in question does obtain. However, this does not necessitate a (pseudo-)incorporation analysis, if we make the reasonable assumption that (low, morphologically simple) adverbs in Turkish demarcate the vP-domain, rather than the VP-domain (as the lowest possibility in the clause). Given that in all ill-formed examples where a non-specific DO (and, later in the paper, a non-specific subject) is not adjacent to the verb, the nominal in question is within the vP-domain (i.e. in the respective specifier positions of vP for the subject, and of AgrOP for the DO), this is expected: these non-specific nominals cannot leave the (lower—see the text about examples (31) and (32)) vP, whose upper boundary is marked by a (low) adverb. The same demarcation can be assumed to hold of certain PPs (e.g. resultatives), whose disruptive effect with respect to the adjacency of non-specific DOs to the verb leads Baker & Vinokurova (2010) to reject a Diesing-type analysis to similar DOM effects in Sakha, and to adopt a pseudo-incorporation account (assuming a Larson-type VP-shell, and viewing the PP as the complement of the verb—the latter a rather problematic assumption). However, I strongly suspect that the analysis I just proposed for Turkish can carry over to Sakha, and to examples involving adverbial or PP "disruptors" of the adjacency effects in question, again without appealing to (pseudo-)incorporation.

18 Non-specific subjects of nominalized embedded clauses which have weak case, i.e. which are not marked genitive, cannot be marked with the plural, while their counterparts in fully verbal clauses can, as we saw earlier. This has been noted by Keskin (2009), as well. I do not have an explanation for this contrast at this point. An anonymous reviewer notes that this could speak in favor of an incorporation analysis. But, if so, this would mean that non-specific subjects with weak Case in tensed clauses are not incorporated, while non-specific subjects with weak Case in nominalized clauses are. Given that non-specific subjects do not differ from each other in tensed versus nominalized clauses otherwise, I would argue that this is not a direction one should pursue at this point of our knowledge.

As stated above, non-specific nominal phrases are trapped within the vP/VP, due to the Diesing Effect; therefore, non-specific subjects cannot move to the canonical subject position of Spec,TP. Depending on one's notion of phrase structure, we will have to say that either there is a non-alternating silent expletive pronoun in that position, or that the position is not realized. Either way, a strong agreement on TP (i.e. overtly plural for a plural third person subject) is not possible, because there is no specific, referential subject in the specifier position; instead, subject agreement will have to have the default shape, i.e. third person singular, and thus be weak. Given that this weak agreement cannot alternate with strong agreement, it is not just a morpho-phonological, stylistic variant of strong agreement; instead, it is truly weak. The specific direct object would need to move to a position higher than the non-specific subject, i.e. it has to leave the vP/VP domain (cf. the Diesing Effect), and it must therefore precede the non-specific subject, rather than following it. In (36), this has not happened, leading to the ill-formedness of the example. Note that the weak subject agreement appears to be sufficient to activate AgrO so as to license the accusative Case on the direct object. This becomes important in D. below, where a different linearization of a specific DO with respect to the non-specific subject is well-formed.

D Specific direct object, non-specific subject (in this order)

(37) [$_{TP,NMLZ}$ [$_{vP}$ *köy-ü$_j$*   [$_{vP}$ *haydut* [$_{AgrOP}$ t$_j$ [$_{vP}$ t$_j$ *bas-tığ-ın-ı*   ]]]]]
              village-ACC   robber   raid-FN-3SG-ACC

duy-du-m.
hear-PST-1SG

'I heard that robbers raided the village.'

This is a version of C, with the specific direct object, marked accusative, having moved out of the vP/VP domain, in observance of the Diesing Effect; hence, the result is well-formed. The non-specific subject remains in the specifier position of VP, where it gets its weak Case licensed by the weak agreement on the nominalized TP.

E Non-specific subject (no direct object)

With *unergative* verbs, non-specific subjects (just like subjects in general) would be base-generated in *Spec*,vP, i.e. just like their counterparts in transitive constructions, e.g. as in D:

(38) [$_{TP.NMLZ}$ [$_{vP}$ *Yol-dan* [$_{vP}$ *(bir) araba* [$_{VP}$ *geç-tiğ-in-i*]]]] *gör-dü-m.*
road-ABL   a   car   go by-FN-3SG-ACC   see-PST-1SG
'I saw a car/cars go by on the road.'

The non-specific, morphologically bare (rather than genitive) subject remains in its base position of Spec,vP; we can see this by the fact that it follows the directional, oblique (ablative) adjunct. The agreement is weak, as expected; it licenses weak (morphologically unrealized) subject Case on the subject which is in-situ. I assume that the agreement morphology can either license Case on an element in the specifier position of TP, or on an element which is in the specifier position of vP (given that vP is the complement of T+Agr, which makes vP's specifier in its left edge accessible), but not both at the same time. What we have here is the latter option. I further assume that the necessity of licensing weak Case is the motivation of having default or weak agreement to begin with.

I'll assume that a non-specific subject in an *unaccusative* construction is base-generated as the complement of V, just like the complement of a transitive verb. However, there is no AgrO associated with unaccusative verbs, which means that this non-specific subject would remain without Case in this position. Therefore, that subject will move to Spec,vP[19] (but not higher, i.e. not to Spec,TP, since it cannot be marked with a strong subject Case), where it will get its weak subject Case licensed by the weak agreement on TP, just like a non-specific subject in an unergative construction:

(39) a. [*Garaj-da* **beş araba(*-nın)** *ol-duğ-un-u*] *bil-iyor-um.*
       garage-LOC **five car(*-GEN)** be-FN-**3SG**-ACC know-PRS.PROG-1SG
       'I know that there are five cars in the garage.'

   b. *[**Beş araba(-nın)** *garaj-da* *ol-duğ-***un**-*u*] *bil-iyor-um.*
       five car(-GEN) garage-LOC be-FN-**3SG**-ACC know-PRS.PROG-1SG
       intended: 'I know that there are five cars in the garage.'
       (The genitive version is OK under the specific reading for the subject: 'I know that the five cars are in the garage.')

---

[19] In contrast with L&P (2015), I do assume the existence of the Case Filter for nominal phrases as a motivator for movement. Thus, what we have here is a lower version of the familiar derivation of passives and of unaccusative constructions in general, with the difference that we are dealing with non-specific nominal phrases, and thus, according to the details of my proposal, the domain of the movement is lower, i.e. it involves only vP/VP, rather than TP.

F Non-specific subject, non-specific direct object

As we saw in the descriptive part of the paper, this is a configuration which is ill-formed when both the subject and the direct object are morphologically bare:

(40) *[$_{TP.NMLZ}$ [$_{vP}$ *Haydut* [$_{AgrOP}$ *köy$_j$* [$_{VP}$ t$_i$ *bas-tığ-ın-ı*]]]] *duy-du-m.*
robber village raid-FN-3SG-ACC hear-PST-1SG

intended: 'I heard that some unspecified robber/robbers raided some unspecified village/villages.'

Why are such examples ill-formed? Accounts based on linearity (e.g. stating that weak, morphologically unrealized Case needs to be licensed by the verb under adjacency—e.g. Keskin 2009, Kornfilt 1984) could explain this easily: only one constituent can be adjacent to the verb.[20] Likewise, accounts based on (pseudo-)incorporation could posit a constraint, under which only one nominal can (pseudo-)incorporate into the verb at a time—a constraint which is easy to formulate, but is not obvious: why shouldn't a second nominal be able to (pseudo-)incorporate into the result of the first application of (pseudo-)incorporation? The approach I have adopted here has a somewhat harder time: It cannot be claimed that weak agreement can do only one thing at a time, e.g. license weak Case on the non-specific subject *or* activate AgrO to license Case on the direct object; this is because examples such as (37) in D are well-formed; the overt accusative on the direct object must have been licensed by the AgrO, in turn activated by subject agreement which also licenses the weak Case on the non-specific subject.

I therefore have to posit a constraint against more than one weak Case in a local domain. This takes care of the ill-formedness of (40).[21]

As we saw earlier in B, the order of *specific (genitive) subject—non-specific (weak-Case) direct object* is fine, since the above-mentioned condition of having

---

[20] Note, however, that accounts such as the proposals in Öztürk (2005, 2009), and others, which assume that non-specific nominal phrases project only up to NP and not DP, and therefore do not need Case, would need some linearization statement which is independent from Case needs, in order to explain the ill-formedness of such examples, e.g. of the type mentioned in the text, positing that only one element can (pseudo-)incorporate into the verb.

[21] One of the anonymous reviewers asks whether such a constraint is equivalent to the proposal by Alexiadou & Anagnostopoulou (2001, 2007), stating that at least one NP needs to move out of the domain of the verbal phrase (thus, for me, out of the *v*P), so that if the subject does not, then the object must. These proposals may indeed be equivalent, and, depending on the ultimate theoretical status of the Case Filter, the proposal made here against two instances of weak Case in the verbal domain may be viewed as a motivation of the proposal made by Alexiadou & Anagnostopoulou.

at most one weak Case at a time is respected. What is interesting is the fact that, at least for some speakers, the genitive subject in this linearization can also have a non-specific meaning, as long as the local agreement is weak. Note that it is only with plural subjects that one can determine the weakness of the agreement; if the genitive subject is singular, the agreement form for third person singular is viewed as strong,[22] and thus the genitive subject is interpreted as specific. This is why, even for such permissive speakers, the secondary interpretation of genitive subjects as non-specific is possible only for *plural* subjects.

G *Non-specific direct object, non-specific subject

(41) *[TP.NMLZ [vP *Köy$_j$* [vP *haydut* [AgrOP t$_j$ [vP t$_j$ *bas-tığ-ın-ı*]]]]]
village   robber   raid-FN-3SG-ACC

duy-du-m.
hear-PST-1SG

intended: 'I heard that some unspecified robber/robbers raided some unspecified village/villages.'

This is a version of the previous example in F (with the bare, non-specific DO scrambled over the non-specific, bare subject), and thus the account given there carries over. Note that this linearization cannot be "saved" by marking the subject with the genitive and assigning it a secondary, non-specific interpretation, because here, we also have a violation of the Diesing Effect: the non-specific direct object has moved out of the *v*P/VP domain.

We have now gone over the main types of constructions involving specific and non-specific subjects and direct objects, and have discussed the licensing of subject cases (nominative and genitive as strong subject cases as well as null as a weak subject case) and of the object case (accusative as the strong version, and null as the weak version) for specific and non-specific subjects and objects, respectively. We did observe correlations between these Cases and subject agreement, and we therefore attributed causality to agreement in the licensing of these Cases. While doing so, however, we relied on configurationality: the activating agreement, i.e. subject agreement, must c-command the activated agreement, i.e. object agree-

---

[22] An anonymous reviewer points out that I am making the assumption here that whenever a certain piece of morphology can be interpreted as "rich" or "strong", it should be so interpreted. It is true that I am indeed making this assumption in the text; there is some independent evidence for this, coming from binding facts. Discussion of this would take us too far afield; in any event, this is a topic which deserves detailed research in the future.

ment. On the other hand, there is no competition between either different agreements, or between different Cases; instead, we have collaboration: the higher, activating agreement allows the lower agreement to be effective as a licenser, and the lower agreement can only be effective under the activation by the higher agreement.

5 Apparent problems: Embedded transitive clauses without subject agreement

So far, I have been mainly interested in the licensing of subject and object Cases. Before turning to a third structural Case, namely the dative, I would like to briefly discuss two contexts, where there is no subject agreement, but where a direct object's accusative Case (as well as weak Case for non-specific objects) is licensed nonetheless: Embedded infinitival clauses with a PRO subject, and exceptional case marking (ECM)-clauses whose subject has risen to the root clause.

5.1 Infinitival clauses with PRO subjects

In Turkish infinitival clauses in obligatory or optional Control contexts have nominalized predicates that lack subject agreement; in the morphological slot for nominal agreement, there is a -k. This is illustrated by the following examples:

(42) Ali$_i$ [PRO$_i$ bütün gün kitab-ı   / kitap oku-mak]-tan bık-tı.
      Ali   entire day book-ACC   book read-INF-ABL bored-PST
      'Ali has gotten bored of reading the book/books all day long.'

The traditional understanding of the nominalization morphology illustrated here is to view the entire sequence of -mAK as the marker of the infinitive predicate. This is the analysis also found in more formal and/or recent literature. However, this analysis leaves no room to posit any agreement element, nor even a morphological slot for agreement. This is not a problem and might even be viewed as an advantage: in Government and Binding approaches to infinitival clauses, the PRO-subject is supposed to be Case-less (e.g. Chomsky 1981 and later work in that framework). Given that in this paper, too, I have assumed that subject Case is licensed by subject agreement for subjects in Spec,TP, the traditional analysis of the Turkish infinitival marker as an agreement-less nominalizer, -mAK, falls into place perfectly. However, this obviously raises the question of how the direct object receives Case—irrespective of whether strong or weak, depending on the specificity of that direct object—in the Case activation approach pursued in this paper, if no subject Case is assigned.

The answer to this potential problem is offered by a different analysis of the infinitival predicate: Control verbs are a subset of verbs which select "non-factive" or "subjunctive" nominalized clauses (see Kornfilt 1997, among others). The morphological marker for those clauses is -*mA*. Those clauses also bear subject agreement markers:

(43) Ali [Oya-nın bütün gün kitab-ı / kitap oku-ma-**sın**-dan]
     Ali   Oya-GEN entire day book-ACC   book read-NFN-**3SG**-ABL
     bık-tı.
     bored-PST
     'Ali has gotten bored with Oya's reading the book/books all day long.'

I propose to analyze the so-called infinitival marker as a sequence of two morphemes: the "non-factive", subjunctive nominalizer -*mA*, and, in the morphological slot for agreement, the anti-agreement -*K*. The anti-agreement marker now becomes the actual infinitive marker; it prevents PRO from receiving regular subject Case (in a language like Turkish where it obviously does not);[23] but, at the same time, by virtue of being in the morphological slot for agreement (and thus also being in the same phrase-structural position as subject agreement), it can also fulfill the function of subject agreement as proposed here (and by Keskin 2009): it activates AgrO, so that the direct object gets its object Case (in either its strong or weak realization) licensed.[24]

---

23 Instead of the regular subject Case, the PRO in infinitival clauses has, I claim, the Null Case proposed by Chomsky & Lasnik (1993), assigned to it by the "anti-agreement" marker -*K*; see also Kornfilt (2018b) for a brief discussion of this view for Turkish infinitivals. (In response to a comment by one of the anonymous reviewers: I have chosen to refer to -*K* as anti-agreement rather than null agreement, given that it is overt, and it blocks any genuine φ-agreement to show up in these infinitival clauses.) Discussing the challenge posed for this proposal by quirky lexical cases in Icelandic would take us too far afield. The potential problem of hosting a DP-trace (which should be altogether devoid of Case, rather than being assigned Null Case) in the subject position of an infinitival clause in Raising constructions does not arise for Turkish given that in potential Subject Raising constructions (whose status as such is somewhat controversial for Turkish and for head-final languages in general) as well as in SOR/ECM constructions, the embedded clause is not infinitival, but rather is tensed. (See the next subsection on ECM as well as the next footnote.)
24 The editors have raised an interesting question: They point out that the approach I have taken in this paper would predict that in clauses that are truncated below inflection, no accusative mark-

5.2 ECM constructions

A small list of verbs in Turkish, all essentially having the semantics of belief, allow for ECM-constructions:

(44) Ali ben$_i$-i [t$_i$ bu kitab-ı   / kitap yaz-dı   ] san-ıyor.
      Ali I-ACC   this book-ACC   book write-PST   believe-PRS.PROG
      'Ali believes me to have written this book/books.'

The embedded clause in ECM constructions in Turkish is not an infinitival as in English; rather, in its primary form, it is a tensed clause which lacks subject agreement marking on the embedded predicate.[25]

Given that there is no subject agreement on the embedded clause, how is either version of object Case licensed? Also, how is the strong object Case licensed on the raised subject?

The second question is answered more readily. Given that the raised subject has risen into the domain of the root clause, and, more specifically, into the specifier position of the matrix AgrO, its object Case, i.e. accusative, is licensed in a straightforward manner: The root clause has strong agreement (with the root subject), and this agreement activates the root AgrO's Case licensing potential. (Also, given that the raised subject is specific, it will not stop in this position; due to the Diesing Effect, it will also raise further and adjoin to the *v*P of the root clause.)

Returning to the first question, I posit a chain effect between the activated AgrO of the matrix clause and the AgrO of the embedded, agreementless clause.

---

ing would be possible; they ask whether this prediction is fulfilled, or whether this is testable at all. The infinitival clauses just discussed in this section are the closest that one would get to a clause "truncated" below inflection, given that there is no subject agreement morphology on such clauses. The discussion in this section anticipates this question (although not under the heading of "truncation"): given that there is no agreement morphology on the predicate, no subject case would be licensed in principle, and therefore, under the proposal of this paper, the DO of a transitive infinitival should bear no accusative morphology. This prediction, if it is one, is not fulfilled. However, under the analysis proposed in this section, there is no truncation below subject agreement in infinitival clauses: the "anti-agreement" morpheme *-K* sits in the position of agreement; it assigns null Case to the PRO-subject; given that the infinitival *is* inflected (with *-K*) under this analysis, there is no truncation of the kind addressed by the question; the subject and its Case (and, thus, AgrO) *are* activated, thus triggering DOM on a qualifying DO.

25 There is also a version of this construction with a local agreement form. I focus on the agreement-less version, given that it is potentially problematic for the approach advanced here. Where the local subject agreement does show up, AgrO in the embedded clause would be activated, and either strong or weak object Case would be licensed. Readers interested in Turkish ECM-constructions are referred to Kornfilt (1977), Moore (1998), and Zidani-Eroğlu (1997).

Given that the subject of the agreementless clause has risen to the specifier position of the matrix AgrO, this triggers a second(ary) activation mechanism: The matrix AgrO, in addition to licensing the object Case on the derived occupant of its specifier position, is now also able to activate the AgrO of the embedded clause; this "chain-building" is made possible by two factors: 1. Lack of subject agreement on the embedded clause (with resulting transparency), and 2. The fact that the clause has lost its subject due to movement, i.e. that (together with the first factor) the trace in Spec,TP lacks Case.

Now that the embedded AgrO is activated, it can license either strong or weak Case on its specifier, i.e. of the direct object of the embedded clause.

I now turn to a brief discussion of the dative as a structural Case.

5.3 Instances of dative as a structural Case, and how to account for it

First, we have to address the question of whether the dative is a lexical Case or a structural Case, or else whether it has to be categorized as either type, depending on its syntactic context. With respect to a number of criteria, the dative in Turkish is a lexical Case in most of its occurrences. I will mention two criteria here:

First, structural object Case, i.e. accusative, disappears under passive; lexical Case does not.

(45) Structural Case

    a. *Ali her gün yol-da bu köpek-ler-i gör-ür.*
       Ali every day road-LOC this dog-PL-ACC see-AOR
       'Ali sees these dogs on the road every day.'

    b. *Bu köpek-ler(*-i) her gün yol-da (Ali tarafından) gör-ül-ür.*
       this dog-PL(-ACC) every day road-LOC Ali by see-PASS-AOR
       'These dogs are seen every day on the road (by Ali).'

(46) Lexical Case: Ablative

    a. *Ali bu köpek-ten kork-ar.*
       Ali this dog-ABL fear-AOR
       'Ali is afraid of this dog.'

    b. *Bu köpek*(-ten) kork-ul-ur.*
       this dog-ABL fear-PASS-AOR
       'This dog is feared.' ('One is afraid of this dog.')[26]

(47) Lexical Case: Dative

    a. *Ali öğrenci-ler-e   yardım ed-er.*
       Ali student-PL-DAT help   do-AOR
       'Ali helps students (habitually).'

    b. *Öğrenci-ler*(-e) yardım ed-il-ir.*
       student-PL-DAT help   do-PASS-AOR
       'Students are helped (habitually).' ('One (habitually) helps students.')

In (45b), we see that the accusative direct object has undergone DP movement; it is the derived subject of the example and is in the nominative; if it were to keep its accusative, this would lead to ill-formedness. In contrast, (46b) and (47b) show that lexical Case cannot be changed into the nominative; it has to remain under "passivization".

Second, derived subjects of "transitive passives" Agree with their predicates; oblique objects do not become subjects and do not Agree with their predicates.

Given that constituents with lexical Case do not "lose" their Case when the predicate is passive, they do not undergo DP movement (given that such movement would be unmotivated for a DP which does bear Case), and thus they do not become derived subjects; this can be seen by the fact that the derived subject in "transitive passives" agrees with the predicate, while the DPs marked with lexical Cases do not:

(48) Transitive passive; derived subject agrees with the predicate

    a. *Ali ben-i çok sev-er.*
       Ali I-ACC very like-AOR
       'Ali likes me a lot.'

    b. *Ben çok sev-il-ir-im.*
       I   very like-PASS-AOR-1SG
       'I am very much liked.'

---

[26] As these examples involving lexical Case and passive show, Turkish allows passives of this sort. However, agent phrases are mostly disallowed in these "non-transitive passives", while such phrases are perfectly fine with passives involving true transitives, as illustrated in (45b). Thus, this can be viewed as an additional criterion to differentiate between structural and lexical cases.

(49) Passive with an oblique (ablative) object; there is no derived subject, hence no agreement with the predicate

  a. *Ali ben-den çok kork-ar.*
     Ali I-ABL very fear-AOR
     'Ali is very afraid of me.'

  b. *Ben-den çok kork-ul-ur(*-um).*
     I-ABL very fear-PASS-AOR(-1SG)
     'I am much feared.'

(50) Passive with an oblique (dative) object; there is no derived subject, hence no agreement with the predicate

  a. *Ali ban-a hep yardım ed-er.*
     Ali I-DAT always help do-AOR
     'Ali always helps me.'

  b. *Ban-a hep yardım ed-il-ir(*-im).*
     I-DAT always help do-PASS-AOR(-1SG)
     'I am always helped.'

There are additional criteria; for example, structural Cases exhibit DOM and DSM-effects, as we have seen earlier in this paper. Lexical Cases do not exhibit such effects. In other words, constituents marked with lexical Cases can be interpreted as specific or non-specific; the latter interpretations hold when a lexical Case is present, and we do not see the variation in overt versus covert Case with respect to specificity which we saw earlier with respect to accusative and genitive, i.e. with respect to structural Cases.[27]

---

[27] For discussion of structural versus lexical Cases in Turkish and for additional examples, the reader is referred to Kornfilt (1984, 1997), and to Keskin (2009). An anonymous reviewer points out that there are languages where DOM-effects are exhibited by lexical cases, as well, and refers to the work of Manzini & Franco (2016). Note that Manzini & Franco's (2016)'s work addresses Indo-European languages; in most Altaic languages exhibiting DOM-effects, we see limitation to structural cases. The same is true for passive as used as a criterion to differentiate lexical from structural cases; it may be possible to get around this in Indo-European, as Caha (2009) shows—another study referred to in this context by the same reviewer. However, it is impossible in Altaic (at least for the Altaic languages such as Turkic and Mongolian languages) to disregard the lexical versus structural Case distinction. Caha does so for the languages he considers, by placing the genitive below accusative (itself below nominative) in the clausal architecture, including all (i.e. personal as well as impersonal) passives, where a nominative subconstituent of a genitive

Having established the dative in Turkish as a lexical Case, we have to see whether there are contexts where the dative might be categorized as a structural Case.

Applying one of the criteria mentioned above for structural case, namely variation of Case, we could classify the dative as a structural Case in causative constructions, because it alternates with the accusative. This is the well-known alternation of the causee's Case as dative versus accusative: When the basic verb is transitive (i.e. when there is an accusative direct object of the basic verb), the causee is dative, and when the basic verb is intransitive (i.e. when the basic verb has no object at all, or if it has an object or adjunct with a lexical Case), the causee is accusative. Obviously, this is a situation which is perfectly tailored for a configurational, competition-based account: the presence versus absence of a nominal phrase with a particular structural Case (here, of an accusative direct object) determines the Case found on another nominal phrase (here, on the causee).

Let us look at the causative version of a transitive simple verb:

(51) a. *Ali Oya-ya mektub-u yaz-dır-dı.*
Ali Oya-DAT letter-ACC write-CAUS-PST
'Ali made Oya write the letter.'

Note that the dative and the accusative can also be in the converse order:

(51) b. *Ali mektub-u Oya-ya yaz-dır-dı.*
Ali letter-ACC Oya-DAT write-CAUS-PST
'Ali made Oya write the letter.'

(or of any other oblique object, even lower than the genitive) moves up to a high position for the checking of nominative (under the "peeling theory" of Starke 2005), just as it would do from out of an accusative, thus making the structural versus lexical case distinction irrelevant, at least for such instances. However, Kornfilt & Whitman (2012) show that, while Japanese genitive subjects are indeed low (i.e. *v*P-internal), Turkish genitive subjects are high; they are *v*P-external and probably as high as nominative subjects, if not even higher, i.e. above the (defective) TP of nominalized clauses. Furthermore, DOs corresponding to accusatives move to this high genitive position in nominalized passive clauses, while Caha's approach prohibits an accusative changing into a genitive, given that for him, the genitive is lower than the accusative in the clausal architecture. Moreover, no "nominative subconstituent" moves to subject position from "out of" an oblique constituent in Turkish and similar languages; such movement would be restricted to application "out of" accusatives only. Thus, neither approach challenges the distinction between structural and lexical case discussed in the text for Turkish nor the criteria used to make that distinction. It is possible that Indo-European is different from other genetically and typologically distinct languages in this respect; future research will address this question.

Native speakers usually judge both orders as equally unmarked, with a possible preference of (51a) as slightly less marked. Given that the same speakers tend to judge the converse order between dative and accusative DPs (i.e. accusative DPs before dative DPs) as less marked in general, i.e. in non-causative contexts, this is an interesting observation whose explanation I leave for future work, because the facts need to be corroborated with a larger number of native speakers than I was able to poll for this paper.

The two configurational rules stated at the beginning of this paper, and in particular (1a) (i.e. B&V's (4a)), which is designed to license datives, might be successful in capturing the dative–accusative alternation in causatives.[28] Note that (1a) must apply first, so that the dative can be licensed (when the simple verb is transitive); if (1b) applies first, the lower NP gets its accusative licensed, and (1a) cannot apply.[29] However, it is not crystal-clear how (1b) (B&V's (4b)) would apply, without being bled. Note that B&V's (4b) was designed to license the accusative under the presence of, and competition with, a *subject*. If their (4a) applies first, and correctly licenses dative Case on the causee, the NP2 of (4b) won't be able to get its accusative licensed, because the NP1 (if this is how we view the "original" subject of the simple verb) already has Case, namely dative. In other words, here, B&V's (4a) has bled (4b), because it seems to have applied to a larger domain than (4b), while (4b) is designed to apply, in general, to a larger domain than (4a).

One way out of this might be not to apply (4b) immediately after (4a), but only after moving the direct object (with its so far unlicensed accusative) of the simple verb out of the VP and adjoining it to the higher verbal domain headed by the causative verb. There, it will be in competition with the subject and have its accusative licensed configurationally. This would derive (51b). Subsequent scrambling would derive (51a) from (51b). This derivation would suggest that (51a) is more marked than (51b) in causatives—a small problem for the derivation, because, as mentioned briefly when first presenting these two examples, native speakers tend to judge (51a) as less marked than (51b). However, given the ten-

---

[28] This is not to say that B&V derive Sakha causatives in the way I discuss their rules for Turkish causatives; as one of the anonymous reviewers points out, for B&V, it is the causer, rather than the causee, that triggers the accusative on the lower DO. However, the Sakha causative facts are somewhat different from those in Turkish, and I leave a detailed comparison of these facts to future research.

[29] Levin & Preminger (2015) note this bleeding relationship, too; they tentatively propose that the ordering of B&V's (4a) before (4b), so as to avoid being bled, can be derived from an Elsewhere Condition (e.g. as in Kiparsky 1983), because their (4a) refers to the VP-phase, and is thus more specific than (4b), which does not refer to any particular phase and thus can be viewed as the "elsewhere case"; thus, the more specific rule would be automatically ordered before the "elsewhere" one.

tative nature of this preference at this point, I don't view this observation as a serious problem for the configuration-and-competition approach and leave this aspect of causatives for future research.

What about causative versions of intransitive constructions? This is illustrated by the following example:

(52) Ali Oya-yı koş-tur-du.
Ali Oya-ACC run-CAUS-PST
'Ali made Oya run.'

Here, the causee would have its accusative licensed under B&V's (4b); under their approach, the causee would be the NP2 of (4b); the subject, i.e. the causer, would be the NP1, on which no Case would have been licensed at the point of the application of (4b). Subsequently, the causer, and thus the subject of the entire construction, would have its subject Case (i.e. nominative in this instance) licensed by subject agreement.

Given that my aim here is to extend an agreement-licensing account for subject Case to other structural Cases, and given that I have done this for object Case (both strong and weak), I must now ask the question of how the agreement-based approach can deal with the alternation between accusative and dative on the causee.

The account for the "causativization" of a simple intransitive verb (whether unaccusative or unergative) is straightforward: I assume that causatives are derived via a "unification" of a complex structure into a simple one. The subject of the clause embedded under CAUS starts as the complement of V, if V is unaccusative, and as the specifier of *v*P, if the verb is unergative. Either way, under clause unification, that subject DP ends up in the specifier position of the resulting causative clause's AgrO, given that the resulting causative predicate is always transitive. That clause has subject agreement, enabling the local AgrO to license accusative on the derived "direct object" of the causative verb.

The account for the "causativization" of a simple transitive verb is more complex. The direct object of that verb starts out as its complement and receives its theta role from it. The subject of that verb starts out as the specifier of *v*P of the embedded clause, and receives its theta role there. After clause unification, the complement of the simple verb checks its accusative case against the AgrO, which forces it to move to the Spec,AgrOP of the resulting causative construction. In other words, the already existing accusative features of the lower DO receive primacy against the causee in moving to the Spec,AgrOP position of the resulting causative. The subject of the original embedded clause adjoins to that AgrOP, where it receives an additional thematic role of causee. The subject agreement of the resulting causative construction activates the AgrO as a Case licenser. The DP in Spec,AgrOP has (had) the accusative Case features checked by AgrO, as mentioned above. The DP adjoined to AgrOP (or, under some approaches to phrase structure, the second specifier of AgrOP) receives the next Case in a Case hierarchy which is widely accepted.

The hierarchy is as follows:

(53)   Nominative/(structural) Genitive > Accusative > Dative > Obliques[30]

The Case immediately after the accusative is dative. No structural Case can be assigned more than once in a local domain,[31] hence the prediction is that the causee of a transitive simple verb will end up marked with the dative, and this is correct.

Note also that this derivation results in the dative causee preceding the accusative DP, which corresponds to the (slight) preference of native informants, as reported earlier.

6 Summary and conclusions

We have seen in this paper that it is possible to construct an account in which subject Case (realized as nominative or genitive, depending on the nature of the associated agreement) is licensed by subject agreement, and where (structural) object Cases (accusative and dative) are licensed by object agreement which is activated by subject agreement.[32] Given that the activation relationship between the two types of agreement is configurational, it is fair to say that the proposed

---

[30] With genitive as a lexical case being one of the oblique cases at the lowest rung of the hierarchy.

[31] Causative constructions in Turkish can have two datives; however, only one of those is structural, namely the causee's dative; the other dative DP bears a lexical dative selected by the simple verb under CAUSE; e.g.:

(i)   Ali   Oya-ya   dün   öğrenci-ler-e   yardım   et-tir-di.
      Ali   Oya-DAT   yesterday   student-PL-DAT   help   do-CAUS-PST
      'Ali made Oya help the students yesterday.'

Here, *Oya*, as the causee, bears structural dative, while *öğrenciler* 'students' bears lexical dative, selected for by the verb *yardım et* 'help'.

[32] An anonymous reviewer refers to Kornfilt & Preminger (2015), where the nominative is analyzed as "no case at all", bringing it up as a potential challenge for the approach to DOM advocated here, presumably because a non-nominative subject (i.e. here, a subject bearing no case at

account is conciliatory as well as unified: it combines Case licensing via functional heads with configurationality, but leaves competition out. Note that the proposal is not a hybrid one, i.e. we don't have certain structural Cases licensed by functional heads, and other structural Cases determined configurationally. A second(ary) proposal was to correlate licensing of strong subject Case (whether nominative or genitive) with strong agreement, and weak subject Case (not realized morphologically) with weak agreement. Furthermore, both weak subject Case and weak object Case for non-specific arguments were claimed to be licensed in specifier positions of functional projections (Spec,vP and Spec,AgrOP, respectively, with the latter projection needing to be activated, too), rather than positing (pseudo)incorporation for such non-specific arguments. When the subject and/or the direct object are non-specific, they would need strong Case, and thus would not be able to remain in these positions of weak Case; they thus raise to higher positions: the specific subject raises to Spec,TP, where its strong subject Case is licensed by strong Agreement; the specific direct object adjoins to vP—a short movement which is nonetheless sufficient for the DO to escape its weak Case position, and, more generally, the lower vP, which is the "Diesing area" for non-specific nominals in need of structural Case. Thus, the issue of syntactic position in the phrase-structural hierarchy of embedded as well as root clauses is an important one in the proposals made here. (Note that the contribution to this volume by Manzini, Savoia & Franco also centrally addresses the question of where DOM objects are positioned.)

All aspects of this proposal are of course open to criticism; one of the objections one could raise is the question of AgrOP: Turkish has no overt object agree-

---

all) might not be able to trigger accusative marking on the DO under the proposed account. However, the problem is only apparent. What is important in my account (and may well be somewhat counter-intuitive, as mentioned earlier) is the influence of *subject* agreement on the shape of the *direct object*: I have proposed that when the subject's nominative (or genitive) case is "activated" by subject agreement, this also activates accusative case on the (specific, referential) DO. But even if one were to adopt the "no case at all" approach to subject case, one could also say, in the spirit of the proposal made here, that the subject itself has to be licensed by subject agreement (which amounts to saying that there must be genuine agreement of features between the subject and the agreement on the predicate), without the subject's case to be activated by the same process. Kornfilt & Preminger (2015) in fact propose that subject case and agreement between the subject and subject agreement marking on the local predicate are independent from each other, and that where there is realization of subject agreement on the predicate, genuine agreement with the φ-features of the subject *must* obtain. Thus, in a marriage of the proposals in this paper with the ideas in Kornfilt & Preminger (2015), it is possible to say that where there is such genuine φ-feature agreement between the subject and the predicate, the subject will indeed be activated in the terms of the present paper, and this will trigger DOM effects on the direct object.

ment morphology; is it insightful enough to posit such an abstract functional projection whose head is not overt? In addition to the question of abstractness, one might worry about a proliferation of functional projections: Do we need an additional functional projection in the verbal domain, given that we also have *v*P?

The answers to such questions depend on the aim of the enterprise: if unification is valued highly enough, then the cost of these details should be worthwhile. We saw, even if briefly, that the other unified account of structural Case licensing, i.e. the one proposed by L&P (2015), faces criticism, as well: their treatment of subject Cases is not completely parallel to their treatment of accusative and structural dative (in which they follow B&V 2010): the licensing of those object Cases is not only configurational, but it also is based on competition, while subject Case is not. Furthermore, the fact that subject Cases go hand-in-hand with subject agreement is not fully captured; moreover, we said that the configurational account given for subject Cases can be viewed as a version of the "traditional" account of subject Cases, whereby those Cases are licensed by functional category heads.

As a matter of fact, the authors of L&P (2015) state themselves that the empirical gains of their paper are modest, and that their account was proposed as a possibly better alternative to a hybrid approach to structural Case, rather than as the only solution to the quandary. In a sense, L&P (2015) is an exercise in attempting to extend a configurational account to structural Case, which is rather intuitive for accusative and dative, to the subject Cases of nominative and genitive, where such an account is much less intuitive, or not intuitive at all. My purpose here has been to attempt a similar extension, but coming from a different direction: To extend an intuitive account of structural subject Cases, based on functional categories as licensers, to structural non-subject Cases, where the account may be less intuitive. In order to do so, I have allowed a measure of configurationality, too, with respect to the licensing agreement elements. I leave an evaluation of these two accounts, both aiming at unification, to future work, as well as to the readers.[33]

---

[33] One of the anonymous reviewers states that it is true that all cases are assigned in the same way, by functional heads, on my view; however, s/he also remarks that "there is still a difference, one step further back: some functional heads are self-starters that don't need any activation (like T) whereas others do need to be activated (like *v*). What is the status of that difference, and why does it exist? Does that detract from the claim that this is a unified theory in the strongest sense?" This is a very wide-ranging question, and one with probably more than one answer. For the time being, I will only point out that we did see in this paper (Section 3.2.2) that not all instances of T are "self-starters"; defective, mixed-category Ts (in the sense of Kornfilt & Whitman 2011) are not, and need activation by a c-commanding, higher functional category, as well.

Acknowledgements

This is an expanded, more detailed version of my presentation at the "non-workshop" on Differential Case Marking, held at the SLE in Leiden, in September 2015. I thank the organizers, András Bárány and Jenneke van der Wal, for a very thought-provoking and enjoyable workshop, and the audience for challenging questions and comments. I am further indebted to András Bárány and to Laura Kalin for contentful comments beyond those of two anonymous reviewers to whom I am very grateful for their detailed and thorough reports and suggestions during the first round of reviews, as well as to a third anonymous reviewer for his or her comments during the second round of reviews. I am further indebted to Omer Preminger for enlightening discussions about some of the issues addressed in this paper. Mistakes and misconceptions are my responsibility.

References

Alexiadou, Artemis & Elena Anagnostopoulou. 2001. The subject-in-situ generalization and the role of case in driving computations. *Linguistic Inquiry* 32(2). 193–231. https://doi.org/10.1162/00243890152001753.

Alexiadou, Artemis & Elena Anagnostopoulou. 2007. The subject-in-situ generalization revisited. In Uli Sauerland & Hans-Martin Gärtner (eds.), *Interfaces + Recursion = Language?*, 31–60. Berlin: De Gruyter. https://doi.org/10.1515/9783110207552.31.

Aydemir, Yasemin. 2004. Are Turkish preverbal bare nouns syntactic arguments? *Linguistic Inquiry* 35(3). 465–474. https://doi.org/10.1162/0024389041402607.

Baker, Mark C. & Nadya Vinokurova. 2010. Two modalities of case assignment. *Natural Language & Linguistic Theory* 28(3). 593–642. https://doi.org/10.1007/s11049-010-9105-1.

Bárány, András & Michelle Sheehan. 2019. When dependent case is not enough. Paper presented at GLOW 42, University of Oslo.

Borsley, Robert D. & Jaklin Kornfilt. 2000. Mixed extended projections. In Robert D. Borsley (ed.), *The nature and function of syntactic categories*, vol. 32 (Syntax and Semantics), 101–131. New York: Academic Press.

Bošković, Zeljko & Serkan Şener. 2014. The Turkish NP. In Patricia Cabredo Hofherr & Anne Zribi-Hertz (eds.), *Crosslinguistic studies on noun phrase structure and reference*, 102–140. Leiden: Brill. https://doi.org/10.1163/9789004261440_006.

Cagri, Ilhan M. 2009. Arguing against subject incorporation in Turkish relative clauses. *Lingua* 119(2). 359–373. https://doi.org/10.1016/j.lingua.2007.10.019.

Caha, Pavel. 2009. *The nanosyntax of case*. University of Tromsø dissertation.

Chomsky, Noam. 1981. *Lectures on government and binding*. Dordrecht: Foris.

Chomsky, Noam. 1995. *The minimalist program*. Cambridge, MA: MIT Press.

Chomsky, Noam & Howard Lasnik. 1993. The theory of principles and parameters. In Joachim Jacobs, Arnim von Stechow, Wolfgang Sternefeld & Theo Vennemann (eds.), *Syntax: An international handbook of contemporary research*, 506–569. Berlin: De Gruyter. https://doi.org/10.1515/9783110095869.1.

Dede, Müşerref. 1981. Grammatical relations and surface cases in Turkish. *Proceedings of the Annual Meeting of the Berkeley Linguistics Society* 7. 40–49. https://doi.org/10.3765/bls.v7i0.2076.

Dede, Müşerref. 1986. Definiteness and referentiality in Turkish verbal sentences. In Dan I. Slobin & Karl Zimmer (eds.), *Studies in Turkish linguistics*, 147–163. Amsterdam: John Benjamins.

Diesing, Molly. 1992. *Indefinites*. Cambridge, MA: MIT Press.

Enç, Mürvet. 1991. The semantics of specificity. *Linguistic Inquiry* 22(1). 1–25.

George, Leland M. & Jaklin Kornfilt. 1981. Finiteness and boundedness in Turkish. In Frank Heny (ed.), *Binding and filtering*, 105–128. Cambridge, MA: MIT Press.

von Heusinger, Klaus & Jaklin Kornfilt. 2005. The case of the direct object in Turkish: Semantics, syntax and morphology. *Turkic Languages* 9. 3–44.

Kennelly, Sarah. 1997. Nonspecific external arguments in Turkish. *Dilbilim Araştırmaları Dergisi* 8. 58–75.

Keskin, Cem. 2009. *Subject agreement-dependency of accusative case in Turkish, or jump-starting grammatical machinery*. Utrecht: LOT.

Kiparsky, Paul. 1983. "Elsewhere" in phonology. In Stephen Anderson & Paul Kiparsky (eds.), *A Festschrift for Morris Halle*, 93–106. New York: Holt, Rinehart & Winston.

Kornfilt, Jaklin. 1977. A note on subject raising in Turkish. *Linguistic Inquiry* 8(4). 736–742.

Kornfilt, Jaklin. 1984. *Case marking, agreement, and empty categories in Turkish*. Harvard University dissertation.

Kornfilt, Jaklin. 1991. Some current issues in Turkish syntax. In Hendrik Boeschoten & Ludo Verhoeven (eds.), *Turkish linguistics today*, 60–92. Leiden: Brill.

Kornfilt, Jaklin. 1994. Some remarks on the interaction of case and word order in Turkish: Implications for acquisition. In Barbara Lust, Margarita Suñer & John Whitman (eds.), *Syntactic theory and first language acquisition: Cross-linguistic perspectives*, vol. 1: Heads, projections, and learnability, 171–199. Hillsdale, NJ: Lawrence Erlbaum.

Kornfilt, Jaklin. 1997. *Turkish*. New York: Routledge.

Kornfilt, Jaklin. 2003a. Scrambling, subscrambling, and case in Turkish. In Simin Karimi (ed.), *Word order and scrambling*, 125–155. Malden, MA: Blackwell. https://doi.org/10.1002/9780470758403.ch6.

Kornfilt, Jaklin. 2003b. Subject case in Turkish nominalized clauses. In Uwe Junghanns & Luka Szucsich (eds.), *Syntactic structures and morphological information*, 129–216. Berlin: De Gruyter. https://doi.org/10.1515/9783110904758.129.

Kornfilt, Jaklin. 2007. Review of Balkız Öztürk: *Case, referentiality and phrase structure. Journal of Linguistics* 43(3). 736–742. https://doi.org/10.1017/s0022226707004859.

Kornfilt, Jaklin. 2008. DOM and two types of DSM in Turkish. In Helen de Hoop & Peter de Swart (eds.), *Differential subject marking* (Studies in Natural Language & Linguistic Theory), 79–111. Dordrecht: Springer. https://doi.org/10.1007/978-1-4020-6497-5.

Kornfilt, Jaklin. 2018a. Adjacency and (apparent) lack thereof in Turkish DOM. In Laura Kalin, Ileana Paul & Jozina Vander Klok (eds.), *Heading in the right direction: Treats for Lisa Travis*, vol. 25 (McGill Working Papers in Linguistics), 232–238. Montreal: McGill University.

Kornfilt, Jaklin. 2018b. Sounds are not equal, but nor is all silence. In Huba Bartos, Marcel den Dikken, Zoltán Bánréti & Tamás Váradi (eds.), *Boundaries crossed: At the interfaces of mor-*

phosyntax, phonology, pragmatics and semantics, 299–317. Dordrecht: Springer. https://doi.org/10.1017/978-3-319-90710-9_19.

Kornfilt, Jaklin & Omer Preminger. 2015. Nominative as *no-case-at-all*: An argument from raising-to-accusative in Sakha. In Andrew Joseph & Esra Predolac (eds.), *Proceedings of the 9th Workshop on Altaic Formal Linguistics (WAFL 9)*, vol. 76 (MIT Working Papers in Linguistics), 109–120.

Kornfilt, Jaklin & John Whitman. 2011. Afterword: Nominalizations in linguistic theory. *Lingua* 121(7). 1297–1313. https://doi.org/10.1016/j.lingua.2011.01.008.

Kornfilt, Jaklin & John Whitman. 2012. Genitive subjects in TP nominalizations. In Gianina Iordăchioaia (ed.), *Proceedings of JeNom 4: 4èmes journées d'étude sur les nominalisations — The 4th workshop on nominalizations*, 39–72. Stuttgart: Online Publikationsverbund der Universität Stuttgart.

Levin, Theodore & Omer Preminger. 2015. Case in Sakha: Are two modalities really necessary? *Natural Language & Linguistic Theory* 33. 231–250. https://doi.org/10.1007/s11049-014-9250-z.

Lewis, Geoffrey. 1967. *Turkish grammar*. Oxford: Oxford University Press.

Manzini, M. Rita & Ludovico Franco. 2016. Goal and DOM datives. *Natural Language & Linguistic Theory* 34(1). 197–240. https://doi.org/10.1007/s11049-015-9303-y.

Marantz, Alec. 1991. Case and licensing. In *ESCOL '91: Proceedings of the eighth Eastern states conference on linguistics*, 234–253. Ohio State University.

Moore, John. 1998. Turkish copy-raising and A-chain locality. *Natural Language & Linguistic Theory* 16(1). 149–189. https://doi.org/10.1023/a:1005911609491.

Öztürk, Balkız. 2005. *Case, referentiality and phrase structure*. Amsterdam: John Benjamins. https://doi.org/10.1075/la.77.

Öztürk, Balkız. 2009. Incorporating agents. *Lingua* 119(2). 334–358. https://doi.org/10.1016/j.lingua.2007.10.018.

Sezer, Engin. 1991. *Issues in Turkish syntax*. Harvard University dissertation.

Slobin, Dan I. & Thomas G. Bever. 1982. Children use canonical sentence schemas: A crosslinguistic study of word order and inflections. *Cognition* 12(3). 229–265. https://doi.org/10.1016/0010-0277(82)90033-6.

Starke, Michal. 2005. Naonsyntax class lectures. Spring 2005, University of Tromsø.

Underhill, Robert. 1976. *Turkish grammar*. Cambridge, MA: MIT Press.

Zidani-Eroğlu, Leyla. 1997. Exceptionally case-marked NPs as matrix objects. *Linguistic Inquiry* 28(2). 219–230.

Vassilios Spyropoulos
Abstract and morphological case in a nominative–accusative system with differential case marking

The case of Asia Minor Greek

Abstract: This paper addresses the issue of the relationship holding between abstract and morphological case by examining differential case marking in Asia Minor Greek. Asia Minor Greek dialects have nominative–accusative case systems with overt case exponents; significantly, in these dialects definiteness affects the case marking of the argument either by forcing it to appear in a default case or by marking the relevant definiteness specification by means of a certain (morphologically overt) case. I argue that these phenomena do not derive from functional factors, such as the typicality of subject/object, distinctiveness or iconicity, and I present evidence that the relevant abstract Case is always licensed on DP-arguments in these dialects, even in differential case marking situations, and that the surface morphological case is conditioned by morphological factors. Based on this evidence, I claim that differential case marking in such systems is morphological in nature and derives from postsyntactic impoverishment rules at Morphological Structure that affect the feature constitution of the case terminal node resulting in its differentiating exponence and the non-isomorphism between abstract and morphological case.

Keywords: differential object marking, differential subject marking, Greek, morphological case, abstract Case

1 Introduction

Differential case marking phenomena have drawn the attention of research through different perspectives, because they raise significant questions regarding the status of case and the licensing of arguments. While *differential object marking* is mostly documented by means of languages with a nominative–accusative case system, *differential subject marking* is usually associated with languages with an ergative–absolutive case system.

Vassilios Spyropoulos, National and Kapodistrian University of Athens

https://doi.org/10.1515/9783110666137-005

Another interesting aspect of the phenomenon is that it usually refers to situations where there is an alternation between presence and absence of case marking, in the sense that the differentiated subject/object is somehow deprived of its expected case marking. In this paper, I document two instances of *differential case marking* with some intriguing properties from Asia Minor Greek. Asia Minor Greek is a branch of Greek which consists of a group of dialects and stray varieties, including Pontic, Cappadocian, Pharasiot, Livisiot, Silliot, which were spoken by the Greek-speaking population of the Asia Minor peninsula, nowadays Turkey, until the population exchange that took place after the Greek–Turkish war in the 1920s (Dawkins 1910, 1916). In some of these dialects, in certain environments the subject/object appears in a case different from that imposed by its syntactic function. Thus, in Pontic Greek,[1] when the DP-subject is definite, the N-head appears in the accusative form instead of the expected nominative (differential subject marking):

(1) Differential subject marking in Pontic Greek

   a. *erθen   enas kaloyero-s*
      come.PST.3SG a   monk(M)-SG.NOM
      'A monk came'

   b. *epiyen   o   kaloyero-n*   (instead of kaloyeros)
      go.PST.3SG the(M) monk(M)-SG.ACC
      'The monk went'

Similarly, in Cappadocian Greek,[2] when the object is indefinite, it appears in the nominative form, instead of the expected accusative (differential object marking):

---

[1] Pontic Greek is an Asia Minor Greek dialect, which was originally spoken in the areas at the north coast of Asia Minor. In its original form it was a dialectal group consisting of various subdialects and varieties (Oeconomides 1908, 1958, Papadopoulos 1953, 1955, Dawkins 1931, 1937, Tombaidis 1988, 1996, Drettas 1997). It is now spoken (a) in Greece, by the descendants of the exchanged population mostly in the form of Pontic Greek Koine (see Tombaidis 1992, 1996, Chadzisavidis 1995 on this development), (b) in Russia, Ukraine, Georgia and other post Soviet Union countries (although most of these speakers have now moved to Greece; Pappou-Zouravliova 2001; see also Topcharas 1998 [1932], Semenov 1934 and Dawkins 1937 for Pontic in Soviet Union), and (c) in certain enclaves in north-east Turkey (e.g. Tonya, Sürmene and the Çaykara provinces) mainly in the form of Ophis Pontic Greek (Mackridge 1987, 1995, 1999, Asan 1996, Revithiadou & Spyropoulos 2012, Sitaridou 2013, 2016, etc.). The Pontic Greek data in the paper have been collected by the author from native speakers of the dialect from Greece by means of elicitation targeting the relevant structures.

[2] Cappadocian Greek was an Asia Minor Greek dialectal group spoken by the indigenous Greek-speaking population in the Cappadocian plateau in central Turkey (Dawkins 1910, 1916). It

(2) Differential object marking in Cappadocian Greek (Axos; Dawkins 1916: 396, 402)

    a. *ama* *traniʒne* *to* *liko*
       when see.3PL the wolf.SG.ACC
       'as soon as they see the wolf'

    b. *ivren*   *ena* *liko-s*   (instead of *liko*)
       find.PST.3SG a wolf-SG.NOM
       'He found a wolf'

Pontic Greek and Cappadocian Greek, as Greek in general, have a nominative–accusative case system and in both dialects the nominative may be expressed by means of a specialized overt suffix, while the accusative in the singular seems to be morphologically under- or un-specified.[3] The *Differential Case Marking* phenomena in these dialects may not involve a retreat to zero case exponence, since in Pontic Greek the alternation is between two overt case forms: /-s/ for nominative, /-n/ for accusative, whereas in Cappadocian Greek it is the differentiating case form that has the overt exponent (that is, the nominative instead of the accusative). In addition, these phenomena are subject to certain morphological and lexical restrictions, since they appear only in the singular and with a certain class of nouns.

In this paper, I examine the properties of these phenomena and I argue that they do not derive from functional factors such as the typicality of subject/object, distinctiveness or iconicity. Instead, I suggest that they are morphological in nature and they derive from postsyntactic impoverishment rules at *Morphological Structure* (MS), which affect the constitution of the case node of the N-head and determine its exponence. These rules are triggered by the [+definite] specification of the D head of the relevant DP-argument. Such impoverishment rules affect parts of the case node and not the case node as a whole, so that alternation between different case forms is derived. My analysis is couched within the *feature*

---

included various subdialects and varieties, such as Delmesos, Potamia, Misti, Axos, Phloita, Malakopi, Fertek, Ulaghatsh, Semendere, etc. It exhibited severe interference at all grammatical levels from Turkish, due to the long-term contact with it (Dawkins 1910, 1916, Janse 2002, 2009a; see also Thomason & Kaufman 1988, Johanson 2002). It is now considered extinct (but see Janse 2009b, 2016, Vassalou & Janse 2016, Papazachariou 2016 on the survival and resurrection of the dialect in villages in Central and Northern Greece).

3 Abstracting away from the relevant details, for which see sections 3.1 and 4 below, accusative forms in the singular either have no overt morphological marking (unspecified) or involve the morphological exponent /-n/ (underspecified), which can also be found in the singular nominative form of certain other nouns (e.g. neuters).

decomposition of case hypothesis (Calabrese 1996, 2008, Halle 1997, Halle & Vaux 1998, McFadden 2004, Alexiadou & Müller 2008) as formulated within the *Distributed Morphology* framework (Halle & Marantz 1993, 1994; see Harley & Noyer 2003 and Embick & Noyer 2007, Siddiqi 2010 for overviews), which allows for postsyntactic morphological operations and morphophonological exponence to refer to (sub)properties of the case node and not the case itself. Then, I put forward the hypothesis that these phenomena are instantiations of a generalized *differential argument (case-)marking* situation in Asia Minor Greek. Finally, I speculate an extension of the proposed analysis to Turkish and suggest that Turkish differential subject and object marking are also morphological in nature and derive from postsyntactic impoverishment rules.

2 Some background: Differential argument marking for case

Differential argument marking (DAM) is a descriptive term, which covers differential subject marking (DSM) and differential object marking (DOM) phenomena and refers to situations where the subjects/objects in a language are differentiated in certain ways. These ways may include case marking on the subject/object, agreement marking on the predicate, inverse systems or even voice alternations (see Bossong 1985, Comrie 1989, Woolford 2001, 2008, Aissen 2003, de Hoop & de Swart 2008b, de Hoop & Malchukov 2007, 2008, Malchukov & de Swart 2009 and Witzlack-Makarevich & Seržant 2018 for descriptions and overviews of DAM phenomena). This paper deals with DAM in terms of case, i.e. with differential case marking (DCM). DCM refers to situations where, depending on various factors, the subject/object appears in a different case from the expected one. There are various approaches to these phenomena, which focus on different factors that may regulate the case properties of the subject/object cross-linguistically, deriving thus some very interesting typologies.

One approach takes DCM to be functionally motivated and be regulated by the properties of the 'typical' subject/object (Comrie 1989, Aissen 2003). A typical subject/object is expected not to have case (exponents), whereas a non-typical subject/object is expected to have the relevant case (exponent), so that it is differentiated from the corresponding object/subject. Typicality is defined in terms of different scales/hierarchies, usually for animacy and definiteness:

(3) Hale/Silverstein Hierarchies (Hale 1972, Silverstein 1976)

a. *Grammatical Function Hierarchy*
Subject > Object

b. *Person/Animacy Hierarchy*
1PL > 1SG > 2PL > 2SG > 3.HUMAN.SG > 3.ANIMATE.PL > 3.ANIMATE.SG > 3.INANIMATE.SG > 3.INANIMATE.PL

c. *Definiteness Hierarchy*
Pronoun > Proper Name > Definite > Indefinite Specific > NonSpecific

Typical subjects refer to the higher members of such hierarchies, whereas objects to the lower ones. Aissen (2003) has formulated this observation by using the notion of the *Harmonic Alignment* of hierarchies/scales (Prince & Smolensky 2004), so that, referring to the hierarchy of definiteness, a pronominal subject is a highly typical subject, whereas a non-specific subject is a non-typical subject, and, vice versa, a non-specific object is a highly typical object, whereas a definite object is a non-typical object:

(4) Aissen's Harmonic Alignment for Grammatical Function and Definiteness

a. Subject/Pronoun ≻ Subject/Proper Name ≻ Subject/Definite ≻ Subject/Indefinite Specific ≻ Subject/NonSpecific

b. Object/NonSpecific ≻ Object/Indefinite Specific ≻ Object/Definite ≻ Object/Proper Name ≻ Object/Pronoun

Typical subjects/objects are expected not to have case (exponents). Take a look at the following DOM examples from Turkish[4] and Hindi:

(5) Turkish (Kornfilt 1997, 2008)

a. *Zeynep adam-ı gör-dü*
Zeynep man-ACC see-PST
'Zeynep saw the man'

---

[4] Turkish DOM is commonly referred to in the literature as a prototypical example of DOM regulated by the functional typicality of the object. However, Turkish also exhibits DSM (Kornfilt 1997, 2008, this volume), which patterns in the completely opposite way, i.e. it is the typical subject (specific) that carries the case, whereas the non-typical one (non-specific) has no case marking. See below and Section 7 on the identificational nature of Turkish DCM in its totality.

b. *Zeynep bir adam gör-dü*
   Zeynep a man see-PST
   'Zeynep saw a man'

c. *Zeynep bir adam-ı gör-dü*
   Zeynep a man-ACC see-PST
   'Zeynep saw a certain man'

(6) Hindi (de Hoop & Narasimhan 2008: 64)
raam=ne patthar=ko / patthar toD/-aa
Raam=ERG stone=ACC stone break-PFV.SG.M
'Raam broke the / a stone'

In the examples above the specific/definite object carries the relevant accusative case marker, whereas a non-specific/indefinite object appears in its bare form without a case marker. The DOM situation is regulated by specificity/definiteness, so that the non-typical object, i.e. the specific/definite one, carries case marking, whereas the typical object, i.e. the non-specific/indefinite one, has no case marking. Such an approach also facilitates the functional notions of distinctiveness and iconicity. Thus, a non-typical object (the specific/definite one in the examples above) carries case marking, so that it is distinguished from subjects and vice versa (distinctiveness). Similarly, case marking is an iconic way to encode functional markedness, as this is expressed by means of the position of the subject/object in the relevant hierarchy. Thus, a non-typical object, e.g. the specific/definite one in the examples above, is a marked object and thus it is expected to be also morphologically marked, in the sense that it is the one that has case exponents (iconicity).

De Hoop & de Swart (2008a) point out that a functional approach to DCM based on the typicality of subjects/objects cannot account for the whole range of facts and, thus, there are other factors that may also trigger DCM. In particular, the typicality of subject/object approach to DCM predicts that DSM is the mirror image of DOM, a prediction that is empirically falsified on many occasions. For example, Turkish also exhibits DSM in nominalised complement clauses: the subject of these clauses carries genitive case marking when it is specific and has no case exponent when it is non-specific:

(7) DSM in Turkish (Kornfilt 1997, 2008, this volume)

    a. *arı-nın çocuğ-u sok-tuğ-un-u duy-du-m*
       bee-GEN child-ACC sting-FN-3SG-ACC hear-PST-1SG
       'I heard that the bee stung the child'

    b. *çocuğ-u arı sok-tuğ-un-u duy-du-m*
       child-ACC bee sting-FN-3SG-ACC hear-PST-1SG
       'I heard that bees stung the child'

    c. *çocuğ-u bir arı sok-tuğ-un-u duy-du-m*
       child-ACC a bee sting-FN-3SG-ACC listen-PST-1SG
       'I heard that a bee stung the child'

    d. *çocuğ-u bir arı-nın sok-tuğ-un-u duy-du-m*
       child-ACC a bee-GEN sting-FN-3SG-ACC listen-PST-1SG
       'I heard that a (certain) bee stung the child'

In these examples, in contrast to what it is predicted by Aissen's approach, it is the typical subject in terms of specificity (i.e. the specific) that is case marked, violating both distinctiveness and iconicity. In fact such examples show that case marking may be associated with a certain property of the subject/object (definiteness/specificity, animacy, agentivity, volitionality); the subject/object that carries this property is overtly case marked, in order to be differentiated from a corresponding subject/object that does not carry this property. Such situations reveal a different type of DCM, which is identificational in nature, in the sense that a case marked subject/object is identified as carrying a certain property (de Hoop & Narasimhan 2005, 2008 on Hindi; Kornfilt 2008 on Turkish).

The case properties of a subject/object may also be regulated by clausal features, such as tense, aspect, mood or even the clause type itself (Kornfilt 2008). For example, in Hindi, a subject liable to ergative case marking may not carry the ergative case exponent when the verb is in the imperfective aspect:

(8) Hindi (de Hoop & Narasimhan 2008: 64)

    a. *raam=ne patthar=ko / patthar toD/-aa*
       Raam=ERG stone=ACC stone break-PFV.SG.M
       'Raam broke the / a stone'

    b. *raam patthar=ko / patthar toD/-taa hae*
       Raam stone=ACC stone break-IPFV.SG.M be.PRS.3SG
       'Raam is breaking the / a stone'

In addition, it has been argued that DCM may also be the result of morphological conditions, such as well-formedness conditions on morphological structure and exponence, restrictions on marked combination of features, etc., or even derive from the syntactic structure itself and/or from syntactic operations and principles that regulate case assignment (Woolford 2008, Kornfilt 2008). Such conditions may block or force case marking on the subject/object, resulting thus in DCM situations.

As obvious from the examples discussed above, differentiation is normally obtained by means of an alternation between overt case exponent and absence of case exponent and, in fact, most approaches to DCM, either explicitly or implicitly, assume that DCM results in absence of case assignment altogether and that the differentiated subject/object with no case exponent has not been assigned case at all. However, Keine & Müller (2008, 2011) and Müller (this volume) show that this is not correct. They explore DCM instances that involve an alternation between different overt case exponents and they observe that differentiation on such occasions involves a retreat to a less specified form. They propose that DCM derives from impoverishment, an operation that deprives the subject/object from certain case properties and results in marking by a less specific morphological exponent, including zero.

Another observation found in the literature is that DSM is cross-linguistically less consistent than DOM (Woolford 2001, de Hoop & Malchukov 2007, de Hoop & de Swart 2008b, Malchukov & de Swart 2009) and it is mainly attested in and documented by ergative languages, where the subject carries overt ergative case morphology, a marked and specific case form.[5] DSM is hardly found in nominative–accusative languages and more specifically in the nominative – accusative case alternation axis, because the case of the subject, i.e. the nominative, is usually manifested by a less specific case form or it is not overtly marked at all; thus, it cannot impoverish further so as to derive a differentiated less specific form. If this line of reasoning is on the right track, then DSM can only be found in nominative – accusative systems in which the nominative is morphologically the more specific form (marked nominative systems; König 2008, 2009).

In the following sections I examine two DCM situations in a nominative – accusative case system that seem not to be directly associated with functional markedness/typicality, but they derive from formal considerations of the syntax-

---

[5] Markedness and specificity are not used here with their functional denotation but strictly in their formal content, i.e. a marked form for case is a form that carries specific overt morphological manifestation for case and a specific (case) form is a form that has a very narrow distribution in the sense that it is used only in a certain (case) environment and it carries specialized (case) exponents, i.e. exponents specified for the relevant grammatical information.

morphology interface. It will be shown that DCM in such cases does not affect the abstract case assigned to the subject/object due to its grammatical function, but it is rather a postsyntactic morphological phenomenon, which concerns the morphophonological manifestation of the relevant case node and it is subject to morphological and lexical restrictions.

3 DSM in Pontic Greek

Pontic Greek has a nominative–accusative case system, according to which all DP-subjects are marked with nominative case irrespective of the type of the predicate (transitive, unaccusative, unergative) and the theta-role they realize and, accordingly, objects are marked with accusative case.[6] However, in certain varieties (e.g. Kerasunda, Kotiora, Trapezunda, Ophis, Surmena, Chaldia), when the DP-subject is definite, its N-head appears in the accusative case form; otherwise, i.e. in indefinite DP-subjects with an indefinite article or in bare generic subjects, the N-head appears in the nominative case:

(9) a. *epiyen   o   kaloyero-n*
       go.PST.3SG the(M)   monk(M)-SG.ACC
       'The monk went'

   b. *erθen   enas kaloyero-s*
       come.PST.3SG   a   monk(M)-SG.NOM
       'A monk came ...'

   c. *o   aðelfo-n   entoken   aton*
       the(M) brother(M)-SG.ACC   hit.PST.3SG CL.3SG.M.ACC
       'The brother hit him ...'

   d. *enas rðako-s   eskotosen   aton*
       a   dragon(M)-SG.NOM   kill.PST.3SG CL.3SG.M.ACC
       'A dragon killed him...'

---

[6] Pontic Greek is in this way similar to Standard Modern Greek except from the fact that in Standard Modern Greek indirect objects are marked with the genitive case or expressed by means of a prepositional phrase. See Holton et al. (2012) on Greek in general and Papadopoulos (1955), Tombaidis (1988), Drettas (1997) on Pontic Greek.

This alternation in the case form of the nominal head has been identified and discussed in the literature on Greek dialects as a prominent feature of the Pontic dialect and it has been attributed to the presence of the definite article and the function of the DP as a subject (Hatzidakis 1892, 1934 [1911/1912], Thumb 1910, Dawkins 1916, 1937, Oeconomides 1908, 1958, Papadopoulos 1955, Tombaidis 1964, 1980, 1988). More specifically, it was noticed that the shift from nominative to accusative occurs in the presence of the definite article, which is the definiteness marker in Greek, only when the relevant DP is a subject and not when it functions as a predicate or a predicative modifier of another DP-subject, on which occasion it maintains its nominative form (see below). However, as Koutita-Kaimaki (1977–1978) has pointed out, the definite article in Pontic Greek may be deleted, due to either phonological reasons or interference from Turkish (Papadopoulos 1955, Oeconomides 1958, Tombaidis 1964, Karatsareas 2013), creating environments in which the shift from nominative to accusative occurs in definite DP-subjects without the (phonological) presence of the definite article.[7] Based on these facts and on the variation in the occurence of the phenomenon in the various Pontic varieties (see Section 6), Koutita-Kaimaki (1977–1978) suggests that this case shift should be attributed to a more general historical development according to which the accusative form is gradually taking over the nominative form in the case system of Pontic and of Asia Minor Greek in general. On the other hand, Henrich (1976) attributes this case shift to the conflation of the old inflectional paradigms of the nouns ending in *-os* and those ending in *-on*. All this literature on the phenomenon is mainly descriptive and historical in nature,[8] and although it offers a detailed description of the facts, it fails at identifying the underlying conditions that regulate its main characteristics, namely (a) the role of definiteness and not of the definite article itself as the trigger of the phenomenon and (b) the spread of the accusative case form due to its under/unspecified morphological status.

By relating this shift in case with definiteness, it looks like we are dealing here with an identificational DSM situation associated with definiteness. That is, the accusative case is associated with definiteness, so that a definite DP-subject is not marked with the 'normal' nominative case, but with the accusative. Notice that such a phenomenon does not facilitate the functional notion of distinctiveness, as this was presented in Section 2, because it is the typical subject in terms of definiteness which is differentiated in a way that it ends up being marked with

---

[7] Thanks to an anonymous reviewer for bringing this detail to my attention. In what follows, I will use examples with overt definite articles, so that the definiteness restriction on the distribution of the phenomenon will be clear.
[8] But see Tombaidis (1980, 1988) for an attempt to provide a synchronic description of the facts by means of distribution rules in a structuralist fashion.

the accusative case, which is the case of the object. Distinctiveness would predict the opposite, i.e. that the typical subject will not be differentiated and remain in its 'normal' case, so that it becomes distinct from the object. In other words, since a definite subject is a typical subject, it need not change its case (i.e. nominative) in order to be differentiated from objects and, crucially, it should not change it to a case (i.e. accusative) that is typical for marking objects.[9]

Coming back to the phenomenon itself, there are some very intriguing details. First it does not apply across the board, in the sense that it is restricted only in the singular of a specific class of nouns, namely masculine nouns ending in -*os*;[10] thus, in the following examples, in which the N-head is a masculine noun ending in -*is* / -*as* (10) or a feminine noun ending in -*i* / -*a* (11), DSM does not occur and the N-head appears in the nominative and not in the accusative:

(10) a. *epiɣen   o   ðespoti-s   / *ðespoti-n*
        go.PST.3SG the(M) bishop(M)-SG.NOM   bishop(M)-SG.ACC
        'The bishop went'

   b. *erθen   enas ðespoti-s*
        come.PST.3SG   a   bishop(M)-SG.NOM
        'A bishop came'

---

[9] An anonymous reviewer suggests that the facts can be viewed in a different way so that they comply with distinctiveness: If the accusative form is the unmarked form, then its appearance in definite subjects is expected, because the definite subject is a typical subject and its subjecthood is evident from the definite article, which identifies its function and differentiates it from the object. Thus, no case marking is necessary for identifying the subject and the latter appears in the unmarked form, i.e. the accusative form. However, such an analysis predicts that in definite objects, i.e. non-typical objects, case marking would be necessary and the N-head should not appear in the unmarked accusative form but rather in the marked nominative form so that the definite object is differentiated from the (definite) subject. This prediction is falsified, since all objects in Pontic Greek appear in the accusative irrespectively of definiteness (see below). In addition, as it was mentioned above, the definite article may be omitted, resulting in situations with subjects in the accusative form and without a definite article. Given that accusative objects without an article are also possible in the language, one can easily find examples in which both the subject and the object appear in the accusative case and with no article. In such examples no differentiation is possible by means of the article.

[10] This ending is segmented as involving the SG.NOM suffix /-s/ and the vowel /-o/, which is a theme vowel occurring between the root/stem and the number.case suffix in the singular. Other theme vowels, defining different inflectional classes, are /-a/, /-i/, /-e/ etc. See Revithiadou & Spyropoulos (2016) and Revithiadou et al. (2017) for the role and the function of theme vowels/elements in the nominal morphological structure of Standard and Asia Minor Greek.

    c. *o   vasilea-s   /*vasilea-n   entoken   aton*
       the(M) king(M)-SG.NOM   king(M)-SG.ACC hit.PST.3SG CL.3SG.M.ACC
       'The king hit him ...'

    d. *enas vasilea-s   eskotosen   aton*
       a   king(M)-SG.NOM kill.PST.3SG CL.3SG.M.ACC
       'A king killed him ...'

(11) a. *epiyen   i   kari-Ø   /*kari-n*
        go.PST.3SG the.F woman(F)-SG.NOM   woman(F)-SG.ACC
        'The woman went'

    b. *erθen   enas kari-Ø*
       come.PST.3SG a   woman(F)-SG.NOM
       'A woman came'

    c. *i   yineka-Ø   / *yineka-n   entoken*
       the.F woman(F)-SG.NOM   woman(F)-SG.ACC   hit.PST.3SG
       aton
       CL.3SG.M.ACC
       'The woman hit him ...'

    d. *enas yineka-Ø   eskotosen   aton*
       a   woman(F)-SG.NOM kill.PST.3SG CL.3SG.M.ACC
       'A woman killed him ...'

Second, Pontic Greek DSM applies only in definite DPs that contain an N-head, and it does not apply on personal pronouns and deictic pronouns and determiners, which are by definition definite and higher in the hierarchy than definite DPs:

(12) a. *epiyen   ato-s   /*ato-n*
        go-PST-3SG PRON.3SG.M.NOM   PRON.3SG.M.ACC
        'He/this one went ...'

    b. *ekino-s   /*ekino-n   eskotosen   aton*
       that-M.SG.NOM   that-M.SG.ACC kill.PST.3SG CL.3SG.M.ACC
       'That one killed him ...'

The facts above indicate that Pontic Greek DSM is not defined in terms of a 'typical' subject referring to the definiteness hierarchy, because such an approach would wrongly predict that personal pronouns would appear in the accusative, as they are higher in the definiteness hierarchy than definite DPs. As illustrated in (13), Pontic Greek DSM refers only to a subpart of the relevant hierarchy:

(13) *Definiteness hierarchy* (Hale 1972, Silverstein 1976)

Pronoun > Proper Name > Definite > Indefinite Specific > Non Specific
*DSM   DSM   DSM   *DSM   *DSM

In fact, Pontic Greek DSM is restricted to lexical heads and it does not apply in functional elements that are inherently specified as [+definite] and realize the relevant features of the D head. Thus, in the following example, the adjective that modifies the N-head in a definite DP-subject also appears in the accusative case:

(14) Pontic Greek

erθen [DP o kalon o
come.PST.3SG the(M).SG.NOM good-M.SG.ACC the(M).SG.NOM

aθropo-n]
man(M)-SG.ACC

'The good man came'

Adjectives in Pontic Greek agree in case with the N-head they modify and inflect accordingly. This may be viewed as the result of a concord process that "copies" the feature specification of nouns onto adjectives.[11] The suffixes employed to manifest the relevant grammatical specifications appear on most occasions to be the same, because nouns and adjectives choose their suffixes from a common pool of formatives. However, since adjectives also fall into various inflectional classes, an adjective may have different suffixes from the N-head it modifies, e.g. *o kalon o vasileas* 'the(M).SG.NOM good-M.SG.ACC the(M).SG.NOM king(M).SG.NOM', *o okneas o aθropon* 'the(M).SG.NOM lazy-M.SG.NOM the(M).SG.NOM king(M).SG.ACC'.[12] Interestingly, the adjective may appear in the accusative form when it belongs to the *-os* class, even if the N-head appears in the nominative form because it does not belong to the *-os* class, and vice versa, the adjective may appear in the nominative form when it does not belong to the *-os* class, although the N-head appears

---

[11] For the purposes of this paper I will take no position as to whether concord is the result of a morphological copying mechanism or of a syntactic agreement operation. See Carstens (2000), Baker (2008), Norris (2014, 2017a,b) and Wechsler & Zlatić (2003) for discussion.

[12] This is more evident in the plural, where the repertoire of suffixes is bigger and certain syncretism rules apply, resulting in varying manifestations of the same feature specification: e.g. *kak-i list-es* 'bad-M.PL.NOM thief(M)-PL.NOM'.

in the accusative form because it belongs to the *-os* class. These facts suggest that adjectives do not copy the relevant case suffix from the N-head they modify, but only its grammatical specification. This grammatical specification is then independently liable to morphological processing and manifestation in the noun and the adjective, which may result in varying surface forms.[13]

Such examples are very interesting from another point of view too. Pontic Greek displays obligatory polydefiniteness, in the sense that, whenever there is an adjective in the DP, the definite article appears both in front of the noun and the adjective. Notice that while the N-head and its adjectival modifier appear in the accusative, the definite articles appear in the nominative. Similarly, when a deictic determiner is present in a differentiated definite DP-subject, this determiner also appears in the nominative and not in the accusative:

(15) a. erθen   auto-s   o   aθropo-n
       come.PST.3SG this-M.SG.NOM   the(M).SG.NOM   man(M)-SG.ACC

   a'. *erθen   auto-n   o   aθropo-n
       come.PST.3SG this-M.SG.ACC   the(M).SG.NOM   man(M)-SG.ACC
       'This man came ...'

   b. ekino-s   o   aθropo-n   entoken
      that-M.SG.NOM   the(M).SG.NOM   man(M)-SG.ACC   hit.PST.3SG
      aton
      CL.3SG.M.ACC

   b'. *ekinon   o   aθropon   entoken
       that-M.SG.ACC   the(M).SG.NOM   man(M)-SG.ACC   hit.PST.3SG
       aton
       CL.3SG.M.ACC
       'That man hit him'

Given that Pontic Greek (like Standard Modern Greek) exhibits obligatory case concord within the DP (see above for adjectives), so that all elements in the DP are case marked with the case relevant to the grammatical function of the DP, the fact that the definite article and the deictic determiners in a differentiated DP-subject appear in the nominative and not in the accusative indicates that the whole DP-subject is case marked for nominative, even though any lexical head inside it, i.e. the N-head and its adjectival modifiers, appear in the accusative. This

---

[13] This means that the concord process takes place before DSM, so that DSM is able to independently affect the morphological shape of adjectives and nouns.

conclusion is very significant, because it shows that DSM in Pontic is not syntactic in nature, in the sense that the definite DP-subject is syntactically assigned the 'normal' nominative case and that DSM later affects the surface (morphological) case of the lexical categories but not the (abstract) case of the whole DP. This is reinforced by case agreement facts in secondary predicative structures. In Pontic Greek the nominal and adjectival predicates, as well as the predicative modifiers, always agree in case with the DP they modify.[14] When such elements modify a differentiated DP-subject, they appear in the nominative, although the N-head of the DP-subject is in the accusative:

(16) Pontic Greek

    a. *o   yjo-n   trano-s   entone*
       the(M).SG.NOM son(M)-SG.ACC big-M.SG.NOM become.PST.3SG
       'The son grew big'

    b. *auto-s   o   aθropo-n   kalo-s*
       this-M.SG.NOM the(M).SG.NOM man(M)-SG.ACC good-M.SG.NOM
       en
       be.3SG
       'This man is good'

    c. *ato-s   kalo-s   aθropo-s   en*
       PRON.3SG.M.NOM good-M.SG.NOM man(M)-SG.NOM be.3SG
       'He is a good man'

    d. *auto-s   o   ðeskalo-n   kalo-s*
       this-M.SG.NOM the(M).SG.NOM teacher(M)-SG.ACC good-M.SG.NOM
       aθropo-s   en
       man(M)-SG.NOM be-3SG
       'This teacher is a good man'

Let us summarize. Pontic DSM is triggered by definiteness but it does not abide by the definiteness hierarchy; it rather refers to the feature itself. It is a DP-internal phenomenon, in the sense that it applies only on the lexical heads of the DP and it does not affect the case properties of the whole DP. It is morphologically conditioned, since it applies only in the singular number of a certain inflectional class of masculine nouns and adjectives. Significantly, the differentiated subject is assigned the expected abstract case for subject (i.e. nominative), which, however,

---

[14] See Spyropoulos (1999, 2005) for the phenomenon in Greek in general.

surfaces in a different case form (i.e. accusative). What is more, the differentiation is not between the presence and the absence of case marking. Both nominative and accusative forms involved in the DSM situations carry suffixes for case, /-s/ for nominative and /-n/ for accusative. Thus, Pontic DSM cannot be accounted for by approaches to DSM that assume the banning of case assignment. All these facts militate against functional approaches that derive DSM by referring to markedness and the typicality of subjects in terms of a definiteness hierarchy as the factors that regulate the presence vs. absence of case. Pontic DSM does not facilitate distinctiveness, as it was explained above and it is rather identificational, in the sense that definiteness seems to be identified with accusative. However, even its identificational aspect is not absolute and it rather refers to its surface effects, because the phenomenon does not apply to all definite elements – it excludes personal pronouns and deictic determiners – and it is restricted to a certain class of masculine nouns in the singular. Moreover, if distinctiveness, markedness and identification were at play, we would expect them to similarly affect the object too, giving rise to DOM. Thus, if accusative were identified with definiteness, we would expect that indefinite objects should display the phenomenon from the opposite side and appear in the nominative. This prediction is not borne out, since Pontic Greek lacks DOM and all objects, definite and indefinite, appear in the accusative:

(17) Pontic Greek

    a. *o vasileas eskotosen ton rðako-n*
        the(M) king(M).SG.NOM kill.PST.3SG the dragon(M)-SG.ACC
        'The king killed the dragon'

    b. *o vasileas eskotosen enan rðako-n*
        the(M) king(M).SG.NOM kill.PST.3SG the dragon(M)-SG.ACC
        'The king killed a dragon'

    b'. **o vasileas eskotosen enan rðako-s*
        the(M) king(M).SG.NOM kill.PST.3SG the dragon(M)-SG.NOM
        'The king killed a dragon'

Putting these facts together, I conclude that Pontic Greek DSM is a postsyntactic morphological phenomenon, which only affects the surface manifestation of the case feature of certain lexical categories inside the DP and it is subject to morphological and lexical restrictions. In what follows I present a formal account of this phenomenon.

3.1 Pontic DSM as a morphological effect

The facts described in the previous subsection show that, syntactically speaking, DP-subjects are always assigned nominative case, but when the D head is specified as [+definite], this feature triggers DSM in all lexical elements inside the DP which are liable to it (i.e. masculine nouns/adjectives ending in -*os*). Functional elements that are inherently specified as [+definite], such as definite articles and deictic pronouns and modifiers, are not affected perhaps because they are inserted under the relevant D head in order to satisfy its requirements.[15] The N-head surfaces in an accusative form, which is also overtly marked. Crucially, the accusative form is morphologically a less specific form than the nominative in singular. Take a look at Tables 1 and 2 which illustrate Pontic Greek noun inflection (a relevant fragment of it; abstracting away from dialectal and lexical variation and heteroclisis):

Tab. 1: Pontic Greek noun inflection, masculine nouns

	MASCULINE NOUNS					
	-o CLASS		-a/e CLASS			
	+ANIMATE	−ANIMATE	+ANIMATE			−ANIMATE
SINGULAR						
NOM	ðéskal-o-s	xor-ó-s	máer-a-s	kólak-a-s	kléft-e-s	mín-a-s
GEN	ðéskal-u	xor-ú	máer-a-Ø	kólak-a-Ø	kléft-e-Ø	mín-a-Ø
ACC	ðéskal-o-n	xor-ó-n	máer-a-n	kólak-a-n	kléft-e-n	mín-a-n
PLURAL						
NOM	ðéskal-i	xor-ús	máer-i	kólak-es	kléft-i	mín-as
GEN	ðeskal-íon	xor-íon	maer-íon	kolak-íon	kleft-íon	min-íon
ACC	ðéskal-us	xor-ús	máer-us	kólak-as	kléft-us	mín-as
	'teacher'	'dance'	'cook'	'cajoler'	'thief'	'month'

---

[15] In this way Pontic DSM does not depend on the presence of the definite article, but on the [+definite] specification of the D head, which the article may manifest. Thus, the omission of the definite article, which is very common in Pontic as mentioned above, does not affect the occurrence of DSM, because the latter refers to the [+definite] feature on D itself and not on the element that may realize it. An anonymous reviewer asks what the conditions are that license the [+definite] feature of the D head in general. This is a very complicated issue, the examination of which goes beyond the scope of this paper. For the purposes of this paper, suffices it to say that [+definite] is typically expressed by the definite article, whereas [−definite] by the indefinite article. In Pontic Greek specificity is not grammatically encoded, so that specific indefinite DP-subjects are treated as indefinite DPs and they do not undergo DSM.

Tab. 2: Pontic Greek noun inflection, feminine and neuter nouns

	FEMININE NOUNS -a/i CLASS			NEUTER NOUNS			
	+ANIMATE	−ANIMATE		-o CLASS	-i CLASS	IMPARISYLLABIC	
SINGULAR							
NOM	θayatér-a-Ø	lír-a-Ø	ník-i-Ø	ksíl-o-n	peð-í-n	stóma-n	rápsim-o-n
GEN	θayatér-a-s	lír-a-s	ník-i-s	ksil-íu	peð-íu	stomat-íu	rapsim-íu
ACC	θayatér-a-n	lír-a-n	ník-i-n	ksíl-o-n	peð-í-n	stoma-n	rápsim-o-n
PLURAL							
NOM	θayatér-es	lír-as	ník-as	ksíl-a	peð-í-a	stómat-a	rapsímat-a
GEN	θayater-íon	lir-íon	nik-íon	ksil-íon	peð-íon	stomat-íon	rapsimat-íon
ACC	θayatér-es	lír-as	ník-as	ksíl-a	peð-í-a	stómat-a	raspímat-a
	'daughter'	'pound'	'victory'	'wood'	'child'	'mouth'	'sewing'

In the singular number of the masculine nouns the nominative case is expressed with the exponent /-s/, which has more specific distribution than the exponent /-n/ of the accusative. The exponent /-n/ is used to express the accusative in masculine and feminine nouns, as well as both the nominative and the accusative in neuter nouns. Since nominative and accusative are syncretic in neuter nouns and given that syncretism involves retreat to a less specific form (Frampton 2002, Harley 2008), I conclude that the exponent /-n/ is an underspecified case exponent for the singular. Thus, the nominative form, which involves the /-s/ exponent is a more marked form than the accusative one, because the exponent /-s/ of the nominative is a more specific (specified) case exponent. This means that this subsystem of Pontic Greek nominal inflection is a marked nominative system and that differentiation in terms of accusative involves a retreat to a less specified form. In contrast, in feminine nouns in the singular, the nominative form is expressed by the elsewhere zero exponent -Ø, which indicates that the nominative is the unmarked form, since /-n/ is more specified than -Ø.[16]

Given that the 'normal' abstract case (nominative) is assigned to the differentiated DP-subject, as evident from its distribution and the case agreement facts, I propose that Pontic DSM is the surface effect of certain operations that take place at the Morphological Structure (MS) after Spell-Out and regulate the insertion of case exponents in the case terminal nodes of the lexical categories. These oper-

---

[16] Notice that in contrast to the elsewhere zero exponent /-Ø/, which carries no feature specification for case, the exponent /-n/ is a case exponent which carries case feature information, even though this is not fully specified (see Section 3.2).

ations have the effect of blocking the insertion of the expected nominative exponent in favour of a less specified one (e.g. the accusative). Such an account can also explain the morphological and lexical restrictions of the phenomenon. Given that syntax is insensitive to such restrictions, they are viewed as grammatical and lexical conditioning in the blocking of the insertion of the relevant exponents.

3.2 The elements of the analysis

As mentioned above, Pontic DSM involves an alternation between two overt case forms, i.e. /-s/ for nominative and /-n/ for accusative, and in particular a retreat to a less specific form, i.e. to the /-n/ form of the accusative. I assume that retreat to a less specific form involves *impoverishment* (Bonet 1991, Noyer 1992, 1998, Halle & Marantz 1993, 1994, 2008, Halle 1997, Bobaljik 2002, 2008a, Frampton 2002, Embick & Noyer 2007, Harley 2008, Calabrese 2008 among others) and that the alternation between two overt case forms for the same grammatical function indicates that only certain properties of the case terminal node are affected and not the case node as a whole. Such facts can be accounted for by an analysis that assumes the *feature decomposition of case hypothesis* (Calabrese 1996, 2008, Halle 1997, Halle & Vaux 1998, McFadden 2004, Alexiadou & Müller 2008, among others)[17], according to which case terminal nodes are decomposed into features, and case exponents refer to these case features and not to the case terminal node as a whole. There are different formulations and proposals regarding the exact nature of these case features. For the purposes of this paper, the discussion will be limited to those that distinguish nominative and accusative from other cases and from each other. Thus, following McFadden (2004), I assume that structural nominative and accusative cases are differentiated from oblique/inherent cases by means of a feature [±oblique]; [+oblique] is assigned to the oblique arguments of verbs and to the complements of nouns.[18] Nominative and accusative cases marking the

---

[17] An idea that goes back to the European Structuralists (Hjelmslev 1935, Jakobson 1971 [1936]) and has been developed extensively in work of all sorts of frameworks since then (Bierwisch 1967, Kiparsky 1997, Wunderlich 1997, among others). See the discussion in Blake (2001, 2009) and in Corbett (2012).

[18] The exact ways of inherent case assignment to oblique arguments need not concern us here. Given the configurational approach to theta-role assignment (Hale & Keyser 1993, 2002, Marantz 1993, Baker 1997 among others), inherent case (i.e. the case that depend on a certain theta-role or is lexically specified) may be taken to be assigned to a DP by virtue of the position that DP occupies in the syntactic configuration and the relation it establishes with a certain functional (*vAPPL*) or lexical head (N) (Ura 2000, McGinnis 2001, Anagnostopoulou 2003, Pylkkänen 2008 among others).

subject and the object respectively are [−oblique] and they are assumed to be differentiated from each other by means of a case feature [±inferior]; [+inferior] is assigned to an argument in the presence of a local case competitor (McFadden 2004, Bobaljik 2008b). Thus, an argument has its case terminal node specified as [+inferior], when this argument is the lower argument in a local configuration/domain in which there is a higher argument subject to structural case assignment. The definition of the relevant case features is given in (18) and the feature constitution of the nominative and accusative terminal nodes is presented in (19):

(18) *Case features*
[±oblique]: [+oblique] is assigned to the oblique arguments of verbs and to the complements of nouns (McFadden 2004).
[±inferior]: [+inferior] is assigned to an argument in the presence of a local case competitor (McFadden 2004, Bobaljik 2008b).[19]

(19) *Case terminal nodes*
nominative: [..., −oblique, −inferior]
accusative: [..., −oblique, +inferior]

The relevant /-s/ and /-n/ exponents in Pontic Greek differ only in that /-s/ is additionally specified as [−inferior]:

(20) *The relevant exponents*
/-s/ ↔ [−plural, ..., −inferior]
/-n/ ↔ [−plural, ...,]

DSM is the result of an impoverishment rule which removes the [−inferior] feature specification from the nominative case node, so that it blocks the insertion of /-s/ and allows the insertion of the less specified exponent /-n/:

---

[19] Alternatively, the [+inferior] feature marks the dependent case(s) in a case hierarchy:

(i) Case Hierarchy (Blake 2001, Malchukov & Spencer 2009)
nominative > accusative > oblique/lexical case
nominative > ergative, accusative > genitive > dative > locative > instrumental, ablative > others

See the discussion in Marantz (1991), Grosu (1994), Bittner & Hale (1996), Vogel (2003), McFadden (2004), Bobaljik (2008b), Legate (2008). See also Baker & Vinokurova (2010) and Baker (2015) for a syntactic implementation of dependent case.

(21) *DSM-triggering impoverishment rule*
[–inferior] → ∅ / [$_{DP}$ [$_D$ +def] [$_{N/A[-o\ class]}$ –plural, –oblique, ___]]

(22) *The derivation of the differentiated subject*
MS representation after Spell-Out:
[D[+def | –pl, –obl, –inf]] [rŏak-o-[–pl, –obl, –inf]]

Impoverishment:
[D[+def | –pl, –obl, –inf]] [rŏak-o-[–pl, –obl]]
↕ ↕
o rŏak-o- n

⟶ o rŏak-o-n 'the dragon-SG.ACC'

The formulation of the impoverishment rule above accounts for the various restrictions on DSM effects by including them as grammatical/lexical conditioning in the structural description of the rule. The rule itself is a postsyntactic morphological operation on a given morphosyntactic structure. Thus, a D head with the relevant [+definite] specification is not subject to the impoverishment rule, because it solely provides the context for the application of the rule, which is in this way restricted to the lexical heads inside the DP. Lexical conditioning regarding the inflectional class and grammatical conditioning regarding the number are encoded as featural specifications within the terminal node of the N-head, which provides the appropriate environment for the application of the rule. This piece of information is incorporated in the N-node by means of the affixation of the relevant functional heads on the N-head. Thus, the structural description of the rule predicts why DSM applies only in the masculine nouns ending in *-os* and only in the singular.[20]

The formulation of the impoverishment rule also explains why Pontic Greek does not exhibit DOM as mentioned above. Given that DOM would require an alternation between a nominative and an accusative form expressing an 'accusative'

---

20 An anonymous reviewer notes that the analysis presented above does not provide an explanation for why Pontic DSM is restricted to this specific lexical class of nouns/adjectives. Synchronically speaking, this restriction seems to be an idiosyncratic property of this class of lexical items and it is not relevant to the morphosyntactic structure in which these lexical items participate. The idiosyncratic lexical status of this restriction is also evident by the fact that in certain varieties DSM had started spreading to other lexical classes of nouns (see Section 6), giving rise to variation. Such idiosyncratic lexical restrictions are formally encoded as lexical conditioning in the application of the rules that underlie the relevant phenomena. Thus, if this restriction on Pontic DSM is a lexical idiosyncrasy, it is formally accounted for by means of lexical conditioning on the postsyntactic DSM-triggering impoverishment rule.

terminal node, a DOM-triggering rule would apply in an environment that forces the insertion of the /-s/ exponent instead of the /-n/. Notice that the accusative terminal node is specified as [+inferior], whereas the exponent /-s/ is specified as [−inferior]. The exponent /-s/ is therefore incompatible with the accusative terminal node specification, because they are specified with conflicting values for the [inferior] feature. Furthermore, no rule can provide the appropriate environment for its insertion. Impoverishment could not save the situation, because removing the conflicting [+inferior] specification would create a case terminal node which is less specified than the relevant exponent /-s/; this exponent could not be inserted under it due to the *Subset Principle*, which requires that an exponent may be inserted under a terminal node only if its specification matches or is a subset of the specification of the terminal node and not vice versa.

(23)   *Subset Principle* (Halle 1997)
       The phonological exponent of a vocabulary item is inserted into a position if the item matches all or a subset of the features specified in that position. Insertion does not take place if the vocabulary item contains features not present in the morpheme. Where several vocabulary items meet the conditions for insertion, the item matching the greatest number of features specified in the terminal morpheme must be chosen.

Notice that, even if impoverishment applied, the only exponent liable for insertion would be again the /-n/ exponent, since this exponent is unspecified for the relevant case features.

The morphological approach to DSM presented above also predicts why such phenomena do not appear in feminine nouns. The nominative singular in feminine nouns carries no overt case marking, unlike all other case forms in all nouns, which indicates that the nominative singular in these nouns is expressed by the elsewhere zero exponent -Ø. This means that the nominative singular terminal node is radically impoverished for case (and possibly number) in all feminine nouns, as an instance of metasyncretism (Harley 2008), so that a potential application of the DSM-triggering impoverisment rule would yield no effects. In any case, the exponent /-n/ could never be inserted in such nodes, because it is more specified than the radically impoverished terminal node.

4 DOM in Cappadocian Greek

Cappadocian Greek varieties in which there is a morphological distinction between nominative and accusative forms in the singular (e.g. Delmeso, Potamia,

Axo) exhibit differential object marking: indefinite and incorporating objects appear in the nominative, instead of the expected accusative (Dawkins 1916, Janse 2004, Spyropoulos & Tilipoulou 2006, Spyropoulos & Kakarikos 2009, 2011, Karatsareas 2011):

(24) a. Potamia (Dawkins 1916: 456)
 istera pikan yamo-s (instead of yamo)
 afterwards make.PST.3PL marriage-SG.NOM
 'After that, they got married'

 b. Axos (Mavroxalyvidis & Kesisoglou 1960: 172)
 meɣa loyo-s mi les (instead of loyo)
 big word-SG.NOM NEG say.2SG
 'Don't say big words'

(25) a. Delmesos (Dawkins 1916: 94)
 ðeke ena layo-s (instead of layo)
 hit.PST.3SG a hare-SG.NOM
 'He hit a hare'

 b. Misti (Dawkins 1916: 94)
 xtinu aðara milo-s (instead of milo)
 build.3PL now mill-SG.NOM
 'They are now building a mill'

 c. Axos (Mavroxalyvidis & Kesisoglou 1960: 169)
 pʃasa ena klefti-s (instead of klefti)
 catch.PST.1SG a thief-SG.NOM
 'I caught a thief'

 d. Axos (Mavroxalyvidis & Kesisoglou 1960: 180)
 to ʃkili feri s ta provata liko-s
 the dog-SG.NOM bring.3SG to the sheep.PL.ACC wolf-SG.NOM
 (instead of liko)
 'The dog brings a wolf to the sheep'

 e. Delmesos (Dawkins 1916: 312)
 iferen paltadʒi-s (instead of paltadʒi)
 bring.PST.3SG wood-cutter-SG.NOM
 'He brought a wood-cutter'

Cappadocian Greek DOM is quite exceptional, because the differentiated object, i.e. the indefinite object, appears in a more marked case form. Indefinite objects, which appear in nominative, carry the exponent /-s/ which is used to express the nominative case, whereas definite objects in accusative carry no overt exponent, since accusative is expressed by the elsewhere zero exponent -Ø.[21] Notice that the exponent /-n/, which is used in Pontic Greek to express the accusative, does not exist in Cappadocian Greek. Thus, Cappadocian Greek has also a marked-nominative case subsystem, where nominative is overtly expressed and accusative has no overt exponent at all. Tables 3 and 4 present the noun inflection of the Cappadocian Greek variety of Delmeso.[22]

Such facts cannot be accommodated by a functional approach to DOM based on markedness, the typicality of object, distinctiveness and iconicity, because it is the unmarked typical object (i.e. the indefinite) that carries the case exponents, violating iconicity. In addition, given that the indefinite object is a typical object, whereas the definite one is non-typical, differentiation in terms of distinctiveness would result in a situation where the non-typical object (i.e. the definite) would carry case exponents, so that it would signify its distinct status as an object and not a subject, contrary to the facts. Thus, Cappadocian Greek DOM seems

---

[21] An anonymous reviewer points out that in terms of case functions Cappadocian Greek DOM seems to have the typical distribution and it looks like Turkish DOM, i.e. the object appears in the accusative when it is high in the definiteness scale (specific/definite) and in the nominative when it is low (indefinite). However, there is a crucial difference from Turkish and other, to the best of my knowledge, typical instances of DOM: in Cappadocian Greek the accusative form is not morphologically marked (i.e. it does not carry a special suffix), whereas in Turkish it is morphologically marked (it is expressed by a specific suffix); conversely, the nominative form is not morphologically marked (i.e. it does not carry a specific suffix) in Turkish, whereas it is morphologically marked (it is expressed by a specific suffix) in Cappadocian Greek. Functional approaches to Turkish and other typical instances of DOM (e.g. Aissen 2003) associate functional markedness, i.e. a high position in the scale, with morphological/formal markedness, i.e. overt or more specific/specialized morphological manifestation (see also Keine & Müller 2008 for the same association in a formal account of DOM facts); thus, DOM involves a retreat to a less marked or even unmarked case form so as to match functional unmarkedness. Cappadocian Greek DOM does not behave like those prototypical DOM instances, in the sense that the more marked object in terms of function appears in a less marked form in terms of morphological specification and, vice versa, a less marked object in terms of function appears in a more marked form in terms of morphological specification. So, Cappadocian Greek objects seem to have the typical distribution in the definiteness hierarchy only if we consider case forms as labels (which may sometimes be illusive and misleading) and they do not have this distribution if we consider these forms in terms of morphological markedness/complexity.

[22] The sounds in parentheses are subject to a deletion phonological rule, which affects unstressed high vowels in word final position.

Tab. 3: Inflection of *áθropos, kléftis, papas, keratás, néka*

	NOM	áθropo-s	klétti-s	papa-s	keratá-s	néka-Ø
SG	GEN	aθróp-(u)	kleft-jú	papað-jú	keratað-jú	néka-s
	ACC	áθropo-Ø	kléft(i)-Ø	papá-Ø	keratá-Ø	néka-Ø
	NOM	aθróp-(i)	kléft-(i)	papáð-es	keratáð-ja	nék-es
PL	GEN					
	ACC	aθróp-us / aθrop-jús	kleft-jús	papáð-es	keratáð-ja	nék-es
		'man'	'thief'	'priest'	'snail'	'woman'

Tab. 4: Inflection of *ðendró, métʃ(i), púma*

	NOM	ðendró-Ø	métʃ(i)-Ø	púma-Ø
SG	GEN	ðendr-ú	metʃjú [< metʃi-u]	pumát-(u)
	ACC	ðendró-Ø	métʃ(i)-Ø	púma-Ø
	NOM	ðendr-á	métʃja [< metʃi-a]	púmat-a
PL	GEN	ðendr-ú	metʃjú [< metʃi-u]	pumát-(u)
	ACC	ðendr-á	métʃja [< metʃi-a]	púmat-a
		'tree'	'shirt'	'cover'

to be identificational in that definiteness is at a surface level associated with the accusative form. Recall that a similar surface effect exists in Pontic Greek DSM, where the definite subject also surfaces in an accusative form.

Notice that, as in Pontic Greek, the accusative form is, morphologically speaking, a less specific form, since it carries the elsewehere zero exponent -Ø. Nominative is marked with the exponent /-s/, which I take to be specified only as [–oblique] and carry no specification for the [inferior] feature, because its distribution is not restricted to the nominative case, but, on certain occasions, it can also spread to other cases (see Section 6 for the somehow erratic behaviour of the /-s/ exponent in Cappadocian Greek). Thus the feature specification of the relevant case nodes and exponents in Cappadocian Greek is as follows:

(26) *Case terminal nodes*
  nominative: [..., –oblique, –inferior]
  accusative: [..., –oblique, +inferior]

(27) *The relevant formatives*
  /-s/ ↔ [–plural, ..., –oblique]
  /-Ø/ ↔ elsewhere

Given that the definite accusative form involves a retreat to a less specified exponence, I propose that Cappadocian Greek DOM is the result of an impoverishment rule, which removes the [−oblique] feature specification from the accusative case node, when the DP-object is specified as [+definite], thus blocking the insertion of the /-s/ exponent. Since the exponent /-n/ does not exist in Cappadocian Greek, the elsewhere exponent -Ø is the only exponent that can be inserted under this node.

(28) *DOM-triggering impoverishment rule*
[−oblique] → Ø / [$_{DP}$ [$_D$ +def] [$_N$ −plural, +inferior, ___]

(29) *The derivation of the indefinite object*
MS representation after Spell-Out:
[D[−def]] [laɣo- [−pl, −obl, +inf]]
  ↕   ↕
  ena   laɣo   -s ⟶ ena laɣo-s 'a hare-SG.NOM'

(30) *The derivation of the definite object*
MS representation after Spell-Out:
[D[+def]] [laɣo-[−pl, −obl, +inf]]

Impoverishment:
[D[+def]] [laɣo- [−pl, +inf]]
  ↕   ↕
  to   laɣo   -Ø ⟶ to laɣo 'the hare-SG.ACC'

Given the identificational nature of the phenomenon, we would expect Cappadocian Greek to also exhibit DSM, according to which definite subjects would appear in the accusative form, i.e. without the exponent /-s/. However this prediction is not borne out and Cappadocian Greek does not have DSM (although there are some sporadic examples with definite DP-subjects without the /-s/ suffix, which however should be attributed to a different source; see Section 6).

(31) Delmesos (Dawkins 1916: 316, 312)

a. na par ke sas to ðjavolo-s
SBJV take.3SG and you.PL the devil-SG.NOM
'May the devil take you!'

b. eljo-s mavrosen to prosopo
sun-SG.NOM blacken.PST.3SG the face.SG.ACC
'The sun blackened my face'

The analysis presented above correctly predicts for this fact, because the DOM-triggering impoverishment rule cannot apply on the nominative terminal node due to its structural description. The nominative case node is specified as [..., −oblique, −inferior], whereas the environment for the application of the DOM-triggering impoverishment rule requires a [+inferior] specification.[23]

5 Pontic DSM + Cappadocian DOM = Asia Minor Greek DAM: A morphological DCM

There are some common properties of Pontic DSM and Cappadocian DOM, which seem not to be accidental. First, they are both triggered by the [+definite] specification of the DP. Second, they are subject to certain morphological restrictions, in the sense that they apply only in the singular and Pontic DSM is restricted to a certain inflectional class. Third, at the surface level, they result in an association of definiteness with the accusative form, so that they are both indentificational (in the sense of de Hoop & Narasimhan 2005, 2008 and Kornfilt 2008), i.e. the differentiated subject/object is identified as definite.

I put forward the hypothesis that Pontic DSM and Cappadocian DOM are surface instantiations of a postsyntactic MS operation existing in Asia Minor Greek in general. This operation is an impoverishment rule which is triggered by the [+definite] specification of the DP and results in blocking the insertion of the exponent of the nominative case in favour of a less specified exponent. In the marked-

---

[23] An anonymous reviewer asks what happens with adjectives and other modifiers in Cappadocian Greek and whether their distribution and case marking can be used as a diagnostic for the case properties of the DP-object in a similar way they are used for DP-subjects in Pontic Greek. Unfortunately, adjectives and other modifiers in Cappadocian Greek do not inflect for case and they have the same form for both nominative and accusative case; thus, they offer no insight on the case properties of the N-head they modify.

nominative subsystems of these dialects this less specified exponent coincides with the accusative exponent resulting in case differentiation. This explains why these phenomena appear only in the singular, because only in the singular is the nominative form more marked than the accusative form; in plural, putting aside various syncretisms, both nominative and accusative are expressed by distinct exponents specified for features that are associated with the feature specifications of the relevant terminal nodes.

Significantly, such DAM situations are clearly morphological in nature, in the sense that the differentiated subject/object is assigned the expected abstract case in syntax, and differential case marking is the result of the way MS processes and manifests the relevant case nodes. Thus, Asia Minor Greek DAM has no functional motivation and this is the reason why it unexpectedly exhibits the opposite behavior regarding distinctiveness, iconicity and the function of the typicality of the subject/object according to the definiteness hierarchy. It only seems to exhibit an identificational effect at a surface level, by associating accusative case with definiteness – but not completely.

Asia Minor Greek DAM is very similar to Turkish DOM (Enç 1991, Kornfilt 1997, 2008, Lyons 1999, Lewis 2000, Göksel & Kerslake 2005, von Heusinger & Kornfilt 2005), where accusative case is identified with specificity:

(32) a. *Zeynep-Ø   adam-ı   gör-dü*
       Zeynep-NOM man-ACC see-PST
       'Zeynep saw the man'

   b. *Zeynep-Ø   bir adam-Ø gör-dü*
      Zeynep-NOM a   man   see-PST
      'Zeynep saw a man'

   c. *Zeynep-Ø   bir adam-ı   gör-dü*
      Zeynep-NOM a   man-ACC see-PST
      'Zeynep saw a certain man'

The examples above show that, when the DP-object is [–specific], it loses the accusative case suffix *-(y)I* and appears in the bare form, which is also the nominative case form (Enç 1991, Kornfilt 1997, 2008, Göksel & Kerslake 2005, von Heusinger & Kornfilt 2005). At a surface level this results in a situation where specificity is associated with the accusative case exponent.

This surface association between definiteness/specificity and accusative case form brings the two systems together in a way that it may be argued that are historically related to each other, either by means of contact or in the context of an Anatolian Sprachbund (Tzitzilis 1989, in press). Asia Minor Greek was in long-term contact with Turkish, and Cappadocian Greek in particular exhibits significant interference from Turkish at all levels (Dawkins 1916, Janse 2009a). Since most Greek speakers in these areas were bilingual in Greek and Turkish, the surface effects of Turkish DOM were interpreted by them as an association between definiteness (Greek does not mark specificity independently of definiteness) and accusative case (see Dawkins 1916, Janse 2004, Karatsareas 2011, 2014). Thus, it can be argued that this pattern of association was transferred to Greek and it was replicated by means of the material shapes of this language (Johanson 2009). It was internalized as an impoverishment rule, triggered by the [+definite] specification of the DP and resulting in blocking the insertion of the exponent of the nominative case. This impoverishment rule was subject to the specific properties of the nominal inflectional system(s) of the recipient dialect(s) and the general conditions that govern the morphological manifestation of the terminal nodes that syntax provides as its output, so that it gave DSM in Pontic and DOM in Cappadocian. However, there are some indications that Pontic DSM may be dated before the establishment of the Turkish rule in the area in the 11th century AD (see Thumb 1906: 258, Dawkins 1916: 94), a fact which may set apart its historical development (see Janse 2004) or suggest that such DCM phenomena are part of a set of DAM and other case shift and neutralization phenomena which occur(red) in the languages of the Anatolia region as an areal feature. For the purposes of this paper I maintain the formal connection between Pontic DSM and Cappadocian DOM as instantiations of a general MS rule which affects the constitution and subsequently the manifestation of the case node and I leave the historical and contact issue open to further research.

6 Some further developments

The impoverishment rules underlying Asia Minor Greek DAM, its identificational status and the surface patterns it resulted in triggered a number of interesting developments. First, since at the surface level accusative case was associated with definiteness, the /-s/ formative of the nominative started being associated with indefiniteness. Sporadically, this /-s/ formative is found expressing the indefinite accusative of nouns which do not have a nominative form with this exponent, such as the nouns that belonged to the old neuter class and the loan words that followed this pattern (Dawkins 1916: 94; see also Janse 2004):

(33) Delmesos (Dawkins 1916: 304)
na   me   vyalis   ena   peyaði-s   (instead of *peyaði*)
SBJV CL.1SG.ACC take out.2SG   a   well-SG.NOM
'Dig me a well'

In example (33) the noun *peyaði* is an 'old' neuter noun; in such nouns the nominative singular, as well as the accusative, is expressed by means of the zero exponent -Ø (see Table 4 above). The appearance of the /-s/ suffix here is totally unexpected and it can only be explained as an indefiniteness marker.

Second, in Cappadocian Greek, DOM interacted with other developments in the nominal inflection of these varieties. Most significantly, inanimate 'old' masculine nouns, including those ending in /-os/, got assimilated to the 'old' neuter inflection, in which nominative and accusative singular are expressed by the zero exponent -Ø. This triggered some further developments: (a) the exponent /-s/ of the 'old' masculine nouns was reanalysed together with the theme vowel /-o/ as belonging to the stem resulting in agglutination (Revithiadou et al. 2017) (34), and/or (b) the exponent /-s/ was omitted irrespective of the function of the DP (35).

(34)   [$_{stem}$ mil][$_{ending}$ [$_{TH}$ -o][$_{number.case}$ -s]] → [$_{stem}$ milos] [$_{number.case}$ -Ø]
  a. [$_{stem}$ milos][$_{SG.NOM/ACC}$ -Ø]   >   milos 'mill-SG.NOM/ACC'
  b. [$_{stem}$ milos][$_{GEN}$ -ju]   >   milozju 'mill-GEN'
  c. [$_{stem}$ milos][$_{PL.NOM/ACC}$ -ja]   >   milozja 'mill-PL.NOM/ACC'

(35)   [$_{stem}$ mil][$_{ending}$ [$_{TH}$ -o][$_{number.case}$ -s]] → [$_{stem}$ milo] [$_{number.case}$ -Ø]
  a. [$_{stem}$ milo][$_{SG.NOM/ACC}$ -Ø]   >   milo 'mill-SG.NOM/ACC'
  b. [$_{stem}$ milo][$_{GEN}$ -ju]   >   miloju 'mill-GEN'
  c. [$_{stem}$ milo][$_{PL.NOM/ACC}$ -ja]   >   miloja 'mill-PL.NOM/ACC'

These further developments resulted in a situation where the nominative and the accusative singular of these nouns were syncretic either with the /-s/ exponent or without it, which in turn created an unpredictable variation in the surface forms and masked the surface effects of DOM. Thus, in (36) the definite subject appears without the nominative marker /-s/, giving the false impression of a DSM situation. Furthermore, in (37) the definite object appears unexpectedly with the /-s/ exponent (expected pattern: definite object = accusative form = -Ø exponent), whereas in (38) the indefinite object appears without the /-s/ exponent in the relevant DOM environment (expected pattern: indefinite object = nominative form = /-s/ exponent):

(36) Definite subject without /-s/

    a. Potamia (Dawkins 1916: 94)

        to   milo en   makrja (instead of *milos*)
        the mill be.3SG far

        'The mill is far away'

    b. Axos (Mavroxalyvidis & Kesisoglou 1960: 196)

        to   milo djavolju yjatax ton   (instead of *milos*)
        the mill devil.GEN shelter be.PST.3SG

        'the mill was the devil's shelter'

(37) Definite object with /-s/, Delmesos (Dawkins 1916: 308)

    ivren   to   milo-s   (instead of *milo*)
    find.PST.3SG the mill-SG.NOM

    'He found the mill'

(38) Indefinite object without /-s/, Axos (Dawkins 1916: 390)

    ivra   ena milo   (expected *milos* due to DOM)
    find.PST.3SG the mill-SG.NOM

    'I found a mill'

The erratic distribution of /-s/ in the above examples indicates that this exponent no longer functions as a case exponent for this class of nouns, but it constitutes part of the stem or it may be omitted altogether from the inventory of the inflectional suffixes. Thus, its distribution is not governed by DOM. Table 5 illustrates the declension of the relevant inanimate nouns exemplified by the noun *milo(s)* 'mill'.

Tab. 5: Declension of inanimate noun *milo(s)* 'mill'

		Delmesos / Potamia	*Axos*	
SG	NOM	milo(s)	milo	milos
	GEN	milu > mil	miloju	milozju
	ACC	milo(s)	milo	milos
PL	NOM	milus	miloja	milozja
	GEN	—	—	—
	ACC	milus	miloja	milozja

Third, the DAM-triggering impoverishment rule started spreading to more nouns, an expected development given that the restriction of its application in certain classes of nouns was the result of postsyntactic lexical conditioning. Thus, in Cappadocian Greek it seems that DOM affects all nouns that have distinct nominative and accusative forms, not only those ending in -*os*:

(39) Cappadocian Greek

    a. Delmesos (Dawkins 1916: 312)

        iferen   *paltadʒi-s*   (instead of *paltadʒi*)
        bring.PST.3SG wood-cutter-SG.NOM
        'He brought a wood-cutter'

    b. Axos (Mavroxalyvidis & Kesisoglou 1960: 169)

        pʃasa   *ena klefti-s*   (instead of *klefti*)
        catch.PST.1SG a   thief-SG.NOM
        'I caught a thief'

Similarly, in some Pontic varieties (e.g. Nikopolis, Oinoe), DSM affects all masculine nouns, including those ending in -*as* and -*is*, and even feminine nouns (cf. examples in (10); Oeconomides 1958: 146).

(40) Nikopolis Pontic (Papadopoulos 1955: 159)

    a. *erθen*   *o*   *ðespoti-n*   *so*   *xorion*
        come.PST.3SG the(M).SG.NOM bishop(M)-SG.ACC in-the village
        'The bishop came to my village'

    b. *o*   *psara-n*   *epiasen*   *enan opsarin*
        the(M).SG.NOM fisherman(M)-SG.ACC catch.PST.3SG a   fish
        'The fisherman caught a fish'

7 A potential extension: Applying the analysis in Turkish

As mentioned above Turkish exhibits both DOM and DSM, which are identificational in nature (Enç 1991, Kornfilt 1997, 2008, Lyons 1999, Lewis 2000, Göksel & Kerslake 2005, von Heusinger & Kornfilt 2005). In DOM situations, when the object is [–specific], it appears in the bare form, i.e. it involves no overt morphology:

(41) a. *Zeynep adam-ı gör-dü*
    Zeynep man-ACC see-PST
    'Zeynep saw the man'

   b. *Zeynep bir adam gör-dü*
    Zeynep a man see-PST
    'Zeynep saw a man'

   c. *Zeynep bir adam-ı gör-dü*
    Zeynep a man-ACC see-PST
    'Zeynep saw a certain man'

Turkish DSM (Kornfilt 1997, 2008, this volume, Göksel & Kerslake 2005) applies in certain nominalized complement clauses, in which the subject appears in the genitive case; in these clauses, when the subject is [–specific], it appears in the bare form:

(42) a. *arı-nın çocuğ-u sok-tuğ-un-u duy-du-m*
    bee-GEN child-ACC sting-FN-3SG-ACC hear-PST-1SG
    'I heard that the bee stung the child'

   b. *çocuğ-u arı sok-tuğ-un-u duy-du-m*
    child-ACC bee sting-FN-3SG-ACC hear-PST-1SG
    'I heard that bees stung the child'

   c. *çocuğ-u bir arı sok-tuğ-un-u duy-du-m*
    child-ACC a bee sting-FN-3SG-ACC listen-PST-1SG
    'I heard that a bee stung the child'

   d. *çocuğ-u bir arı-nın sok-tuğ-un-u duy-du-m*
    child-ACC a bee-GEN sting-FN-3SG-ACC listen-PST-1SG
    'I heard that a (certain) bee stung the child'

However, DOM and DSM fail to apply on certain occasions (Kornfilt 2008). Thus, in constructions where the object is assigned an oblique or a lexical case, the non-specific object does not appear in the bare form and carries the relevant oblique/lexical case exponent:

(43) a. *Hasan kitab-ı çocuğ-a / *bir çocuk ver-di*
    Hasan book-ACC child-DAT a child give-PST
    'Hasan gave a book to the/a child'

    b. *Hasan at-a   /*at   biner*
       Hasan horse-DAT horse ride-HAB
       'Hasan rides horses' or 'Hasan rides the horse'

Second, in constructions in which the object/subject carries an agreement suffix, e.g. in partitive constructions (Kornfilt 2008), case marking is obligatory and it appears even when the subject/object has a non-specific reading:

(44) Blocked DOM: Partitive as object (Kornfilt 2008: 88)

    a. *Kitap-lar-ın iki-sin-i   al,   geri-sin-i   kutu-da bırak*
       book-PL-GEN two-3-ACC buy.IMP remainder-3-ACC box-LOC leave.IMP

    b. **Kitap-lar-ın iki-si al,   geri-sin-i   kutu-da bırak*
       book-PL-GEN two-3 buy.IMP remainder-3-ACC box-LOC leave.IMP

    c. *Kitap-lar-dan iki-sin-i   al,   geri-sin-i   kutu-da*
       book-PL-ABL two-3-ACC buy.IMP remainder-3-ACC box-LOC
       bırak
       leave.IMP

    d. **Kitap-lar-dan iki-si al,   geri-sin-i   kutu-da bırak*
       book-PL-ABL two-3 buy.IMP remainder-3-ACC box-LOC leave.IMP
       'Take (any) two of the books and leave the rest in the box' (both specific and non-specific readings)

(45) Blocked DSM: Partitive as a subject in complement clause (Kornfilt 2008: 89)

    a. *Kitap-lar-ın iki-sin-in kaybol-duğ-un-u   bil-iyor-um*
       book-PL-GEN two-3-GEN disappear-FN-3SG-ACC know-PROG-1SG

    b. **Kitap-lar-ın iki-si kaybol-duğ-un-u   bil-iyor-um*
       book-PL-GEN two-3 disappear-FN-3SG-ACC know-PROG-1SG

    c. *Kitap-lar-dan iki-sin-in   kaybol-duğ-un-u   bil-iyor-um*
       book-PL-ABL two-3-GEN disappear-FN-3SG-ACC know-PROG-1SG

    d. **Kitap-lar-dan iki-si kaybol-duğ-un-u   bil-iyor-um*
       book-PL-ABL two-3 disappear-FN-3SG-ACC know-PROG-1SG
       'I know that (any) two of the books got lost' (both specific and non specific)

That DSM and DOM fail to apply in certain constructions indicates that the expected abstract case is always assigned to the relevant argument and that DOM and DSM mask its overt manifestation. When they fail to apply, the expected case surfaces as normal.

There is a striking similarity between Asia Minor Greek DAM and the Turkish DSM and DOM, in that they all involve a retreat to an unmarked form, which results in a situation where the abstract case assigned to the subject/object is manifested by means of a less specified exponent. This may be taken as an indication that Turkish DOM and DSM involve some kind of postsyntactic operation; when this operation fails to apply for some reason, the expected DOM and DSM effects do not appear.

Based on this observation, I put forward the hypothesis that Turkish has a DCM-triggering rule similar to that of Asia Minor Greek. That is, I proppose that Turkish DSM and DOM phenomena are the surface effects of an impoverishment rule that deletes certain features from the case node, blocking, thus, the insertion of the accusative and genitive formatives in favour of the zero exponent -Ø, which is also the exponent of the nominative, since there is no overt specialized nominative formative in the language. The relevant feature may be [–oblique], since DOM/DSM does not affect lexical/oblique cases. As in Asia Minor Greek DAM, it can also be assumed that this impoverishment rule affects only the case nodes on lexical categories and not the functional elements.

(46) *Turkish DOM/DSM rule*
 [–oblique] → Ø / [$_{DP}$ [$_D$ –spec] [$_N$,...., ___]]

The formulation of the rule explains the blocking of DOM/DSM on the relevant occasions. The impoverishment rule affects only the [–oblique] feature, which can be argued to be included in the specification of both the accusative and the genitive case nodes, given that the genitive case in Turkish is 'structural' in the sense that it depends on agreement checking (Kornfilt 2003, 2006, 2008). Lexical and other 'inherent' cases are [+oblique], thus they are not affected by the impoverishment rule. Similarly, failure of DSM/DOM to apply due to the existence of an Agr morpheme can be explained by the fact that the the case morpheme, i.e. the case terminal node, depends, i.e. attaches, on the Agr morpheme (Kornfilt 2008), which is a functional element. If so, then the failure of application derives from the fact that the impoverishment rule does not affect case terminal nodes on functional elements.

8 Conclusions

Pontic Greek DSM and Cappadocian Greek DOM exhibit some very interesting properties: (a) the differentiation involves retreat to a less specific case marking, which may be overt, (b) they obey certain morphological and lexical restrictions, and (c) they cannot be accommodated within a functional approach that capitalizes on the role of distinctiveness, iconicity and the typicality of subject/object in terms of a definiteness hierarchy. It was also shown that, no matter how it surfaces, the relevant abstract case is always assigned to the subject/object. DCM forces this abstract case to be expressed by means of a less specific form in terms of morphological manifestation. This form happens to coincide with the accusative form in a marked-nominative system like the one exhibited by Asia Minor Greek. Thus, Asia Minor Greek DCM is morphological in nature and reveals a non-isomorphism between abstract and morphological case. The relation between abstract case and morphological (surface) case form on such occasions can be captured by means of a *feature decomposition of case* approach and postsyntactic operations at MS that affect the feature constitution of the case terminal node resulting in differentiating exponence. The facts from Asia Minor Greek DCM shows that DSM and DOM effects are not uniform phenomena cross-linguistically and may derive from different sources, including PF-interface properties and postsyntactic morphophonological processing.

A final note before closing: Baker (2015) proposes an analysis of DOM, which relies on the assumption that differentiated objects occupy different positions in the syntactic structure. Given that objects are assigned a dependent case, in the sense that their case 'depends' on the case of a higher argument (i.e. the subject) in a local configuration, the assignment of this dependent case may be cancelled if the relevant argument occupies (perhaps by means of movement) a position in which it is no more 'dependent' on another argument in a given Spell-Out domain. In view of Cappadocian Greek DOM, such an analysis would provide a syntactic/architectural motivation for the impoverishment rule, in the sense that the absence of the relevant case feature could be attributed to the fact that the relevant argument occupies a syntactic position where this case property is no longer assigned. Such an analysis would imply that differentiated objects in Cappadocian Greek occupy different structural positions. However, there is no evidence that objects occupy different positions relevant to their case marking in Cappadocian Greek (see Janse 2006 for a discussion of object positioning in Cappadocian Greek). In addition, such an approach would miss the correlation with Pontic Greek DSM and it cannot account for the various morphological/lexical restrictions. I leave the issue open to future research.

Acknowledgements

Parts and versions of this paper have been presented at the *Workshop on Differential Subject Marking and Ergative Phenomena* during the *46th Annual Meeting of the Societas Linguistica Europaea* (University of Split, 18–21 September 2013), the *36th Annual Meeting of the Section of Linguistics of the School of Philosophy of the Aristotle University of Thessaloniki* (24–25 April 2015) and the *48th Annual Meeting of the Societas Linguistica Europaea* (Leiden University, 2–5 September 2015). I wish to thank the audiences for their constructive comments, suggestions and criticism. The paper has also been greatly benefited by the comments of the editors and three anonymous reviewers, which are kindly acknowledged. The usual disclaimers apply.

References

Aissen, Judith. 2003. Differential object marking: Iconicity vs. economy. *Natural Language & Linguistic Theory* 21(3). 435–483. https://doi.org/10.1023/A:1024109008573.

Alexiadou, Artemis & Gereon Müller. 2008. Class features as probes. In Asaf Bachrach & Andrew Nevins (eds.), *Inflectional identity*, 101–155. Oxford: Oxford University Press.

Anagnostopoulou, Elena. 2003. *The syntax of ditransitives: Evidence from clitics*. Berlin: De Gruyter.

Asan, Ömer. 1996. *Pontos kültürü [The culture of Pontus]*. Istanbul: Belge Yayınları.

Baker, Mark C. 1997. Thematic roles and syntactic structure. In Liliane Haegeman (ed.), *Elements of grammar*, 73–137. Dordrecht: Kluwer.

Baker, Mark C. 2008. *The syntax of agreement and concord*. Cambridge: Cambridge University Press.

Baker, Mark C. 2015. *Case: Its principles and its parameters*. Cambridge: Cambridge University Press.

Baker, Mark C. & Nadya Vinokurova. 2010. Two modalities of case assignment. *Natural Language & Linguistic Theory* 28(3). 593–642. https://doi.org/10.1007/s11049-010-9105-1.

Bierwisch, Manfred. 1967. Syntactic features in morphology: General problems of so-called pronominal inflection in German. In *To honor Roman Jakobson*, vol. 1, 239–270. The Hague: Mouton.

Bittner, Maria & Ken Hale. 1996. Ergativity: Toward a theory of a heterogeneous class. *Linguistic Inquiry* 27(4). 531–604.

Blake, Barry. 2001. *Case*. Cambridge: Cambridge University Press.

Blake, Barry. 2009. History of the research on case. In Andrej Malchukov & Andrew Spencer (eds.), The Oxford Handbook of Case, 1–26. Oxford: Oxford University Press.

Bobaljik, Jonathan David. 2002. Syncretism without paradigms: Remarks on Williams 1981, 1994. In Geert Booij & Jaap van Marle (eds.), *The Yearbook of Morphology 2001*, 53–85. Dordrecht: Kluwer.

Bobaljik, Jonathan David. 2008a. Paradigms (optimal and otherwise): A case for scepticism. In Asaf Bachrach & Andrew Nevins (eds.), *Inflectional identity*, 29–54. Oxford: Oxford University Press.

Bobaljik, Jonathan David. 2008b. Where's phi? Agreement as a postsyntactic operation. In Daniel Harbour, David Adger & Susana Béjar (eds.), *Phi-theory*, 295–328. Oxford: Oxford University Press.

Bonet, Eulàlia. 1991. *Morphology after syntax: Pronominal clitics in Romance*. MIT PhD dissertation.

Bossong, Georg. 1985. *Differentielle Objektmarkierung in den Neuiranischen Sprachen*. Gunter Narr.

Calabrese, Andrea. 1996. Some remarks on the Latin case system and its development in Romance. In José Lema & Esthela Treviño (eds.), *Theoretical analyses on Romance languages: Selected papers from the 26th linguistic symposium on Romance languages*, 71–126. Amsterdam: John Benjamins.

Calabrese, Andrea. 2008. On absolute and contextual syncretism: Remarks on the structure of case paradigms and on how to derive them. In Asaf Bachrach & Andrew Nevins (eds.), *Inflectional identity*, 156–205. Oxford: Oxford University Press.

Carstens, Vicki. 2000. Concord in minimalist theory. *Linguistic Inquiry* 31(2). 319–355.

Chadzisavidis, Sophronis. 1995. Τα ποντιακά στον ελλαδικό χώρο [Pontic in Greece]. *Αρχείον Πόντου [Pontus Archive]* 46. 47–72.

Comrie, Bernard. 1989. *Language universals and linguistic typology*. Chicago, IL: University of Chicago Press.

Corbett, Greville G. 2012. *Features*. Cambridge: Cambridge University Press.

Dawkins, Richard. 1910. Modern Greek in Asia Minor. *The Journal of Hellenic Studies* 30. 109–132 & 267–291.

Dawkins, Richard. 1916. *Modern Greek in Asia Minor: A study of the dialects of Sílli, Cappadocia and Phárasa with grammar, texts, translations and glossary*. Cambridge: Cambridge University Press.

Dawkins, Richard. 1931. Notes on the study of the modern Greek of Pontos. *Byzantion* 6. 389–400.

Dawkins, Richard. 1937. The Pontic dialect of modern Greek in Asia Minor and Russia. *Transactions of the Philological Society* 36. 15–52. https://doi.org/10.1111/j.1467-968X.1937.tb00672.x.

Drettas, Georges. 1997. *Aspects pontiques*. Publié avec le concours du Centre National du Livre. Paris: Association de recherches pluridisciplinaires.

Embick, David & Rolf Noyer. 2007. Distributed morphology and the syntax-morphology interface. In Gillian Ramchand & Charles Reiss (eds.), *The Oxford handbook of linguistic interfaces*, 289–324. Oxford: Oxford University Press.

Enç, Mürvet. 1991. The semantics of specificity. *Linguistic Inquiry* 22(1). 1–25.

Frampton, John. 2002. Syncretism, impoverishment and the structure of person features. In Mary Andronis, Erin Debenport, Anne Pycha & Keiko Yoshimura (eds.), *CLS 38: The main session. Papers from the 38th Meeting of the Chicago Linguistic Society*, vol. 1, 207–222. Chicago: Chicago Linguistic Society.

Göksel, Aslı & Celia Kerslake. 2005. *Turkish: A comprehensive grammar*. London: Routledge.

Grosu, Alexander. 1994. *Three studies in locality and case*. London: Routledge.

Hale, Ken. 1972. A new perspective on American Indian linguistics. In Alfonso Ortiz (ed.), *New perspectives on the pueblos*, 87–103. Albuquerque: University of New Mexico Press.

Hale, Ken & Samuel Jay Keyser. 1993. On argument structure and the lexical expression of grammatical relations. In Kenneth Hale & Samuel J. Keyser (eds.), *The view from Building 20*, 53–109. Cambridge, MA: MIT Press.

Hale, Ken & Samuel Jay Keyser. 2002. *Prolegomenon to a theory of argument structure*. Cambridge, MA: MIT Press.

Halle, Morris. 1997. Distributed morphology: Impoverishment and fission. In Yoonjung Kang Benjamin Bruening & Martha McGinnis (eds.), *PF: Papers at the interface*, vol. 30 (MIT Working Papers in Linguistics), 425–449. Cambridge, MA: MIT Working Papers in Linguistics.

Halle, Morris & Alec Marantz. 1993. Distributed morphology and the pieces of inflection. In Ken Hale & Samuel Jay Keyser (eds.), *The view from building 20*, 111–176. MIT Press.

Halle, Morris & Alec Marantz. 1994. Some key features of distributed morphology. In Heidi Harley & Colin Phillips (eds.), *The morphology–syntax connection*, vol. 21 (MIT Working Papers in Linguistics), 275–288.

Halle, Morris & Alec Marantz. 2008. Clarifying "blur": Paradigms, defaults, and inflectional classes. In Asaf Bachrach & Andrew Nevins (eds.), *Inflectional identity*, 55–72. Oxford: Oxford University Press.

Halle, Morris & Bert Vaux. 1998. Theoretical aspects of Indo-European nominal morphology: The nominal declensions of Latin and Armenian. In Jay Jasonoff, H. Craig Melchert & Lisi Oliver (eds.), *Mír Curad: Studies in honor of Calvert Watckins*, 223–240. Innsbruck: University of Innsbruck.

Harley, Heidi. 2008. When is a syncretism more than a syncretism? Impoverishment, metasyncretism and underspecification. In Daniel Harbour, David Adger & Susana Béjar (eds.), *Phi theory*, 251–294. Oxford: Oxford University Press.

Harley, Heidi & Rolf Noyer. 2003. Distributed morphology. In Lisa Lai-Shen Cheng & Rint Sybesma (eds.), *The second Glot International state-of-the-article book*, 463–496. Berlin: De Gruyter.

Hatzidakis, Georgios. 1892. *Einleitung in die neugriechische Grammatik*. Leipzig: Druck und Verlag von Breitkopf & Härtel.

Hatzidakis, Georgios. 1934 [1911/1912]. Περί της Ποντικής διαλέκτου και ιδία περί των εν αυτή αναλογικών σχηματισμών [On the Pontic dialect with particular emphasis on its analogical formations]. In Georgios Hatzidakis (ed.), *Γλωσσολογικαί έρευναι, τόμος 1 [Linguistic Investigations, Vol. 1]*, 265–291. Athens: Academy of Athens.

Henrich, Günther Stefen. 1976. *Κλητικές και Γενικές σε -ο από αρσενικά σε -ος στα Μεσαιωνικά και Νέα Ελληνικά [Vocative and genitive forms in -o from masculines in -os in Medieval and Modern Greek]*. Aristotle University of Thessaloniki dissertation.

von Heusinger, Klaus & Jaklin Kornfilt. 2005. The case of the direct object in Turkish: Semantics, syntax and morphology. *Turkic Languages* 9. 3–44.

Hjelmslev, Louis. 1935. *La catégorie des cas: Étude de grammaire générale*. Vol. 7.1 (Acta Jutlandica: Aarsskrift for Aarhus Universitet). Copenhagen: Munksgaard.

Holton, David, Irene Philippaki-Warburton Peter Mackridge & Vassilios Spyropoulos. 2012. *Greek: A comprehensive grammar*. 2nd edn. London: Routledge.

de Hoop, Helen & Andrej L. Malchukov. 2007. On fluid differential case marking. *Lingua* 117(9). 1636–1656. https://doi.org/10.1016/j.lingua.2006.06.010.

de Hoop, Helen & Andrej L. Malchukov. 2008. Case-marking strategies. *Linguistic Inquiry* 39(4). 565–587. https://doi.org/10.1162/ling.2008.39.4.565.

de Hoop, Helen & Bhuvana Narasimhan. 2005. Differential case marking in Hindi. In Mengistu Amberber & Helen de Hoop (eds.), *Competition and variation in natural languages: The case for case*, 321–346. London: Elsevier.

de Hoop, Helen & Bhuvana Narasimhan. 2008. Ergative case marking in Hindi. In Helen de Hoop & Peter de Swart (eds.), *Differential subject marking* (Studies in Natural Language & Linguistic Theory), 63–78. Dordrecht: Springer. https://doi.org/10.1007/978-1-4020-6497-5_4.

de Hoop, Helen & Peter de Swart. 2008a. Cross-linguistic variation in differential subject marking. In Helen de Hoop & Peter de Swart (eds.), *Differential Subject Marking* (Studies in Natural Language & Linguistic Theory), 1–16. Dordrecht: Springer. https://doi.org/10.1007/978-1-4020-6497-5_1.

de Hoop, Helen & Peter de Swart (eds.). 2008b. *Differential subject marking* (Studies in Natural Language & Linguistic Theory). Dordrecht: Springer. https://doi.org/10.1007/978-1-4020-6497-5.

Jakobson, Roman. 1971 [1936]. Beitrag zur allgemeinen Kasuslehre: Gesamtbedeutungen der russischen Kasus. In *Selected writings, Volume 2: Word and language*, 23–71. The Hague: Mouton.

Janse, Mark. 2002. Aspects of bilingualism in the history of the Greek language. In James Noel Adams, Mark Janse & Simon Swain (eds.), *Bilingualism in ancient society: Language contact and the written word*, 332–390. Oxford: Oxford University Press.

Janse, Mark. 2004. Animacy, definiteness, and case in Cappadocian and other Asia Minor Greek dialects. *Journal of Greek Linguistics* 5(1). 3–26. https://doi.org/10.1075/jgl.5.03jan.

Janse, Mark. 2006. Object position in Cappadocian Greek and other Asia Minor Greek dialects. In Mark Janse, Brian Joseph & Angela Ralli (eds.), *Proceedings of the 2nd International Conference on Modern Greek Dialects and Linguistic Theory*, 115–129. Patra: University of Patras.

Janse, Mark. 2009a. Greek–Turkish language contact in Asia Minor. *Études Helléniques / Hellenic Studies* 17. 37–54.

Janse, Mark. 2009b. The resurrection of Cappadocian (Asia Minor Greek). *AΩ International* 11. 10–15.

Janse, Mark. 2016. Cappadocian in the social media era. Paper presented at the *7th International Conference on Modern Greek Dialects and Linguistic Theory*, 6–8 October 2016, Rethymnon.

Johanson, Lars. 2002. *Structural factors in Turkic language contacts*. London: Curzon.

Johanson, Lars. 2009. Case and contanct linguistics. In Andrej Malchukov & Andrew Spencer (eds.), *The Oxford handbook of case*, 494–501. Oxford: Oxford University Press.

Karatsareas, Petros. 2011. *A study of Cappadocian Greek nominal morphology from a diachronic and dialectological perspective*. University of Cambridge dissertation.

Karatsareas, Petros. 2013. Understanding diachronic change in Cappadocian Greek: The dialectological perspective. *Journal of Historical Linguistics* 3. 192–229.

Karatsareas, Petros. 2014. The short-lived trajectory of differential object marking in Cappadocian Greek: Language contact, typological anomaly and morphological change. Paper presented at the *Differential Object Marking and Language Contact International Workshop*, Institut national des langues et civilisations orientales (INaLCO), Paris, 5–6 December 2014.

Keine, Stefan & Gereon Müller. 2008. Differential argument encoding by impoverishment. In Marc Richards & Andrej L. Malchukov (eds.), *Scales* (Linguistische Arbeitsberichte 86), 83–136. Leipzig: Universität Leipzig.

Kiparsky, Paul. 1997. The rise of positional licensing. In Ans van Kemenade & Nigel Vincent (eds.), *Parameters of morphosyntactic change*, 460–494. Cambridge: Cambridge University Press.

König, Christa. 2008. *Case in Africa*. Oxford: Oxford University Press.

König, Christa. 2009. Case in an African language: Ik – how defective a case can be. In Andrej Malchukov & Andrew Spencer (eds.), *The Oxford handbook of case*, 730–741. Oxford: Oxford University Press.

Kornfilt, Jaklin. 1997. *Turkish*. New York: Routledge.

Kornfilt, Jaklin. 2003. Subject case in Turkish nominalized clauses. In Uwe Junghanns & Luka Szucsich (eds.), *Syntactic structures and morphological information*, 129–215. Berlin: De Gruyter.

Kornfilt, Jaklin. 2006. Agreement: The (unique and local) syntactic and morphological licenser of subject. In João Costa & Maria Christina Figueiredo Silva (eds.), *Studies on agreement*, 141–171. Amsterdam: John Benjamins.

Kornfilt, Jaklin. 2008. DOM and two types of DSM in Turkish. In Helen de Hoop & Peter de Swart (eds.), *Differential subject marking* (Studies in Natural Language & Linguistic Theory), 79–111. Dordrecht: Springer. https://doi.org/10.1007/978-1-4020-6497-5.

Koutita-Kaimaki, Myrto. 1977–1978. Η ονομαστική σε -ν των αρσενικών ονομάτων της ποντιακής [The nominative in -n of the masculine nouns in Pontic]. *Αρχείον Πόντου [Pontus Archive]* 34. 259–298.

Legate, Julie Anne. 2008. Morphological and abstract case. *Linguistic Inquiry* 39(1). 55–101. https://doi.org/10.1162/ling.2008.39.1.55.

Lewis, Geoffrey. 2000. *Turkish grammar*. 2nd edn. Oxford: Oxford University Press.

Lyons, Christopher. 1999. *Definiteness*. Cambridge: Cambridge University Press.

Mackridge, Peter. 1987. Greek-speaking moslems of north-east Turkey: Prolegomena to a study of the Ophitic sub-dialect of Pontic. *Byzantine and Modern Greek Studies* 11. 115–137.

Mackridge, Peter. 1995. Pontic in contemporary Turkey: Ancient features in the dialect of Ofis. *Αρχείον Πόντου [Pontus Archive]* 46. 133–161.

Mackridge, Peter. 1999. The Greek spoken in the region of Pontus. In *Dialect enclaves of the greek language*, 101–105. Athens: Centre for the Greek Language.

Malchukov, Andrej & Andrew Spencer. 2009. Typology of case systems: Parameters of variation. In Andrej Malchukov & Andrew Spencer (eds.), *The Oxford handbook of case*, 651–667. Oxford: Oxford University Press.

Malchukov, Andrej & Peter de Swart. 2009. Differential case marking and actancy variations. In Andrej Malchukov & Andrew Spencer (eds.), *The Oxford handbook of case*, 339–355. Oxford: Oxford University Press.

Marantz, Alec. 1991. Case and licensing. In *ESCOL '91: Proceedings of the eighth Eastern states conference on linguistics*, 234–253. Ohio State University.

Marantz, Alec. 1993. Implications of asymmetries in double object constructions. In Sam Mchombo (ed.), *Theoretical aspects of Bantu grammar*, 113–150. Stanford, CA: CSLI Publications.

Mavroxalyvidis, Georgios & Iordanis I. Kesisoglou. 1960. *Το Γλωσσικό Ιδίωμα της Αξού [The dialect of Axos]*. Athens: French Institute of Athens Publications, Centre for Asia Minor Studies.

McFadden, Thomas. 2004. *The position of morphological case in the derivation.* University of Pennsylvania dissertation.
McGinnis, Martha. 2001. Variation in the phrase structure of applicatives. *Linguistic Variation Yearbook* 1(1). 105–146. https://doi.org/10.1075/livy.1.06mcg.
Norris, Mark. 2014. *A theory of nominal concord.* University of California Santa Cruz dissertation.
Norris, Mark. 2017a. Description and analyses of nominal concord (Pt I). *Language and Linguistics Compass* 11(11). https://doi.org/10.1111/lnc3.12266.
Norris, Mark. 2017b. Description and analyses of nominal concord (Pt II). *Language and Linguistics Compass* 11(11). https://doi.org/10.1111/lnc3.12267.
Noyer, Rolf. 1992. *Features, positions and affixes in autonomous morphological structure.* MIT dissertation.
Oeconomides, D. E. 1908. *Lautlehre des Pontischen.* Leipzig: Deichert'sche Verlagsbuchhandlung.
Oeconomides, D. E. 1958. *Γραμματική της ελληνικής διαλέκτου του πόντου [Grammar of Pontic Greek].* Athens: Academy of Athens.
Papadopoulos, Anthimos. 1953. Χαρακτηριστικά της ποντικής διαλέκτου [Features of the Pontic dialect]. *Αρχείον Πόντου [Pontus Archive]* 18. 83–93.
Papadopoulos, Anthimos. 1955. *Ιστορική γραμματική της ποντικής διαλέκτου [Historical Grammar of Pontic Greek].* Athens: Committee for Pontian Studies.
Papazachariou, Dimitrios. 2016. Comparing the vowel systems of Pontic and Cappadocian, as they are spoken today: Dialects in contact in Greek environment. Paper presented at the *7th International Conference on Modern Greek Dialects and Linguistic Theory*, 6–8 October 2016, Rethymnon.
Pappou-Zouravliova, Ekaterini. 2001. Οι Έλληνες της Σοβιετικής Ένωσης και οι διάλεκτοί τους [The Greeks in Soviet Union and their dialects]. In *Greek linguistics '99: Proceedings of the 4th International Conference on Greek Linguistics, Nicosia, September 1999*, 495–502. Thessaloniki: University Studio Press.
Prince, Alan & Paul Smolensky. 2004. *Optimality theory: Constraint interaction in generative grammar.* Malden, MA: Blackwell.
Pylkkänen, Liina. 2008. *Introducing arguments.* Cambridge, MA: MIT Press.
Revithiadou, Anthi & Vassilios Spyropoulos. 2012. *Οφίτικα: Πτυχές της Γραμματικής Δομής μίας Ποντιακής Διαλέκτου [Ofitika: Aspects of the grammatical structure of a Pontic dialect].* Thessaloniki: Kyriakidis Brothers.
Revithiadou, Anthi & Vassilios Spyropoulos. 2016. Stress at the interface: Phases, accents and dominance. *Linguistic Analysis* 42. 1–71.
Revithiadou, Anthi, Vassilios Spyropoulos & Giorgos Markopoulos. 2017. From fusion to agglutination: The case of Asia Minor Greek. *Transactions of the Philological Society* 115(3). 297–335. https://doi.org/10.1111/1467-968X.12091.
Semenov, A. 1934. Der nordpontische Dialekt des Neugriechischen. *Glotta* 23(1–2). 96–107.
Siddiqi, Daniel. 2010. Distributed morphology. *Language and Linguistics Compass* 4(7). 524–542. https://doi.org/10.1111/j.1749-818x.2010.00212.x.
Silverstein, Michael. 1976. Hierarchy of features and ergativity. In R. M. W. Dixon (ed.), *Grammatical categories in Australian languages*, 112–171. Canberra: Australian Institute of Aboriginal Studies.
Sitaridou, Ioanna. 2013. Greek-speaking enclaves in Pontus today: The documentation and revitalization of Romeyka. In Mari Jones & Sarah Ogilvie (eds.), *Keeping languages alive: Lan-*

guage endangerment: Documentation, pedagogy and revitalization, 98–112. Cambridge: Cambridge University Press.

Sitaridou, Ioanna. 2016. Reframing the phylogeny of Asia Minor Greek: The view from Pontic Greek. *CHS Research Bulletin, Center for Hellenic Studies, Harvard University* 4(1). 1–17.

Spyropoulos, Vassilios. 1999. *Agreement relations in Greek*. University of Reading dissertation.

Spyropoulos, Vassilios. 2005. Agreement and multiple case licensing in Greek. In Melita Stavrou & Arhonto Terzi (eds.), *Advances in Greek generative grammar*, 15–39. Amsterdam: John Benjamins. https://doi.org/10.1075/la.76.03spy.

Spyropoulos, Vassilios & Konstantinos Kakarikos. 2009. Aspects of dialectal variation in the Greek declension: A feature-based approach. In Geert Booij, Angela Ralli & Sergio Scalise (eds.), *Morphology and dialectology: On-line proceedings of the 6th Mediterranean Morphology Meeting (MMM6)*, 49–62. Patras: University of Patras.

Spyropoulos, Vassilios & Konstantinos Kakarikos. 2011. A feature-based analysis of cappadocian Greek nominal inflection. In Mark Janse, Brian Joseph, Pavlos Pavlou, Angela Ralli & Spyros Armosti (eds.), *Studies in Modern Greek Dialects and Linguistic Theory*, 203–213. Nicosia: Research Centre of Kykkos Monastery.

Spyropoulos, Vassilios & Marianna Tilipoulou. 2006. Definiteness and case in Cappadocian Greek. In Mark Janse, Brian Joseph & Angela Ralli (eds.), *Proceedings of the 2nd International Conference on Modern Greek Dialects and Linguistic Theory*, 366–378. Patras: University of Patras.

Thomason, Sarah Grey & Terrence Kaufman. 1988. *Language contact, creolization, and genetic linguistics*. Berkeley, CA: University of California Press.

Thumb, Albert. 1906. Prinzipienfragen der Koine-Forschung. In Johannes Ilberg & Bernhard Gerth (eds.), *Neue Jahrbücher für das Klassische Altertum Geschichte und Deutsche Literatur und für Pedagogik*, vol. 17, 246–263. Leipzig: Druck & Verlag von B.G. Teubner.

Thumb, Albert. 1910. *Handbuch der neugriechischen Volkssprache: Grammatik, Texte, Glossar*. Second, corrected and expanded edition. Strassburg: Verlag von Karl J. Trübner.

Tombaidis, Dimitrios. 1964. Ποντιακά γραμματικά [Pontic grammar notes]. *Αρχείον Πόντου [Pontus Archive]* 26. 150–158.

Tombaidis, Dimitrios. 1980. Συμβολή στην έρευνα του ονοματικού συνόλου της ποντιακής [A contribution to the investigation of the nominal group of Pontic]. *Αρχείον Πόντου [Pontus Archive]* 36. 220–237.

Tombaidis, Dimitrios. 1988. *Η ποντιακή διάλεκτος [The Pontic dialect]*. Athens: Committee for Pontian Studies.

Tombaidis, Dimitrios. 1992. Η τύχη των μικρασιατικών ιδιωμάτων στον ελληνικό χώρο [The fate of the Asia Minor dialects in Greece]. *Centre for Asia Minor Studies Bulletin* 9. 241–250.

Tombaidis, Dimitrios. 1996. Η ποντιακή διάλεκτος [The Pontic dialect]. In Dimitrios Tombaidis (ed.), *Η Ποντιακή διάλεκτος [Studies on the Pontic dialect]*, 222–233. Thessaloniki: Kodikas.

Topcharas, K. 1998 [1932]. *Η Γραμματική της Ποντιακής: I Γραμματικι τι Ρομεικυ τι Ποντεικυ τι Γλοσας [The grammar of Pontic Greek]*. Reproduction of the original 1932 Rostov-on-Don edition. Thessaloniki: Kyriakidis Brothers.

Tzitzilis, Christos. 1989. Zu den griechisch-türkischen Sprachbeziehungen. *Linguistique Balkanique* 32. 185–197.

Tzitzilis, Christos. In press. Sprachbund and etymology: Turkish etymology and the Anatolian Sprachbund. In Gebhard J. Selz (ed.), *The Tietze Symposium Proceedings (Vienna 14–17, July 2014)*. Vienna: Institut für Orientalistik, University of Vienna.

Ura, Hiroyuki. 2000. *Checking theory and grammatical functions in universal grammar.* Oxford: Oxford University Press.

Vassalou, Dimitris Papazachariou, Nikoleta & Mark Janse. 2016. Methodological principles of mišótika cappadocian data collection. Paper presented at the *7th International Conference on Modern Greek Dialects and Linguistic Theory*, 6–8 October 2016, Rethymnon.

Vogel, Ralf. 2003. Surface matters: Case conflict in free relative constructions and case theory. In Ellen Brandner & Heike Zinsmeister (eds.), *New perspectives in case theory*, 269–300. Stanford, CA: CSLI Publications.

Wechsler, Stephen & Larisa Zlatić. 2003. *The many faces of agreement.* Stanford, CA: CSLI Publications.

Witzlack-Makarevich, Alena & Ilja A. Seržant. 2018. Differential argument marking: Patterns of variation. In Alena Witzlack-Makarevich & Ilja A. Seržant (eds.), *Diachrony of differential argument marking*, 1–40. Berlin: Language Science Press. https://doi.org/10.5281/zenodo.1228243.

Woolford, Ellen. 2001. Case patterns. In Géraldine Legendre, Jane Grimshaw & Sten Vikner (eds.), *Optimality-theoretic syntax*, 509–543. Cambridge, MA: MIT Press.

Woolford, Ellen. 2008. Differential subject marking at argument structure, syntax and PF. In Helen de Hoop & Peter de Swart (eds.), *Differential subject marking* (Studies in Natural Language & Linguistic Theory), 17–40. Dordrecht: Springer. https://doi.org/10.1007/978-1-4020-6497-5.

Wunderlich, Dieter. 1997. Cause and the structure of verbs. *Linguistic Inquiry* 28(1). 27–68.

M. Rita Manzini, Leonardo Savoia, and Ludovico Franco

DOM and dative in (Italo-)Romance

Abstract: We aim at showing that the superficial identity of DOM internal arguments and of goal dative involves no accidental homophony or syncretism, but rather an underlying identical structure of embedding. Specifically, we conclude that DOM arguments are syntactically oblique (Section 2). We introduce the matter by detailing referential/animacy splits in Italo-Romance microvariation (Section 1.1). We show that in Italian varieties goal arguments can be introduced by prepositions different from *a*; the same oblique morphology is then associated with animate/definite (DOM) objects (Section 1.2). In Section 5, the existence of both *leísta* varieties (Ibero-Romance) and *loísta* varieties (in Italo- and Ibero-Romance) in clitic doubling provide further evidence in favour of a common treatment for goal and DOM datives.

Keywords: differential object marking, dative, locative, clitic doubling, Italo-Romance

1 DOM in Italian varieties

This section details microvariation in differential object marking (DOM) in Central and Southern Italian varieties, in Sardinian, in the dialects of Romagna and Montefeltro, in Corsican and in Romansh.[1] In Section 1.1 we order our data according to the categories of animacy and definiteness/specificity that are generally held to be descriptively relevant for the distribution of DOM. In Section 1.2 we address the nature of the preposition that lexicalizes DOM in the relevant languages and its relation to the preposition lexicalizing dative. This latter issue is directly relevant for the analysis of DOM as obliquization in Section 2 and for the subsequent discussion of the issues this proposal raises (Sections 2 to 5).

---

[1] The data collected here are mainly taken from the corpus of Manzini & Savoia (2005), and are made available for non-Italian speaking scholars. The IPA transcription is simplified by the elimination of stress diacritics.

M. Rita Manzini, Università degli studi Firenze
Leonardo Savoia, Università degli studi Firenze
Ludovico Franco, Università degli studi Firenze

https://doi.org/10.1515/9783110666137-006

1.1 Animacy and definiteness splits

As is well-known from both the historical-typological and the formal literature, the set of DPs undergoing DOM crosslinguistically may be characterized in terms of a hierarchy on whose descriptive content there is considerable agreement, though it is not obvious what exactly orders it: whether classical notions of animacy and/or definiteness (Aissen 2003) or more abstract notions (Kiparsky 2008). It is not an aim of the present contribution to advance new proposals in this respect. However it is convenient to introduce the morphosyntactic microvariation of Central and Southern Italian varieties in this way. This also allows us to make a general point on the nature of microvariation.

To begin with, in the varieties in (1), the presence of (obligatory) DOM is limited to 1/2 personal pronouns (Loporcaro 1988: 269 for the Altamura dialect). While DOM is generally restricted to noun phrases characterized by a high position in the animacy hierarchy, the maximum of animacy in such a hierarchy is attributed to the discourse participants (henceforth 1/2P). 1/2P elements admit of a straightforward denotational characterization as the speaker, hearer coordinates of the universe of discourse. In (1) the (a), (b) examples illustrate DOM; the (a′), (b′) examples set up the contrast with object DPs (including 3P personal pronouns) not undergoing DOM.

(1) Colledimacine (Abruzzi)

    a.   *a   camatə a   mme / a   nnu*
          he.has called DOM me   DOM us
          'He has called me / us.'

    a′. *a   camatə frattə   tiə   / kwiʎʎə*
          he.has called brother mine   him
          'He has called my brother / him.'

Cagnano Amiterno (Abruzzi)

    b.   *camanu a   tti / a   mmi / a   nnu / a   vvu*
          they.call DOM you DOM me   DOM us   DOM you.PL
          'They call you / me / us / you.PL'

    b′. *camanu frate   tu   / issi / issu*
          they.call brother yours them him
          'They call your brother / them / him.'

In other dialects, DOM is restricted to personal pronouns (1/2/3P), as in (2).

(2) Torricella Peligna (Abruzzi)

    a. kwillə vaitə a   mmɛjə / a   nniəwə / (a)   kkwillə
       he   sees DOM me   DOM us   DOM him
       'He sees me / us / him.'

    a'. so   camætə frɔt-tə   / kellə femənə
       I.have called brother-yours that woman
       'I have called your brother / that woman.'

Canosa Sannita (Abruzzi)

    b. ji camə a   ttɛ / a   vvo   / (a) kkullu
       I call DOM you   DOM you.PL DOM him
       'I call you / him.'

    b'. ji camə fratə-tə
       I call brother-yours
       'I call your brother.'

Several varieties differentiate pronouns and kinship terms, which are obligatorily introduced by the DOM preposition, from other DPs, including human animate ones. This split, privileging kinship terms, evokes the fact that kinship terms have a number of properties more reminiscent of proper names than of other DPs.[2] Therefore the languages in (3) correspond to a high cut of the animacy hierarchy, namely proper name–like DPs as opposed to other human/animate DPs.

(3) Accettura (Lucania)

    (addʒə camə:tə) ...
    I.have called

    a. a   jeddə / a   tta feɲə   a'. (a) kɛdda: femənə
       DOM him   DOM your son   DOM that woman
       'I have called him / your son / that woman.'

---

[2] Specifically, Longobardi (1994) argues that proper names in a language like Italian raise from N to the D position, so that they are in complementary distribution with D elements. While singular count nouns in Italian require an overt D, kinship terms exclude it – which is also true in the varieties in (3). In this respect, kinship terms are formally (not just cognitively) close to proper names.

Celle di Bulgheria (Campania)
(camu) ...
I.call

b. *a   iddu / a   ffrati-tu*   b'. *(a)   dd ɔmu*
    DOM him   DOM brother-yours   DOM the man
'I call him / your brother / the man.'

Nocara (Calabria)
(addʒə camə:tə) ...
I.have called

c. *a   ɲellə / a   ffrɜ:tə tujə*   c'. *(a)   kkiəlla fiəmmənə*
    DOM him   DOM brother yours   DOM that   woman
'I have called him / your brother / that woman.'

Ittiri (Sardinia)
(appɔ ʒamaɾu) ...
I.have called

d. *a   issu / a   bbabbu ɾou*   d'. *(ai) kussa femina*
    DOM him   DOM father yours   DOM that   woman
'I have called him / your father / that woman.'

Paulilatino (Sardinia)
(appɔ bbistu) ...
I.have seen

e. *a   issu / a   ffiddzu ðu*   e'. *(ai) ɣuɖɖ ommine*
    DOM him   DOM son   yours   DOM that man
'I have called him / your son / that man.'

Tempio Pausania (Sardinia)
(camu) ...
I.call

f. a iḍḍu / a ttɔ vraeḍḍu   f'. (a) kissa vɛmina
    DOM him DOM your brother   DOM that woman

'I call him / your brother / that woman.'

Munacia d'Auddè (Corsica)
(aɟɟu istu) ...
I.have seen

g. a kkwiḍḍu / a to sureḍḍa   g'. (a) kwiḍḍa fɛmmina
    DOM him DOM your sister   DOM that   woman

'I have seen him / your sister / that woman.'

In many varieties a DP is, or may be, introduced by the DOM preposition if it has a human denotation, regardless of its definite/indefinite status, as illustrated in (4). The first example of each pair presents DOM with an indefinite human object — while the second example contrasts it with a non-human definite, establishing that definiteness does not enter in the equation.

(4) Scuol (Engadine)
(klɔma) ...
call

a. (ad) yn om   a'. il tʃaŋ
    DOM   a   man   the dog

'Call a man / the dog!'

S. Vittore (Lazio)
(addʒə camatə) ...
I.have called

b. a nnu kriturə   b'. ʎu kaːnə
    DOM a   child   the dog

'I have called a child / the dog'

Gallo Matese (Campania)

(γɛ cɔ:mə) ...
I call

c.	a	nə ɣwaʎʎoːnə	c'.	ru	kuɔnə
	DOM	a boy		the	dog

'I call a boy / the dog'

Giovinazzo (Apulia)

(sɔ cameːtə) ...
I.have called

d.	(a)	nu mənɪːnə	d'.	u	keːnə
	DOM	a boy		the	dog

'I have called a boy / the dog'

Orroli (Sardinia)

(appu tserriau) ...
I.have called

e.	(a)	un ommini	e'.	su	ɣani
	DOM	a man		the	dog

'I have called a man / the dog'

Alimena (Sicily)

(ji camu) ...
I call

f.	a	un uəmʊ	f'.	u	kanɪ
	DOM	a man		the	dog

'I call a man / the dog'

In other varieties, DOM is triggered by definiteness/specificity. The data in (5) present systematic contrasts between definite noun phrases in the left-hand column, which are introduced by the DOM preposition, and indefinite ones in the right-hand column, which are not introduced by the DOM morpheme or only optionally so. Definite inanimates are associated with DOM in the (b″), (c″), (e″) examples, establishing the fact that definiteness is paramount in these instances.[3]

---

[3] The possibility for inanimates to be DOM objects is pointed out by Rohlfs (1971).

The optionality effect in the right-hand column, can be attributed to the fact that so-called indefinites have at least two readings: a properly indefinite reading by which they represent true variables, and a specific one.[4]

(5) Minervino Murge (Apulia)

(jaɲɲə camæːtə) ...
I.have called

a.	a	kkwɛraː fɛmənə	a'.	na	fɛmənə
	DOM	that woman		a	woman

'I have called that / a woman'

Gorgoglione (Lucania)

(addʒə camɛːtə) ...
I.have called

b.	ɔ	kriatuːrə	b'.	nu	kriatuːrə
	DOM	the		a	child

'I have called the / a child'

(miəttə) ...
put

b".	a	kkeistə
	DOM	this

'Put this in!'

Guardia Perticara (Calabria)

(addʒə camaːtə) ...
I.have called

c.	ɔ	ɣwaʎʎoːnə	c'.	nu	kriatuːrə
	DOM	the		a	child

'I have called the / a child'

(miəttə) ...
put

---

[4] Some of the varieties exemplified in (5), namely Nocara, also appear in the set of examples in (3). They make a three-way distinction: kinship terms (obligatory DOM), definite human DPs (possible DOM), indefinites (no DOM).

c″. *a   kkwestə kkwa*
    DOM this   here
'Put this one in!'

Nocara (Calabria)

(*εddʒə camɜːtə*) ...
   I.have called

d. (*a*)   *kkiəlla fiəmmənа*　　　　d′. *na fiəmmənа*
    DOM that   woman　　　　　　　　　a   woman
'I have called that / a woman'

Camerota (Campania)

(*addʒu vistu*) ...
   I.have called

e. *a   kkilli waʎʎuni*　　　　　　e′. (*a*)   *nu waʎʎuni*
    DOM that boy　　　　　　　　　　　　DOM a   boy
'I have seen that / a boy'

(*ɲdʒi lεvu*)   ...
   there I.take.away

e″. *a   kkistu*
    DOM this
'I take this away from it'

Làconi (Sardinia)

(*a   βiu*) ...
   he.has seen

f. (*ai*) *kussas feminaza*　　　　f′. *una vemina*
    DOM those   women　　　　　　　　　　DOM a
'He has seen those women / a woman'

Modica (Sicily)

(*vitti*) ...
   I.saw

g. *ɔ   kani*　　　　　　　　　　　g′. *n uommənu*
   DOM the　　　　　　　　　　　　　　　　a man
'I saw the dog / a man'

Some varieties associate DOM with definite/specific human referents – while both definite non-humans and indefinite humans are not introduced by DOM. Some examples are in (6).

(6) Albidona (Calabria)

(ddʒə vistə) ...
I.have seen

    a.   a   kwəllu krəstia:nə   a'. u   kuanə / nu krəstia:nə
        DOM that person   the dog   a   person

'I have seen that / a person / the dog'

Cirò Marina (Calabria)

(ε camate) ...
I.have called

    b.   a   kkira fimmənə / a   n ɔmənə ε kirə
        DOM that woman   DOM a man of those

    b'. nu ɔmənə / u   kanu tɔjə
        a man   the dog yours

'I have called that woman / one of those men / a man / your dog'

Ittiri (Sardinia)

(appɔ ʒamaru) ...
I.saw

    c. (ai) kussa femina   c'. un omine / zu ɣanε
        DOM that woman   a man   the dog

'I saw the dog / a man'

Further restrictions have been suggested by the literature to be relevant for the distribution of DOM, such as a notion of affected object for Spanish (Torrego 1998). Nevertheless, according to the corpus study of von Heusinger & Kaiser (2011) all definite animate internal arguments in Spanish are associated with DOM, independently of the nature (affecting/non affecting) of the predicate. In addition, in Spanish, DOM with indefinite animate arguments is in fact more systematic with verbs classes such as perception verbs or psych verbs that have non-affected objects. One of the core verbs used in the Italo-Romance examples in (1)–(6) is *see*, which takes a non-affected object.

The description of splits along the so-called animacy/definiteness hierarchy would not be complete without mentioning the fact that quantifiers such as *no one, someone, who* are usually introduced by the DOM preposition. Of particular relevance in this respect are the varieties that display sensitivity to a high cut in the hierarchy, such as Munacia or Paulilatino in (3). As shown in (7b) and (7c) DOM is not merely possible, but obligatory with *nobody* and with *who*. In the variety of Celle di Bulgheria in (7a) *somebody* also behaves in the same way.

(7) Celle di Bulgheria

    a. *nu ccamu a nniʃʃuni*
        not I.call DOM nobody
        'I do not call anybody.'

    a'. *a kki cami*
        DOM who you.call
        'Who do you call?'

    a''. *camu a kkwakkunu*
        I.call DOM somebody
        'I call somebody.'

Paulilatino

    b. *nɔ appɔ bbistu a nnɛmmɔzɔ*
        not I.have seen DOM nobody
        'I haven't seen anybody.'

    b'. *a kkiɛ a βistu*
        DOM who he.has seen
        'Who has he seen?'

Munacia

    c. *un aɟɟu istu a nnimu*
        not I.have seen DOM nobody
        'I haven't seen anybody.'

    c'. *a kkwali cammani*
        DOM who they.call
        'Who do they call?'

Other varieties of special interest are those in (5) that display sensitivity to definiteness. The data in (8) shows that they also introduce DOM in front of quantifiers like *nobody* and *who*.

(8) Gallo Matese

    a. *nə ca:mə a nnəʃʃu:nə*
       not I.call DOM nobody
       'I do not call anybody.'

    a'. *a kki camə*
       DOM who you.call
       'Who do you call?'

Minervino Murge

    b. *nan aɟɟə cammætə a nnəʃʃɛunə*
       not I.have called DOM nobody
       'I haven't called anybody.'

    b'. *(a) tʃə a cammætə*
       DOM who you.have called
       'Who did you call?'

Nocara

    c. *ɔnn ɛddʒə camɜ:tə a nnəʃʃunə*
       not I.have called DOM nobody
       'I haven't called anybody.'

    c'. *a kkɪ ɛi βɪstə*
       DOM who you.have seen
       'Who did you see?'

Làconi

    d. *nɔ βiaɾa a nnɛmmɔzɔ*
       not he.sees DOM nobody
       'He hasn't seen anybody.'

    d'. *a ttʃinni tserriaza*
       DOM who you.call
       'Who do you call?'

Modica

    e. *n tʃamai a nnuɖɖu*
       not I.called DOM nobody
       'I didn't call anybody.'

e'. a   kku ʃamaʃti
    DOM who you.called
    'Who did you call?'

It is true that the quantifiers in (7)–(8) have human referents and they may be attributed to the same D category as personal pronouns. As animate pronouns they may therefore jump to the top of the hierarchy. Alternatively, however, the data in (7)–(8) may suggest that a correct understanding of the referential scale governing the distribution of DOM requires its interaction with information flow at the Conceptual–Intentional (C–I) interface to be considered, hence a notion of topicality (É. Kiss 2017). As indicated at the beginning, these themes are largely beyond the scope of the present work.

At the same time, the detailed evidence we presented allows us to make an important point on the nature of parameterization, since in the dialectological domain of Italian varieties we can see displayed all (and only) the parameters normally arising between different language families. Thus Aissen (2003) reviews well-known facts about DOM privileging a definiteness cut in Iranian but an animacy cut in Indo-Aryan. As for Spanish, Aissen takes it to exemplify a language where animacy and definiteness are both relevant. In the microcosm of Italian dialects we find replicated the same variation found in the macrocosm of the Indo-European family, it would appear that this variation is hardly dictated by areal or other external considerations, but is endemic to grammatical systems.

In the next section we will get closer to our theoretical aims, by presenting a further data set, which illustrate Italian varieties where the preposition that introduces DOM is not *a* 'to'. Crucially we will find that even though different prepositions may be involved, if they externalize DOM, they also externalize goal datives. This sets the stage for the theoretical discussion in Section 2, where we argue that DOM (in Romance and Indo-European languages) is indeed obliquization.

1.2 DOM = dative

From the point of view adopted in this paper, as will become more explicit from the analysis that we will provide in Section 2, the most notable syntactic property of the Romance DOM is its morphological coincidence with the dative, introduced by the preposition *a* (Jaeggli 1981, Torrego 1998, Manzini & Franco 2016). Our idea is that this coincidence reflects a real underlying (syntactic and interpretative) identity. Prima facie evidence for such a claim comes from variation in prepositional systems. Some varieties from the Montefeltro use the prepositional morpheme *ma* for the DOM argument, while Gallo-Italic dialects of Sicily use the preposition *da* (Rohlfs 1969 [1954]: §632). Crucially, dative arguments are consistently introduced by the same morphemes. Hence, there is systematic co-variation between the preposition used to introduce the descriptive dative and the descriptive DOM.

Relevant data from some Montefeltro varieties are reproduced in (9)–(11). The preposition *ma* introduces the DOM internal argument, as in (a), and the goal dative argument, as in (b) — as well as locatives, with a restricted set of lexical items, as in (c). Importantly, it is not just the case that the *a* preposition is not available in these languages; rather it is found with locatives and as the prepositional introducer of infinitival control complements, as in (d)–(d′).[5]

(9) Mercato Saraceno (Romagna)

  a. *a tʃəm m(a) e   tu   fradɛl*
     I call DOM the your brother
     'I call your brother.'

  b. *a l dɛg ma lu*
     I it say to him
     'I say it to him.'

  c. *l ɛ ma kəza / ma la təvla / ma la porta*
     he is at home at the table at the door
     'He is at home / at the table / at the door.'

  d. *a sɔː a maɲɲa / a tʃezəna*
     I am at eat   in Cesena
     'I am eating / in Cesena.'

  d′. *a veg a kəza / a maɲɲa / a tʃezəna*
      I go to home to eat   to Cesena
      'I go home / to eat / to Cesena.'

(10) Sant'Agata Feltria (Marche)

  a. *cɛma ma la tu   surɛla*
     call DOM the your sister
     'Call your sister!'

---

[5] In the Manzini & Savoia (2005) corpus, similar data are reported for the varieties of Urbania, Piobbico, Tavullia (Marche) and Rontagnano (Romagna). According to Rohlfs (1969 [1954]: §639), the *ma* preposition is etymologically connected to Lat. *in medio ad* 'into the middle of'.

b. u   n   da   ɲint   ma niʃoɲ
   he of.it gives nothing to no one
   'He doesn't give anything to anyone.'

c. l   ɛ ma la porta / la tɜvla / kɛza
   he is at the door   the table   home
   'He is at at the door / at the table / at home.'

d. l   ɛ a maɲe:
   he is at eat
   'He is eating.'

d'. a vag a le   / a la   / a roma
    I go to there   to there above to Rome
    'I go there / over there / to Rome.'

(11) Mercatello sul Metauro (Marche)

a. ɔ   vist   ma   l   tu   fratɛl
   I.have   seen   DOM the your brother
   'I have seen your brother.'

b. l ɔ   dat   ma lʊ
   it I.have given to   him
   'I have given it to him.'

c. lʊ ɛ   ma kɛza / ma la   tavla / ma la   pɔrta
   he is home   at the table   at the door
   'He is at home / at the table / at the door.'

d. lʊ ɛ a urbiŋ
   he is in Urbino
   'He is in Urbino.'

d'. va a kɛza / a urbiŋ / a veda
    go to home   to Urbino   to see
    'Go home / to Urbino / to see!'

In Italian, the same lexicalization space is uniformly taken by *a* 'at/to' as in (12).

(12) Italian
   a. *Ho   dato   il   libro a Gianni*
      I.have given the book to Gianni
      'I have given the book to Gianni.'
   b. *Sono a casa / a tavola / alla   porta / a Firenze*
      I.am at home   at table   at.the door   in Florence
      'I am at home / the table / at the door / in Florence.'
   c. *Vado a casa / a tavola / alla   porta / a Firenze*
      I.go to home   to table   to.the door   to Florence
      'I go home to the table to the door to Florence.'

In the variety of Avigliano Umbro, *da* lexicalizes goals, as in (13b) and DOM, as in (13a) — further strengthening the conclusion that the coincidence of goal and DOM arguments is not a matter of accidental syncretism.[6] Importantly, the language does have the *a* preposition, lexicalizing locative state, or motion to, as in (f). In (c)–(d), locations at deictic or human referents are expressed by *da*, independently of whether it is a state as in (d) or a motion to, as in (c). Otherwise *da* specializes for motion from, in (e).

(13) Avigliano Umbro (Umbria)
   a. *camo da   esso*
      I.call DOM him
      'I call him.'
   b. *lo ɾajo da mmi fratɛllo*
      it I.give to my brother
      'I give it to my brother.'
   c. *vajo lla   da esso*
      I.go there to him
      'I go to him there.'
   d. *stɔnno   lla   da esso*
      they.are there by him
      'They are by him.'

---

6 Similar data are reported by Manzini & Savoia (2005) for Macchie Amelia (Umbria).

e. vɛŋgo da su / ju kkasa
I.come from up down home
'I come from up / down home.'

f. vajo a ttɔdi
I.go to Todi
'I go to Todi.'

The occurrence of *da* with highly ranked locations may not be irrelevant for its occurrence in DOM/dative contexts in (13). However, there is no causal connection between the two, since the distribution of *da* in Avigliano Umbro is as in Italian (14), covering location-at and motion-to with highly ranked referents, and all motion-from.

(14) Italian

a. *Vengo da casa / Firenze*
I.come from home Florence
'I come from home / Florence.'

b. *Sono / vado da lui / Maria*
I.am I.go by/to him Maria
'I am by / I go to him / Maria.'

In Gallo-Italic varieties of Sicily, the preposition *da* also introduces goal datives, as in (15b), and DOM, as in (15a). However with ablatives we find the preposition *ɾa/ða* 'of' as in (15c), which also introduces genitives. As for the preposition introducing locatives with highly ranked referents, in Aidone we find the item *nnə*, as in (15d-e) which does not have independent prepositional uses, but rather occurs as the wh-pronoun for 'where'. Thus the data of Aidone strengthen the generalizations that we have been drawing so far — essentially that dative and DOM are interrelated.

(15) Aidone (Sicily)

a. stawə tʃamannə ɾa iwə / ɾa ti / ɾa tta fra / ɾa
I.was calling DOM him DOM you DOM your brother DOM
ḍḍa fumənə
the woman
'I was calling him / you / your brother / the woman.'

b. *u stawə ðaʒinnə ðatta fra / ð ɛ karoʒə*
   it I.was giving to your brother / to the children
   'I was giving it to your brother / to the children.'

c. *stawə vəninnə rə n kazə mijə / ðə məssinə / ðə ŋ*
   I.was coming from in house mine / from Messina / from in
   kambaɲɲə
   countryside
   'I was coming from home / Messina / the countryside.'

d. *iwə vɛŋə nnə/ndə mi*
   he comes to me
   'He comes to me.'

e. *jɛ nn/nd iwə*
   he.is by him
   'He is by him.'

In short, though prepositions introducing goal datives vary, the same preposition that introduces datives introduces DOM arguments in Romance. Eastern Romance is an exception to this generalization, but still falls under a slightly broader generalization to the effect that DOM arguments are introduced by oblique prepositions (see footnote 13). The DOM/dative connection is generally true in Indo-European languages (and Basque, Odria 2014),[7] suggesting that DOM arguments may be not just accidentally or superficially connected to datives – but they may really be obliques (Manzini & Franco 2016).[8] This is the analysis we will develop in Section 2 — in contrast both with traditional, descriptive approaches which treat DOM as a

---

[7] An anonymous reviewer enquires whether DOM in Basque may be triggered by language contact with Spanish. This may well be so, but it is hardly relevant, given that DOM=Dative syncretism is a widespread feature of natural languages, independently of areal considerations. Just to give an example, Amharic (Afro-Asiatic, Amberber 2012) is one of the many non-Indo-European languages displaying DOM=Dative. Furthermore, one cannot really invoke genetic continuity for the Indo-European spread of the phenomenon, since no morphological continuity is involved. Thus Italian *a* for dative is a neo-formation entirely independent of the other neo-formation, as e.g. -*ko* of Hindi. The same point holds of the *a* of Italian vs. *ma* of (9)–(11). Finally one may want to raise the question whether grammaticalization can provide an alternative account for the link between datives and DOM (in terms of a semantic shift from dative to accusative, or vice versa). The point is that grammaticalization is a weaker explanation than the one entertained here, namely actual identity. Therefore compelling empirical reasons are required to retreat to it.

[8] See Manzini & Franco (2016: 228-230) for discussion of some languages (Turkish, Finnish) in which DOM does not seem to take the form of obliquization of highly ranked referents. Franco &

special accusative ('prepositional accusative') and to generative treatments (Jaeggli 1981, Torrego 1998) which adopt the same accusative view. The analysis of systems, including the connection between dative/DOM and locative, is the object of a separate study (Franco et al. to appear).

2 DOM as an oblique Case

In Section 2.1 we provide a characterization of the dative Case/preposition as an elementary predicate introducing a part-whole (possession) relation; we further propose that DOM instantiates the same elementary predicate. Therefore, DOM applies to highly ranked referents within the VP raising them to the role of possessor. This approach faces potential problems whenever DOM arguments pattern with direct objects rather than indirect objects in a number of respects; in Section 3, we consider passivization. In Section 4 we provide a brief outline of how the micro-variation presented in Section 1 fits in with the proposed analysis.

2.1 The nature of oblique Case and of DOM

Our framework is defined by current minimalist models of generative grammar (Chomsky 1995, 2001), which in part also provide a framework theory of Case. We take a view under which the lexicon precedes syntax, and in fact projects it, in keeping with the minimalist postulate of Inclusiveness (Chomsky 1995). Within the minimalist approach, properties such as gender (nominal class), number and person, which are intrinsically associated with nominal constituents, are features. However, relations, such as theta-roles, are not features, but correspond simply to syntactic configurations. From this perspective, it is potentially problematic to find that Case is treated as a feature, i.e. as nominal class or number rather than as theta-roles. The fact that Case is the only feature in Chomsky (1995) which is radically uninterpretable (i.e. which does not have an interpretable counterpart) is a reflex of the deeper difficulty in reconciling the traditionally relational core of this notion with its feature status. The solution to which Chomsky (2001) arrives is that the real underlying relation between Case assigner and Case assignee is

---

Manzini (2017a), take into consideration languages (Slavic, Eastern Iranian) and Finnic in which a genitive=DOM syncretism applies (cf. also Kaiser *et al.* this volume).

an agreement relation, involving phi-features; Case is but a reflex of this relation which appears on nominal constituents.[9]

As far as we can tell, the empirical range of Chomsky's proposal only directly covers nominative and accusative (reflexes of phi-feature checking on T and *v* respectively). If we ask ourselves how Chomsky's approach could be applied to obliques, the literature on the functional head Appl comes naturally to mind (Pylkkänen 2008, Cuervo 2003, Pineda 2016). According to this literature, a functional head Appl checks the descriptive dative. We could therefore say that dative is but the reflex of phi-feature agreement between Appl and a DP. However, in the languages we are considering there is no evidence for applicative verbal affixes – on the contrary, there is abundant evidence of adnominal morphology (Case, prepositions). We therefore avoid taking the circuitous route of attributing such overt morphology to feature checking with an abstract Appl.

A fairly obvious intuition on oblique Cases, originally formalized by Fillmore (1968), is that they are the inflectional equivalent of prepositions (English *to* = dative, English *of* = genitive, etc.). If a preposition is a predicate introducing a relation between the argument it selects and another argument, so therefore is oblique Case. If we say that (oblique) Case has a relational content (it is effectively an inflectional counterpart of elementary predicates like Ps), then it is evident that we take the category Case, or to be more precise, oblique Case, to be interpretable – i.e. endowed with some interpretive content, albeit elementary. Based on these considerations, Manzini & Savoia (2011), Manzini & Franco (2016) propose an analysis of dative and genitive Case as elementary relators, extended then to DOM.

Genitive Case, or the preposition *of*, are canonically taken to introduce the possession relation. An idea put forth in very similar terms by various strands of literature is that possession is in fact a surface manifestation of the more elementary part-whole, inclusion relation. Belvin (1996) argues that the predicate *have* does not denote possession or ownership, but rather it means *include*. Inclusion, as defined by Belvin, is not concerned with the member-set relation, but rather with the concept of zonal inclusion, where the notion of zone refers to "a region of space-time". Belvin assumes there is only one *have* with a fixed inclusion meaning, and semantic variation arises from the context. Belvin & den Dikken (1997: 170) define the relation introduced by *have* as zonal inclusion in the following terms: "Entities have various zones associated with them, such that an object or eventuality may be included in a zone associated with an entity without being

---

[9] Baker & Vinokurova (2010), writing on Sakha (Turkic), argue that Case cannot be reduced *in toto* to phi-feature agreement; for accusative they suggest reverting to the dependent Case algorithm of Marantz (2000). This matter is orthogonal to the present discussion, which is concerned with obliques – assuming that DOM is an oblique as well.

physically contained in that entity... The type of zones which may be associated with an entity will vary with the entity". Manzini & Savoia (2005, 2007) propose that the Romance genitive/partitive clitic *ne* introduces a pronominal set which is a "superset-of" some other argument of the sentence (the internal argument).[10]

On the basis of this construal of possession, let us consider datives. The line of analysis of ditransitive verbs initiated by Kayne (1984) is characterized by the assumption that verbs like *give* take a predication as their complement; the content of this predication is a possession relation between the accusative direct object (the possessum) and the dative (the possessor). For Pesetsky (1995) the predicate head is *to*, as in (16a). The same is true for Harley (2002) who takes English *to* to be a P_{LOC} as in (16b).[11] Beck & Johnson (2004) follow Larson (1988) in adopting a

---

10 In many languages the ablative lexicalizes partitives (e.g. in Turkic languages, Koptjevskaja-Tamm 2009); this is also true of the *ne* clitic, which can convey motion-from. As already mentioned, the connection between possession/inclusion obliques and obliques is left for a separate study. Our idea goes against the grain of classical assumptions about the primitive nature of the spatial system, in proposing that eventual meanings are derived from inclusion (Franco et al. to appear). Thus the ablative meaning 'y out of x' is dependent on inclusion, i.e. 'y in x'; note that English also uses *out of* in partitive expressions.

11 Here we reject the characterization in favour of an inclusion one (see the discussion below). Miyagawa & Tsujioka (2004) argue that, in Japanese, there are two distinct goal positions, a possessor goal and a locative goal, though both are encoded by the *ni* morpheme. Their evidence includes the fact that when both goals appear in the same sentence, the word order is quite rigid and the low goal cannot precede the high goal as in (i)-(ii); note that the goal can independently precede the theme, though it need not to.

(i) Japanese
Taroo-ga Hanako-ni Tokyo-ni nimotu-o okutta.
Taro-NOM Hanako-DAT Tokyo-to package-ACC sent
'Taro sent Hanako a package to Tokyo.'

(ii) Japanese
*Taroo-ga Tokyo-ni Hanako-ni nimotu-o okutta.
Taro-NOM Tokyo-to Hanako-DAT package-ACC sent
'Taro sent Hanako a package to Tokyo.'

In the terms of footnote 10, the basis for the syncretism between goal dative and motion-to in Japanese (as in English *to*, Romance *a* etc.) is the common notion of inclusion (Franco et al., to appear). At the same time the two arguments differ in that the inclusion relation is locatively restricted in motion-to contexts. It is this restriction that implies different attachments; recall that in English dative *to* but not *to* undergoes dative shift.

variant of the same fundamental structure where the DP and *to*-DP complements occupy the Spec and sister position of V respectively, as in (16c).

(16) a. ... give a letter [PP to Sue]   (Pesetsky 1995)
    b. ... CAUSE [PP a letter [[P-LOC to] Mary]]   (Harley 2002)
    c. ... [VP the guide [V' send to Satoshi]]   (Beck & Johnson 2004)

In present terms, if the *to* preposition (or dative Case) heads a possession predication, then it is associated with the inclusion (part-whole) content. We notate inclusion with (⊆), though as indicated by the discussion that precedes, the inclusion relation is to be construed not mathematically but as a looser zonal inclusion one. Prepositions like English *to* or Italian *a* that have (⊆) content are notated P(⊆), as in the structure of Italian (17) in (18). In (18), P(⊆) takes as its internal argument its sister DP *Gianni* and as its external argument the sister to its projection, i.e. the DP *il libro* 'the book'. Correspondingly, the second internal argument of *dare* 'give', i.e. the traditional dative, participates in fixing the reference of the first internal argument, i.e. the accusative, by denoting a superset/domain/zone including it.

(17) Italian
    Ho   dato   il   libro   a   Gianni
    I.have given the book   to Gianni
    'I have given the book to Gianni.'

(18)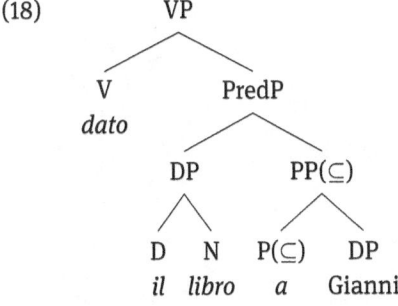

An issue arises in connection with datives that are complements of unergative verbs. Evidently, in the absence of an internal argument, we cannot run the analysis in (18) for examples like Italian (19a); conversely, we need an analysis capable of differentiating the dative internal argument in (19a) from the accusative (direct object) in (19b).

(19) Italian

    a. *Parla   a Gianni*
       he.talks to Gianni
       'He talks to Gianni.'

    b. *Chiama Gianni*
       he.calls Gianni
       'He calls Gianni.'

We propose that in (19a) the two arguments of P(⊆) are again the DP embedded under it and, as we propose, an eventive constituent, adapting the characterization of so-called high Appls.[12] Intuitively, transitive predicates can be paraphrased as consisting of an elementary predicate associated with an eventive name. Hale & Keyser (1993), Chomsky (1995) formalize this intuition about the complex nature of transitive predicates by assuming that they result from the incorporation of an elementary state/event into a transitivizing predicate (CAUSE). In minimalist syntax the transitivizing predicate is standardly built into the structure in the form of a *v* functional head. Within such a conceptual framework, (19a) can be informally rendered as 'He causes him to be on the receiving end of some talk', or more directly 'He causes him talk (i.e. to be talked to)', corresponding to the *v*-V organization of the predicate in structure (20).

(20)

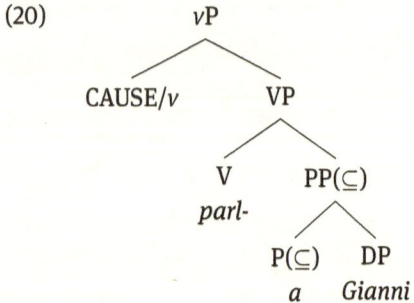

By contrast, despite the causative, two-layered organization of the predicate, complements of *chiamare* 'call' (or rather 'cause call'), as in (19b), are embedded in a canonical transitive structure comprising a nominative agent and an accusative theme. In other words, in Italian, *chiamare* 'call' behaves as a single predicate,

---

12 See Boneh & Nash (2012) for a review of problems arising in classifying French datives according to the categories low and high Appl, as understood by Pylkkänen (2008).

its complementation structure displaying no sensitivity to the presence of (potential) subevents/states in it. Vice versa, the dative with *parlare* 'talk' is a result of the sensitivity of argument structure to the finer event articulation of the predicate. In this respect we agree with Svenonius (2002: 202) that "there is no such thing as idiosyncratic lexical Case; that is, ... that a verb takes a dative object is ... not entirely independent of event structural properties". At the same time, we also expect a certain amount of crosslinguistic variation in the externalization of complements as either direct objects or obliques (see Manzini & Franco 2016: 217–218 on *help*, Svenonius 2002 on Icelandic vs. English).

Summarizing so far, we take a fairly classical possession approach to dative goals, as schematized in (18). We extend this treatment to non-ditransitive contexts, where we propose that the oblique Case/preposition introduces a possession/part-whole relations involving a (sub)event, as in (20). These are the fundamental ingredients that we need for our analysis of DOM as an oblique. Let us start with the varieties where DOM has a particularly restricted distribution, namely 1/2P elements, as in (1a), repeated below in (21a) for ease of reference. We take the syncretism of DOM and dative in Italian varieties to point to a common underlying structure. So the structure in (21b) must parallel that provided in (20) for dative complements – which is also the fundamental insight of Torrego (2010), Pineda (2014). Specifically, following the interpretation that we have imputed to structures like (20), we will say that the internal argument with Participant (speaker, hearer) reference in (21) is construed as a possessor/locator of the VP subevent.

(21) a. *a   camatə   a   mme / a   nnu*   (=(1a))
        he.has   called   DOM   me   DOM   us
        'He called me/us.'

   b.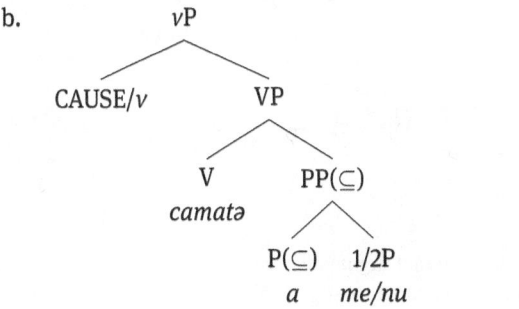

The question is whether this extension of the treatment of datives to DOM provides an adequate, or eventually revealing, match to known empirical evidence.

It is worth noticing that though any number of abstract logics can be imposed on natural languages, one of the few insights that we can have into their real underlying logic is provided by lexicalization patterns. In Section 2.1 dative complements imply sensitivity to the two-layered structure of transitive/unergative complements, while direct objects imply insensitivity to it. Similarly according to Svenonius (2002), the presence of a dative complement implies the activation of a split eventive structure – though only in some languages and for some predicates. dative complements are clues to underlying structural and interpretive differences, albeit subtle ones. The same logic applies to (21). There is no *a priori* reason why an argumental frame including a Participant internal argument should reflect a complex organization of the event with verbs like *call* in (21) – and one where the Participant plays the role of possessor (locator) of the VP event. However, the lexicalization patterns of the dialects reviewed in Section 1 suggest that this is what happens. In other words, the surfacing of highly ranked (DOM) internal arguments as datives is no morphological accident – nor does it reflect a merely morphological regularity. DOM arises in the syntax, reflecting a slightly different structuring of the event with Participant internal arguments.

At the same time there is a profound difference between dative arguments, e.g. in (20), and DOM arguments in (21). With goal datives, the $P(\subseteq)$ constituent is required by the predicate – it is in effect what Chomsky (1986) calls an inherent Case, i.e. a Case required by the verb (or perhaps at the interpretive level by the eventive content). By contrast, making explicit what the discussion so far merely suggests, the DOM dative is a $P(\subseteq)$ headed constituent required by the referential properties of the internal argument. Languages with DOM datives are those where an argument with certain referential properties can never be inserted VP-internally except under $P(\subseteq)$.[13] In (21), it is Participant arguments that must be embedded under $P(\subseteq)$ when inserted as internal arguments. The constraint can be formulated as in (22), leaving for the time being open the range of DPs that can undergo DOM beyond 1/2P.

(22) DOM
     $[_{VP}$ V $[$ *$P(\subseteq)$ DP $]]$ where DP=1/2P etc.

---

[13] In Romanian, animate/definite internal arguments are introduced by the preposition *pe*, which is independently attested in Romanian as a(generally rendered as 'on') (see Irimia, this volume). We have already suggested in footnote 10 that locatives (for instance *a* locatives) can be construed in terms of a restriction on the $(\subseteq)$ relation, namely 'x included by y, y a location'. Suppose we apply this general suggestion to Romanian *pe*. The realization of DOM arguments by *pe* will involve the basic predicate $(\subseteq)$ minus the locative restriction.

The constraint in (22) says that a Participant argument cannot be embedded under VP as a theme object; rather it can be embedded in VP only as long as it is construed as entailing a possessor (locator, etc.) relation to the event. This is not a translation in structural terms of commonly held views about DOM. Specifically, (22) does not connect to the idea that DOM is a way of providing a "differential marking" for an accusative object – notably for reasons of distinctiveness, as implied by functionalist approaches. On the contrary, DOM consists in the obliquization of a direct object – consequent to the fact that in some languages only a suitably low ranked referent can be a bare object, while a highly ranked referent is interpreted as the possessor/locus of the event.[14]

3 The passive issue

The reason that is often put forth in the descriptive and theoretical literature in favour of a characterization of DOM as a special accusative morphology, is the fact that it can be passivized. This contrasts with the behaviour of datives, which cannot be promoted to subject at all, in Romance languages. Before proceeding to the analysis (following Manzini & Franco 2016: 219–222), we briefly illustrate passivization in Italian dialects with DOM using examples with Middle-Passive (MP) clitic *si*. We break our examples in three sets, but the facts are identical throughout (23)-(25).[15] (23) illustrates passivization in dialects with a high cut in the animacy/definiteness hierarchy — namely just deictic arguments (Canosa Sannita) or proper names/kinship terms. In the relevant languages, the 3P pronoun found in the subject position of the passive would obligatorily undergo DOM in object position. In this sense, DOM object passivize in these languages.

(23) a. Canosa Sannita
 kwillə tsi vedə sɛmbrə a ppas'sa
 they MP see.3SG always to pass.by
 'They are always seen passing by.'

---

[14] This conceptualization is not found in other formal literature. From a cognitive viewpoint, similar considerations are advanced by Enghels (2007) (cf. Enghels & Vanderschueren 2009), who argues that dative-marked internal argument are semantically interpreted as owners/subjects of an embedded sub-event, based on a series of quantitative studies on perception verbs in Spanish.
[15] We report the data in some detail because Fábregas (2013), following Spanish-speaking literature, mentions comparable examples in Spanish as being ill-formed. The Italian data show that the Spanish phenomenon does not have any deep connections to DOM or other pan-Romance parameters.

b. Celle di Bulgheria

iddu si viði / lɔru si viðinu sɛmbi pas'sa
he MP see.3SG they MP see.3PL always pass.by
'He is / they are always seen passing by.'

c. Ittiri

issu s iðɛ / issɔs s iðɛnɛ ssɛmprɛ ßassɛndɛ
he MP see.3SG they MP see.3PL always passing.by
'He is / they are always seen passing by.'

d. Tempio Pausania

iɖɖu s iði / iɖɖi s iðini zɛmpri passɛndi
he MP see.3SG they MP see.3PL always passing.by
'He is / they are always seen passing by.'

e. Munacia d'Auddè

iɖɖu zi iði / iɖɖi zi iðini zɛmpri pas'sa
he MP see.3SG they MP see.3PL always pass.by
'He is / they are always seen passing by.'

Passivization is possible along the same lines in varieties which have a rather lower cut of acceptance of DOM, namely with human and/or definite referents, selectively illustrated in (24).

(24) a. S. Vittore

issə sə verə / verənə ʃpissə
he/they MP see.3SG see.3PL often
'He is / they are often seen.'

b. Camerota

jissu si viri / lɔru si virənu sɛmbə pas'sa
he MP see.3SG they MP see.3PL always pass.by
'He is / they are always seen passing by.'

c. Minervino Murge

luərə sə vɛrənə sɛmbə də passæ
they MP see.3PL always of pass.by
'They are always seen passing by.'

d. Albidona
   jillə sə ßiðə / ɣuərə sə ßiðənə ssɛmbə
   he   MP see.3SG   they MP see.3PL always
   'He is / they are always seen.'

e. Cirò Marina
   sə viðə/ viðənə ssɛmpə passarə ɛ   kka
   MP see.3SG see.3PL always pass   this way
   'He is / they are always seen pass this way.'

f. Modica
   iḍḍu si viri   / iḍḍi si virunu sɛmpri
   he   MP see.3SG   they MP see.3PL always
   'He is / they are always seen.'

g. Làconi
   si bbiara / bbianta zɛmpra ßassandu
   MP see.3SG   see.3PL always passing.by
   'He is / they are always seen passing by.'

In (25) we illustrate passive in some of the varieties displaying parameterization in the prepositional system, reported in Section 1.2.

(25) a. Mercatello sul Metauro
   sə vedə / vedənə sɛmpr a pa'sɛ
   MP see.3SG see.3PL always to pass.by
   'He is / they are always seen passing by.'

b. Avigliano Umbro
   loro se verono sɛmpre pas'sa
   they MP see.3PL always pass.by
   'They are always seen passing by.'

c. Aidone
   kuḍḍə sə virənə simbrə a pas'sɛ
   they   MP see.3PL always to pass.by
   'They are always seen passing by.'

By contrast, passives (*si* passives or others) involving the promotion of a goal dative to subject are generally not attested. Thus the passivization of Italian (24a) in (26) is ill-formed.

(26) Italian

*Gianni viene parlato
Gianni is talked
'John is talked (to).'

If the structure of goal dative in (20) and that of DOM in (21b) are the same, how come (20) cannot passivize, but (21b) can? Let us begin with (20). Given an underlying cause-result articulation of the event, P(⊆) introduces an argument construed as being a possessor-possessed relation with the result sub-event. Crucially, this dative is selected by the predicate, i.e. it depends on the shape of the event, not on the referential properties of the argument which P(⊆) embeds. We use this property of goal datives to explain why they cannot undergo passivization, raising to the Spec, IP/nominative position. Italian is a language where *parlare* 'talk' is always treated as a complex bi-eventive predicate, and P(⊆) is required by the predicate itself. In order to satisfy this selectional requirement, a P(⊆) internal argument must be merged under passive as well, as in (27). This means that precisely because of its inherent Case properties/embedding under PP, this internal argument is not available for movement.

(27) a.   [$_{VP}$ parlato [$_{P(⊆)}$ a Gianni]]

b. *[$_{VP}$ parlato [$_{DP}$ Gianni]]

On the contrary, we predict that there is nothing wrong with a passive structure where the goal dative is not raised to nominative. In other words, we correctly allow an impersonal passive where only arbitrarization of the external argument takes place, as in (28).

(28) Italian

È   stato parlato (di questo) a Gianni
it.is been talked of this   to Gianni
'Gianni has been talked to about this.'

At this point, we must explain why any internal argument of *see* raises to the Spec,IP/nominative position in the *si* passives in (23)–(25) — so that under passive, highly ranked referents, undergoing DOM behave just like lower ranked referents embedded as bare objects. Consider for instance the passivization in (29), from the Corsican variety of Munacia. The derivation of (29b) proceeds as in (29c). In passive, there is no *v*P phase (Chomsky 1995), the external argument is either not realized (and interpreted by existential closure) or demoted to oblique, and the extended projection principle (EPP) position is satisfied by the internal argument (*iɖɖu*) which receives nominative Case.[16] The DOM constraint in (22) does not apply to (29c) insofar as the relevant configuration is not defined, i.e. there is no referentially high ranked internal argument in VP that requires to be lexicalized as possessor/locus of the event. Had the DOM constraint been applied at First Merge, assigning oblique to the internal argument *iɖɖu*, the latter would not have been available for movement, blocking passive.

(29) Munacia d'Auddè (Corsica)

    a. *aɲu   istu a   kkwiɖɖu*   (=(3g))
        I.have seen DOM him
        'I have seen him.'

    b. *iɖɖu zi iði*   (=(23f))
        he   MP see.3SG
        'He is seen.'

    c. [$_{IP}$ iɖɖu [$_I$ si iri [$_{VP}$ ~~iði~~ [~~iɖɖu~~]]]]

As shown by the data in (7)-(8) in Section 1, DOM is also assigned to wh-phrases; a relevant example for Munacia is reproduced in (30a), with the derivation in (30b). Therefore DOM Case is preserved under wh-movement in (30b) though not under passivization in (30). This is because in (30) Case must be satisfied in the VP and cannot be satisfied at any other point in the derivation. Hence the DOM constraint in (22) is activated and oblique assigned.

(30) Munacia

    a. *a   kkwali cammani*   (=(7c'))
        DOM who   they.call
        'Who do they call?'

    b. [$_{CP}$ a kkwali [$_{IP}$ cammani [$_{vP}$ [$_{VP}$ ~~cammani a kkwali~~]]]]

---

[16] In (29c) we omit various details, such as the precise structure of the clitic *si*, which are of great importance in themselves, but irrelevant in the context of the present discussion (Manzini et al. 2016: see).

In short, goal obliques are selected by certain predicates (or events); this requirement cannot be circumvented derivationally. On the contrary, DOM obliques are enforced by (22), i.e. by a requirement on VP-internal high ranked referents; this constraint can be circumvented derivationally, i.e. by extracting the highly ranked referent to a VP-external position. Therefore, it is not necessary to hold that DOM objects are deep accusatives, or to deny that they are obliques, as they superficially appear to be, in order to predict that inherent obliques, but not DOM, interfere with passivization. An independently postulated distinction is sufficient, namely that, goal obliques are inherently Case marked (Chomsky 1986), while DOM arguments are assigned oblique Case structurally.

Importantly, some variation is also possible, in the sense that some languages treat the two types of obliques, DOM internal arguments and goal datives, in a unified way. This is the case at least for Apulian varieties, as illustrated in (31), where the goal argument of the verb *write* passivizes.[17]

(31) Minervino Murge

    a. jaɲɲə skrittə a jiddə
        I.have written to him
        'I have written to him.'

    b. jiddə jɛ statə skrittə (da la suərə)
        he is been written by the sister
        'He has been written (by the sister)'

It is tempting to interpret the data in (31) as implying that in these varieties goals are treated like DOMs. So, there are languages in which goal and DOM datives are identified as internal arguments, independently of the different eventive structure.

---

[17] The possibility of passivizing indirect objects in Apulian varieties with DOM is reported in the literature, as in (i)–(ii).

(i)   Bari, Apulia (Pineda 2014)
       Maríjə ha státə təlefonátə dò marítə
       'Maria has been phoned by the husband'

(ii)   Altamura, Apulia (Loporcaro 1988: 290ff)
       pəppinə venə skrittə do lɛttərə
       'Peppino is written two letters'

In other words, goal dative is dealt with as a type of DOM. If so, the data potentially reinforce our case in favour of the underlying similarity of DOM and goal datives, perhaps pointing to the generalization of the treatment of dative as a structural Case.

4 Further issues: referential ranking, predicate classes

In Section 1 we displayed a number of finely parameterized properties characterizing DOM. In this section, we briefly indicate how the relevant parameters fit in with the present account of DOM. The first issue that faces us is defining the classes of DPs that undergo DOM. Under (22), Participant clitics cannot be embedded in a predicate unless they are part of a possessor substructure. Languages without DOM are simply languages for which (22) holds of the empty set of referents, hence is void/undefined. On the other hand we know that referential splits can oppose not only Participants to other arguments, but also personal pronouns to other referents; or personal pronouns and proper names/kinship terms to other referents. We may further define a value in the parametric scale defined by the conjunction of human and definite properties. After this, descriptive definiteness and animacy properties diverge. In other words, the distribution of DOM may be determined by animacy or by definiteness disjunctively (Aissen 2003). These largely shared assumptions (see Kiparsky's 2008 D-hierarchy) are represented in what we label the Referential Hierarchy in (32b).

(32) a. DOM Constraint
 $[_{VP} \text{ V } [*(P\subseteq) \text{ DP }]]$

 b. Referential Hierarchy
 DP = (1/2P (& D pronoun (& name/kinship DP (& human definite DP (& human DP or definite DP)))))

Universal Grammar defines the Referential Hierarchy; however there is no prediction as to where a language will cut it. Evidently, the child who learns a language will have to fix where her/his language puts the boundary between lower ranked referents that allow for bare accusative embedding, and higher ranked referents that require the more complex oblique embedding. A number of issues are left open by the descriptive systematization in (32) – for instance, why human and definite properties, in principle distinct, enter into the same scale of higher and lower ranked referents. As already mentioned, the definition of the hierarchy is outside the scope of the present contribution. Our aim was simply to show that parametric variation can be written into our account of DOM by providing a DP scale, as in (32b), feeding the DOM constraint in (32a).

Next, a gradation between different types of predicates, favouring/requiring or disfavouring/disallowing DOM has often been argued for. Von Heusinger & Kaiser (2011: 611) observe such a gradation with indefinite animate objects in Spanish. As already mentioned in Section 1, all definite animate objects in their corpus are attached via DOM irrespective of the nature of the predicate. Furthermore, with indefinite human objects, verb classes that display DOM attachment include non affecting verbs (perception verbs, psych verbs). Therefore, affectedness does not seem to play a role. Our examples from Italian varieties in Section 1.1 confirm this conclusion, since one of the core verbs we used is non-affecting *see*.

The issue of verbal classes, like that of the Referential Hierarchy, is outside the scope of the present contribution. At the same time, it is worth pointing out that our analysis makes certain predictions. In essence, DOM amounts to the fact that highly ranked DPs enforce an attachment where they have an oblique/possession relation to the VP sub-event/state. Therefore we may surmise that in situations where the ranking of the argument makes it possible but not necessary for DOM attachment to take place, the likelihood of DOM depends on the accessibility of the two-layered *v*-V structure required by $P(\subseteq)$ attachment. Thus our analysis implies that in Spanish action predicates, psychological predicates and perception predicates have more transparent *v*-V structures than, say, non-psychological stative predicates.

In fact, some predicates exclude DOM independently of the definite/human nature of the object, specifically verbs of possession/ownership like *avere* or *tenere* 'have'. In the Romansh variety of Müstair in (33a–a′), we contrast a core stative, non-affecting verb (*know*), still displaying a DOM object, with *have*. In the Southern Italian variety of Cirò Marina, *tenere* 'have' excludes DOM, while *tenere* 'hold' displays DOM with definite human objects in (33b–b′).

(33) Müstair (Grisons)

    a. *jau kanoːʃ a kweːs omants*
       I know DOM those men
       'I know those men.'

    a′. *jau na trai filts / kweːs kindɛlts*
        I have three sons those children
        'I have three sons / those children.'

Cirò Marina

b. tɛnənə   a   kkirə ɣwaɲɲunə
they.hold DOM those boys
'They are holding those boys.'

b'. tɛnənə   kirə   ɣwaɲɲunə
they.have those boys
'Those boys are their sons.'

It is natural to surmise that the pattern in (33) depends on the fact that the content of the verb *have* is the reverse of the content of the dative preposition/Case. Since we notated the latter as ($\subseteq$) we may suggest ($\supseteq$) as the content of *have*, as in (34).[18] It would appear therefore the grammar avoids duplication of the possession structure – or perhaps specifically the combination of the dative inclusion relator and its reverse.

(34)   [$_{VP\supseteq}$ tɛnənə [(*P$\subseteq$) kirə ɣwaɲɲunə]]

In conclusion, the questions briefly noted in this section (referential hierarchy, predicate gradation) are amply discussed in the literature. The presentation here merely scratches the surface. At the same time, it was important to indicate that the proposal put forth here does not interfere with known approaches to referential hierarchies and may actually contribute to an understanding of predicate gradation.

5 Cliticization of DOM arguments

The main aim of the present article is to show that the morphological coincidence of goal datives with the DOM in many languages should be building it into the syntax, implying that DOM arguments are not differentially marked accusatives, but rather obliques. In Section 3 we have considered perhaps the most important difficulty with this conclusion, concerning movement. As anticipated there, another notable computational processes with which our hypothesis potentially interacts is agreement. Relevant languages for observing this interaction are those

---

[18] According to Franco & Manzini (2017b), ($\supseteq$) is also the content of instrumentals and comitatives, as externalized by the preposition *with* (Italian *con*). Most transparently, *the girl with a hat* expresses the same relation between the two arguments as *the girl has a hat* – which reverses the dative (or genitive) relation: *(give) a hat to the girl* or *the hat of the girl*.

that display overt agreement of the verb with the accusative object – or in ergative languages (e.g. the Indo-Aryan languages) with the absolutive object. In principle two configurations may arise, as indicated in (35).

(35) Possible (object) agreement configurations with DOM and goal arguments
   a. DOM arguments agree with the verb, inherent dative arguments do not
   b. DOM and inherent dative arguments do not agree with the verb

Indo-Aryan languages verify the existence of both pattern (35b), which is expected under the present approach, and pattern (35a), which is expected under the assumption that DOM is a deep accusative. For instance, lack of agreement of both DOM and inherent datives characterizes Hindi and Punjabi, which therefore instantiate patterns (35b). Indo-Aryan languages which implement the scenario in (35a) include Rajasthani, where DOM and absolutive objects agree, though goal datives do not (Manzini & Franco 2016 and references quoted there).

When it comes to Romance, a number of reasons conspire to restrict the range of Romance data bearing on this research question. First, Ibero-Romance does not display object agreement at all. Italian varieties do display object agreement, but normally only with elements that have moved to the left of the perfect participle (either to the Spec, IP position or cliticized), as indicated by Kayne (1989). Therefore, testable varieties are restricted to a set of Central and Southern Italian varieties displaying agreement with the object *in situ* (including those in D'Alessandro & Roberts 2010). Many of these varieties phonologically reduce final vowels (to schwa) so that agreement can only be seen by the presence of metaphony (Ablaut) on the tonic vowel of strong (rhizotonic) participles. This conspiracy of factors means that Romance data on the agreement question as formulated in (35) are not readily available.[19]

We will therefore move our research to the domain of Romance cliticization, and ask the following variant of the agreement question: to the extent that doubling is possible/required with DOM objects, which clitics surface in doubling

---

19 Central-South Italian varieties in the Manzini & Savoia (2005) corpus where DOM and agreement with the object in situ both occur include at least Gallo Matese, S. Vittore, Colledimacine, Torricella Peligna, Roccasicura. The corpus includes no evidence as to the interaction of the two phenomena. According to Manzini & Franco (2016), Manzini & Savoia (to appear) there is independent evidence that Romance displays the same alternations as Indo-Aryan. They argue that 1/2P object clitics in Italian (and most other Romance languages, though not in Romanian) are subject to DOM. They further observe that 3P accusatives always trigger agreement with the perfect participle, while 1/2P objects (DOM by hypothesis) may or may not trigger it. They argue that this optionality is a reflex of the parameter in (35) seen on a larger scale in Indo-Aryan.

structures – accusative or dative ones? In general, which clitics pronominalize DOM objects? Recall that in the third person, Romance varieties generally distinguish an accusative clitic (inflected for number and gender) from a dative clitic. For instance the accusative series of Italian is *lo/la/li/le* 'him/her/them(M)/them(F)', while the dative clitic is *gli/le* 'to him/to her' (plural *loro* 'to them' is not a clitic). In Spanish the accusative series is *lo/la/los/las* 'him/her/them(M)/them(F)', while dative comes in a SG/PL pair *le/les* 'to him/to her, to them'.

Traditional approaches hold that DOM objects are deep accusatives; therefore the prediction is that they are doubled/pronominalized by accusative clitics, even though goal datives are doubled/pronominalized by dative clitics, as in (36a). However, if DOM arguments share deep morphosyntactic properties with inherent datives, as assumed here, we predict that both are doubled (or more generally pronominalized) by the same clitics, as in (36b). In turn, the option in (36b) may be taken to imply either (i) that both DOM and goal datives correspond to dative clitics or (ii) that both correspond to accusative clitics. Perhaps surprisingly, all three possibilities in (36) are attested by the data.

(36) Possible cliticization configurations with DOM and goal arguments
   a. Clitics doubling/pronominalizing DOM arguments belong to the accusative series, clitics doubling/pronominalizing goal datives belong to the dative series;
   b. Clitics doubling/pronominalizing DOM and goal datives belong to the same series:
      (i) both belong to the dative series
      (ii) both belong to the accusative series.

We review the data instantiating the various possibilities in (36) in Section 5.1. In Section 5.2, we provide a preliminary analysis for them.

5.1 Cliticization and doubling

We begin our review of the interactions between DOM and cliticization by considering clitic doubling contexts. Early formal studies within the generative framework theorize that DOM enables clitic doubling in Spanish and its dialects, as both the clitic and the argument that doubles it independently receive Case (Jaeggli 1981), namely the clitic receives accusative, while DOM is introduced by the Case marker *a* — so clitic doubling implies DOM. A different correlation is suggested by Dobrovie-Sorin (1994: 235), who notes that DOM is necessarily doubled by a clitic in Modern Romanian — so DOM implies clitic doubling. Already Suñer (1988) however highlights Spanish contexts in which clitic doubling is possible without the presence of DOM. Vice versa, the situation depicted by our examples of Italian varieties is one where without exception DOM is attested in the absence of clitic doubling. Therefore, the first important empirical conclusion to be retained is that, considering the entire spectrum of Romance variation, the two phenomena overlap but are not in an implicational relation.

Next, while Spanish and Romanian are uncontroversially taken to instantiate clitic doubling, Italian is normally taken to be a non-clitic doubling language. Actually, this is true at best of normative Italian. All Italian varieties, including the colloquial standard, display clitic doubling with the dative of highly ranked referents, as shown in (37) with Central and Southern Italian varieties that have been used to illustrate DOM in previous sections. Clitic doubling is favoured with pronouns, and is generally possible with definite human referents, in line with the referential hierarchy.

(37) a. Italian (non-normative)
Dammelo a me!
give-to.me-it to me
'Give it to me!'

b. Sant'Agata Feltria
u j / m el da m el tu fradɛl / mu mɛ
he him me it gives to the you brother to me
'He gives it to me / to your brother.'

c. Colledimacine
kwiʎʎə jə / ʎə da a nnu / a ddissə
he us him gives to us to him
'He gives it to us / to him.'

d. Torricella Peligna
jə lə dæ a kkwissə
him it he.gives to him
'He gives it to him.'

e. Minervino Murge
nə la dɔnnə a jeddə
him it he.gives to him
'He gives it to him.'

f. Aidone

   ɟ   u   da   a   iwə
   him it he.gives to him
   'He gives it to him.'

g. Làconi

   (si) / (mi) ɖɖu anti   a ffraɾi ɾua   / a mmimmi
   him   me   it   they.give to brother yours   to me
   'They give it to me / to your brother.'

h. Paulilatino

   (si) / ti ɖu jattsɔ a ffardɛ ɾu   / a ttiɛ
   him   you it I.give to brother yours   to you
   'I give it to you / to your brother.'

i. Munacia

   da-ɖɖi-lu   a iɖɖu
   give-him-it to him
   'Give it to him!'

Doubling with the dative of highly ranked referents characterizes Northern Italian dialects as well. In fact, in contexts involving pronouns, and in particular those pronouns denoting discourse participants (speaker, hearer), DOM prepositions can also surface in Northern Italian. Such examples are reported from the Trieste dialect in Ursini (1988: 548), e.g. *el te ga bastonado a ti*, lit. 'he you has beaten DOM you'; in (38a) we reproduce just an example from Modena. (38b) shows clitic doubling with human referents in the dative, as anticipated.

(38) Modena (Emilia)

   a. *i   m   tʃamen sɛmper a   mɛ*
      they me call   always DOM me
      'They always call me.'

   b. *a g   al dag   a   lo   / a   pirein*
      I   to.him it give to him   to Peter
      'I give it to him / to Peter.'

Clitic doubling with DOM objects is systematically attested in our data by varieties from the Montefeltro (with the DOM argument introduced by the preposition *ma*), as in (39). Clitic doubling with 1/2P pronouns is preferred in the variety of

Rontagnano, though 3P referent display DOM and no clitic doubling. In the variety of Mercato Saraceno doubling is allowed with a specific human DOM object, though the non-specific reading of the same DP is incompatible with both DOM and doubling.

(39) Rontagnano (Romagna)

a. tʃame-m mu   me
   call-me DOM me
   'Call me!'

a'. a t   ɔ   tʃa'mɜ ma teə
    I you have called DOM you
    'I have called you.'

a". aj ɔ   tʃa'mɜ ma lu / m   e   tu fraɛl
    I have called DOM him DOM the your brother
    'I have called him / your brother.'

Mercato Saraceno

b. a l ɔ   tʃ'ama m   un operai
   I him have called DOM a worker
   'I have called a worker.'

b'. a ɔ   tʃa'ma un operai
    I have called a worker
    'I have called a worker.'

What precedes however is sufficient to depict a picture of Italian varieties making them much more similar to Spanish than it is usually assumed. In essence, Standard Spanish has clitic doubling with pronouns, whether direct or indirect objects, and with indirect objects, while it excludes doubling with direct object — albeit highly ranked in the animacy hierarchy and therefore lexicalized by DOM. Most Italian varieties pattern with standard Spanish in presenting doubling with dative objects and with pronouns. This contrasts with the situation depicted for Rio de la Plata Spanish (Jaeggli 1981, Suñer 1988), where highly ranked referents that undergo DOM also undergo clitic doubling. Some Italian varieties (here Mercato Saraceno) seem to display an extension of doubling comparable to less restrictive varieties of Spanish.

With this much background we are now ready to consider the data that directly address the variation schema in (36) in Italo- and Ibero-Romance. The pattern in (36bii), whereby accusative clitics lexicalize both theme and goal arguments is robust in Central and Southern Italian varieties (Rohlfs 1969 [1954]: §633, Formentin 1998 on Old Neapolitan, Ledgeway 2000, 2009). Examples of this pattern from some of the varieties used here to exemplify DOM are reported in (40), covering Central and Southern Italy and Sardinia. In (b)-(f) we show that exactly the same clitics are lexicalized with the transitive verbs *see*, *call* and with the intransitive verb *speak* (which requires a *to* object in English as well). The data in (a) show the free alternation of dative and accusative clitics with *speak* in the dialect of S. Vittore. For Làconi in (g) we display both the lexicalization of the accusative with *speak* and *see*, and the possible alternative lexicalization of the dative with *speak*. The accusative clitic can be doubled by an *a* phrase, as shown in particular in (b). What is particularly worth noting about the parallelism between *call/see* and *speak* is that in perfect participle contexts in Sardinian, such as (f)-(g), both verbs can be seen to fully Agree with the clitic. For the reasons seen earlier, namely the phonological neutralization of final vowels to schwa, these data are simply difficult or impossible to see in Central and Southern varieties.

(40) S. Vittore

    a.   ʎə   /   la   parlə
           to.her   her   I.speak
           'I speak to her.'

    a'.   ʎ   /   l   addʒə parlaːtə
           to.him   him   I.have spoken
           'I have spoken to him.'

Celle di Bulgheria

    b.   u   parlanu   /   viɾinu   (a   iddu)
          him   they.speak   they.see   to/DOM   him
          'They speak to / they see him.'

Camerota

    c.   nunn   u   /   a   /   iː   parlu   /   viyu
          not   him   her   them   I.speak   I.see
          'I do not speak to / I see him / her / them.'

Nocara

    d.   u   /   a   /   i   parlə   /   viyə
          him   her   them   I.speak   I.see
          'I speak to / I see him / her / them.'

Guardia Perticara

e. u / a / lə parlə / cæ:mə
him her them I.speak I.call
'I speak to / I call him / her / them.'

Tempio Pausania

f. lu / la / li vaeḍḍu / iku
him her them I.speak I.see
'I speak to / I see him / her / them.'

f'. l aɟɟu vaiḍḍatu / vaiḍḍata / vaiḍḍati
him/her/them I.have spoken.M.SG spoken.F.SG spoken.PL

    vistu / vista / visti
    seen.M.SG seen.F.SG seen.PL

'I have spoken to / seen him / her / them.'

Làconi

g. ḍḍu / ḍḍa / ḍḍus / ḍḍas yistjɔnnɔ / bbiu
him her them.M them.F I.speak I.see
'I speak to / I see him / her / them.'

g'. ḍḍ appu kistjɔnnau / kistjɔnnara
him her I.have spoken.M.SG
'I have spoken to him / her.'

g''. ḍḍi yistjɔnnɔ
to.him/her I.speak
'I speak to him / her.'

The phenomenon illustrated in (40), namely the extension of accusative clitics to the complements of dative verbs, is known as *loísmo* in the Spanish literature, robustly attested in some varieties (Alvar 1996: 162, Fernández-Soriano 1999, Zdrojewski & Sanchez 2014). Henceforth we adopt the label *loísmo* to refer to the pattern in (36bii). The data in (40), especially in (40f) and (40g) allow us to check how clitics behave with respect to agreement with the perfect participle – a phenomenon absent from Ibero-Romance. The answer is that accusative clitics trigger agreement on both transitive and inherent dative participles. In other words, the relevant clitics do not just have the morphological form of accusatives – they behave like accusatives syntactically (D'Alessandro & Roberts 2010).

The conclusion that we are not witnessing a surface morphological phenomenon is further supported by dialects where a morphologically dative form is also possible, for instance S. Vittore in (a) or Làconi in (g); in other words, the accusative clitic is not merely repairing the absence of a specialized dative. In fact, dialects in (40) generally have a morphological dative clitic, which regularly shows up in ditransitive contexts. Some examples are provided in (41). Specifically, we display another couple of minimal pairs, in Celle di Bulgheria (a) and in Gorgoglione (b), showing the contrast between intransitive *write* with an accusative goal and transitive *write* with a dative goal. The example of Guardia Perticara in (c) forms a minimal pair with that displayed in (40).

(41) Celle di Bulgheria

    a. u / a ʃkrivu (a iddu / a issa)
       him her I.write to him to her
       'I write him / her a letter.'

    a'. li   ʃkrivu na littira
       to.him I.write a letter
       'I write him a letter.'

    Gorgoglione

    b. u / a / ɔ   skrivə
       him her them he.writes
       'He writes him / her / them.'

    b'. lə   skrivə na lɛittərə
       to.him I.write a letter
       'I write him a letter.'

    Guardia Perticara

    c. lə   rannə   kwestə
       to.him they.give this
       'They gave him this.'

    Làconi

    d. ɖɖi   a   kkustu
       to.him he.gives this
       'He gives him this.'

Recall that we have proposed a uniform treatment for all the noun phrases introduced by the preposition *a* in Italo-Romance, namely for both traditional datives and DOM. Under this treatment, one can expect that there are clitic systems in which both DOM and dative are doubled/pronominalized by the same clitic series. This prediction finds important support from the *loísmo* varieties reviewed so far, where both clitics show up in the accusative and Agree with the perfect participle. Importantly, the relevant varieties have also dative clitics, which are however constrained to ditransitive contexts, with a lexicalized accusative theme.

We will return to the syntactic analysis of *loísmo* in Section 5.2. Before doing so, however, other predictions regarding (36) need to be checked, beginning with (36bi). Are there languages where both inherent datives and DOM objects are lexicalized by dative clitics? Relevant examples of this pattern are not found in Italo-Romance, but are robustly documented in Spanish dialects, under the label *leísmo*; the phenomenon is widespread in Spanish varieties spoken in Central and South America (Alvar 1996: 63, 108, 205) and in Central Spanish and Basque varieties (Fernández-Soriano 1999, Ormazabal & Romero 2013). In *leísmo* varieties, the accusative clitic, e.g. *lo* in (42a), picks up an inanimate referent and does not enter doubling, while the *le* clitic, identical to the goal dative, picks an animate referent, eventually doubling a DOM object, as in (42b).

(42) Spanish (Basque Leísta Dialect, Ormazabal & Romero 2013: 316)

a. *Lo vi   / *lo vi   el libro*
   it I.saw it I.saw the book
   'I saw it / the book.'

b. *Le   vi   (al   niño / a   la niña)*
   to.him/her I.saw DOM.the boy   DOM the girl
   'I saw him / her / the boy / the girl.'

Within the present analysis, it is natural to conclude that the clitics in (42) reflect the same Case organization as their doubled DPs — hence goal and DOM datives coincide on the dative clitic *le*. Ormazabal & Romero (2007) reject the possibility that *le* in (42b) is a dative. One of their objections is that (42a) and (42b) can both passivize, while goal datives cannot. In view of the discussion in Section 3, this objection can be overcome. The main objection we are left with is that "unlike accusative *le*, dative *le* is not selective with respect to animacy". For instance examples like (43) are attested in Spanish, where the dative clitic doubles an inanimate goal.

(43) Spanish

Le   puse   el azúcar al   café
To.it I.put the sugar   to.the coffee
'I put the sugar in(to) the coffee.'

But what seems a problem to Ormazabal & Romero is the predicted outcome under present assumptions. Inherent datives such as the one in (43) are selected by the verb, and are assigned to arguments irrespective of their position in the Referential Hierarchy, hence to animates and inanimates alike. On the other hand only animate 3P clitics are embedded as DOM structural datives, on a par with their lexical DP counterparts in (42b); inanimates correspond to ordinary accusatives, as in (42a).[20]

Let us return to the schema in (36) once more. We have now seen that the pronominalization/doubling of DOM arguments by the same clitics as inherent datives is robustly attested – whether accusative clitics (*loísmo*) or dative clitics (*leísmo*) are involved. We must now consider the possibility that the two sets of elements have a different clitic counterpart or clitic doubling, as in (36a). This possibility is instantiated in some of the best known varieties of Spanish, namely the Standard – and the earliest of the dialects to be studied in the formal literature, namely Rioplatense Spanish (cf. also Leonetti 2008). In standard Spanish, animate and inanimate internal arguments are pronominalized by an accusative clitic, though doubling is not allowed, as in (44a); a DP lexicalizing a goal dative is doubled by a dative clitic, as in (44b). In Rioplatense Spanish, what changes is simply the possibility for the accusative clitic to double a DOM object, as in (45).

(44) Spanish (standard)
    a. Lo   vio   (*a   Juan)
       him he.saw DOM Juan
       'He saw him / Juan.'
    b. Le   dio   el libro (a Juan)
       to.him he.gave the book to Juan
       'He gave him the book (to John).'

---

20 Gallego (2013) strikes an intermediate position. He argues that *leísmo* involves a process of dative (as here), but derived from an accusative via movement to a functional head. However dativization *en route* seems to require a violation of Inclusiveness and in any event a realizational morphology. As an anonymous reviewer points out, there exists Spanish varieties (e.g. Basque Country Spanish) involving so-called *leísmo de cosa*, namely *leísmo* extended to inanimate participants. This is reminiscent of the fact that in more relaxed varieties of Romance, including Rioplatense Spanish (Suñer 1988), as well as the Southern Italian varieties in (5), an inanimate object can undergo DOM if it is definite/specific enough.

(45) Spanish (Rioplatense)
   Lo   vio   (a   Juan)
   him he.saw DOM Juan
   'He saw him / Juan.'

This well-known pattern appears to favour the view that the *a* phrase in (44a) is an underlying accusative, determining doubling by an accusative clitic. But the overall picture presents equally strong *prima facie* evidence in favour of the view supported here, namely that DOM results from the promotion of a highly ranked internal argument from theme to possessor, via merger of the (⊆) content — coming from *loismo* and *leísmo* dialects. We will now briefly outline a way of incorporating the parametric variation just observed into the present account.

5.2 Analysis

Let us begin with the simple observation that clitic doubling involves obligatory agreement (or non-distinctness) in phi-features. We may adopt the view that clitics and DPs are each separately merged in their relevant domains (Sportiche 1996), and then connected by Agree; the clitic in the inflectional domain serves as a probe for the DP in situ.[21] At the same time, the clitic and the doubled DP do not necessarily Agree in Case.

Consider first the *leísmo* pattern, exemplified in (42) above. From the present point of view, this pattern is one where the clitic and the DP it doubles/pronominalizes Agree in Case, namely in dative Case. It is therefore a fully expected pattern. More formally, they share the (⊆) property, lexicalized by P in front of the lexical DP and by dative Case on the clitic, as schematized in (46). What needs to be said in order to capture varieties like (46) is simply that in the relevant varieties the conditions attaching to VP-internal embedding of full DPs, also hold for the insertion of D heads in the clitic domain. So (*contra* Ormazabal & Romero 2013) there is no formal Agree relation with respect to Case — but it so happens that the same lexicalization conditions prevail in the predicative domain (full DP arguments) and in the inflectional domain (clitic D arguments).

---

[21] In conventional minimalist terms this implies that the phi-features of the clitic are uninterpretable/unvalued (Roberts 2010), so that something more should be said about instances where the same clitics occur alone with referential import. In reality it is far from obvious why agreement, *qua* identity, could not hold of two identical sets of valued/interpreted features (Manzini & Savoia 2007, 2011); see Manzini & Savoia (to appear) for a recent implementation of this idea.

(46) Spanish (Leísmo dialects)
 [$_{\text{IP}}$ [$_{\text{D}(\subseteq)}$ le] [$_{\text{I}}$ vi [$_{\text{VP}}$ v̵i̵ [$_{\text{PP}(\subseteq)}$ a la niña]]

Let us then consider the mismatch of an accusative clitic with a dative argument (*loísmo*), schematized in (47) for Celle di Bugheria's example in (40b). In present terms, there is a ($\subseteq$) Case mismatch not only when the DP argument corresponds to an inherent dative (with the verb *speak (to)*) but also when it corresponds to a DOM dative (with the verb *see*). Recall that inherent dative and DOM arguments can be distinguished among others on the basis of passivization; DOM datives passivize, while inherent datives with *speak (to)* do not passivize. The parallel behavior of goal and DOM *a* phrases under *loísmo* tendentially supports their unification.

(47) Celle di Bulgheria
 [$_{\text{IP}}$ [$_{\text{D}}$ u] [$_{\text{I}}$ parlanu/viðinu [$_{\text{VP}}$ p̵a̵r̵l̵a̵n̵u̵/̵v̵i̵ð̵i̵n̵u̵ [$_{\text{PP}(\subseteq)}$ a iddu]]

The discussion above suggests that DPs and clitics represent two separate implementations of the argument structure of the sentence. If so, (47) simply shows that each domain (the predicative domain and the inflectional domain) may have its own specific case pattern. To be more precise, in the clitic domain in (47) all internal arguments are simply lexicalized by Ds, bearing nominal class (gender) and number properties — but no oblique ($\subseteq$) property, irrespective of whether such a property is selected by the verb within VP or it is not.[22] One may wonder why the reverse asymmetry (i.e. bare DP arguments in VP and oblique clitics) does not seem to be attested. Ultimately, the answer must be that clitics have referential properties partially different from those of lexical elements. More precisely, P($\subseteq$) is required by the high referential ranking/goal status of lexical DPs; in the clitic domain no such requirement is present, insofar as 3P clitics do not reflect or codify any referential ranking.[23]

There is an important exception to the generalization that in languages like Celle di Bulgheria any internal argument is lexicalized by a bare D clitic (i.e. a so-called accusative). This is that in ditransitive configurations, goal clitics surface in the dative, as in structure (48), corresponding to example (41a'). In a functionalist vein, one may of course be tempted to invoke the need for disambiguation. There are formal means to implement the same basic idea. For instance, assuming the clitic to act as a probe for phi-features Agree in (48), we may consider that its closest goal is the direct object, yielding a reading different from the intended one. In

---

[22] Phi-feature Agree takes place between the D clitic and the DP argument embedded under the ($\subseteq$) oblique layer, which is therefore structurally transparent.
[23] On the contrary, 1/2P clitics necessarily codify DOM, if footnote 16 is correct.

other words, the right reading can be achieved only by having recourse to the specialized dative clitic. Economy considerations privilege the simpler lexicalization in (47) where possible.

(48) [$_{IP}$ [$_{D(⊆)}$ li] [$_I$ ʃkrivu [$_{VP}$ ~~ʃkrivu~~ na littira [$_{PP(⊆)}$ a iddu]]

The apparently most problematic configuration from the present point of view arises in the standard variety of Spanish or in Rioplatense dialects, where DOM obliques are doubled by accusative clitics, while goal datives are doubled by dative clitics, along the lines of (49), corresponding to examples (44)–(45).

(49) Spanish (standard/Rio de la Plata)
    a. [$_{IP}$ [$_D$ lo] [$_I$ vio [$_{VP}$ ~~vio~~ [$_{PP(⊆)}$ a Juan]]
    b. [$_{IP}$ [$_{D(⊆)}$ le] [$_I$ dio [$_{VP}$ ~~dio~~ el libro [$_{PP(⊆)}$ a Juan]]

It is a fact that in languages like (49) cliticization distinguishes lexical datives and DOM objects, while the present approach to DOM predicts a unified treatment for them. On the other hand, nothing we have said so far is incompatible with the conclusion that in the clitic domain, themes and goals are assigned accusative and dative respectively, and no DOM applies – even though DOM applies to lexical DPs in the predicative domain. This is simply another consequence of the assumption made at the outset, that the case array of clitics in the inflectional domain does not necessarily match the case array of lexical DPs in the predicative domain.

In short, the complex Standard Spanish vs. *loísmo* vs. *leísmo* parameter can be expressed within the present approach. Some additional assumptions may be involved in capturing the range of observed variation, but this is true of any approach. For instance, Ormazabal & Romero (2013) invoke the distinction between clitics *qua* D heads and clitics *qua* pure agreement heads (*leísmo*). The choice between the account we offered and alternative accounts is empirical; for instance one would need to evaluate present conclusions against other accounts drawing in not only *leísmo* but also *loísmo*.

6 Conclusions

We have argued that the superficial identity of DOM internal arguments and of goal datives involves no accidental homophony or syncretism, but rather an underlyingly identical syntactic structure of embedding. We have shown that in each Italo-Romance variety considered the same oblique morphology is consistently associated both with indirect objects and with animate/definite direct objects, though the particular preposition chosen may vary from language to language (Section 1.2). We have analyzed DOM arguments as syntactically datives, linking them to possession (Section 3) and further reducing possession to a surface manifestation of a more elementary part-whole relation (Section 2.1). We have addressed the main difficulties raised by the formal and traditional literature against the structural identification of DOM and dative, dealing with passive in Section 3. In Section 5, we have considered cliticization and clitic doubling, reviewing different possible Case matches between clitics and direct objects, DOM objects, goal datives (the Standard Spanish pattern, *loísmo, leísmo*), showing how they can be made consistent with the present proposals.

Acknowledgements

We thank our anonymous reviewers for useful comments and criticism. The authors contribute equally to this work. For Italian administrative purposes, Ludovico Franco takes responsibility of Section 2.

References

Aissen, Judith. 2003. Differential object marking: Iconicity vs. economy. *Natural Language & Linguistic Theory* 21(3). 435–483. https://doi.org/10.1023/A:1024109008573.
Alvar, Manuel. 1996. *Manual de dialectología hispánica: El español de América*. Barcelona: Ariel.
Amberber, Mengistu. 2012. Differential case marking of arguments in Amharic. In Andrej Malchukov & Andrew Spencer (eds.), *The Oxford handbook of case*, 742–755. Oxford: Oxford University Press.
Baker, Mark C. & Nadya Vinokurova. 2010. Two modalities of case assignment. *Natural Language & Linguistic Theory* 28(3). 593–642. https://doi.org/10.1007/s11049-010-9105-1.
Beck, Sigrid & Kyle Johnson. 2004. Double objects again. *Linguistic Inquiry* 35(1). 97–123. https://doi.org/10.1162/002438904322793356.
Belvin, Robert S. 1996. *Inside events*. University of Southern California dissertation.
Belvin, Robert & Marcel den Dikken. 1997. There, happens, to, be, have. *Lingua* 101(3-4). 151–183. https://doi.org/10.1016/S0024-3841(96)00049-6.
Boneh, Nora & Léa Nash. 2012. Core and non-core datives in French. In Beatriz Fernández & Ricardo Etxepare (eds.), *Variation in datives*, 22–49. Oxford: Oxford University Press.
Chomsky, Noam. 1986. *Barriers*. Cambridge, MA: MIT Press.
Chomsky, Noam. 1995. *The minimalist program*. Cambridge, MA: MIT Press.
Chomsky, Noam. 2001. Derivation by phase. In Michael Kenstowicz (ed.), *Ken Hale: A life in language*, 1–52. Cambridge, MA: MIT Press.

Cuervo, María Cristina. 2003. *Datives at large*. Cambridge, MA: MIT dissertation.

D'Alessandro, Roberta & Ian Roberts. 2010. Past participle agreement in Abruzzese: Split auxiliary selection and the null-subject parameter. *Natural Language & Linguistic Theory* 28(1). 41–72. https://doi.org/10.1007/s11049-009-9085-1.

Dobrovie-Sorin, Carmen. 1994. *The syntax of Romanian*. Berlin: De Gruyter.

É. Kiss, Katalin. 2017. The person-case constraint and the inverse agreement constraint are manifestations of the same inverse topicality constraint. *The Linguistic Review* 34(2). 365–395. https://doi.org/10.1515/tlr-2017-0004.

Enghels, Renata. 2007. La semántica de los verbos de percepcíon y la variacíon de régimen en español. *Revue de Linguistique Romane* 71. 73–98.

Enghels, Renata & Clara Vanderschueren. 2009. La construcción infinitiva tras verbos de percepción visual y auditiva: Un análisi comparative entre el portugués y el español. *Revue Romane* 44(1). 25–46.

Fábregas, Antonio. 2013. Differential object marking in Spanish: State of the art. *Borealis*: An International Journal of Hispanic Linguistics 2(2). 1–80. https://doi.org/10.7557/1.2.2.2603.

Fernández-Soriano, Olga. 1999. El pronombre personal: Formas y distribución: Pronombres átonos y tónicos. In Ignacio Bosque & Violeta Demonte (eds.), *Gramática descriptiva de la lengua española*, 1209–1275. Madrid: Espasa.

Fillmore, Charles. J. 1968. The case for case. In Emmon Bach & Robert Harms (eds.), *Universals in linguistic theory*, 1–88. New York: Holt, Rinehart, & Winston.

Formentin, Vittorio. 1998. Commento linguistico. In *Loise De Rosa, Ricordi, I*. Roma: Salerno.

Franco, Ludovico & M. Rita Manzini. 2017a. Genitive/'*Of' arguments in DOM contexts. *Revue Roumaine de linguistique* 62. 427–444.

Franco, Ludovico & M. Rita Manzini. 2017b. Instrumental prepositions and case: Contexts of occurrence and alternations with datives. *Glossa* 2(1), 8. 10.5334/gjgl.111.

Franco, Ludovico, M. Rita Manzini & Leonardo M. Savoia. To appear. Locative Ps as general relators: Location, direction, DOM in Romance. *Linguistic Variation*.

Gallego, Ángel. 2013. Syntactic variation in Romance *v*. Handout of a paper presented at the workshop 'Towards a Theory of Syntactic Variation', Bilbao, June 5–7, 2013.

Hale, Ken & Samuel Jay Keyser. 1993. On argument structure and the lexical expression of grammatical relations. In Kenneth Hale & Samuel J. Keyser (eds.), *The view from Building 20*, 53–109. Cambridge, MA: MIT Press.

Harley, Heidi. 2002. Possession and the double object construction. *Linguistic Variation Yearbook* 2(1). 31–70. https://doi.org/10.1075/livy.2.04har.

von Heusinger, Klaus & Georg A. Kaiser. 2011. Affectedness and differential object marking in Spanish. *Morphology* 21(3-4). 593–617. https://doi.org/10.1007/s11525-010-9177-y.

Jaeggli, Osvaldo. 1981. *Topics in Romance syntax*. Dordrecht: Foris.

Kayne, Richard S. 1984. *Connectedness and binary branching*. Dordrecht: Foris.

Kayne, Richard S. 1989. Facets of Romance past participle agreement. In Paola Benincà (ed.), *Dialect variation and the theory of grammar*, 85–103. Dordrecht: Foris.

Kiparsky, Paul. 2008. Universals constrain change; Change results in typological generalizations. In Jeff Good (ed.), *Linguistic universals and language change*, 23–53. Oxford: Oxford University Press.

Koptjevskaja-Tamm, Maria. 2009. A lot of grammar with a good portion of lexicon: Towards a typology of partitive and pseudo-partitive nominal constructions. In Johannes Helmbrecht,

Yoko Yoko, Shin Yong-Min, Stavros Skopeteas & Elisabeth Verhoeven (eds.), *Form and function in language research*, 329–346. Berlin: De Gruyter.

Larson, Richard K. 1988. On the double object construction. *Linguistic Inquiry* 19(3). 335–391.

Ledgeway, Adam. 2000. *A comparative syntax of the dialects of southern italy: A minimalist approach*. Oxford: Blackwell.

Ledgeway, Adam. 2009. *Grammatica diacronica del napoletano*. Berlin: De Gruyter.

Leonetti, Manuel. 2008. Specificity in clitic doubling and differential object marking. *Probus* 20(1). 33–66. https://doi.org/10.1515/PROBUS.2008.002.

Longobardi, Giuseppe. 1994. Reference and proper names: A theory of n-movement in syntax and logical form. *Linguistic Inquiry* 25(4). 609–665.

Loporcaro, Michele. 1988. *Grammatica storica del dialetto di altamura*. Pisa: Giardini.

Manzini, M. Rita & Ludovico Franco. 2016. Goal and DOM datives. *Natural Language & Linguistic Theory* 34(1). 197–240. https://doi.org/10.1007/s11049-015-9303-y.

Manzini, M. Rita, Anna Roussou & Leonardo M. Savoia. 2016. Middle-passive voice in Albanian and Greek. *Journal of Linguistics* 52(1). 111–150. https://doi.org/10.1017/S0022226715000080.

Manzini, M. Rita & Leonardo M. Savoia. 2005. *Morfosintassi generativa*. 3 vols. Alessandria: dell'Orso.

Manzini, M. Rita & Leonardo M. Savoia. 2007. *Studies in romance and albanian varieties*. London: Routledge.

Manzini, M. Rita & Leonardo M. Savoia. 2011. Cambridge: Cambridge University Press.

Manzini, M. Rita & Leonardo M. Savoia. To appear. Person splits in Romance varieties: Implications for parameter theory. In András Bárány, Theresa Biberauer, Jamie Douglas & Sten Vikner (eds.), *Nominal architecture and its consequences: Synchronic and diachronic perspectives*.

Marantz, Alec. 2000. Case and licensing. In Eric Reuland (ed.), *Arguments and case*, 11–30. Amsterdam: John Benjamins. https://doi.org/10.1075/la.34.04mar.

Miyagawa, Shigeru & Takae Tsujioka. 2004. Argument structure and ditransitive verbs in Japanese. *Journal of East Asian Linguistics* 13(1). 1–38. https://doi.org/10.1023/b:jeal.0000007345.64336.84.

Odria, Ane. 2014. Differential object marking and the nature of dative case in Basque dialects. *Linguistic Variation* 14(2). 289–317. https://doi.org/10.1075/lv.14.2.03odr.

Ormazabal, Javier & Juan Romero. 2007. The object agreement constraint. *Natural Language & Linguistic Theory* 25. 315–347. https://doi.org/10.1007/s11049-006-9010-9.

Ormazabal, Javier & Juan Romero. 2013. Differential object marking, case and agreement. *Borealis: An International Journal of Hispanic Linguistics* 2(2). 221–239. https://doi.org/10.7557/1.2.2.2808.

Pesetsky, David. 1995. *Zero syntax*. Cambridge, MA: MIT Press.

Pineda, Anna. 2014. What lies behind dative/accusative alternations in Romance. In Stefania Marzo & Karen Lahousse (eds.), *Romance languages and linguistic theory 2012: Selected papers from 'Going Romance' Leuven 2012*, 123–139. Amsterdam: John Benjamins. https://doi.org/10.1075/rllt.6.06pin.

Pineda, Anna. 2016. *Les fronteres de la (in)transitivitat: Estudi dels aplicatius en llengües romàniques i basc*. Barcelona: Institut d'Estudis Món Juïc.

Pylkkänen, Liina. 2008. *Introducing arguments*. Cambridge, MA: MIT Press.

Roberts, Ian. 2010. *Agreement and head movement*. Cambridge, MA: MIT Press.

Rohlfs, Gerhard. 1969 [1954]. *Grammatica storica della lingua italiana e dei suoi dialetti: Sintassi e formazione delle parole*. Torino: Einaudi.

Rohlfs, Gerhard. 1971. Autour de l'accusatif prépositionnel dans les langues romanes. *Revue de Linguistique Romane* 35. 312–334.

Sportiche, Dominique. 1996. Clitic constructions. In Johan Rooryck & Laurie Zaring (eds.), *Phrase structure and the lexicon*, 213–276. Dordrecht: Kluwer.

Suñer, Margarita. 1988. The role of agreement in clitic-doubled constructions. *Natural Language & Linguistic Theory* 6(3). 391–434. https://doi.org/10.1007/BF00133904.

Svenonius, Peter. 2002. Icelandic case and the structure of events. *Journal of Comparative Germanic Linguistics* 5(1–3). 197–225. https://doi.org/10.1023/A:1021252206904.

Torrego, Esther. 1998. *The dependencies of objects*. Cambridge, MA: MIT Press.

Torrego, Esther. 2010. Variability in the case patterns of causative formation in Romance and its implications. *Linguistic Inquiry* 41(3). 445–470. https://doi.org/10.1162/LING_a_00004.

Ursini, Flavia. 1988. Varietà venete in friuli – venezia giulia. In Michael Metzeltin Günter Holtus & Christian Schmitt (eds.), *Lexikon der Romanistischen Linguistik*, vol. IV, 538–550. Tübingen: Niemeyer.

Zdrojewski, Pablo & Liliana Sanchez. 2014. Variation in accusative clitic doubling across three Spanish dialects. *Lingua* 151(B). 97–240. https://doi.org/10.1016/j.lingua.2014.08.003.

Pei-Jung Kuo
Topicality and differential object marking in Mandarin Chinese: Identity and variety in an array of structures

Abstract: In this paper I discuss differential object marking in Mandarin Chinese. In addition to the BA construction examined by Yang & van Bergen (2007), I demonstrate that differential object marking is also observable in the verb copying construction and the transitive V–O compound verb construction. Essentially, I propose that differential object marking in these three constructions is closely related to internal topicalization. Structurally, comparison of the relevant features of internal topicalization among these three constructions reveals individual differences. Finally, the case of external topicalization is also addressed to complete the picture of differential object marking in Mandarin Chinese.

Keywords: BA construction, verb copying construction, transitive V–O compound verbs, internal topicalization, external topicalization

1 Introduction

Mandarin Chinese is well-known as an isolating language, such that there are no overt case markers or agreement systems available in Chinese syntax. As such, it is probably quite unexpected that differential object marking is available in Chinese since, in most other languages, differential object marking is strongly associated with agreement or case systems.[1] In the following discussion, however, I will argue that differential object marking is indeed available in Mandarin Chinese. Moreover, differential object marking in Mandarin Chinese correlates with/reflects topicalization. A relation between differential object marking (DOM) and topicalization has been argued to exist in other languages, as argued by García García (2005) for Spanish, Guntsetseg (2009) for Mongolian, Dalrymple & Nikolaeva (2011) for Tundra Nenets (Uralic) and Tigre, and many others.

Since there are no overt case markers or agreement systems available in Chinese, the focus of syntactic study is placed greatly on the word order. The typical

---

[1] Note that differential object marking here is defined as a syntactically derived mechanism, rather than a morpho-phonological marking.

Pei-Jung Kuo, National Chiayi University

word order for a declarative sentence in Chinese is shown in example (1). As one can see, the word order follows the pattern Subject–Verb–Object.

(1) *Zhangsan mai-le zhe-ben shu*.
Zhangsan sell-ASP this-CLF book
'Zhangsan sold this book.'

Sometimes, in order to stress how the subject deals with the object in a disposal manner, Chinese employs the BA construction to illustrate intention. The BA construction counterpart of example (1) is shown in (2). The underlined object in example (1) now takes a preverbal position in example (2), preceded by a BA marker. In the literature, the disposal function of the BA construction has received the most attention and has also been widely discussed (see Y.-H. A. Li 2006 for summary). However, Yang & van Bergen (2007) (see also van Bergen 2006) observed another special property of the BA construction. That is, they propose that the lexical item BA in the BA construction serves as a type of differential object marker in Mandarin Chinese.

(2) *Zhangsan ba zhe-ben shu mai-le.*
Zhangsan BA this-CLF book sell-ASP
'Zhangsan sold this book.'

A well-known feature of DOM cross-linguistically is that the use of the marking is sensitive to the [±definiteness] and [±animacy] of the object NP (i.e. Bossong 1985 and Aissen 2003). For example, van Bergen (2006), has proposed the following universal prominence scales for definiteness and animacy, as show in (3) and (4) respectively.

(3) *Definiteness scale*
Pronoun > Proper Noun > Definite NP > Indefinite Specific NP > Indefinite Non-specific NP

(4) *Animacy scale*
Human > Animate > Inanimate

The BA construction shows an interesting correspondence with the two scales of DOM. In example (5a), when the object NP is a generic or specific/definite [–animate] NP, BA is optional.² However, an obligatory BA marker results in ungrammaticality when the object is an indefinite non-specific [–animate] NP as in (5b).

(5) a. *Zhangsan (ba) shu / zhe-ben shu shuai-chuqu-le.*
Zhangsan BA book this-CLF book throw-out-ASP
'Zhangsan threw the book / this book away.'

b. **Zhangsan ba yi-ben shu shuai-chuqu-le*
Zhangsan BA one-CLF book throw-out-ASP
intended: 'Zhangsan threw a book away.'

Note that in the definiteness scale, it is possible that the BA NP can be indefinite but specific (see Li & Thompson 1981). Hence example (5b) can be grammatical if the denotation by the speaker is 'Zhangsan threw a certain book away.' This indefinite but specific NP refers to a certain book known by the speaker but not known by the listener.

On the other hand, when the object NP following BA is [+animate] in the BA construction, the BA marker is obligatory, as in (6a).³ However, if the [+animate] NP is substituted for an indefinite non-specific NP, the sentence becomes ungrammatical even with the presence of BA, as in (6b).⁴

(6) a. *Zhangsan *(ba) Lisi shuai-chuqu-le.*
Zhangsan BA Lisi throw-out-ASP
'Zhangsan threw Lisi away.'

b. **Zhangsan ba yi-ge ren shuai-chuqu-le.*
Zhangsan BA one-CLF person throw-out-ASP
intended: 'Zhangsan threw a person away.'

---

2 Hence BA in example (2) can be omitted without change in the word order as well since the following object NP is a definite [–animate] NP.

3 Languages may differ in defining what counts as specificity or animacy for differential object marking. In Mandarin Chinese, only a [+human] NP can be considered animate (see also the scale in (4)). As shown in example (i), when the object NP is an animate animal NP, BA is also optional, similar to the generic or specific/definite [–animate] NP in (5a).

(i) *Zhangsan (ba) zhu mai-le.*
Zhangsan BA pig sell-ASP
'Zhangsan sold the pigs.'

4 Although BA is obligatory for examples like (6a), BA in fact can be omitted under particular circumstances. See Section 4 for further discussion.

Therefore we can see that indefinite non-specific objects are not allowed in a BA construction, whether [+animate] or [–animate]. For generic or specific [–animate] objects, the BA marker is optional. However, if the generic or specific object NPs are [+animate], the BA marker becomes necessary. In the following discussion, I will demonstrate two more constructions in Mandarin Chinese which exhibit relevant features of differential object marking; namely the verb copying construction and the transitive V–O compound verb construction. Among these three constructions, I propose that differential object marking in Mandarin Chinese is only observable with preposed object NPs inside the *v*P/TP domain. That is, differential object marking is correlated with internal topicalization in Mandarin Chinese.

This paper is organized as follows: In Section 2, I introduce the verb copying construction and the transitive V–O compound verb construction. The role of [±definiteness] and [±animacy] in these two constructions will be discussed as well. In Section 3, I discuss the commonalities among these three constructions and propose that internal topicalization is the common property which determines the presence of differential object marking in these three constructions. Furthermore, the various differences among these three constructions will also be discussed. In Section 4, two issues of differential object marking with external topicalization in Mandarin Chinese will be presented. I conclude the paper in the last section.

2 Two more constructions

In this section, I will discuss two more constructions which also exhibit the same patterns observed in the BA construction outlined in Section 1. These two constructions are the verb copying construction and the transitive V–O compound verb construction.

2.1 The verb copying construction

The verb copying construction has received a great deal of attention in the literature on Chinese syntax, such as in the research of Li & Thompson (1981), C.-T. J. Huang (1982, 1984), Gouguet (2006), Fang & Sells (2007), Cheng (2007), Hsu (2008), and Tieu (2009). The most salient property of the verb copying construction is that the main verb emerges twice in the sentence.[5] An example is shown in (7). In this example, the main verb *qi* ('to ride') appears twice and is marked in bold. The first verb is referred to as the "copied verb" in the literature, and is followed by the object NP.

(7) Zhangsan **qi** ma **qi** de hen quai.
    Zhangsan ride horse ride DE very quick
    'Zhangsan rode the horse very fast.'

Although the copied verb appears as a verb in example (7), studies argue that the copied verb does not behave like a typical transitive verb in Mandarin Chinese. For example, Tsao (1987b) shows that a typical transitive verb in Mandarin Chinese can take aspect markers, as shown in (8a), whereas it is not acceptable for copied verbs to take aspect markers, as shown in (8b).

(8) a. Zhangsan qi-le/zhe/guo ma.
       Zhangsan ride-ASP horse
       'Zhangsan rode/is riding a horse.'

   b. *Zhangsan qi-le/zhe/guo ma qi-de hen kuai.
       Zhangsan ride-ASP horse ride-DE very fast

In addition, a typical transitive verb in Mandarin Chinese can form an A-not-A question to ask a yes-no question, as shown in (9a). However, it is simply ungrammatical for a copied verb to form an A-not-A question, as show in (9b).

(9) a. Zhangsan qi-bu-qi ma?
       Zhangsan ride-not-ride horse
       'Does Zhangsan ride horses?'

   b. *Zhangsan qi-bu-qi ma qi-de hen kuai?
       Zhangsan ride-not-ride horse ride-DE very fast

One may wonder what the copied verb really is if it does not behave like a typical verb. Based on a review of the literature, there is little discussion about the function of the copied verb in the verb copying construction. Here I would like to make

---

[5] The verb copying construction adopted here is a general term for any construction containing two identical main verbs in a single sentence. There are several different subtypes noted in the literature (i.e. Li & Thompson 1981). Here the verb copying construction illustrated is also known as the manner V-*de* construction.

the following suggestion (also see Kuo 2015 for details). I propose that the real function of the copied verb is not revealed unless one examines both the copied verb and the following object NP. More specifically, I propose that the copied verb is a type of differential object marker. If this is true, it is then expected that [±definiteness] and [±animacy] should influence the copied verb in the verb copying construction. This prediction is borne out in both (10) and (11).

(10) a. *Zhangsan (fan) shu / zhe-ben shu fan-de hen yongli.*
Zhangsan (flip) book this-CLF book flip-DE very hard
'Zhangsan flipped the book / this book very hard.'

b. **Zhangsan fan yi-ben shu fan-de hen yongli.*
Zhangsan flip one-CLF book flip-DE very hard
intended: 'Zhangsan flipped a book very hard.'

(11) a. *Zhangsan *(ti) Lisi ti-de hen yongli.*
Zhangsan kick Lisi kick-DE very hard
'Zhangsan kicked Lisi very hard.'

b. **Zhangsan ti yi-ge ren ti-de hen yongli.*
Zhangsan kick one-CLF person kick-DE very hard
intended: 'Zhangsan kicked a person very hard.'

As shown in (10a), the copied verb is optional when the following [−animate] object NP is generic or specific/definite. However, in the case of (10b), the verb copying construction is not allowed for an indefinite non-specific [−animate] object NP. In (11a), a definite/specific [+animate] object NP is only compatible with an obligatory copied verb. However, as shown in (11b), the verb copying construction is not allowed for an indefinite non-specific [+animate] object NP.

Overall, the [±definiteness] and [±animacy] features of the object NP in the verb copying construction have similar limitations to those observed in the BA construction presented previously.

2.2 The transitive V–O compound verb construction

In this section I will discuss another construction which is related to differential object marking in Mandarin Chinese. I call this construction the transitive V–O compound verb construction (see also Li & Thompson 1981, Chang et al. 1988, Paul 1988, T.-C. C. Tang 1988, C.-R. Huang 1989, Mo 1990, and Her 1997). As the name indicates, the transitive V–O compound verb plays an important role in this construction. A typical example is shown in (12). In this example, the transitive V–O compound verb is *guan-xin* ('to care'), where the verbal part is *guan* ('to involve'), and the object part is *xin* ('heart'). In (12a), the transitive V–O compound verb *guan-xin* behaves as a transitive verb, taking a direct object NP. Interestingly, the transitive V–O compound verb *guan-xin* also allows for another syntactic pattern. In (12b), the transitive V–O compound verb is seen to function intransitively, with its object NP taking a preverbal position, preceded by the preposition *dui* ('to').[6] In Chinese, the preposition *dui* ('to') is a common preposition preceding object NPs as shown in (13).

(12) a. *Zhangsan hen guan-xin Lisi.*
    Zhangsan very care   Lisi
    'Zhangsan cares about Lisi a lot.'

   b. *Zhangsan **dui** Lisi hen guan-xin.*
    Zhangsan to Lisi very care

(13) a. *Zhansan dui Lisi hen hao.*
    Zhangsan to Lisi very good
    'Zhangsan is very good to Lisi.'

   b. *Wo dui zhe-jing shi   meiyou yijian.*
    I   to this-CLF matter no   opinion
    'I do not have any opinion regarding this matter.'

Although the preposition *dui* in (12b) appears similar to the examples in (13), they, in fact, behave differently. Here I compare the transitive V–O compound verb *guan-xin* to a semi-transitive V–O compound verb whose object is introduced by a real preposition. The relevant examples are shown in (14). The semi-transitive V–O compound verb illustrated here is *kai-dao* ('to operate, lit. open knife'). In (14a), the direct object NP of the semi-transitive V–O compound verb cannot appear postverbally. The only legitimate option is to employ the preposition *gei* ('to') to introduce the direct object NP, as in (14b).[7]

---

[6] In the literature, there are few examples of the so-called transitive V–O compound verbs which exhibit two syntactic patterns (see T.-C. C. Tang 1988).
[7] Although prepositional phrases usually occur preverbally in Mandarin Chinese, this is not always the case. For example, the PP of the ditransitive *song* ('give') appears postverbally, as in example (i).

(14) a. *Yi-sheng kai-dao Dongni.
       doctor   operate Tony
       intended: 'The doctor operated on Tony.'

   b. Yi-sheng [gei Dongni] kai-dao.
      doctor   to Tony   operate
      'The doctor operated on Tony.'

There are at least three salient differences regarding the preposition *dui* ('to') in (12b) and the preposition *gei* ('to') in (14b): PP mobility, preposition omissibility, and PP syntactic range. The first difference lies in the mobility/immobility of the prepositional phrases. For the transitive V–O compound verb *guan-xin*, its prepositional phrase can be moved to the sentence-initial position, as shown in (15). However, the prepositional phrase of the semi-transitive V–O compound verb *kai-dao* cannot be moved, as in (16).

(15) [dui Kaite], Dongni hen   guan-xin.
      to Kate   Tony   very care
     'Tony cares about Kate a lot.'

(16) *[gei Dongni], yisheng mingtian kai-dao
      to   Tony   doctor tomorrow operate
     intended: 'The doctor will operate on Tony tomorrow.'

The second difference is whether the preposition can be omitted in the sentence-initial position for these two V–O compound verbs. In other words, this concerns the property of whether these two V–O compound verbs allow bare object NPs in sentence-initial positions. For *guan-xin*, the preposition *dui* can be omitted and the object NP can stand alone, as in (17). However, the preposition *gei* cannot be omitted for *kai-dao* in the sentence-initial position, which means that a bare object NP is not allowed, as in (18).

(i) Zhangsan song-le   yi-ben   shu   [$_{PP}$ gei Lisi].
    Zhangsan give-ASP one-CLF book   to Lisi
    'Zhangsan gave a book to Lisi.'

(17) Kaite, Dongni hen guan-xin.
    Kate Tony very care
    'Tony cares about Kate a lot.'

(18) *Dongni, yisheng mingtian kai-dao
    Tony   doctor   tomorrow operate
    intended: 'The doctor will operate on Tony tomorrow.'

Lastly, the PPs' syntactic positions are also quite different. As shown in (19) and (20), the *dui*-PP can precede or follow the dynamic modal *ken* ('be willing to'), but the *gei*-PP can only follow it. As argued in Hsu (2005), dynamic modals mark the *v*P periphery. Therefore, this shows that the *dui*-PP has a wider syntactic range than the *gei*-PP, which is inside the *v*P domain.[8]

(19) Dongni (ken)   dui Kaite (ken)   guan-xin.
    Tony be-willing-to to Kate be-willing-to care
    'Tony is willing to care about Kate.'

(20) Yisheng (ken)   gei Dongni (*ken)   kai-dao.
    doctor be-willing-to to Tony   be-willing-to operate
    'The doctor is willing to operate on Tony.'

From the above comparison, it is evident that the preposition *dui* for the transitive V–O compound verb *guan-xin* does not behave like a typical preposition. Notice that the preposition *dui* is followed by an object NP in the examples. After examining the interaction between *dui* and the following object NP, I propose that *dui* is not a typical preposition, but a kind of differential object marker. This proposal is inspired by the [±definiteness] and [±animacy] elements of the transitive V–O compound verb *guan-xin* in (21) and (22). In (21), when the object NP is a generic or a specific/definite [−inanimate] NP, *dui* is optional, whereas an obligatory *dui* results in an ungrammatical sentence in conjunction with an indefinite non-specific [−inanimate] NP.

---

8 In addition to the syntactic position difference, one of the reviewers wondered if they involve the same derivation as *dui*-PPs and if *gei* can be deleted if the object NP is [−animate] and [+specific]. However, since the verb *kai-dao* ('operate') requires an [+animate] object NP semantically, this possibility is not testable.

(21) a. Zhangsan (dui) shi / zhe-jian shi hen guan-xin.
Zhangsan (to) matter this-CLF matter very care
'Zhangsan cared about the matters / this matter a lot.'

b. *Zhangsan dui yi-jian shi hen guan-xin.
Zhangsan to one-CLF matter very care
intended: 'Zhangsan cared about a matter a lot.'

As for the definite/specific [+animate] object NP in (22a), the preposition is required. Once the definite/specific [+animate] object NP becomes indefinite non-specific [+animate], the sentence becomes ungrammatical, as in (22b).⁹

(22) a. Zhangsan *(dui) Lisi hen guan-xin.
Zhangsan to Lisi very care
'Zhangsan cared about Lisi a lot.'

b. *Zhangsan dui yi-ge ren hen guan-xin.
Zhangsan to one-CLF person very care
intended: 'Zhangsan cared about a person a lot.'

In short, what is observed is that the transitive V–O compound verb construction for *guan-xin* is exactly the same when compared to previous patterns observed for the BA construction and the verb copying construction.

---

9 Concerning examples of ungrammatical inclusion of indefinite, non-specific, inanimate objects with the V–O compound verb in (21b) and (22b), one of the reviewers asked how to express grammatical counterparts in Mandarin Chinese. Note that the V–O compound verb in (21b) and (22b) can take an object NP postverbally or preverbally. If the indefinite, non-specific, inanimate objects are placed in the postverbal object position, we derive grammatical sentences as in examples (i) and (ii). There are no definiteness or animacy restrictions in the postverbal object position.

(i) Zhangsan hen guan-xin yi-jian shi.
Zhangsan very care one-CLF matter
'Zhangsan cared about a matter a lot.'

(ii) Zhangsan hen guan-xin yi-ge ren.
Zhangsan very care one-CLF person
'Zhangsan cares about a person a lot.'

3 Similarity and differences

In this section I discuss a shared property related to differential object marking phenomena among the three constructions: the BA construction, the verb copying construction, and the transitive V–O compound verb construction. The individual differences among these three constructions will also be addressed.

3.1 Internal topicalization

One may notice that a shared property among the three constructions examined in Section 1 and 2 is that the differential object markers (BA, the copied verb, and *dui*) and the object NPs are all in preverbal positions. More specifically, the differential object markers and the object NPs are in a position between the subject and the verb.[10] There are interesting proposals in the literature regarding the syntactic position of the object NPs falling between the subject and the verb. For example, Tsao (1987a) proposed that the BA NP in the BA construction is a secondary/internal topic. In addition, Paul (2002, 2005) and Hsu (2008) propose that the bare preposed object NPs between the subject and the verb are internal topics in Mandarin Chinese. This internal topic proposal is reminiscent of the discussion of Belletti (2004) and others cross-linguistically. However, as pointed out by Paul (2005), there is only partial correspondence between the left periphery of the low TP area in Italian and Chinese. For example, no topic is allowed under focus in Chinese.[11]

Therefore I believe a better way to argue for the existence of internal topics is to compare them to the well-known external topics in Mandarin Chinese. In the literature, it has been proposed that Mandarin Chinese is a topic-prominent language. Examples like (23) and (24) taken from Li & Thompson (1981) are indeed quite common in Chinese. In (23), the predicate *hen da* 'very big' modifies the subject *ye-zi* 'leaf'. Furthermore, *Na-ke su* ('that tree') functions as a topic, which takes a comment *ye-zi hen-da* ('leaves very big').[12]

---

10 Yang & van Bergen (2007) have proposed that the syntactic position of the BA NP is also a factor which can influence differential object marking.
11 In addition, the preposed object is not a case of object shift as observed in Scandinavian languages. As proposed in Huang et al. (2009), in Mandarin Chinese, the highest position that a verb can move to is the *v* position. According to Holmberg's generalization, the verb moving up to T is a required element for object shift in Icelandic or Danish.
12 The non-topicalized version of example (23) is shown in (i), in which *na-ke shu de ye-zi* functions as the subject.

(23) Base-generation
   Na-ke   shu ye-zi hen da.
   that-CLF tree leaf very big
   'That tree, its leaves are very big.'

Another typical topic-comment example is shown in (24), which is somewhat different from (23). Note that the topic in (23) is a base-generated topic, since there is no place in which we can place it back in the comment part. In contrast to the topic in (23), the topic in (24) is a moved topic. The topic has been argued to have moved from the postverbal object position (i.e. C.-C. J. Tang 1990).

(24) Movement
   Na-ben shu$_i$, wo yijing   kan-kuo-le t$_i$.
   that-CLF book I already see-ASP-ASP
   'That book, I have already read it.'

As pointed out by Paul (2005), one salient property of topics in Mandarin Chinese is that they do not always associate with old or given information. In other words, topics in Chinese can convey new information as well, as shown in (25) and (26).[13]

(25) External topic: old information
   A: *Zhangsan qu Taibei le ma?*
      Zhangsan go Taipei ASP Q
      'Did Zhangsan go to Taipei?'
   B: *Taibei a,   ta miantian cai yao qu ne!*
      Taipei EXCL he tomorrow CAI will go EXCL
      'Taipei, he won't go there until tomorrow.'

(i) *Na-ke   shu de ye-zi hen da.*
     that-CLF tree DE leaf very big
     'That tree's leaves are very big.'

13 Paul (2005) argues that this particular new-information carrying property is partly the cause of why topic cannot occur under focus in Chinese.

(26) External topic: new information
 Taibei a, wo zhen xiang xiangzai jiu qu!
 Taipei EXCL I really want now JIU go
 'Taipei, I really want to go there now!'

In (25), the topic of Taipei had been mentioned in a previous question, thus is old/given information in the reply. However, the sentence in (26) can be uttered by a husband to his wife while watching a television program introducing Taipei. No previous mention of Taipei is needed in this discourse context.

Also note that for NP topics in examples like (23) and (24) are in the sentence-initial position. These sentence-initial topics have been observed to show a particular property (see Li & Thompson 1981, Liu 1997, Bender 2000, and others). That is, only generic and definite/specific NPs can serve as external topics. If the NP is indefinite, it cannot serve as a topic. This contrast is shown in (27a) and (27b).

(27) a. *Gou / zhe-zhi gou, Zhangsan hen xihuan.*
 dog this-CLF dog Zhangsan very like
 'Zhangsan likes dogs / this dog very much.'

 b. **Yi-zhi gou, Zhangsan hen xihuan.*
 one-CLF dog Zhangsan very like
 intended: 'Zhangsan likes a dog very much.'

Consequently, if NPs located between the subject and the verb are indeed topics, we expect that they exhibit the same or similar properties as external topics. Firstly, internal topics can show old/given or new information as external topics. Examples for the three constructions are shown in examples (28) through (32).

(28) The BA construction: old information
 A: *Ni kan-jian [wo zuotian mai-de shu]$_i$ ma?*
 you see-see I yesterday buy-DE book Q
 'Did you see the book that I bought yesterday?'
 B: *Wo ba ta$_i$ fang-zai shuguai li le.*
 I BA it put-in bookshelf inside ASP
 'I put it in the bookshelf.'

(29) The BA construction: new information
Ni ba na-jian jifu na-gei wo qiaoqiao.
you BA that-CLF cloth take-GEI I look
'Give me that piece of cloth so that I can take a look of it.'

(30) The verb copying construction: old information
A: *Zhe-ben shu zhe-me popolanlan de?*
this-CLF book how crappy DE
'Why this book is so crappy?'
B: *Yingwei Zhangsan fan zhe-ben shu fan-de hen yongli.*
because Zhangsan flip this-CLF book flip-DE very hard
'Because Zhangsan flipped this book very hard.'

(31) The verb copying construction: new information
Wo xie-zi xie-de hen quai! Ni yao kan-kan ma?
I write-word write-DE very quick You want see-see Q
'I wrote quickly! Would you like to take a look at it?'

(32) The transitive V–O compound verb construction: old information
A: *Zhangsan zhe-me kandai zhe-jian shi?*
Zhangsan how treat this-CLF matter
'How does Zhangsan see this matter?'
B: *Zhangsan dui zhe-jian shi hen guan-xin.*
Zhangsan to this-CLF matter very care
'Zhangsan cares about this matter a lot.'

(33) The transitive V–O compound verb construction: new information
Ni dui zhe-jian shi you sheme kanfa?
you to this-CLF matter have what point-of-view
'What is your point of view of this matter?'

From the above examples, it is clear that these three constructions can carry old/given information, following previous discourses. Moreover, similar to external topics, these constructions can also be uttered independently in appropriate contexts without previous utterances.

Secondly, similar to the external topic in (27), only generic and definite/specific NPs can be internal topics, while indefinite NPs cannot. This prediction is borne out for NPs in the three constructions in examples (34) through (36). The internal NPs in the three constructions can be generic or definite NPs, but an indefinite non-specific internal NP is simply prohibited.[14]

(34) The BA construction

    a. *Zhangsan (ba) shu / zhe-ben shu shuai-chuqu-le.*
       Zhangsan BA book this-CLF book throw-out-ASP
       'Zhangsan threw the book / this book away.'

    b. **Zhangsan ba yi-ben shu shuai-chuqu-le.*
       Zhangsan BA one-CLF book throw-out-ASP
       intended: 'Zhangsan threw a book away.'

(35) The verb copying construction

    a. *Zhangsan (fan) shu / zhe-ben shu fan-de hen yongli.*
       Zhangsan flip book this-CLF book flip-DE very hard
       'Zhangsan flipped the book/this book very hard.'

    b. **Zhangsan fan yi-ben shu fan-de hen yongli.*
       Zhangsan flip one-CLF book flip-DE very hard
       intended: 'Zhangsan flipped a book very hard.'

(36) The transitive V–O compound verb construction

    a. *Zhangsan (dui) shi / zhe-jian shi hen guan-xin.*
       Zhangsan to matter this-CLF matter very care
       'Zhangsan cares about the matters/this matter a lot.'

---

14 There is a slight difference between the external topic and the internal topic in terms of their acceptability for indefinite NPs. When an indefinite NP has a specific reading, this is acceptable for bare internal topics. However, an indefinite specific NP is unacceptable for bare external topics. An indefinite specific external topic must be preceded by *you* ('to have') as shown in (i), which is also known as the existential construction in Mandarin Chinese.

(i) *You yi-ge ren, wo hen xihuan.*
   have one-CLF person, I very like
   'There is someone whom I like very much.'

b. *Zhangsan dui yi-jian shi hen guan-xin.
   Zhangsan to one-CLF matter very care
   intended: 'Zhangsan cares about a matter a lot.'

Therefore we can see that the NPs in these three constructions are indeed topic-like. In addition, one may notice that from examples (34) through (36), when the internal topics are generic or definite/specific, BA, the copied verb and use of *dui* in fact are optional. On the other hand, while the internal topics are indefinite NPs in these three constructions, the sentences are ungrammatical even with the presence of BA, the copied verb, or *dui*.[15] This contrast reminds us of the [±definiteness] feature of DOM in the previous section. Moreover, we have seen that the [±animacy] feature of the object NP also affects the presence of BA, the copied verb, and *dui* in these constructions. Examples are illustrated as follows:

(37) a. *Zhangsan *(ba) ren / Lisi shuai-chuqu-le.*
        Zhangsan BA people Lisi throw-out-ASP
        'Zhangsan threw someone / Lisi away.'

   b. **Zhangsan ba yi-ge ren shuai-chuqu-le.*
        Zhangsan BA one-CLF person throw-out-ASP
        intended: 'Zhangsan threw a person away.'

(38) a. *Zhangsan *(ti) ren / Lisi ti-de hen yongli.*
        Zhangsan kick people Lisi kick-DE very hard
        'Zhangsan kicked people / Lisi very hard.'

   b. **Zhangsan ti yi-ge ren ti-de hen yongli.*
        Zhangsan kick one-CLF person kick-DE very hard
        'Zhangsan kicked Lisi / *one person very hard.'

---

15 One reviewer mentioned that the preposed internal topics are reminiscent of Tsai (2001) who also discussed the definite and nonspecific properties of preposed objects with realis and irrealis tenses. The nonspecific reading in Tsai (2001) basically equates to the generic reading employed in this paper. As far as I can see, the preposed topics in Tsai (2001) could also take optional DOMs, and it does not matter whether these generic NPs are interpreted as definite or nonspecific.

(39) a. *Zhangsan *(dui) ren   / Lisi hen guan-xin.*
       Zhangsan to   people / Lisi very care
       'Zhangsan cares about people / Lisi a lot.'

   b. **Zhangsan dui yi-ge   ren   hen guan-xin.*
       Zhangsan to one-CLF person very care
       intended: 'Zhangsan cares a person a lot.'

As shown from examples (37) through (39), when the object NP is an [+animate] generic or definite/specific NP, BA, the copied verb and *dui* are obligatory. However, when an [+animate] NP is also an indefinite non-specific NP, the sentence is ungrammatical. The above phenomena therefore links DOM to internal topics directly in these three constructions.[16,17] In addition, the differentiation of [-specific] objects as non-occurring NPs in these three constructions is due to their inability to constitute internal topics. This further illustrates that DOM in these three constructions are syntactically derived.

3.2 The differences

Although Section 3.1 has illustrated how DOM in the BA construction, the verb copying construction, and the transitive V–O compound verb construction are related to internal topics, in this section I discuss three differences among these three constructions.

First of all, one salient difference among these three constructions is that the DOM employed in these three constructions are quite different. The BA construction, the verb copying construction, and the transitive V–O compound verb construction are repeated as follows and their DOM markers are shown in bold:

(40) *Zhangsan **ba** zhe-ben shu   mai-le.*
     Zhangsan BA this-CLF book sell-ASP
     'Zhangsan sold this book.'

---

16 Cross-linguistically, Kannada, a Dravidian language spoken in India, has similar DOM phenomenon as observed in Chinese. In Kannada, [+animate] objects have to be marked. However, [-inanimate] objects can optionally have a DOM if they are specific.
17 Paul (2005) also cites Hou's (1979) observation in which [+human] DPs including proper names of persons and pronouns cannot be preposed in Mandarin Chinese. Therefore the grammatical examples in her paper are all inanimate NPs and therefore doe not have the animacy restriction exhibited in example (37) to (39).

(41) Zhangsan **qi** ma qi-de hen quai.
Zhangsan ride horse ride-DE very quick
'Zhangsan rides horses very quickly.'

(42) Zhangsan **dui** xuengsheng hen guan-xin.
Zhangsan to student very care
'Zhangsan cares about students a lot.'

As shown from examples (40) through (42), the differential markings are *ba*, the copied verb *qi*, and *dui*. A quick glance at the three differential object markers seems to suggest no shared properties. We may simply conclude that the markers of DOM vary widely in Mandarin Chinese. However, one possibility may exist to connect these three markers. That is, BA, the copied verb and *dui* are all verb-related historically. Although BA simply functions as a disposal marker for the BA construction in contemporary Mandarin, Sun (1996) argued that BA was originally as a verb in archaic Chinese, as illustrated in (43). As shown by the gloss, BA means 'to hold' in this example.[18] Similar to BA, we can also find examples of *dui* functioning as a verb in archaic Chinese. The example is shown in (44), where *dui*'s verbal meaning is 'to face'.[19] As for the copied verb, it is a copy of the main verb in the sentence. Therefore the verb-related property seems to be the link among these three DOM markers which are superficially heterogeneous.

(43) from *Shi Ji*, 91 AD
zuo qian yang, you ba mao, xi xing er qian yi gao.
left drag goat right hold lance knee precede then front to tell
'(Someone) dragged a goat on his left hand, and held a lance on his right hand, preceding to the front by his knees to tell something.'

(44) from *Shi Ji*, 91 AD
han chu zhan bei, kui bu neng dui.
sweat out wet back ashamed not can face
'The sweat wet the back, and the person was so ashamed to face (someone)'

---

18 Later BA becomes a preposition in around the Tang Dynasty (618 AD–907 AD), and becomes a disposal marker in modern Chinese (see Zou 1995 and Sun 1996).
19 As a verb, *dui* can also mean 'to answer' or 'to treat' in archaic Chinese.

Secondly, although the object NPs in the relevant three constructions are all located between the subject and the verb according to the surface order, they involve several different syntactic features. The first difference is that BA and the BA NP in the BA construction are in the vP domain. However, the copied verb and the object NP in the verb copying construction and *dui* and the object NP in the transitive V–O compound construction can range from the vP domain to the TP domain.

Domain differences can be observed from the interaction between the modals and object NPs in these three constructions. Hsu (2005) has proposed the following modal hierarchy in Mandarin Chinese, as shown in (45). The modal projections are basically located in the TP domain. As one can see, the deontic modals in Mandarin Chinese mark the vP periphery.[20]

(45) [$_{TopP}$ Topic [$_{TP}$ Outer subject [$_{MP}$Epi Epistemic modal [$_{MP}$Deo Deontic modal [$_{MP}$Dyn Dynamic modal [$_{vP}$ Inner subject v [$_{VP}$ ...]]]]]]]

For the BA construction, in (46), we can see that BA and the BA NP have to occur following the dynamic modal *ken* ('be willing to'). If BA and the BA NP are prior to the dynamic modal, the sentence becomes ungrammatical.

(46) Zhangsan (ken)   ba zhe-jian shi   (*ken)   zuo-wan.
      Zhangsan be-willing-to BA this-CLF matter be-willing-to do-finish
      'Zhangsan is willing to finish this matter.'

This result in (46) is not surprising since, in the literature, it has been proposed that the BA NP is located at Spec,vP, while BA is the overt realization of the vP head, as in C.-T. J. Huang (1997) and Lin (2001). Y.-H. A. Li (2006) and Huang et al. (2009) suggest that the BA NP is located at the specifier position of a *Ba*P, which is right above vP. In either proposal, BA and the BA NP are located in the vP periphery.

As for the verb copying construction and the transitive V–O compound verb construction, they behave consistently. As shown below, the dynamic modal can be either lower or higher than the copied verb and the object NP in (47) and *dui* and the object NP in (48). This indicates that the copied verb and the object NP in (47) and *dui* and the object NP in (48) can be higher than the vP periphery.

---

20 Recently there are different proposals regarding relative modal positions in Mandarin Chinese. For example, Tsai (2010) has argued that the epistemic modal projection is higher than the outer subject position, while the dynamic modal projection has been argued to be located inside the vP domain. If this analysis for modals is adopted, the relevant position of BA and the BA NP must be reanalyzed as well. I leave this question for further research.

(47) *Zhangsan (ken)   qi   na-pi   ma   (ken)   qi   de*
    Zhangsan be-willing-to ride that-CLF horse be-willing-to ride DE
    hen quai.
    very fast
    'Zhangsan is willing to ride that horse very fast.'

(48) *Dongni (ken)   [dui Kate] (ken)   duo   guan-xin*
    Tony   be-willing-to   to   Kate   be-willing-to much care
    yi-dian.
    one-point
    'Tony is willing to care about Kate more.'

Moreover, the following examples further illustrate that the copied verb and the object NP and the *dui*-PP can also be in the TP domain. As shown in (49) and (50), the copied verb and the object NP and the *dui*-PP can both higher than the epistemic modal *yinggai* ('should').

(49) *Zhangsan (yinggai) qi   na-pi   ma   (yinggai) qi   de hen quai.*
    Zhangsan should   ride that-CLF horse   should ride DE very fast
    'Zhangsan must ride that horse very fast.'

(50) *Dongni (yinggai) [dui Kate] (yinggai) duo   guan-xin yi-dian.*
    Tony   should   to   Kate   should   much care   one-point
    'Tony must care about Kate more.'

Therefore from the interactions with modals, we can see that basically BA and the BA NP are restricted to the *v*P domain. On the other hand, the copied verb and the object NP and the *dui*-PP have a wider syntactic domain range. They can either be located in the *v*P or the TP domain. Although the object NPs in the BA construction, the verb copying construction, and the transitive V–O compound verb construction are internal topics, they are in different syntactic domains.

In addition to differences in syntactic domain, the BA NP and the object NP following the copied verb or *dui* also differ in their syntactic positions. For example, Y.-H. A. Li (2006) proposes that the BA NP is located at the specifier position of *v*P taken by a functional *Ba*P which hosts BA. This seems to be a fixed position. However, as just shown, the object NPs following the copied verb or *dui* can be higher than epistemic modal and lower than dynamic modal. If the modals have fixed syntactic position, as shown in (45), this implies that the object NPs following the copied verb or *dui* do not have certain fixed syntactic positions. Therefore, no matter whether one adopts Paul (2002, 2005), who proposes that the internal topic is located at the specifier of a FP above *v*P and below TP, or Hsu (2008), who proposes an independent functional TopicP in the TP domain, this topic projection has to be "mobile" (see also Rizzi 1997, Roussou 2000, and Belletti 2004). This is why Kuo (2009) proposed that internal topics may be located at any specifier position of functional projection available within the TP domain.[21] For ease of discussion, I simply assume that the internal topic is located at Spec,FP, no matter whether this FP is an independent topic projection or an existing functional projection in the TP domain. Importantly, this mobile property of the object NP following the copied verb or *dui* is essentially different from the BA NP which is always in Spec,*v*P.

Finally, the internal topics in these three constructions also have different syntactic formation strategies. While the internal object NP in the BA construction can be formed via base-generation or movement, the internal object NP in the verb copying construction has been argued to be formed via base-generation (i.e. Cheng 2007). On the other hand, the internal object NP in the transitive V–O compound verb construction involves movement.

It is well-known that the BA construction can be formed by movement or by base-generation. These two syntactic strategies are illustrated in (51) and (52). In (51), the object NP is moved from the postverbal position to a preverbal position. This kind of movement has been argued to be an A-movement by Goodall (1987), Sybesma (1999), Paul & Whitman (2010), and others.

(51) a. *Zhangsan mai-le na-ben shu.*
       Zhangsan sell-ASP that-CLF book
       'Zhangsan sold a book.'

    b. *Zhangsan **ba** na-ben shu$_i$ mai-le t$_i$.*
       Zhangsan BA that-CLF book sell-ASP

On the other hand, the BA NP can also be base-generated, as shown in (52). In this example, the main verb is *bo* ('to peel'), and its direct object is *pi* ('skin'). Apparently, the BA NP *juzi* ('orange') is not the direct object of the main verb. However, the BA NP is semantically related to the direct object NP since the skin is located on the orange. The base-generated BA NP therefore maintain a possessor-possessee relationship with the direct object in example (52).

---

[21] See Kuo (2009) for further details of this proposal.

(52) *Zhangsan **ba** juzi bo-le pi.*
     Zhangsan BA orange peel-ASP skin
     'Zhangsan peeled the skin of the orange.'

As for the verb copying construction, Cheng (2007) has argued that the copied verb and the followed direct object are formed by base-generation. To be more specific, the copied verb and the following direct object merge to the structure via sideward movement (i.e. Nunes 2001, 2004). An example of the verb copying construction is shown in (53).

(53) *Zhangsan qi (na-pi) ma qi de hen quai.*
     Zhagnsan ride that-CLF horse ride DE very fast
     'Zhangsan rode that horse very fast.'

To form example (53), the main verb *qi* ('ride') first merges with a *de*P in (54a). The direct object stands alone. Then the verb in (54a) is copied and merges with the independent direct object to form a VP as in (55b). Finally the VP containing the copied verb and the direct object NP merges with the original VP as in (56).

(54) a. K = [$_{VP}$ ride [$_{deP}$ de very fast]]
     b. L = [$_{NP}$ (that) horse]

(55) a. K = [$_{VP}$ ride [$_{deP}$ de very fast]]
     b. M = [$_{VP}$ **ride** [$_{NP}$ (that) horse]]

(56) [[$_{VP}$ **ride** [$_{NP}$ (that) horse]] [$_{VP}$ ride [$_{deP}$ de very fast]]]

Although the copied verb and the direct object have been proposed to enter the structure via sideward "movement", they show up in the structure by base-generation according to steps (54) to (56).

The transitive V–O compound verb construction is shown in (57). In (57a) the direct object is in a postverbal position. In (57b), the direct object has moved to a preverbal position, preceded by *dui* ('to'), following T.-C. C. Tang (1988).

(57) a. *Zhangsan hen guan-xin Lisi.*
        Zhangsan very care Lisi
        'Zhangsan cares for Lisi a lot.'

     b. *Zhangsan **dui** Lisi$_i$ hen guan-xin t$_i$.*
        Zhangsan to Lisi very care

The internal topics between the *v*P and the TP domains involve A-movement, according to Shyu (1995), Ting (1996) and J.-I. J. Li (1999), because of locality, lack of weak-cross-over effect, lack of restriction effects, and anaphor binding facts. However, Kuo (2009) has argued that internal topics in fact show mixed A/A'-movement properties. If this is on the right track, this again differentiates the object NP following *dui* from the BA NP, although both internal topics are derived by movement.[22]

Note that although we see different formation methods for internal topics, this is in fact expected. Recall that for external topics, the topics can be derived by movement or base-generation, as in (58) and (59) (i.e. C.-C. J. Tang 1990). Compared to internal topics, the movement of external topics has been argued to be A'-movement in the literature.

(58)   *Meiguihua$_i$, wo hen xi-huan t$_i$.*
       rose   I   very like
       'I like roses a lot.'

(59)   *Hua,   wo zui   xi-huan meiguihua.*
       flower I   most like   rose
       'As for flowers, I like roses most.'

The three structural differences among the BA construction, the verb copying construction, and the transitive V–O compound verb construction are summarized in Table 1.

From this table, we can see that there are significant differences among the BA construction, the verb copying construction, and the transitive V–O compound

---

22 One reviewer points out that the *dui*-PP is reminiscent of the DOM = dative proposal as discussed by Manzini, Savoia, and Franco (this volume). Indeed, *dui* ('to') in Chinese can also introduce a goal dative argument as in (i).

(i)   *Wo dui ta   shuo-le.*
      I   to him say-ASP
      'I told him.'

However, an essential part of the DOM = dative proposal is that that the internal argument can never be inserted VP-internally without a DOM dative. This is not the case that we have observed for the transitive V–O compound verb construction (i.e. (57b) versus (57a)). In addition, the emergence of the *dui*-PP is also in a different syntactic domain. Hence the case of the transitive V–O compound verb construction in Chinese is not compatible with the DOM = dative proposal.

Tab. 1: Differences among BA, verb copying and transitive V–O compound verb constructions

Constructions	Features			
	Differential object marking	Syntactic domain	Object NP position	Preverbal object NP formation
The BA construction	BA	vP	Spec,vP	A-movement or base-generation
The verb copying construction	the copied verb	vP ~ TP	Floated Spec,FP	base-generation
The transitive V–O compound verb construction	*dui*	vP ~ TP	Floated Spec,FP	A/A'-movement

verb construction. These differences may be due to the particular requirements of the constructions themselves. Hence there are different formation options, different syntactic positions and domains, and different differential object markings. However, we also see a way to unite these three constructions, which is internal topicalization. From the discussion so far, it seems hard to conclude that the internal topic status is derived from a particular functional head. But if one follows the mapping theory, such as in the work of Neeleman & van de Koot (2008), these internal topics with or without specific locations do show the topic-comment property since they are all in the domain between the subject and the verbal part of sentences. If we follow this analysis, the internal topic status of these constructions can be derived in a unified manner.

To summarize, we may conclude that although internal topicalization is the unified answer to explain the DOM phenomenon in these three constructions, there are existing structural differences based on the construction employed.[23],[24]

---

[23] One reviewer wonders how the DOM is derived in these three constructions. I propose that differential object marking can be seen as a Last Resort strategy for internal topics in Mandarin Chinese, following Rodríguez-Mondoñedo (2007). I assume that the vP and the FP which host internal topics in Mandarin Chinese are lacking [+person] features. Hence [+animate] object NPs, which have [+person] features, cannot be licensed if they are internally topicalized. The derivation can be saved when DOMs which have full phi-features are introduced to the structure. The internalized objects can then undergo covert movement to the specifier of the projection projected by the DOM and check all their features.

[24] Under the above proposal, the functional projections which can host internal topics are considered to be phi-feature deficient and therefore DOMs are required. Although the DOM seems to appear only TP/vP-internally, this does not imply that TP/vP-internal NPs always demand DOMs.

4 External topicalization

In this section I discuss two topicalization-related issues. I first discuss whether DOM is available in external topicalization in Mandarin Chinese. In addition, I discuss the interesting phenomenon of the omission of the obligatory differential object marker in relevant constructions.

First, I examine the possibility of DOM with external topicalization in Mandarin Chinese. So far, we have seen that differential object marking can be found in Mandarin Chinese for internal topicalization. Since external topicalization also exists in Mandarin Chinese, one may wonder if differential object marking is available in external topicalization as well. It appears that this is not possible, since we cannot find [±definiteness] and [±animacy] differences for external topics.

Note that for the three constructions discussed, the external topics are only available for the verb copying construction and the transitive V–O compound verb construction. The external topic is not available for the BA construction. This is because the BA marker has been functioning as an anchor marking the *v*P periphery, as discussed previously. Therefore we are left with the other two constructions. The verb copying construction with external topics are shown in (60) and (61). As these two examples show, no matter whether the object NP in the external topic position is generic or specific or animate, the copied verb is always optional.

(60) *(qi) ma / na-pi ma, Zhangsan qi-de hen quai.*
   ride horse that-CLF horse Zhangsan ride-DE very quick
   'As for riding horses/that horse, Zhangsan rides very fast.'

(61) *(da) Lisi, Zhangsan da-de hen yongli.*
   hit Lisi Zhangsan hit-DE very hard
   'Zhangsan hit Lisi very hard.'

For example, unlike the cases discussed in this chapter, the indefinite non-specific NP in the focus *lian ... dou/ye* construction is acceptable (see Shyu 1995).

(i) *Zhangsan lian yi-zhe mayi dou/ye bu gan shanghai.*
   Zhangsan even one-CLF ant all/too not dare hurt
   'Zhangsan cannot even hurt an ant.'

Hence in general, the DOM in Chinese is a TP/*v*P-internal phenomenon, and it is only available for internal topics which are hosted by phi-feature deficient functional projections.

The object NPs in the transitive V–O compound verb constructions can become external topics as well. The relevant examples are shown in (62) and (63). Similar to the verb copying construction, when the object NPs in the external topic position are generic, specific or animate, *dui* is also optional.

(62) (dui) quojiadashi / zhe-jian shi, Dongni hen guan-xin.
 to national-matter this-CLF matter Tony very care
 'Tony cares about this matter/national matters a lot.'

(63) (dui) Kaite, Dongni hen guan-xin.
 to Kate Tony very care
 'Tony cares about Kate a lot.'

Apparently there is no distinction available based on the different features of the object NPs in the external topic position. Since the generic, definite/specific, and animate NPs can stand alone in the external topic position, we may conclude that differential object marking is not required for external object NPs. This conclusion has two interesting consequences.[25] Firstly, this shows that the preposed objects in Mandarin Chinese do not come with an animacy restriction themselves. Otherwise bare animate/inanimate external topics would not be possible. Secondly, DOM is not the trigger, with the output interpreted as topicalization. Since external topics may exist independently, this potential relation between DOM and topicalization has to be rejected.

However, we do see the optional copied verb and *dui* in the above examples. If differential object marking is not available for external topics, we need to explain the emergence of the copied verb and *dui* in the external topic position. In fact, the copied verb and *dui* are not really unexpected since they may show up in the external topic position via movement. That is, the copied verb and *dui* emerge when the object NPs are in the internal topic position. Later, the internal object NPs and the differential object markers together undergo movement to the external topic position. Here I show the movement with an [+animate] NP in both the verb copying construction and the transitive V–O compound verb construction.

(64) a. Zhangsan [da Lisi] da-de hen yongli.
 Zhangsan hit Lisi hit-DE very hard
 'Zhangsan hit Lisi very hard.'

---

[25] The author would like to thank one of the reviewers who points out these potential problems to the current analysis.

b. [da Lisi]ᵢ, Zhangsan tᵢ da-de hen yongli.
   hit Lisi   Zhangsan   hit-DE very hard

(65) a. Dongni [dui Kate] hen guan-xin.
        Tony   to Kate   very care
        'Tony cares about Kate a lot.'

   b. [dui Kate]ᵢ, Dongni tᵢ hen guan-xin.
      to Kate   Tony   very care

Recall that if the object NP in the internal topic position is an [+animate] NP, a differential object marker is required. Hence in (64a), the copied verb is required for the verb copying construction. According to Cheng (2007), the copied verb and the object NP form a VP constituent. This VP constituent may undergo further movement to the external topicalization as in (64a). A similar situation can be found in the transitive V–O compound verb construction in (65). In (65a), the [+animate] object NP needs *dui* and these two elements form a PP. This PP moves to the external topic position in (65b). In this way, we then explain why differential object markers can emerge in the external topic position even if external topicalization is not correlated with DOM in Mandarin Chinese.

Finally, although external topics do not exhibit the relevant properties of DOM in Mandarin Chinese, they can still be related to DOM in some respects. Recall that for [+animate] generic or definite/specific object NPs, differential object markers are obligatory in the three constructions discussed, as repeated in (66) through (68).

(66) Zhangsan *(ba) Lisi da-le   yi-duan.
     Zhangsan   BA Lisi beat-ASP once
     'Zhangsan beat Lisi once.'

(67) Zhangsan *(da) Lisi da-de   hen yongli.
     Zhangsan   beat Lisi beat-ASP very hard
     'Zhangsan beat Lisi very hard.'

(68) Zhangsan *(dui) xuengsheng hen guan-xin.
     Zhangsan   to   student   very care
     'Zhangsan cares about students a lot.'

The restriction is definitely true if these object NPs in the above examples are interpreted as objects. Interestingly, the examples from (66) through (68) without the differential object markers in fact can be acceptable under different readings. As shown from (69) through (71), the examples from (66) through (68) are judged to be grammatical without the differential object markers. However, in these newly constructed examples, the object NPs from (66) through (68) are interpreted as subjects, while the subject NPs from (66) through (68) are interpreted as external topics instead.

(69)   *Zhangsan Lisi da-le yi-duan.*
       Zhangsan Lisi beat-ASP once
       'Lisi beat Zhangsan once.'

(70)   *Zhangsan Lisi da-de hen yongli.*
       Zhangsan Lisi beat-DE very hard
       'Lisi beat Zhangsan very hard.'

(71)   *Zhangsan xuengsheng hen guan-xin.*
       Zhangsan student very care
       'Students care about Zhangsan a lot.'

Since [+animate] definite or generic external topics do not require differential object markers, this kind of interpretation is, therefore, a way out after the differential object markers are removed.

5 Conclusion

Recently, Dalrymple & Nikolaeva (2011) have argued that [±definiteness] and [±animacy] features are not the only factors to determine differential object marking cross-linguistically. They show that information structure is also a huge factor. Therefore, there are three types of languages with differential object marking based on the interaction between the semantic features and information structure. These three types are listed as follows (Dalrymple & Nikolaeva 2011: 215):

Type 1   Languages where DOM is regulated solely by information structure; correlations with semantic features are only tendencies (no spreading or narrowing).
Type 2   Languages where DOM is regulated solely by semantic features; correlations with information structure are only tendencies (loss of connection to information-structure role via narrowing or spreading).

Type 3 Languages where DOM is regulated both by information structure and semantics:
(a) Languages where DOM applies to topical objects and non-topical objects with certain semantic features (spreading to arguments with topic-worthy features while also retaining a connection to information-structure role).
(b) Languages where DOM applies to topical objects only if they have certain semantic features (narrowing to arguments with topic-worthy features bearing the appropriate information-structure role).

According to the discussion so far, Mandarin Chinese should belong to the third type, which is also the most common cross-linguistically (Dalrymple & Nikolaeva 2011). Moreover, Chinese belongs to subtype 3b, where differential object marking is only observable on internal topics and is determined by the [±definiteness] and [±animacy] semantic features of the object NPs.

To recap, in this paper I discuss the phenomenon of differential object marking in Mandarin Chinese. We have seen that the DOM phenomena can be observed in the BA construction, the verb copying construction, and the transitive V–O compound verb construction. The shared syntactic property of these three constructions and the DOM phenomena is internal topicalization, though there are also differences which vary from construction to construction. Most importantly, the examination of the verb copying construction and the transitive V–O compound verb construction in this paper not only supplements our understanding of differential object making in Mandarin Chinese, but also shows a stronger importance of the factor of information structure in the study of differential object marking.

Acknowledgements

This paper is part of my research sponsored by the Ministry of Science and Technology, Taiwan (Grant No. MOST 103-2410-H-415-021). I hereby acknowledge the financial support of the MOST. The author would also like to thank the three anonymous reviewers for their valuable comments and suggestions on the previous version of this paper. All errors remain mine.

References

Aissen, Judith. 2003. Differential object marking: Iconicity vs. economy. *Natural Language & Linguistic Theory* 21(3). 435–483. https://doi.org/10.1023/A:1024109008573.

Belletti, Adriana. 2004. Aspects of the low IP area. In Luigi Rizzi (ed.), *The structure of CP and IP*, vol. 12 (The cartography of syntactic structures), 16–51. New York: Oxford University Press.

Bender, Emily. 2000. The syntax of Mandarin BA: Reconsidering the verbal analysis. *Journal of East Asian Linguistics* 9. 105–145.

van Bergen, Geertje. 2006. *To ba or not to ba: Differential object marking in Chinese*. Nijmegen: Radboud University MA thesis.

Bossong, Georg. 1985. *Differentielle Objektmarkierung in den Neuiranischen Sprachen*. Gunter Narr.

Chang, Li-ping, Chu-Ren Huang & Keh-jian Chen. 1988. The phenomenon of Mandarin pseudo-transitive verbs. In *The 2nd Conference of Mandarin Teaching*, 213–222.

Cheng, Lisa Lai-Shen. 2007. Verb copying in Mandarin Chinese. In Norbert Corver & Jairo Nunes (eds.), *The Copy Theory of Movement*, 151–174. Amsterdam: John Benjamins. https://doi.org/10.1075/la.107.07che.

Dalrymple, Mary & Irina Nikolaeva. 2011. *Objects and information structure*. Cambridge: Cambridge University Press.

Fang, Jie & Peter Sells. 2007. A formal analysis of the Verb Copy Construction in Chinese. In Tracy Holloway King & Miriam Butt (eds.), *Proceedings of the LFG07 conference*, 198–213. Stanford, CA: CSLI Publications.

García García, Marco. 2005. Differential object marking and informativeness. In Klaus von Heusinger, Georg A. Kaiser & Elisabeth Stark (eds.), *Proceedings of the workshop "Specificty and the evolution / emergence of nominal determination systems in Romance"*, 17–31. Konstanz: Universität Konstanz.

Goodall, Grant. 1987. On the argument structure and L-Marking with Mandarin Chinese *Ba*. In Joyce McDonough & Bernadette Plunkett (eds.), *NELS 17: Proceedings of the seventeenth annual meeting of the North East Linguistic Society*, 232–242. Amherst, MA: GLSA Publications.

Gouguet, Jules. 2006. Adverbials and Mandarian argument structure. In Olivier Bonami & Patricia Cabredo Hofherr (eds.), *Empirical issues in syntax and semantics*, vol. 6, 155–173.

Guntsetseg, Dolgor. 2009. Differential object marking in (Khalkha-)Mongolian. In Ryosuke Shibagaki & Reiko Vermeulen (eds.), *Proceedings of the 5th Workshop on Altaic Formal Linguistics (WAFL 5)*, vol. 58 (MIT Working Papers in Linguistics), 115–129. Cambridge, MA: MIT.

Her, One-Soon. 1997. *Interaction and variation in the Chinese VO construction*. Taipei: Crane Publishing.

Hou, John Yien-Yao. 1979. *Grammatical relations in Chinese*. University of Southern California dissertation.

Hsu, Yu-Yin. 2005. *The syntactic structure and pedagogical grammar of modals in Mandarin Chinese*. National Taiwan Normal University MA thesis.

Hsu, Yu-Yin. 2008. The sentence-internal topic and focus in Chinese. In Marjorie K.M. Chan & Hana Kang (eds.), *Proceedings of the twentieth North American Conference on Chinese Linguistics (NACCL-20)*, 635–652. Columbus, OH: The Ohio State University.

Huang, C.-T. James. 1982. *Logical relations in Chinese and the theory of grammar*. MIT dissertation.

Huang, C.-T. James. 1984. Phrase structure, lexical integrity, and Chinese compounds. *Journal of the Chinese Language Teachers Association* 19. 53–78.

Huang, C.-T. James. 1997. On lexical structure and syntactic projection. *Chinese Languages and linguistics* (3). 45–89.

Huang, C.-T. James, Audrey Li & Yafei Li. 2009. *The syntax of Chinese*. Cambridge: Cambridge University Press.

Huang, Chu-Ren. 1989. Subcategorized topics in Mandarin Chinese. Paper presented at the 1989 CLTA Annual Meeting, Boston, 17–19 November 1989.

Kuo, Pei-Jung. 2009. *IP internal movement and topicalization*. Storrs, CT: University of Connecticut dissertation dissertation.

Kuo, Pei-Jung. 2015. The components of sideward movement in the verb copying construction in Mandarin Chinese. *Studies in Chinese Linguistics* 36(1). 35–58. https://doi.org/10.1515/scl-2015-0003.

Li, Charles N. & Sandra A. Thompson. 1981. *Mandarin Chinese: A functional reference grammar*. Berkeley: University of California Press.

Li, Jen-I Jelina. 1999. The structural position of preposed objects in Mandarin. In Chaofen Sun (ed.), *Proceedings of the 10th North American Conference on Chinese Linguistics (NACCL-10)*, vol. 1, 187–204. Los Angeles, CA: GSIL Publications.

Li, Yen-Hui Audrey. 2006. Chinese Ba. In Martin Everaert & Henk van Riemsdijk (eds.), *The Blackwell companion to syntax*. Vol. 1, 374–468. Oxford: Blackwell.

Lin, T.-H. Jonah. 2001. *Light verb syntax and the theory of phrase structure*. University of California, Irvine dissertation.

Liu, Feng-Hsi. 1997. An aspectual analysis of BA. *Journal of East Asian Linguistics* 6(1). 51–99. https://doi.org/10.1023/A:1008287920948.

Mo, Ruo-Ping. 1990. *Mandarin Chinese subcategorized topics: A Lexical Functional Grammar account*. Taipei: Fujen Catholic University MA thesis.

Neeleman, Ad & Hans van de Koot. 2008. Dutch scrambling and the nature of discourse templates. *The Journal of Comparative Germanic Linguistics* 11. 137–189. https://doi.org/10.1007/s10828-008-9018-0.

Nunes, Jairo. 2001. Sideward movement. *Linguistic Inquiry* 31(2). 303–344. https://doi.org/10.1162/00243890152001780.

Nunes, Jairo. 2004. *Linearization of chains and sideward movement*. Cambridge, MA: MIT Press.

Paul, Waltraud. 1988. *The syntax of verb–object phrases in Chinese: Constraints and reanalysis*. Paris: Editions Languages Croisés.

Paul, Waltraud. 2002. Sentence-internal topics in Mandarin Chinese: The case of object preposing. *Language and Linguistics* 3(4). 695–714.

Paul, Waltraud. 2005. Low IP area and left periphery in Mandarin Chinese. *Recherches linguistiques de Vincennes* 33. 111–134.

Paul, Waltraud & John Whitman. 2010. Applicative structure and Mandarin ditransitives. In Maia Duguine, Susana Huidobro & Nerea Madariaga (eds.), *Argument structure and syntactic relations: A cross-linguistic perspective*, 261–282. Amsterdam: John Benjamins. https://doi.org/10.1075/la.158.15pau.

Rizzi, Luigi. 1997. The fine structure of the left periphery. In Liliane Haegeman (ed.), *Elements of grammar*, 281–337. Dordrecht: Springer.

Rodríguez-Mondoñedo, Miguel. 2007. *The syntax of objects: Agree and differential object marking*. University of Connecticut dissertation.

Roussou, Anna. 2000. On the left periphery: Modal particles and complementisers. *Journal of Greek Linguistics* 1(1). 65–94. https://doi.org/10.1075/jgl.1.05rou.

Shyu, Shu-ing. 1995. *The syntax of focus and topic in Mandarin Chinese*. University of Southern California dissertation.
Sun, Chaofen. 1996. *Word order change and grammaticalization in the history of Chinese*. Stanford, CA: Stanford University Press.
Sybesma, Rint. 1999. *The Mandarin VP*. Dordrecht: Kluwer.
Tang, C.-C. Jane. 1990. *Chinese phrase structure and the extended X-bar theory*. Ithaca, NY: Cornell University.
Tang, T.-C. Charles. 1988. On the notion "possible verbs of Chinese". *Tsing Hua Journal of Chinese Studies* 18(1). 43–69.
Tieu, Lyn Shan. 2009. Standard vs. sideward movement in verb copying. In Yun Xiao (ed.), *Proceedings of the 21st North American Conference on Chinese Linguistics (NACCL-21)*, vol. 2, 584–600. Smithfield, RI: Bryant University.
Ting, Jen. 1996. Deriving the secondary topic in Mandarin Chinese. In Tsai-Fa Cheng, Yafei Li & Hongming Zhang (eds.), *Proceedings of the Joint Meeting of the 7th North American Conference on Chinese Linguistics (NACCL-7) and the 4th International Conference on Chinese Linguistics (ICCL-4)*, vol. 1. Madison, WI: University of Wisconsin.
Tsai, W.-T. Dylan. 2001. On object specificity. *ZAS Papers in Linguistics* 22. 173–190.
Tsai, W.-T. Dylan. 2010. Tan hanyu motaici qi fenbu yu qunshi de duiying guanxi [On the syntax semantics correspondences of Chinese modals]. *Zhongguo Yuwen [Studies of the Chinese Language]* 3. 208–221.
Tsao, Feng-fu. 1987a. A topic-comment approach to the *Ba* construction. *Journal of Chinese Linguistics* 15(1). 1–55.
Tsao, Feng-fu. 1987b. On the so-called verb-copying construction in Chinese. *Journal of the Chinese Language Teachers Association* 22(2). 13–44.
Yang, Ning & Geertje van Bergen. 2007. Scrambled objects and case marking in Mandarin Chinese. *Lingua* 117(9). 1617–1653. https://doi.org/10.1016/j.lingua.2006.06.009.
Zou, Ke. 1995. *The syntax of the Chinese ba-construction and verb compounds: A morphosyntactic analysis*. University of Southern California dissertation.

Elsi Kaiser, Merilin Miljan, and Virve Vihman
Estonian speakers' representation of morphological case

Implications for Case/Agree

Abstract: In this paper, we focus on three cases in Estonian (nominative, partitive, genitive) that are used to mark core arguments (subject, object, possessor). We address fundamental questions about the concept of case, including whether abstract case should be related to morphologically overt case. We strive to bring together formal analyses of case with experimental data on the interpretation of case-marked nouns. The chapter reports on a sentence-completion experiment on Estonian speakers' interpretations of nouns presented in the three different cases, each of which is syntactically ambiguous and provides under-determined cues about the grammatical role of the noun. Our data suggest that grammatical case interpretation is not based purely on structure. Instead, we find that morphological case constrains the distribution of a nominal to specific syntactic functions, and the actual function of each case-marked noun is determined in interaction with other factors. Indeed, the more (syntactically) underspecified a case-marker is, the more other cues (in our study, animacy, number, and linear position) interact with it.

Keywords: morphological case, Estonian, Case and Agree, language processing

1 Introduction

In this paper, we report on a sentence completion experiment that investigated Estonian speakers' interpretations of morphological case. We combine formal theories of morphosyntax and a psycholinguistic approach to explore the phenomenon of case from two different perspectives. Case lies in an unsettled place in grammar, with many as yet unresolved issues, particularly regarding the links between morphological form, grammatical function and language processing.

Elsi Kaiser, University of Southern California
Merilin Miljan, University of Tartu
Virve Vihman, University of Tartu

https://doi.org/10.1515/9783110666137-008

Generative linguistic theory assumes two kinds of case: morphological and abstract. Abstract case is a uniquely syntactic concept, a "primitive feature that reflects a relationship between an argument and its syntactic context" (Polinsky & Preminger 2014: 7–8). It is assigned in the syntax and may be — but does not have to be — realized in morphology. Yet there is no consensus on how abstract case is assigned in the syntax or what the role of morphological case should be.

Two main approaches to explaining the assignment of case dominate in generative theory: Agree-based theories and configurational theories. In the Agree-based case theory (Chomsky 2000, 2001, *i.a.*), abstract case is essentially a *by-product* of agreement, which is a basic grammatical operation in minimalist syntax. More specifically, case (as a grammatical feature) is defined as a relationship between a noun phrase and a nearby c-commanding functional head: some functional head F assigns a specific case feature to a noun phrase under an agreement relationship (i.e. Agree). Typically, the finite tense projection (T/Infl) assigns nominative under Agree, v/Voice (the active verb form) assigns accusative, and inside noun phrases, D (possessive, seen as a determiner) assigns genitive. Although this approach to case assignment has been influential in theoretical work, it faces questions about the range of agreeing and case-assigning functional heads (see e.g. Baker 2015: 28), and how crucial the presence of some functional head is to the assignment of case, not to mention the status of agreement relations (Agree) in syntactic theory more generally (cf. Chomsky 2015).

The configurational approach, e.g. Dependent Case Theory (Marantz 1991, McFadden 2004, Bobaljik 2008, Baker 2015), does not regard case assignment as a side effect of an agreement relation, but as independent of it. Abstract case is seen as a relationship between two nominals within the same local domain, and case values are assigned to noun phrases by configurational rules (dependent case rules; e.g. Baker 2015: 79). The idea is that the assignment of one case typically depends on the presence of another case-marked noun phrase in its local vicinity, e.g. accusative is only assigned when a nominative subject is present in the clause. This approach to case assignment assumes several kinds of case, all determined by the conditions of their assignment: lexical, dependent, or assigned by default (see also Section 2.2). We discuss the viability of this approach in accounting for differential case marking in Section 2.2.

Case marking can also be approached from a comprehension-based, psycholinguistic angle. It is known that real-time language processing is incremental (e.g. Altmann & Kamide 1999, Kaiser & Trueswell 2004, Tanenhaus et al. 1995, *i.a.*). That is, a comprehender starts building an interpretation incrementally, before the end of the sentence, when the syntactic information is still potentially ambiguous. Research has shown that the extent to which the language comprehension system considers or 'activates' alternative structures during this parsing process is influenced by multiple types of information — including case-marking on nouns (e.g. Kaiser & Trueswell 2004, Lamers & de Swart 2012, Bornkessel & Schlesewsky 2006).

Thus, from a psycholinguistic perspective, morphological case-marking is an influential cue that actively guides the syntactic structures that comprehenders activate during real-time language processing. This comprehension-oriented view of case-marking as a signal for syntactic structure building contrasts with the more production-oriented conceptualization of case exhibited by both Agree-based and configurational approaches. These approaches largely view case as a reflex or consequence of a certain syntactic configuration. Although these views may be not mutually exclusive, they represent two different ways of conceptualizing the role that case-marking plays in language. Indeed, the fundamental aims of psycholinguistic theories of incremental processing and theoretically-oriented Agree-based and configurational approaches are quite distinct, and cannot be directly compared — especially given that theoretical approaches to case are normally not intended to be models of the language processing system or parser.[1]

In this paper, our aim is not to argue in favor of one of these approaches over the others, or to advocate for a specific view of the relationship between grammar and processing. Instead, we aim to use insights from both theoretical and psycholinguistic work to inform our investigation of how case marking guides language processing in Estonian. Thus, the paper has two distinct foci — grammatical knowledge and performance — in order to study case from an interdisciplinary perspective.

Specifically, in this paper we investigate the interpretation of three different case markers in Estonian, each of which is syntactically ambiguous and thus does not provide fully deterministic cues about the grammatical role of the noun. Estonian is well-suited for our investigations because it has a rich morphological case system which nevertheless includes syntactically ambiguous cases, meaning that case-markers do not 'pin down' the grammatical role of the relevant noun. Moreover, both subjects and objects exhibit semantically-motivated case alternations (differential case marking). Thus, comprehenders face the question of how to interpret partially ambiguous case-marking. In order to focus specifically on the information provided by the case markers themselves, we look at the interpretation of case-marked nouns in isolation, without additional syntactic context. This al-

---

[1] However, consider Radford (2004: 228) who points out that a fundamental principle of Universal Grammar, a Locality Principle, "suggests a processing explanation" (see Chomsky 2001: 13), as according to this principle all relations (probe, goal), or grammatical operations, must be local "in order to minimise search", that is, to "process limited amounts of structure at one time".

lows us to identify what kind of structural information (if any) the morphological case of a noun contributes, from the perspective of the language comprehender.

We also investigate whether and how the semantic properties of nouns — specifically animacy and countability — interact with the syntactic information signaled by case marking. Although the effects of countability (or number) have not received much attention in this context, prior psycholinguistic work on other languages shows that animacy guides the interpretation of syntactically ambiguous case-marked nouns. For example, in German constructions which include arguments in nominative and dative, either of the arguments could be interpreted as subject or object. In such instances, the parser is said to rely on animacy information: notwithstanding the information derived from case-marking, animate entities are more preferred as subject (actor) arguments than inanimate ones, leading to a favored linearisation of animate-before-inanimate (e.g. Schlesewsky & Bornkessel 2004, Grewe et al. 2006).

In this paper, we focus on the grammatical cases — that is, cases used to mark the core arguments subject, object and possessor. Generative approaches to case-marking tend to draw a sharp distinction between syntactic uses of case (argument encoding) and semantic uses (adjunct encoding), even when the same morphological form is used for both functions. The Estonian system allows us to interrogate the nature of syntactic, as opposed to semantic case, leading also to more fundamental questions about the concept of 'abstract case', that is, case which is structurally assigned, and regarded separate from surface, morphological case forms. Thus, our study raises important questions about the surface morphology of the language: What is the motivation for abstract case alongside the surface forms in a language with overt case-marking? How should abstract case be related to morphologically overt case?

The paper is structured as follows: first we give a brief overview of differential case-marking in Estonian and discuss how Finnic data has been analyzed within the frameworks of Agree-based and configurational theories of case assignment. Sections 3 and 4 describe two experiments we carried out on the interpretation of Estonian grammatical cases, reviewing the first, published in Miljan et al. (2017), as it provides the background and motivation for the second, reported here for the first time. In Section 5 we connect the results to their implications for case theory, and finish with general discussion and conclusions.

2 Differential case marking in Estonian (and Finnish)

In our discussion of Estonian case marking, let us start with the key observation that Estonian exhibits differential case marking (DCM) on both subjects and objects. As we will see, the case alternations are associated with differences in interpretation, and also pattern in different ways for singular and plural nouns. We first consider case alternation on objects and then turn to subjects.

Unlike languages with typical differential object marking (DOM), in which some objects are unmarked whereas others have distinctive case-marking, Estonian (like its close relative Finnish) shows alternation between two overt case markers on singular direct objects: *partitive* and *genitive*. This variation between partitive (as in (1a)) and genitive marking (1b) signifies a difference in boundedness, either in the amount of the affected object or in grammatical aspect, or perfectivity (Erelt & Metslang 2017, Ogren 2015, 2018). (Objects in the scope of negation must be in partitive case and do not show the genitive/partitive alternation.)

(1) a. Imperfective
 Poiss sõi suppi.
 boy.NOM.SG eat.PST.3SG soup.PART.SG
 'The boy was eating soup.' / 'The boy ate (some) soup.'

 b. Perfective
 Poiss sõi supi (ära).
 boy.NOM.SG eat.PST.3SG soup.GEN.SG PTCL
 'The boy ate the soup (up).'

(2) Imperfective
 Juhan kirjutas luuletusi.
 Juhan.NOM write.PST.3SG poem.PART.PL
 'Juhan wrote (some) poems.' / 'Juhan was writing poems.'

(3) Perfective
 Juhan kirjutas luuletused.
 Juhan.NOM write.PST.3SG poem.NOM.PL
 'Juhan wrote (the) poems.'

In the case of plural direct objects, the alternation is between *partitive* (2) and *nominative* (3). In the literature on case marking in Estonian and Finnish, genitive on the affected object is described in some traditions as accusative, realized by morphological genitive in singular (1b) and nominative in plural (3). While reference grammars of Estonian (e.g. Erelt et al. 1993, 2007, Erelt & Metslang 2017) state that there is no morphologically distinct accusative case in Estonian, its existence is nevertheless debated (see, e.g. Hiietam 2003, Caha 2009, Norris 2018a). In Finnish, pronouns and some wh-words exhibit a morphologically distinct accusative form (see, e.g. Kiparsky 2001, Hakulinen et al. 2004).

In addition to this alternation between object cases, Estonian (like Finnish) also exhibits differential case marking on the *subject*. With count nouns, this tends to happen with plurals (compare (5a) and (5b))[2], and involves alternation between nominative and partitive subjects with intransitive (activity) verbs: the nominative in (4) gives rise to a perfective reading and the counterpart partitive in (5) gives rise to an imperfective or partially affected reading. (We say more about the verb agreement patterns in Section 2.1)

(4)   Külalised   saabusid.
       guest.NOM.PL arrive.PST.3PL
       'The guests (have) arrived.'

(5) a.   Külalisi   saabus.
       guest.PART.PL arrive.PST.3SG
       '(Some) guests arrived.' / 'Guests were arriving.'

---

2 In addition to plural and mass nouns, singular partitive count nouns can also take the subject role, but then the interpretation of that noun assumes a context of a 'universal grinder', as in, e.g. one apple is divided between several people (i). Example (5b) above is ungrammatical because there is no context which supports the interpretation of that partitive noun in the subject role. If one replaces the verb 'arrive' with 'suffice' in (5b), it would be grammatical, as in (ii).

(i)   Õuna   jagus   kõigile.
      apple.PART.SG suffice.3SG.PST everyone.ALL
      '(The) apple was divisible between everyone.' / 'There was enough of the apple for everyone.'

(ii)   Külalist   jagus   kõikjale.
      guest.PART.SG suffice.PST.3SG everywhere.ALL
      'The presence of (the) guest could be felt everywhere.'

b. *_Külalist_   _saabus._
   guest.PART.SG arrive.PST.3SG
   resulting reading: '(Part of) a guest arrived.'

Thus, partitive is involved in differential case marking on both subjects and objects, and the details depend on number (and countability). In the contexts in which differential marking occurs, the interpretation of nominative and genitive contrasts with partitive: partitive alternates with (i) genitive for singular nouns in differential object marking (example (1)), and (ii) nominative in differential subject marking (see the examples in (4–5)) as well as for plural nouns in differential object marking (examples (2–3)). While partitive conveys semantic partiality ('some' or 'part of'), nominative and genitive are interpreted as 'all' or 'whole' in these contexts; while a partitive object signals imperfectivity, genitive on the object is taken to mean perfectivity (for more on these pragmatic effects of case variation in Estonian, see e.g. Cann & Miljan 2012).

The differential case marking of Finnic poses a challenge for derivational accounts of case. One main question is: How to establish unified explanations for all the instantiations of DCM in Estonian specifically or in Finnic more generally?[3] In the remainder of Section 2, we provide an overview of the theoretical accounts proposed for Finnic, of which we are aware.

2.1 Agree and DCM in Estonian and Finnish

In this section, we discuss the assignment of Estonian 'grammatical' cases (nominative, genitive, partitive) from the perspective of Agree-based case theory, and then turn to configurational approaches, in particular Dependent Case Theory, in the following section.

Recall that according to Agree-based case theory, some functional head has to be postulated to assign a structural case feature to a noun phrase, which then enters into an agreement relationship with that head. Two fundamental questions emerge from this approach: first, is the presence of a functional head crucial to the assignment of structural case (see also Baker 2015); second, how do the surface morphological facts relate to syntax?

---

[3] There are accounts which have attempted a unified analysis of partitive for Finnish within the framework of Minimalism, e.g. Csirmaz (2012), which relates partitive to a semantic property of divisibility of a phase: if a phase is interpreted as divisible after Spell-out, the syntactic case [Case] is realized as morphological partitive. However, this account does not extend to partitive marking on subjects.

There is some evidence in Estonian morphology for an agreement relationship between nominative case assignment and the finite Tense/Inflection head (henceforth T/Infl). As shown in (6), the finite verb agrees in person and number with a nominative noun in the subject position:

(6) a. Tõnis **ostab** uue laeva.
Tõnis.NOM buy.PRS.3SG new.GEN.SG ship.GEN.SG
'Tõnis (will) buy a new ship.'

b. Ma / sa **ostan** / **ostad** uue laeva.
1SG.NOM 2SG.NOM buy.PRS.1SG buy.PRS.2SG new.GEN.SG ship.GEN.SG
'I / you (will) buy a new ship.'

Yet this is only part of the story, since non-finite clauses can also have nominative subjects in Estonian, as in (7)–(8). These examples are grammatical, freestanding clauses (i.e. not ellipsis or fragments), in which the non-finite verb (the infinitive in (7) and the *vat*-evidential in (8)) conveys the evidential meaning of hearsay.

(7) Erelt et al. (2007: 264)
Mari **olla** *väga jutukas.*
Mari.NOM be.INF very talkative.NOM.SG
'Mari (is said) to be very talkative.'

(8) *Tõnis* **tahtvat** *uut laevakaupa teha.*
Tõnis.NOM want.INF new.PART.SG ship-deal.PART.SG do.INF
'Tõnis (is said) to want to make a new ship deal.'

Examples like (7) and (8) show that nominative case does not depend on finite T/Infl being present. The data indicate that nominative case-marking is not dependent on agreement in Estonian. Rather, agreement is dependent on nominative case on the subject: when the verb shows agreement, it only agrees with the nominative subject (see, e.g. partitive subject in (5) above, with no agreement). Thus, it looks like Estonian has case-sensitive agreement, as opposed to case-assigning agreement (see also, e.g. Bobaljik 2008 who states that it is more common for case-marking to determine agreement, in line with what we see in Estonian, than the other way around).

There is no morphological object agreement in Estonian that would support object case assignment under the relationship of Agree. The object can occur in three different forms: genitive ((1), (6)), nominative ((3)), or partitive ((1), (2), (8), (9)). Some treatments analyze the genitive as accusative on the basis of syntactic structure: the syntactic accusative is then realized by morphological genitive in singular and nominative in plural, as in (3), repeated here as (10) and contrasting with (9).

(9) *Juhan   kirjutas   luuletust   / luuletusi.*
    Juhan.NOM write.PST.3SG poem.PART.SG   poem.PART.PL
    (i) 'Juhan was writing (a) poem/ poems.'
    (ii) 'Juhan wrote (some) poems.'

(10) *Juhan   kirjutas   luuletuse   / luuletused.*
     Juhan.NOM write.PST.3SG poem.GEN.SG   poem.NOM.PL
     'Juhan wrote (a/the) poem / poems.'

Since no account has been proposed for differential case marking in Estonian from the perspective of derivational grammar,[4] we now turn to object case-marking patterns in Finnish, which have mainly been analyzed from the perspective of traditional (Government and Binding) and Agree-based accounts. In order to capture the distribution of morphological genitive and partitive in Finnish, most syntactic analyses invoke the concept of abstract accusative and partitive. (Finnish, unlike Estonian, has a morphologically-distinct accusative form which is visible on direct-object pronouns, see e.g. Hakulinen et al. 2004.) To explain differential case marking, functional categories with differential movement positions are posited (e.g. Nelson 1995, Ritter & Rosen 2001, Svenonius 2002). More recent accounts do not necessarily posit an accusative. Poole (2015), for example, argues for a configurational approach to Finnish structural cases, referring to alternation between partitive and nonpartitive (i.e. genitive/nominative), which he relates to different movement positions associated with aspect.

The most common strategy for explaining the genitive/partitive alternation on objects in Finnish is to associate the assignment of one of the two alternating cases with some marked (specified) feature and the assignment of the other case with an unmarked (unspecified) feature. Specifically, such approaches observe that the abstract accusative occurs only on the object and nowhere else, and analyze it as being introduced by an independent functional head, Aspect (i.e. telicity/boundedness of the predicate which relates accusative to the perfective interpretation). The assignment of accusative (the abstract case) is thus determined by the presence of the functional head Aspect. In related work, Vainikka (1993) posits

---

[4] See, however, Norris (2018b) who accounts for Estonian data from the perspective of derivational grammar, but focuses on the structure of nominals.

that in Finnish, only verbs with the feature [+completed] assign accusative. More recently, Ritter & Rosen (2001) proposed that in Finnish an event is quantized[5] when the direct object is quantized. Under their account, when a verb is specified for the [Quant] feature, an object that bears the feature [Quant] moves to Spec-Agr-O to check the [Quant] feature as well as the Accusative Case. If the verb does not have a [Quant] feature, the object stays in VP and receives Partitive Case. See also Kratzer (2004) for related work.

As partitive case has a wider distribution than accusative (e.g. partitive can occur on subjects, objects, adjuncts), partitive is analyzed as the default or elsewhere case for complements (e.g. Vainikka 1993, Kiparsky 1998), or the basic unmarked case for objects, related to the interpretation of 'non-boundedness' (e.g. de Hoop & Malchukov 2007), or non-aspectual theta-role (Nelson 1995).

Although the above analyses work for a set of core examples in Finnish and Estonian, there are some major complications for Agree-based accounts, including: (i) unexpected partitive in [+bounded] situations, and (ii) constructions in which verbs are [+bounded] but the object is [-bounded]. We discuss these below:

(i) Unexpected partitive in [+bounded] situations

Plenty of Estonian examples can be found with a [+bounded] verb and [+bounded] noun phrase, which nevertheless surfaces with partitive, as in (11)–(12).

(11) *Ta   tervitas   presidenti.*
     3SG.NOM greet.PST.3SG president.PART.SG
     'S/he greeted (the) president.'

(12) *Ta   külastas   näitust.*
     3SG.NOM visit.PST.3SG exhibition.PART.SG
     'S/he visited (the) exhibition.'

To accommodate examples like (11)–(12), a set of partitive-assigning verbs may be defined, e.g. Kiparsky (1998, 2001) on Finnish. This gives us two different types of partitive in one language: one partitive is assigned by default, and the other is assigned lexically.[6] Indeed, it has been proposed that one case can be assigned

---

5 Cf. Krifka's (1992) concept of quantization with respect to nominals and events.
6 See also Kaiser 2002, 2004 for discussion of other instances of unexpected partitive case and optional case alternations related to pragmatic factors.

in multiple ways (see e.g. Brattico 2011 for Finnish). However, one may wonder whether it is possible to avoid this kind of multiplicity. When case is analyzed as being assigned in multiple ways, the function of case-marking becomes obscured, for example, Brattico (2011: 1065) refers to this as "purposeless feature distribution".

(ii) [+bounded] verbs and [-bounded] objects

In a large set of examples in both Estonian and Finnish, the functional head Aspect is not able to determine case assignment on noun phrases under agreement. In order to assign case at all, another functional head needs to be posited for a noun phrase, referred to as a null quantifier in the literature (e.g. Kiparsky 2001). This pertains to verbs with the feature [+bounded], when the object noun phrase is [-bounded] and receives partitive case, as in (13)–(14), paraphrasable as 'some gold' or 'some typos', respectively. Singular count nouns, as in (15), are [+bounded] and behave differently with the same [+bounded] verbs: they do not allow the reading of unboundedness, i.e. [-bounded] on the noun, hence partitive is excluded on such nominals and syntactic accusative (realized by genitive) is assigned instead.

(13) *Ta   leidis   kulda.*
 3SG.NOM find.PST.3SG gold.PART
 'S/he found (some) gold.'

(14) *Ta   leidis   kirjavigu.*
 3SG.NOM find.PST.3SG typo.PART.PL
 'S/he found (some) typos.'

(15) *Ta   leidis   *raamatut   / raamatu.*
 3SG.NOM find.PST.3SG book.PART.SG   book.GEN.SG
 'S/he found a book.'

In sum, postulating the relation of Agree does not help us fully capture the differential object case marking patterns in Estonian and Finnish, at least not in a straightforward way.

What about differential case-marking on subjects, as in (5) above? As we saw in (5), subjects of intransitive verbs can occur in nominative or partitive case. We now briefly discuss prior accounts of differential subject marking. In general, researchers have argued for a structural explanation which says that the single argument of an unaccusative verb is syntactically equivalent to an internal argument (object) and hence receives partitive marking as a default complement case (e.g. Nelson 1995 on Finnish). However, this account on its own is not sufficient for Finnish and Estonian,[7] as the single argument of an unergative verb (derived in the top of the shell/vP/preverbal position and thus syntactically equivalent to the subject of a transitive verb) can also have a partitive marked subject in Estonian (e.g. verbs such as 'to fly', 'to drive', 'to run', etc.), as in (16).

(16) a. *Inimesi sõitis maale.*
 people.PART.PL drive.PST.3SG countryside.ADE
 '(A number of) people were driving to the countryside.'

 b. *Mehi jooksis mäest üles.*
 men.PART run.PST.3SG mountain.ELA up
 '(A number of) men ran up the hill.'

2.2 Dependent case analysis of DCM in Finnish (Baker 2015)

Having reviewed work on Agree-based theories of Finnish case, we now turn to configurational approach, e.g. Dependent Case Theory (Marantz 1991, McFadden 2004, Bobaljik 2008, Baker 2015). In this theory, abstract Case is a relationship between two *nominals* within the same local domain: case values are assigned to noun phrases independent of agreement by configurational or dependent case rules (e.g. Baker 2015: 79). Consequently, there are several kinds of case, as in Marantz's (1991) *Case realization disjunctive hierarchy* (as cited in Baker 2015: 47–48), which has four:
1. Lexically assigned case (e.g. inherent case)
2. Dependent case, where case assignment depends on the presence of some other case in the local domain (e.g. accusative and ergative)
3. Unmarked case (e.g. nominative or absolutive)
4. Default case, assigned to any noun phrase which is not otherwise marked for case.

---

[7] Note that these intransitive constructions are slightly different in Estonian and Finnish (for more detail on the differences and similarities of intransitive sentences in Finnish and Estonian, see Spoelman 2013).

Since Dependent Case Theory has not been applied to Estonian, in our review of existing work we focus on Finnish, based on Baker (2015), but see also Poole (2015). According to dependent case analysis, differential case marking patterns can only be explained by a strategy which considers one of the alternating cases to be assigned and the other to be the default or unmarked case. For Finnish, Baker (2015) proposes that partitive is the unmarked case in the VP domain, assigned to a noun phrase that is not otherwise case-marked. Baker (2015: 19) claims that accusative (the feature value [ACC]) exists in Finnish grammar and that there is an accidental homophony between accusative and genitive in singular (non-pronominal) nouns, and between accusative and nominative in plural (non-pronominal) nouns. (Recall that in Finnish, accusative case is morphologically distinct from genitive and nominative on pronouns). Since the assignment of accusative is seen to depend on whether a nominative argument is present, Baker analyzes accusative as dependent case.

Baker suggests that in Finnish, differential object marking takes place in narrow syntax (i.e. c-command relationships), whereas in some other languages it takes place at the phonological form (PF). For the assignment of dependent case, i.e. accusative, Baker assumes a [+bounded] v or Aspect head that attracts a [+bounded] noun phrase to its specifier (Spec) position to check its [+bounded] feature value (Baker 2015: 143). Otherwise, partitive case is assigned in VP, and is regarded as the unmarked case in VP (it is assigned when no other, "more interesting", case has been assigned). Note that nominative (the subject case) is, according Baker (2015: 145), an unmarked case of the TP domain.

As for differential marking between nominative and partitive subjects in Finnish, Baker (2015) follows a traditional syntactic explanation: noun phrases which have not moved out of VP are taken as internal arguments and assigned partitive case (see also Nelson 1995, Kiparsky 2001). That is, partitive subjects are taken to be part of VP, as in (17).

(17) Finnish (Kiparsky 2001: 345)
 Nyt [$_{VP}$ *tule-e uutis-i-a*].
 now come-3SG news-PL-PART
 'Now there comes (some items of) news.'

Yet there are some complications for this approach, as already pointed out in section 2.1, part (ii). First, in Finnish as well as in Estonian, a partitive subject may precede the verb, hence the partitive subject can occur outside VP, as in (18)–(19). This can be attributed to scrambling – as both Finnish and Estonian have flexible word order – but this raises the new question of what triggers the scrambling to a VP-external position. While this in itself does not argue against Baker's account, it highlights some open questions which need to be addressed. Poole (2015), for example, states explicitly that partitive on subjects is the DP-level partitive (i.e. partitive related only to nominals), and sets the issue aside.

(18) Finnish
Vieraita   saapuu.
guests.PART.PL arrive.PRS.3SG
'(Some) guests were arriving.'

(19) Estonian
Külalisi   saabus.
guest.PART.PL arrive.PRS.3SG
'(Some) guests were arriving.'

Second, imperative constructions turn out to be problematic for the assignment of nominative. The subject of an imperative verb can be optionally overt in Estonian, as in (20), as well as in Finnish, but the object is still marked by nominative and not accusative, as would be expected by dependent case assignment. That is, when another structurally case-marked nominal/DP is present in the case-assignment domain (the noun *sina* 'you' carrying nominative), the other argument (*koer* 'dog') should be assigned a dependent case, accusative.

(20) *Vii   sina   koer   jalutama.*
take.IMP.SG 2SG.NOM(=overt subject) dog.NOM.SG(=object) walk.INF
'You take the dog for a walk!' (imperative)

Baker (2015: 141, 207–209) offers a solution to this for Finnish by connecting the subject of an imperative verb to PRO.[8] (In non-derivational accounts, it has been suggested that the postverbal subject, as well as the preverbal one, are discourse vocatives, e.g. Kiparsky 2001, Miljan & Cann 2013; Erelt et al. 2007 mention that the subject may also be used for contrasting different addressees).

In summary, both Agree-based case theory and Dependent Case Theory aim to explain the *syntax* of case assignment. They treat case as a reflex (or a consequence) of a syntactic relationship. Because they are concerned with the syntactic configurations involved in case assignment, these accounts focus on the structure of the clause and the positions of noun phrases in it. Yet, as pointed out above (Sections 2.1 and 2.2), these approaches face empirical challenges.

---

8 We are grateful to an anonymous reviewer for pointing this out to us.

In the rest of this paper, we discuss two psycholinguistic experiments that investigate what assumptions native Estonian speakers make about case-marked nouns when given no syntactic information about the structure of the clause. Thus, we essentially 'reverse' the approach taken by most syntactic theories – rather than using syntactic configurations to explain case assignment, we ask: if someone is given a case-marked noun with no syntactic cues, what assumptions does that person make about the syntactic role of the noun? Before discussing the logic of the experiments more explicitly in the next section, let us summarize the basic assumptions that both theoretical approaches make about nominative, genitive and partitive case – the three cases investigated in the experiments.

Both Agree-based and Dependent Case Theory approaches tend to postulate the existence of a (syntactic) accusative underlying the morphological genitive on direct objects. Accordingly, morphological **genitive** is assumed to be syncretic, essentially functioning as two separate (syntactic) cases: (i) nominal/possessive genitive and (ii) accusative (realized as genitive in singular). Thus, under this view, whether a noun with genitive morphology is genitive or accusative-realized-as-genitive essentially depends on whether or not it is syntactically a direct object.

Both of these accounts view **partitive** as the object case, or a case belonging within the verb phrase; it is assumed to be the unmarked or default case in the VP because its distribution is broader than that of the accusative. Cann & Miljan (2012), on the other hand, argue that partitive marks the core meaning of semantic partitivity, and that genitive case is the underspecified, unmarked oblique case (see also Miljan & Cann 2013). Csirmaz (2012) takes a similar stance on Finnish cases within a derivational approach by relating partitive directly to divisibility and arguing that accusative (realized by morphological genitive) is the default case. Thus, under the partitive-is-default view, a noun with partitive morphology can occur in a wide range of complement positions in the VP, but under the partitive-marks-partitivity view, a noun with partitive morphology occurs in constructions involving partitivity/divisibility.

Theoretical approaches agree that **nominative** is the subject or default case of the finite verb projection, TP.

In the next section, we report two experiments investigating the role that overt case morphology plays in the interpretation of noun phrases and whether morphological (i.e. paradigmatic) case can predict syntax. Thus, rather than taking syntax as our starting point and asking how different syntactic configurations result in a noun being assigned a particular case (case as a *reflex* of a syntactic relation), we take as our starting point the surface case forms (i.e. case-marked nouns themselves) and ask what follows if we regard case markers as *active* contributors to language processing. In a morphologically rich, yet partially ambiguous, system like Estonian, what information do the morphological case markers on their own convey about syntactic structure? When Estonian speakers encounter a case-marked noun, what grammatical role do they associate with the noun? Does this interact with other factors, such as the number and animacy of the noun? If we assume an admittedly over-simplified, purely syntactic theory of case, it is not clear how such semantic factors could play a role. In contrast, if we assume a psycholinguistic perspective, according to which the language processing system is highly sensitive to multiple sources of information, we expect factors like number and animacy to modulate the syntactic interpretation of case-marked nouns. Indeed, according to this kind of view, the situations where the case marker is syntactically most ambiguous might be the situations where we see the clearest effects of semantic factors such as animacy and number.

3 Psycholinguistic experiments

To take the surface, case-marked forms as a starting point and investigate what information they carry for Estonian speakers, we devised two sentence-completion experiments using nominative, genitive and partitive nouns. Participants saw case-marked prompt nouns (e.g. *sõbra* 'friend.GEN.SG'), and their task was simply to use this noun in a sentence. In forming a sentence, participants necessarily assign some grammatical function to each noun, from which we can observe their preferred production patterns with a given form. In work using sentence-completion methodology, it is assumed that speakers' production patterns (in this case, the grammatical role assigned to a noun) provide an indication of their interpretation preferences (e.g. Trueswell et al. 1993, Snedeker & Trueswell 2004 for related work). When faced with a case-marked noun (or any other linguistic element), participants first need to interpret it before providing a continuation and embedding it in a linguistic context. Thus, frequent continuations reflect frequent interpretations. Sentence-completion methodology has been successfully used within psycholinguistics to tap into a variety of questions related to language processing. We wished to explore how speakers interpret nouns bearing case without any syntactic context to guide them.

In our target items, we examined the effects of the noun's (i) animacy (animate, inanimate) and (ii) number (singular, plural). As regards **animacy**, prior work in other languages has found an 'animacy-first' bias: Psycholinguistic research has found that speakers tend to mention animate before inanimate nouns (e.g. Bock 1986, Ferreira 1994, see also Prat-Sala & Branigan 2000). Relatedly, corpus work in various languages has found that subjects tend to be animate and objects tend to be inanimate (e.g. Dahl 2000, Dahl & Fraurud 1996, Dahl 2008, many others). Thus, we wanted to see to what extent animate and inanimate nouns with the same (ambiguous) case marker would receive different syntactic interpretations.

Number is also relevant because the case-marking system of Estonian is sensitive to number: certain syntactic functions are expressed with different case marking depending on the number of the noun (see Section 2). For example, genitive plural nouns never occur in the direct object function (only singular nouns do). We also tested mass nouns, but here we only report results for count nouns. More generally, interactions between number, grammatical role assignment, and case-marking have not received much attention from either theoretical or empirical psycholinguistic perspectives. Typological research on number has tended to focus on verb agreement. Psycholinguistic studies on number have also largely focused on subject-verb agreement effects in comprehension and production (see Lago et al. 2015 for a review). We aimed to find out how the syntactic interpretation of nominative, genitive and partitive nouns is influenced by whether the nouns are singular or plural. For some case-number combinations, this is grammatically restricted, as with the genitive plurals mentioned above, but others are more probabilistic.

We first briefly review the first experiment (published as Miljan et al. 2017), which provides important background information for the new experiment reported on in this paper. The design of the studies is parallel, with one crucial difference in the constraints imposed on the position of the target noun. The same nouns were used as prompts in both studies, but in our first study, the nouns were presented as *sentence-initial* (e.g. *Sõbra ...*) and in the instructions, participants were explicitly instructed to begin their sentences with the prompt noun. In the second study, reported here, participants were instructed to formulate a sentence using the noun *anywhere in the sentence*.

We manipulated the constraints on noun position to gain insights into different types of information signaled by case-marking. The first experiment, with sentence-initial nouns, aims to mimic the incrementality of real-time language processing in a minimally-constraining context — recall that prior work on case-marked nouns has shown that people start to interpret words based on their case-marking immediately, before they have seen the rest of the sentence (for studies of the processing of case-marking, see, e.g. Kamide et al. 2003, Schlesewsky & Bornkessel 2004, Grewe et al. 2006, Şükrü et al. 2008, Bornkessel-Schlesewsky & Schlesewsky 2009). Thus, by asking people to continue fragments, we can see what grammatical roles are most frequently attributed to *sentence-initial nouns* with particular morphological cases, thus mimicking online language processing.

All the cases used in the experiment, when used in sentence-initial position, can in principle signal more than one structural position. Examples (21a-c) show some possible continuations for a prompt word in genitive case.

(21) **Sõbra ...**
 'friend.GEN.SG' ...

    a. [**Sõbra**   **ema**]$_{NP}$ *tuli*   *külla.*
         friend.GEN.SG mother.NOM.SG come.PST.3SG to visit
         '(A) friend's mother came to visit.'

    b. [**Sõbra**]$_{NP}$ *kutsus*   *ta*   *pulma.*
         friend.GEN.SG invite.PST.3SG 3SG.NOM wedding.SG.ILL
         'S/he invited a friend to the wedding.'

    c. [**Sõbra**   **juures**]$_{PP}$ *vaatasid*   *nad*   *filmi.*
         friend.GEN.SG at   watch.PST.3PL 3PL.NOM film.PART.SG
         'At (their) friend's house, they watched a film.'

As can be seen here, flexible word order in Estonian means that sentence-initial nouns are not restricted to the subject role. However, although nouns in a variety of grammatical roles can occur in sentence-initial position, some grammatical roles – especially subjects – are more frequent sentence-initially than others. In (21a), the possessive target noun is embedded in a sentence-initial subject constituent. In (b) and (c), however, the subject is postverbal, with the genitive noun receiving a direct object (21b) or postpositional complement (21c) interpretation. Although Estonian has flexible word order, corpus studies have shown that SV(X) constituent order is the most frequent; Lindström (2004) reports that in spoken Estonian, 41% of all sentences have SV(X) order, (X) indicating any constituent optionally following the verb.

The sentence-initial nouns in our first study allow for the noun to be interpreted without any previous information about the verb or the syntactic structure of the clause: the only available information is the noun itself, with its case and semantic properties. This can be compared to a situation where an Estonian reader or listener encounters a sentence beginning with *sõbra* 'friend.GEN.SG': What grammatical roles does the listener/reader consider at the point where she has heard only the initial case-marked noun, disregarding previous context? While context-free (i.e. discourse-initial), isolated nouns may not be highly frequent, the sentence-completion task allows us to investigate what structures speakers are likely to construct, based solely on information contained in the noun. Our sentence completion task aimed to mimic this situation.[9]

In our second experiment, participants could use the prompt noun in any position in forming their sentence, including non-initial positions, as in (22). The flexibility of using the noun in any position addresses one of the limitations of our first study, namely the fact that the sentence-initial position in Estonian is likely to favor certain grammatical roles (especially subjects or subject-internal roles) than others (see discussion above). Thus, to gain a clearer sense of what grammatical role information is provided by case-markers, in the new experiment we eliminated the requirement for the noun to be in sentence-initial position, allowing for completed sentences such as those in (22).

(22) a. *Ma   leidsin   trennist   endale [toreda*
       1SG.NOM find.PST.3SG gym.SG.ELA   myself   nice.GEN.SG
       sõbra].
       friend.GEN.SG
       'I found myself a nice friend in (the) gym.'

   b. *Vennale   meeldib   tihti   [**sõbra**   juures] käia.*
       brother.SG.ALL like.PRS.3SG often   friend.GEN.SG at   go.INF
       'My brother often likes to visit his friend's place.'

In sum, our first study looks at the interpretation of case-marking in a situation similar to incremental language comprehension, whereas the second study (noun in any position) looks at the interpretation of case-marking in a flexible context, to see how people interpret case-marking without word order constraints.

3.1 Results of earlier work: Interpretation of case-marking on sentence-initial nouns

In our first experiment (reported fully in Miljan et al. 2017), participants were asked to write a sentence beginning with the prompt noun. This method taps into grammatical-role expectations triggered in participants' minds by information from case-marked nouns, in a context where no information is available about

---

[9] It is important to note that the processing perspective aims for a different type of information: the information which becomes available at each point in the input sequence incrementally. This is in stark contrast to theories of grammar that focus on the representation of the information of entire phrase/clause/sentence.

the verb or clause structure. We report data for count nouns in the nominative, genitive and partitive case.

3.1.1 Experimental set-up of our prior study

Forty-two adult native Estonian speakers participated in an internet-based study implemented with Limesurvey (https://www.limesurvey.org/). Participants saw nouns and were asked to write a sentence beginning with the noun provided. We manipulated the number (singular, plural) and case-marking (nominative: NOM, partitive: PART, genitive: GEN) of the initial noun in a 2x3, Latin square design. In addition, we controlled for animacy (animate, inanimate) between items, ensuring that each participant saw a balanced number of animate and inanimate nouns. Example items are in Table 1.

Tab. 1: Examples of animate noun *rebane* 'fox' and an inanimate noun *raamat* 'book'

Noun	Animate 'fox'	Case form	Inanimate 'book'
SG	*rebane*	NOM.SG	*raamat*
	rebast	PART.SG	*raamatut*
	rebase	GEN.SG	*raamatu*
PL	*rebased*	NOM.PL	*raamatud*
	rebaseid	PART.PL	*raamatuid*
	rebaste	GEN.PL	*raamatute*

We tested 18 target count nouns (as well as 9 mass nouns and 6 time expressions, not reported here) and 32 filler items, which involved a range of different cases and parts of speech (e.g. *kaua* 'long.time', *pargis* 'park.INE', *kiiresti* 'fast', *suuri* 'large.PART.PL').

Two trained coders analyzed the grammatical role assigned to the case-marked noun in participants' continuation sentences (e.g. *subject, object, possessor of subject, possessor of object*).[10] See Miljan et al. (2017) for a full discussion of the coding labels.

---

[10] 28% of the data was fully double-coded to ensure consistency across coders in their use of the coding labels.

3.1.2 Results and discussion: Our prior study

With **nominative nouns,** there was an overwhelming bias to interpret the noun as a subject: approximately 90% (or more, in certain conditions) of nominative nouns are interpreted as subjects, regardless of whether the noun is singular or plural, animate or inanimate. In other words, we find no effects of animacy or number in nominative case. The strength of the bias to *interpret nominative nouns as subjects* is presumably at least partly due to the initial position. This finding is in line with corpus frequencies aligning nominative case in sentence-initial position with subjects (e.g. Lindström 2004). We address this question in our new experiment, where nouns are not limited to initial position.

Partitive nouns show greater sensitivity to number and animacy than nominative nouns. Partitive nouns are most frequently interpreted as *objects* (80.9% of animate singulars, 60.3% of animate plurals, 55.5% of inanimate singulars, 65% of inanimate plurals) – but with animate nouns, the strength of this bias depends on number: Animate nouns result in more object interpretations when they are singular than plural, but inanimate nouns show no significant effects of number. We also found that partitive *subject* continuations, which were used only with plural nouns, occur more with animates than inanimates (34.9% of animate plurals and 14.3% of inanimate plurals). We attribute this to a general preference to *interpret animate nouns as subjects*, combined with the preference for sentence-initial nouns to be subjects. Inanimate partitive nouns are also interpreted fairly often as adverbial complements (17.5% of inanimate plurals, 33.3% of inanimate singulars), which fits with cross-linguistic observations about *objects being prototypically inanimate* (e.g. Hopper & Thompson 1980, Dowty 1991). This suggests that the link between objects and inanimates extends also to objects inside gerund clauses, even in sentence-initial position.

As a whole, the continuation patterns with partitive case show that Estonian speakers' expectations regarding the grammatical role of a sentence-initial partitive noun is sensitive to *both* number and animacy.[11] Nouns in partitive case can be interpreted as objects or as subjects, with frequencies depending on the noun's number and animacy.

When it comes to **genitive nouns,** both animacy and number influence the grammatical role attributed to the noun. The most frequent grammatical role assigned to *animate* genitive nouns is possessor-of-subject (69.8% of singular ani-

---

[11] As mentioned in Section 2, objects in the scope of negation are also marked with partitive case in Estonian. However, Miljan et al. (2017) shows in detail that the high rate of object continuations observed in the dataset for partitive nouns as a whole is not simply due to participants producing a high rate of negative sentences.

mate genitive nouns, 49.2% of plural animate genitive nouns). This contrasts with *inanimate* genitive nouns (only 22.2% of singular inanimates, 30.2% of plural inanimates are possessors-of-subject). Inanimate genitive nouns also occur in modifier structures where the noun is an object inside a nominalized structure (20.6% of singular inanimates, 41.3% of plural inanimates), which fits with the crosslinguistically observed association between objects and inanimates.

The preference to interpret animate genitive nouns as possessors of the subject might be related to a general preference for animates to be possessors, which may, in turn, be related to the semantics of possession as well as frequencies of occurrence in the language (Rosenbach 2017). Moreover, the tendency to interpret these animate genitive nouns more specifically as possessors of subjects may well be attributed to the general preference for subject-initial orders, as discussed above (see also MacDonald 2013).

It is worth noting that none of the animate nouns and only 13% of the genitive singular inanimate nouns were interpreted as the direct object of a transitive verb. This low rate may be related to word order effects: object-initial orders are less frequent in Estonian than subject-initial orders. We return to this question below.

3.1.3 Summary of our prior study

Our earlier experiment shows that (i) although nominative case strongly signals that the noun is a subject, genitive and partitive are not unambiguously associated with any single grammatical role, and (ii) speakers' expectations regarding the grammatical roles of nouns are influenced by cues such as animacy and number, and by morphological case-marking. Generally speaking, most of the animacy effects we find can be derived from a bias to interpret animates as subjects and inanimates as objects. Most of the number effects we find can be derived from either syntactic constraints (e.g. genitive plural cannot mark a direct object) or the semantically- and/or pragmatically-based constraint against animate count nouns as partitive subjects.

4 Experiment: Interpretation of case-marking on nouns in any position

Given that the sentence-initial position of the nouns in our prior study may have influenced the results, we conducted a new experiment using the same nouns and the same design, but allowed participants to use the noun anywhere in forming a sentence, i.e., no word-order constraints were imposed. This allows us to see what grammatical role(s) are most closely associated with the different cases – and whether this is influenced by animacy and number – in the absence of any word order information.

4.1 Method

4.1.1 Participants

Forty-two native adult Estonian speakers participated over the Internet. None of them had participated in our earlier study.

4.1.2 Materials and design

The materials and design were the same as in the first study: We used the same target nouns and the same filler items. We manipulated the number (singular, plural) and case-marking (nominative, partitive, genitive) of the initial noun, and included both animate and inanimate nouns. As in the first study, we used a Latin square design, common in psycholinguistic research, to ensure that each participant saw each specific noun only once, and saw equal numbers of nouns in all six conditions. Each participant saw equal numbers of animate and inanimate nouns.

4.1.3 Procedure

The sentence-completion task was conducted over the Internet with LimeSurvey. Participants saw nouns and were asked to use each noun in a sentence. Instructions and examples made clear that they could use the noun in *any position they wanted* (including sentence-initial). Participants were not informed that our aim was to investigate case or grammatical roles. Their comments after the experiment suggest that they remained unaware of our aims.

4.2 Data analysis

We analyzed the grammatical role that participants assigned to the case-marked noun in their continuation sentence. The data was coded by a native Estonian speaker (a trained coder from the first study). Half the data was also coded by a second trained coder (from the first study), and points of uncertainty were resolved through discussion between coders. The most frequent grammatical role labels are in Table 2. Examples are given in (23)–(30).

Tab. 2: Summary of the main coding labels used in data analysis

Category label	Grammatical Roles
subj	subject, e.g. (23)
part-subj	partitive subject, e.g. (24)
poss-subj	possessor of the subject, e.g. (25)
obj	object, as in earlier ex. (22a)
obj-PP	object of an adposition, as in earlier ex. (22b)
poss-obj	possessor of an object, e.g. (26)
poss-adv	possessor of an adverbial, e.g. (27)
compx-obj	object inside a complex structure, e.g. (28), (29)
pred-compl	predicative complement, e.g. (30)
obj-adv	object inside a gerund clause, e.g. (31)

(23) *hiired* (mouse-NOM.PL) [subj]
 Talveks tulevad tuppa hiired.
 winter.SG.TRANSL come.3PL.PRS room.SG.ILL mouse.NOM.PL
 'For the winter, mice come into the room.'

(24) *vett* (water-PART.SG) [part-subj]
 Kraanist tuleb vett, mida on hea vahepeal
 tap.SG.ELA come.3SG.PRS water.PART.SG that is good meantime
 juua.
 to drink
 'From the tap comes water, which is good to drink occasionally.'

(25) *vee* (water-GEN.SG) [poss-subj]
 Selle vee maitse on väga imelik.
 this.GEN water.GEN.SG taste.NOM.SG be.PRS.3SG very strange
 'The taste of this water is very strange.'

(26) *mehe* (man-GEN.SG) [poss-obj]
Me   ei   taha selle   mehe   mõtteid   kuulata.
1PL.NOM NEG want this.GEN   man.GEN.SG   thought.PART.PL   to listen
'We do not want to listen to this man's thoughts.'

(27) *sõprade* (friend-GEN.PL) [poss-adv]
Sõprade   ringis   on   mõnus olla.
friend.GEN.PL   circle.SG.INE be.PRS.3SG good   be.INF
'It's good to be among friends.'

(28) *raamatute* (books-GEN.PL) [compx-obj]
Raamatute   lugemine   aitab   puhata.
book.GEN.PL   reading.NOM   help.PRS.3SG rest.INF
'Reading books helps (you) rest.'

(29) *verd* (blood-PART.SG) [compx-obj]
Aktiivselt   verd   annetanud   inimesed   saavad
actively   blood.PART.SG   donate.PTCP   people.NOM.PL   get.3PL.PRS

Elroni   rongides   detsembris   soodustust.
Elron.GEN.SG   train.PL.INE   December.SG.INE   discount.PART.SG
'People who have actively donated blood will get a discount on Elron's train tickets in December.'

(30) *jänes* (hare-NOM.SG) [pred-compl]
See   pikk-kõrv   seal   on   jänes.
this.NOM   long-eared.NOM.SG   there   be.3.PRS   hare.NOM.SG
'The long-eared one there is a hare.'

(31) *luuletust* (poem-PART.SG) [obj-adv]
Luuletust   kuulates   jäi   Peeter   tukkuma.
poem.PART.SG   listening   stay.3SG.PST Peeter.NOM   doze.INF
'Listening to the poem, Peeter dozed off.'

In the next section, we report the most common grammatical roles for each case. The other, less frequent grammatical roles are grouped together in the 'other' columns for ease of presentation.

To analyze the data statistically, we used mixed-effects regression models (lmer, R Core Team, http://www.R-project.org/). Mixed-effects models are better suited for this kind of categorical data than analyses of variance. When assessing whether the proportion of initial uses of a noun differs from chance (0.5) — to see whether initial vs. non-initial uses are more frequent — we fitted an intercept-only model for each condition, with random intercepts for subject and item whenever possible. When analyzing effects of animacy and number, we analyzed the continuation patterns for each of the three cases separately, with animacy (animate, inanimate) and number (singular, plural) as the independent variables in each analysis. Our mixed-effects models used the maximal random effect structure justified by the design, with random slopes and intercepts for subjects and items. (If the maximal model did not converge, we simplified the model, beginning with removal of a random slope for the interaction, until it converged.) In cases where there are no datapoints for a certain condition/level, planned comparisons were conducted on the other conditions/levels.

4.3 Results and discussion

When analyzing our results, we first consider the grammatical roles of nouns used in sentence-initial position, as compared to non-initial position (Section 4.3.2). There are differences in the basic positional preferences of each case (initial/non-initial), and these preferences are modulated by animacy and number. Thus, in the subsequent sections (Sections 4.3.3 to 4.3.5), we present the grammatical role data for each case (nominative, partitive and genitive) as a function of whether the noun was used in sentence-initial position or non-initial position. (Before turning to these results, in Section 4.3.1 we also briefly address effects of pre-nominal elements, especially quantifiers, on Estonian case.)

As will become clear, the three cases differ in the extent to which their interpretation is influenced by animacy and number. *Nominative* nouns are relatively impervious to effects of animacy or number, and show a strong tendency to be interpreted as subjects, especially when sentence-initial: Upon encountering a nominative noun, Estonian speakers show a preference for associating it with the subject role. *Partitive* nouns show a more nuanced pattern: Although partitives used in sentence-initial position seem to be more associated with subjecthood, partitive nouns in non-initial position are mostly objects, regardless of animacy or number. Notably, partitive case on its own (i.e., without accounting for other noun properties) does not provide a very reliable cue for any particular grammatical role, at least in sentence-initial position. When it comes to *genitive* nouns used sentence-initially, the grammatical roles that people assign to them are influenced by animacy: (i) animate nouns are mostly interpreted as possessor-of-subject, but (ii) inanimate nouns are split between different grammatical roles. Genitive singular nouns in non-initial position, in contrast, tend to be interpreted as objects, regardless of animacy.

4.3.1 Bare vs. modified nouns

Before turning to the details of the results, we consider a complication that results from the open-ended nature of the fragment-completion task. A noun's case in Estonian can be impacted by the presence of certain modifiers (e.g. a numeral greater than 'one') and certain quantifiers (e.g. *palju* 'a lot/many', *mitu* 'how many/several') which require partitive case on the noun. However, not all prenominal modifiers require partitive case (e.g. *mõni* 'some'). Thus, a subject noun that would otherwise be nominative (e.g. (9), (11), (23)) – or an object that would otherwise be genitive (22a) – will occur in partitive when preceded by certain quantifiers, e.g. *rohkem* 'more' (32), or a numeral higher than 'one' (33). Whether the modified noun is plural or singular depends on the modifier: crucially, numerals over 'one' require partitive singular nouns. Adjectives and demonstratives agree with the case of the head noun (e.g. (22a), (25), (26), (33)).

(32) *Rohkem tüdrukuid   võiks   tunda   huvi   robootika*
       more   girl.PART.PL could   feel.INF   interest.PART.SG robotics.GEN
      vastu.
       towards
      'More girls could feel interested in robotics.'

(33) *Ma   leidsin   trennist   kaks   toredat*
       1SG.NOM   find.PST.3SG   gym.SG.ELA   two.NOM.SG   nice.PART.SG
      sõpra.
       friend.PART.SG
      'I found two nice friends in (the) gym.'

Hence, the use of modifiers can 'muddy the waters' if our aim is to gain insights into the relationship between case and grammatical role. In our dataset, 54.8% of the sentences produced by participants used the target nouns as bare (unmodified) nouns, whereas 35.8% of the sentences involved a target noun with some kind of modifier (some of which trigger partitive case).[12] For purposes of

---

[12] The remaining 9.4% of continuations were excluded from subsequent analyses because they could not be analyzed with respect to the noun's grammatical role, for example they were not

data analysis in this paper, we examine only the bare nouns. This allows us to keep the results maximally comparable to our prior study (where the noun was given sentence-initially, making modifiers less likely), and also circumvents potential complications regarding the relationship between grammatical role and case. However, we emphasize that the question of how quantifier-triggered and numeral-triggered case-assignment relate to existing theories of subject and object case assignment is an important question for future work.

4.3.2 Frequencies of case-marked nouns in initial vs. non-initial position

Before considering effects of number and animacy on comprehenders' interpretation of the different cases, we investigated how often nouns in the different conditions were used sentence-initially vs. in another position. Figure 1 shows, for the bare nouns in responses in each condition, what proportion of nouns were produced in sentence-initial and non-sentence-initial position. The graph shows that for each case, at least 25% of nouns were freely produced in sentence-initial position. This shows that our approach of providing sentence-initial nouns in our prior work, although constraining, is not an unusual or impossible situation: When given the choice of using a noun anywhere in the sentence, people still produced it in sentence-initial position at least 25% of the time.

Figure 1 clearly shows that different cases elicit different rates of sentence-initial vs. non-initial nouns. Overall, nominative and genitive nouns are more likely to be sentence-initial than not, whereas partitive nouns are more likely to be non-initial. When we take a closer look at the patterns as a function of noun number and animacy, as shown in Figure 2, the same overall patterns persist, yet we also see moderating effects of number and animacy.

With **nominative** nouns, we see an overall preference to use the noun in sentence-initial position, regardless of number. However, we find a difference between animate and inanimate nouns: while the rate of sentence-initial uses is significantly higher than chance (0.5) with *animate nominative* nouns, it does not reach significance with *inanimates* (see Table 3 for statistics). With **genitive** nouns, we find that the rate of sentence-initial uses is significantly higher than chance with both singular and plural animate nouns, but with inanimate nouns this only holds with plural nouns; singular inanimate genitive nouns are split be-

---

complete sentences (e.g. contained no verb, e.g. 'the boys' song'), involved an error (e.g. participant changed the case of the noun), or used the noun inside a compound noun (e.g. 'carrot' used in the compound 'carrot pieces').

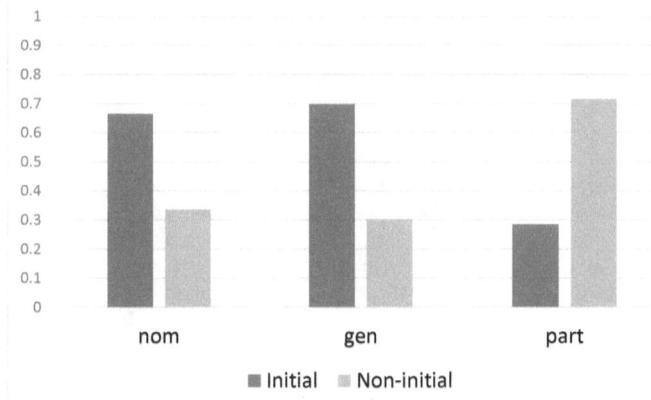

Fig. 1: Linear order patterns of bare nouns: Out of the bare nouns in each case, what proportion occurs in sentence-initial vs. non-initial position? (collapsing number and animacy)

tween sentence-initial and non-initial uses. As a whole, these patterns largely fit with prior observations from production experiments in other languages which found an 'animacy-first' bias: Speakers tend to mention animate nouns before inanimate nouns (e.g. Bock 1986, Ferreira 1994, see also Prat-Sala & Branigan 2000).

With **partitive** nouns, the overall numerical preference is for a non-initial position (unlike nominative and genitive nouns), and this is significantly higher than chance with inanimate but not significant with animate nouns. In other words, inanimate partitive nouns show a stronger non-initial preference than animate partitive nouns. This makes sense if we think about the interplay of the 'animacy-first' bias (which would push animate nouns to a sentence-initial position) and the partitive case's preference for a non-initial position.

4.3.3 Nominative nouns

Because we found differences in the basic positional preferences of each case (initial/non-initial), and because animacy and number differ in how they impact the different cases, in this section and the subsequent ones we present the grammatical role data for each case separately, and as a function of whether the noun was used in sentence-initial position or non-initial position. For nouns in each position, we look at the grammatical roles that participants assign to those nouns, and test statistically whether they are influenced by the noun's animacy or num-

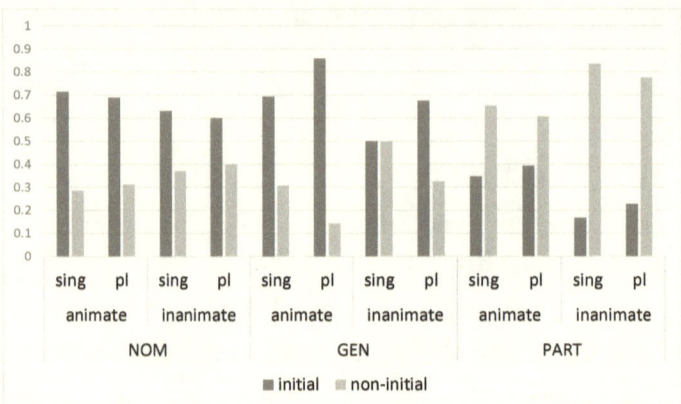

Fig. 2: Linear order patterns of bare nouns: Out of the bare nouns in each condition, what proportion occurs in sentence-initial vs. non-initial position?

ber, or an interaction of these two factors. Let's start with the nominative conditions.

In our prior experiment (discussed in Section 3.1), responses showed a strong bias to assign the subject function to nominative nouns, even though Estonian also allows morphological nominative case in other functions (e.g. singular and plural objects in imperatives, plural affected nouns as direct objects, see Section 2 above). In the current study, as shown in Figure 3, nominative nouns produced in **sentence-initial position** (the most frequent position for nominatives) again have an extremely strong subject bias.

However, when we look at **non-initial nominative nouns** (Figure 4), a more nuanced picture emerges. When we consider the proportion of *subject continuations* statistically, we find a main effect of animacy ($\beta = 0.922$, $z = 2.362$, $p<.02$), a main effect of number ($\beta = -1.091$, $z = -2.793$, $p<.01$) and no number-by-animacy interaction ($\beta = -0.229$, $z = 3.463$, $p>.55$). In other words, when participants chose to use a nominative noun in a non-initial position, subject continuations were more likely with animate nouns than inanimate nouns, and more likely with plural nouns than with singular nouns.

Let us now turn to the proportion of *object continuations* with non-initial nominative nouns. Although it may seem surprising that nominative nouns are used in object position, recall that Estonian allows morphologically nominative nouns in non-subject positions (see Section 2 above). In our data, singular nominatives only occur in object position if they are inanimate, never when they are animate. This reflects the well-known bias to match subjecthood with animacy. Echoing a similar pattern, nominative nouns that are plural occur numerically more fre-

Tab. 3: Statistical analyses of the data in Figure 2. Is the proportion of initial uses significantly different from chance? Shaded cells differ significantly from chance.

Condition	Intercept	SE	z value	Pr(>|z|)
Nom_anim_sing	1.034	0.431	2.398	0.0165
Nom_anim_pl	0.799	0.3156	2.534	0.0113
Nom_inanim_sing	0.566	0.487	1.162	0.245
Nom_inanim_pl	0.405	0.373	1.088	0.277
Gen_anim_sing	0.895	0.405	2.21	0.0271
Gen_anim_pl	1.792	0.408	4.389	<.0001
Gen_inanim_sing	−0.005	0.354	−0.016	0.987
Gen_inanim_pl	0.728	0.325	2.238	0.025
Part_anim_sing	−10.97	16.34	−0.672	0.502
Part_anim_pl	−5.002	4.328	−1.156	0.248
Part_inanim_sing	−1.837	−0.661	−2.778	0.0055
Part_inanim_pl	−1.2322	0.429	−2.868	0.00413

quently in object position when they are inanimate than when they are animate, but this pattern does not reach significance. (This is not surprising: The size of this data subset is small — since most nominative nouns are sentence-initial — and so statistical analyses for seemingly clear patterns may fail to reach significance due to lack of power.)

With singular nominatives in non-initial position, we also find more *predicate complement* constructions (copular constructions, e.g. (30) above) with animate than inanimate nouns, though the difference does not reach significance.

Comparison with our earlier experiment: Overall, the results for *sentence-initial* nominative nouns are in line with our first study, which found a high rate of subject continuations. While *non-initial* nominatives still show a numerical subject preference as well, it is clear from Figure 4 that the animacy of the noun – as well as its number in some instances – plays a role. Thus, upon encountering a nominative noun, Estonian speakers show a preference for associating it with the subject role, but this preference is not absolute.

4.3.4 Partitive nouns

In our first study, partitive nouns were most frequently — but not exclusively — interpreted as objects, and this pattern also obtains in the new experiment, as can be seen in Figures 5 (initial position) and 6 (non-initial position). This is espe-

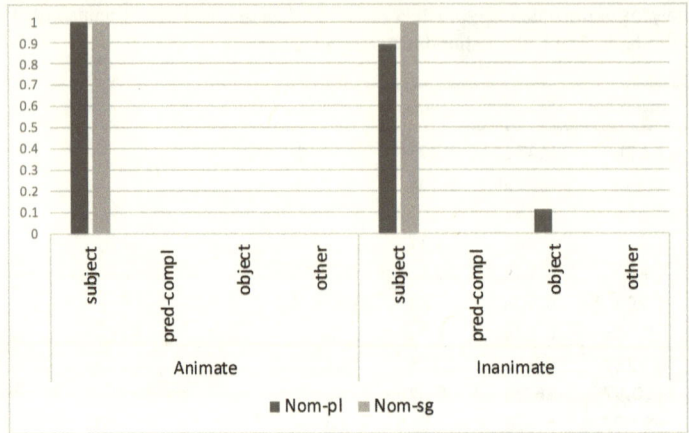

Fig. 3: Bare nominative nouns (n=93) in sentence-initial position: Grammatical role as a function of animacy and number.

cially clear with singular (count) nouns, in contrast to plural (count) nouns (see Section 2 for discussion).

Let us first consider the partitive nouns used in **initial position**. The most common continuation types are object, compx-obj (i.e. object complement in nominalization, as in (29)), partitive subject (24), and obj-adv (i.e. object inside a gerund clause, as in (31)).

When we assess the rate of object continuations statistically, we find no significant effects of animacy or number: The object preference is equally strong with animates and inanimates, and singular as well as plural nouns. (As in Section 4.3.3, the small size of the dataset means that lack of power may prevent statistical analyses from reaching significance.)

We also find no significant effects of animacy on the rate of partitive-subject continuations (that is exclusively used with plurals) or compx-obj continuations.[13] However, although the patterns do not reach significance, the rate of partitive-subject continuations is numerically higher with animates (27.3%) than with inanimates (14.3%; almost twice as many), which is in the same direction as our prior study, which found that (plural) animate nouns were used significantly more often as partitive subjects than inanimate nouns.

---

[13] In cases where there are no datapoints in one of the animacy categories, as is the case with obj-adv continuations with bare partitive nouns used in sentence-initial position (these occur with inanimates but not with animates in our data), statistical analyses of animacy were not conducted.

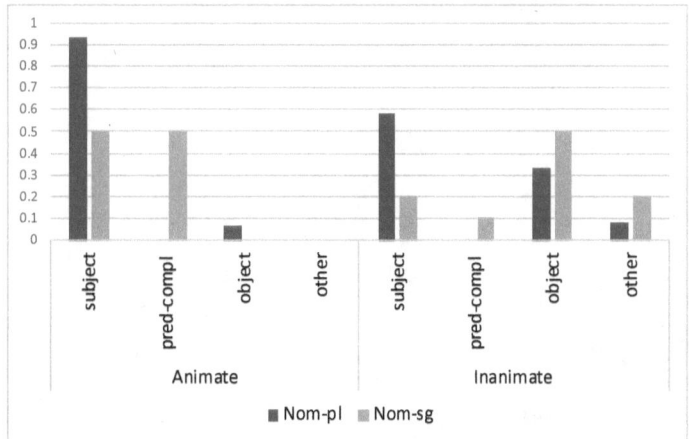

Fig. 4: Bare nominative nouns in non-initial position (n=47): Grammatical role as a function of animacy and number.

Another parallel with our prior study comes from the adverbial complement (gerund) continuations (obj-adv): In the new experiment, *no* animate nouns are interpreted as adverbial complements, whereas 28.6% of plural partitive inanimates and 25% of singular partitive inanimates are. This echoes our prior study, where inanimates had much higher rates of adverbial complement interpretation than animates. These patterns fit with the basic idea that inanimate nouns tend to be objects.

Overall, echoing our prior study, singular partitive nouns used in sentence-initial position in the current experiment occur in a variety of object positions (direct object, obj-adv and compx-obj), whereas plural partitive nouns, though still mostly being objects, are also sometimes realized as subjects, especially when animate.

Let us now turn to the grammatical roles assigned to partitive nouns used in **non-initial position**. Compared to sentence-initial partitive nouns, the non-initial ones show a stronger object preference, especially in the case of animate nouns. That is, when people want to use partitive plural as partitive subject, they tend to use it sentence-initially.

As Figure 6 shows, there is a clear overall object bias with both animates and inanimates. Indeed, statistical analyses reveal no significant effects of animacy or number on the rate of object continuations – object continuations are equally likely with animates and inanimates, and singular as well as plural nouns. We see numerical indications of object interpretations being more likely with singular

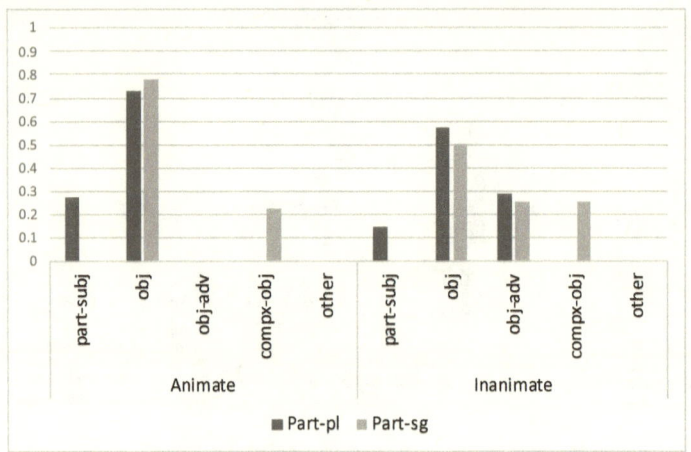

Fig. 5: Bare partitive nouns in sentence-initial position (n=31): Grammatical role as a function of animacy and number.

nouns, echoing some of the results from our prior study, but this is not significant in the smaller dataset of the current study.

The rate of (plural) partitive subject continuations is higher with animate nouns (17.6%) than inanimate nouns (4.2%) – although this is not significant, it is in exactly the same direction as we saw in our prior work and with the initial nouns in the current study as well. We see in Figure 6 that a plural partitive noun that is animate is numerically more likely to be a subject than a plural partitive noun that is inanimate. No partitive, singular count noun was interpreted as a subject.

Comparison with our earlier experiment: Overall, these results fit with our prior study in indicating that partitive case is not a strong cue for a particular syntactic role, in contrast to nominative case, and its interpretation can be modulated by the noun's number and animacy. Furthermore, the new study reveals an asymmetry in the grammatical roles of partitive nouns used sentence-initially and non-initially: When a speaker chooses to use a partitive noun in sentence-initial position (current experiment) or is required to use it in sentence initial-position (our prior experiment), that noun is fairly often the subject (and also plural and often animate). This contrasts with partitive nouns used in non-initial position, which are much more likely to be objects or object complements (and thus more likely to be singular as well as inanimate). Overall, partitive case on its own (without noun semantics) does not necessarily provide a very reliable cue for any particular grammatical role, at least in sentence-initial position.

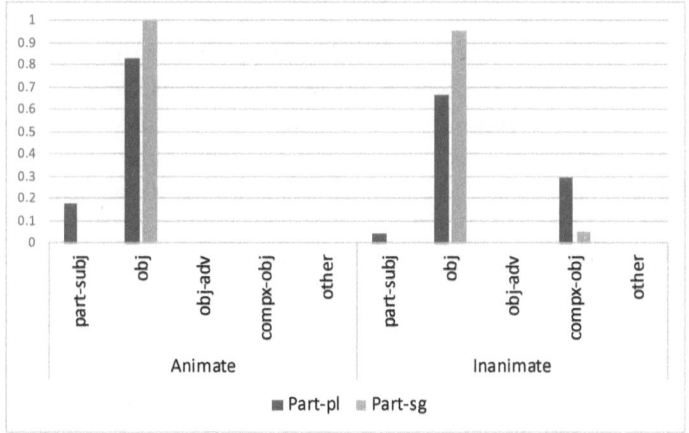

Fig. 6: Bare partitive nouns in non-initial position (n=78): Grammatical role as a function of animacy and number

4.3.5 Genitive nouns

As in our prior study, when we look at the **sentence-initial uses** of genitive nouns in the new experiment (Figure 7), we again find that (i) animate nouns are mostly interpreted as possessor-of-subject, whereas (ii) inanimate nouns are split between different grammatical roles. In particular, we see that inanimate genitives are split between possessor-of-subject, object of an adpositional phrase, and modifier structures where the noun is embedded as an object inside a nominalized structure (compx-obj) (as in (28) above). Thus, the animacy of the noun influences the grammatical role that people assign to it.

When we assess these patterns statistically, we find that the rate of possessor-of-subject continuations shows a significant effect of animacy ($\beta=0.871$, $z=3.429$, $p<.001$), no effect of number ($\beta =0.438$, $z =1.526$, $p>.12$) and no interaction ($\beta=0.286$, $z=1.201$, $p>.22$). In other words, just like in our prior work, animate genitive nouns are interpreted as possessors of the subject at a higher rate than inanimate nouns – which we attribute to a connection between animacy, subjecthood and sentence-initial position, as mentioned earlier.

The frequency with which participants interpret genitive nouns as objects of an adpositional phrase shows no significant effects of number or animacy, and no interaction. However, the rate of compx-obj continuations (modifier structures where the target noun is an object of a nominalized structure) is significantly higher with inanimate plural genitive nouns than with animate plural genitive nouns ($\beta=-1.126$, $z=-2.381$, $p<.02$). This same pattern is echoed with singular nouns, albeit on a smaller scale: there are *no* cases of singular genitive animate nouns being used in sentence-initial position in the compx-obj construction, but there *are* cases of singular genitive *inanimate* nouns in this construction. This bias for inanimates fits with what we saw before, and given that compx-obj continuations embed the noun as an object inside a complex nominalized structure, this pattern makes sense in light of the cross-linguistically observed association between objects and inanimates.

As in the first study, it is striking that hardly any genitive nouns in sentence-initial position are objects (no singular animates and only 11.8% of singular inanimates[14]).

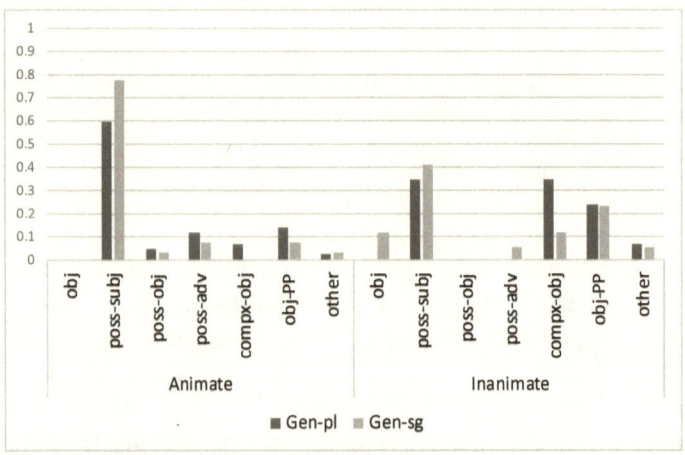

Fig. 7: Genitive nouns in sentence-initial position (n=115): Grammatical role as a function of animacy and number.

When we consider genitive nouns used in **non-initial position** (Figure 8), a striking difference emerges, namely the increased rate of object interpretations, at least with singular nouns: 66.7% of singular animate genitive nouns and 88.2% of singular inanimate genitives are interpreted as objects. Indeed, with both animate and inanimate singular nouns, object interpretations are now the most frequent option. This contrasts strikingly with what we saw in our prior study and in the sentence-initial usage in the current study. These patterns make sense, given that sentence-initial objects, although grammatical, are less frequent in Estonian than sentence-initial subjects (Lindström 2004, Tael 1988). However, the asym-

---

14 As explained in Section 2 above, plural objects occur only in nominative or partitive.

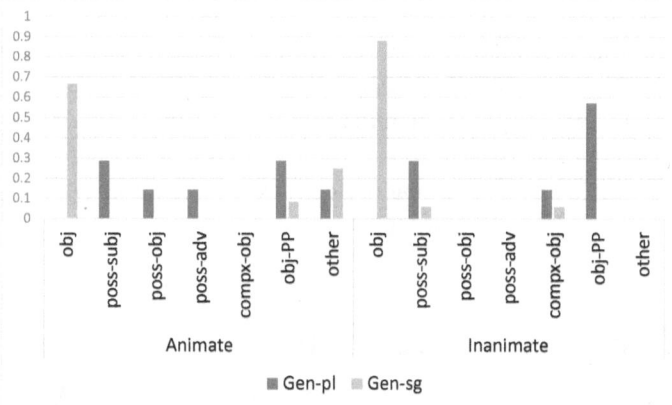

Fig. 8: Genitive nouns in non-initial position (n=50): Grammatical role as a function of animacy and number.

metry in the rate of object interpretations in our data is worth emphasizing, because it shows that comprehenders' expectations about how a noun with genitive case is to be interpreted (our prior study), or their choices about how to 'use' a genitive-marked noun (the new study), critically depend on the linear position of that noun. Thus, both the morphological case-marker and the 'linguistic context' (in this case: initial vs non-initial position) influence what grammatical role people associate with a particular case-marker.

The rate of object continuations with singular genitive nouns shows no significant effect of animacy, which is also true of the rate of possessor-of-subject continuations with plural genitive nouns and the rate of object-of-adpositional-phrase continuations with plural genitive nouns. Numerically, however, we find more object interpretations and more object-of-adpositional-phrase interpretations with inanimate than animate nouns, which seems to fit with the basic association between objects and inanimates. However, further data collection would be needed to see if the numerical patterns are meaningful, as our dataset is rather small.

Comparison with our earlier experiment: Again for genitive nouns, the results of this study corroborate and expand on our earlier study. We found an interaction with animacy in both studies, in sentence-initial position: animate nouns in genitive case are most strongly associated with the role of possessor of subject, whereas inanimates are also interpreted as object inside a nominalized construction, particularly plurals. Very few sentence-initial genitives are interpreted as object. However, as with partitive case, the second study reveals that sentence position plays an important role in the interpretation of genitive case. The majority of non-initial singular genitive nouns are interpreted as object, regardless of animacy. Plural genitive nouns, which do not function as objects, are assigned various grammatical roles in non-initial position. Genitive singular nouns were assigned the role of object proportionally less than partitives, yet were much more likely to be given an object interpretation in the second study, with unrestricted sentence position. Genitive nouns overall do not point strongly toward a particular syntactic role, especially in sentence-initial position, but in non-initial position, genitive singulars show a clear preference for object.

5 Implications for theories of case

What should we make of these empirical results in the light of the theories of case discussed in Sections 2.1 and 2.2? We can start with a bigger picture question from derivational theories: why is there case/Case at all? Our data suggest that morphologically overt case is not a redundancy in grammar, nor a reflex of syntactic configuration. Morphological case form constrains the distribution of nominals to specific syntactic functions, even if it does not directly predict grammatical roles.

As the experiments show, nouns in nominative overwhelmingly signal that they are the subject in a sentence (although the object function is also available in the grammar); nouns in genitive indicate an oblique, non-subject function (with more specific functions heavily dependent on the noun's linear position and animacy), and nouns marked by partitive tend to be associated with the object argument function (more with singulars, less with plural nouns). Yet there is no straightforward, one-to-one, match between form and function.

In order to come up with a plausible theory of case, i.e., a theory which also takes into account surface case morphology, one needs to capture the **distribution** of morphological case markers. This is evident in Section 2.2 above, in discussing the theory of Dependent Case: although this is a theory of morphological case, it does not address or incorporate the distribution of morphological case markers, e.g. partitive, but rather accounts for the case realization in each syntactic configuration separately. Thus, partitive on an internal argument is related to VP and its aspectual properties (unboundedness), while partitive on an external argument is associated with properties of the DP. This is essentially a construction-specific approach to case: Each type of syntactic configuration assigns the same case feature (e.g. partitive) that is associated with a different syntactic/interpretational effect (e.g. either DP-partitive or VP-partitive). Yet, as our results clearly show, one surface/morphological case marker (e.g. genitive, partitive) predicts a specific range of syntactic functions. Hence, one might expect a unifying property to relate these different syntactic functions to a specific morphological case marker, in other words, account for its distribution.

However, although in our data the overt case form specifies constraints on the possible syntactic functions of the noun, the actual function of each case-marked noun is determined in interaction with other factors. For all three cases, the data showed interactions with animacy, to a greater or smaller extent: animate nouns showed a strong tendency to appear in linear order before inanimate ones, through assuming relevant syntactic functions, e.g. subject for nominative, possessor of subject for genitive. Especially noteworthy is the finding that a single semantic factor, animacy, together with linear position (initial vs. non-initial), differentiated between argument and adjunct (such as PP complement) uses of one and the same case marker, for both genitive and partitive case. This calls into question the empirical basis for the distinction between purely syntactic (argument-encoding) and semantic (adjunct-like) case, or structurally and semantically (lexically) assigned case. This distinction may emerge from a complex combination of noun semantics, structural syntax, and the nature of a case-marker. Essentially, the interaction between a case-marker and the relevant factors indicates that the case marker on its own is underspecified. This is one of the main generalizations from our findings: The more (syntactically) underspecified a case-marker is, the more other cues (in our study, animacy, number, and linear position) interact with it.

Specifically, nouns in **nominative** showed a strong preference for acting as subject, especially in sentence-initial position. When the participants were free to use any word order possible, they interpreted nominative inanimate nouns as subjects less often than expected.

Genitive case proved to be the most syntactically underspecified morphological noun form in our data (as also argued by Csirmaz 2012 for Finnish, Miljan & Cann 2013 for Estonian). The range of functions assigned to genitive nouns by participants spanned from possessor and direct object to complements of adpositions. Moreover, the position of a genitive-marked noun in a sentence (initial vs non-initial) was significant for its interpretation: An animate singular noun in genitive typically prompted speakers to avoid using it as an object in sentence-initial position, assigning it a possessor function instead (cf. Fig 7 and 8). In our data, animate nouns in genitive are never interpreted as objects in sentence-initial position. For inanimate singular nouns, a similar pattern emerges, though less absolute.

Thus, for genitive-marked nouns, both possessor and object interpretations are available, but which of these functions is chosen depends on animacy and sentence position. This strongly indicates that in Estonian, relating genitive to *one* particular syntactic function (e.g. accusative or possessor) is not empirically justifiable, since genitive systematically occurs in possessor, direct object and complement positions. An account which takes the surface morphology as a starting point should be able to address this diverse distribution of genitive, e.g. via some form of 'unified' analysis.

Partitive is a case-marker with specific constraints. Partitive nouns were predominantly assigned the syntactic role of object, but this pattern was weaker with plural animate nouns, which are often associated with the subject function.

The predominant object interpretation of partitives was further boosted for singular nouns: all singular partitive nouns were interpreted as objects (or objects of nominalizations and of adverbial clauses, i.e. obj-adv) and none as subjects (see Figures 5 and 6). Also noteworthy is that the object interpretation was the only possible option for singular (count) *animate* nouns in partitive, as no other grammatical role was assigned to these (not even obj-adv, which was assigned to *inanimate* singular count nouns). These data on partitive case suggest an interesting question: Why is partitive, often analyzed as a default, structural case (see Section 2 above) so 'sensitive' to number and animacy, such that singular, animate count nouns in partitive case can only be assigned the object function? No other case (nominative, genitive) shows this type of 'sensitivity'.

The other striking result regarding partitive, in comparison with the other two cases (nominative, genitive), is that with free word order, partitive-marked nouns were mostly used in non-initial sentence position, regardless of animacy. Moreover, the non-initial partitive nouns show a stronger object preference than sentence-initial ones, especially in the case of animate nouns. That is, when people want to use partitive plural as a partitive subject, they tend to use it sentence-initially. This is a surprising result in light of the literature on Estonian partitive subjects and Finnish ones (e.g. Huumo & Lindström 2014).

5.1 A speculative proposal of Estonian grammatical cases based on experimental data

In this section, we look more closely at how the theoretical analysis of Finnic case is borne out by data on the use of case in language processing. Does the processing perspective provide us with information which might illuminate the representation of case in formal grammatical theory? We believe the results indicate the following theoretical claims:

1. No abstract case is necessary. Our results point toward a surface-oriented theory of case, as discussed in Section 5 above. That is, each morphological case under study (nominative, genitive, partitive) constrains the possible syntactic functions of the noun, with none of them related to a specific syntactic position. Abstract case, which is tied to specific syntactic positions, does not help to capture the distribution of surface cases. The notion of syntactic case is not helpful here, if this notion is related to specific syntactic positions and is meant to account for NP movement.

2. Grammatical case interpretation is not based purely on structure. The interactions we found between case markers and noun semantics (animacy, number) can be taken to indicate that case may not be best accounted for in terms of purely syntactic (i.e. rule-based) allocation of (case) features, or their assignment via structural positions. None of the cases in our study were related to only one syntactic position: nominative was used for subject and object functions; genitive was used for an array of functions, excluding the subject; and partitive was used for both object and subject functions. Two of the cases – genitive, partitive – were interpreted with respect to the properties of a noun (animate, inanimate; singular, plural). This suggests that case interpretation cannot be reduced to solely syntactic structure (or positional features).

3. Case markers are underspecified. The Estonian data clearly show (i) interactions between case-markers, noun semantics (animacy), number (cf. partitive), and linear position; and (ii) that more syntactically ambiguous case markers interact more strongly with other cues. In order to allow for the variable interpretations reflected in these interactions and capture the relevant generalizations, an account based on the concept of underspecification would be promising. Underspecified case markers can then be specified in particular constructions via compositional interaction.

4. Nominative is not a case. Our experimental results suggest that nominative form is strongly associated with the subject function, but this only holds for initial, preverbal position. In non-initial position, nominative signals the subject most strongly when the noun is animate and plural. Basically, nouns in nominative seem to be interpreted based on their position (preverbal) and semantics (animacy). Nominative nouns are used with both core arguments (subject, object) and as predicate complements. This all points to the generalization that nominative form is no case form, and does not 'add' anything to the noun. Speakers interpret the noun relying on other cues (initial position, animacy, number). Thus, analyses which treat nominative as an 'elsewhere' case, meaning it is assigned to any noun which is not assigned case otherwise, are supported by these findings, e.g. Miljan & Cann (2013), and by extension also Kiparsky (2001) on Finnish.

5. Genitive is the default case in Estonian (Finnic). Our results can be taken as an indication that genitive would best be analyzed in a unified way, as an oblique, i.e. non-subject, case: In our participants' responses, genitive was associated with an array of functions, except for subject. We propose that the sole function of genitive is to indicate *syntactic dependency to the closest syntactic head*, either at DP-level (e.g. possessive) or VP-level (e.g. object, adjunct). The (syntactic) interpretation of a noun in genitive seems to adhere to minimal locality or adjacency, as also shown by the striking interaction of linear position in a sentence: the non-initial genitive is likely to be structurally closer to the verb, that is, part of VP, hence the object or adjunct.

The minimal locality principle captures the different syntactic functions of genitive. A genitive noun that is closest to another (non-genitive) noun (i.e. head noun) invites the inference that the noun in genitive is a possessor; in our data, possessors are predominantly, but not necessarily, animate. However, a genitive noun whose closest head is a deverbal noun (as in, e.g. *Juhani.GEN jooksmine.NOM* 'John's running'), invites the inference that the genitive noun is the agent of the running event expressed by the noun phrase.

Further, a genitive noun whose closest head is the verb invites the inference that the noun in genitive is the direct object, and so on. Note that this explanation neatly captures the difference between objects and adjuncts: when either of them is a single dependent of the verb, the distinction in Estonian boils down to noun semantics, see examples in (34a–b). However, if both an internal argument and an adjunct are present, the adjunct is coded differently, e.g. by a 'semantic' case comitative (34c).

(34) a. *Ta   kirjutas   luuletuse.*
        3SG.NOM write.PST.3SG   poem.GEN.SG
        'S/he wrote a poem.'

   b. *Ta   kirjutas   terve   päeva.*
        3SG.NOM write.PST.3SG   whole.GEN.SG   day.GEN.SG
        'S/he wrote for the whole day.'

   c. *Ta   kirjutas   luuletuse   päevaga.*
        3SG.NOM write.PST.3SG   poem.GEN.SG   day.SG.COM
        'S/he wrote a poem in a day.'

Yet the above is not to say that the genitive can indicate syntactic dependency in an unconstrained manner. For example, genitive singular nouns cannot combine with imperative verbs. The specifics of this particular constraint are most likely related to the verb form, so that noun morphology (case marking) and verb morphology (active, passive, imperative) interact, but we leave the details of these constraints for future work, as our main observation here is that a genitive-marked noun needs to combine with another category (nouns, verbs, postpositions, etc.) for its interpretation.

Under this kind of approach, there is no need to postulate an abstract accusative case, nor syncretism between genitive and accusative. Instead, possessive and syntactic functions are encoded by the same overt, syntactically underspecified, case-marker.

6. There is more to partitive than meets the eye. Unlike what is often suggested in the literature (see Sections 2.1 and 2.2), according to which partitive is analyzed as an unmarked (or default) case assigned in VP, partitive appears to exert some semantic effect on the noun it marks. This is most straightforwardly shown in our data by singular count nouns, uniformly assigned the object function. These data allow us to address a chicken-and-egg issue: Is partitive case licensed by divisible constituents (cf. Csirmaz 2012, or Kiparsky 2001 who refers to unbounded constituents), or does partitive trigger the interpretation of divisibility/unboundedness/partitivity on the noun it marks?

The speakers in our study avoided assigning any other grammatical role for partitive, singular, animate count nouns than object. One possible explanation is that partitive triggers the reading of divisibility on the noun it marks, and the only way to interpret that noun is in the scope of VP, in terms of imperfective aspect (see, e.g., Verkuyl 1993). Plural nouns can easily be interpreted as divisible, and this is why they were assigned the subject function (outside the scope of VP) in our data (most often to animate plurals).

6 Conclusion

This paper argues that language processing is highly relevant to language competence: we bring together experimental data on the interpretation of case-marked nouns and formal analyses of case. We believe both approaches can be strengthened if they can inform and test each other. We argue for a unifying approach based on surface case forms, underspecification and interactions between factors. In the future, these results should be compared with data from corpora and other psycholinguistic paradigms.

References

Altmann, Gerry T.M. & Yuki Kamide. 1999. Incremental interpretation at verbs: Restricting the domain of subsequent reference. *Cognition* 73(3). 247–264. https://doi.org/10.1016/S0010-0277(99)00059-1.

Baker, Mark C. 2015. *Case: Its principles and its parameters*. Cambridge: Cambridge University Press.

Bobaljik, Jonathan David. 2008. Where's phi? Agreement as a postsyntactic operation. In Daniel Harbour, David Adger & Susana Béjar (eds.), *Phi-theory*, 295–328. Oxford: Oxford University Press.

Bock, J.K. 1986. *Meaning, sound, and syntax: Lexical priming in sentence production*. Vol. 12. 575–586.

Bornkessel-Schlesewsky, Ina & Matthias Schlesewsky. 2009. *Processing syntax and morphology: A neurocognitive perspective*. Oxford: Oxford University Press.

Bornkessel, Ina & Matthias Schlesewsky. 2006. *Generalised semantic roles and syntactic templates: A new framework for language comprehension*. Ina Bornkessel, Matthias Schlesewsky & Angela D. Comrie Bernard kand Friederici (eds.). Berlin: De Gruyter. 327–353.

Brattico, Pauli. 2011. Case assignment, case concord, and the quantificational case construction. *Lingua* 121(6). 1042–1066. https://doi.org/10.1016/j.lingua.2011.01.004.

Caha, Pavel. 2009. *The nanosyntax of case*. University of Tromsø dissertation.

Cann, Ronnie & Merilin Miljan. 2012. *Syntactic descriptions and pragmatic explanations*. Vol. 29. Differential case-marking. 585–605. https://doi.org/10.1515/tlr-2012-0021.

Chomsky, Noam. 2000. Minimalist inquiries: The framework. In Roger Martin, David Michaels & Juan Uriagereka (eds.), *Step by step: Essays on minimalist syntax in honor of Howard Lasnik*, 89–155. Cambridge, MA: MIT Press.

Chomsky, Noam. 2001. Derivation by phase. In Michael Kenstowicz (ed.), *Ken Hale: A life in language*, 1–52. Cambridge, MA: MIT Press.

Chomsky, Noam. 2015. *The minimalist program*. 20th Anniversary Edition. Cambridge, MA: MIT Press.

Csirmaz, Aniko. 2012. The case of the divisible phase: Licensing partitive case in Finnish. *Syntax* 15(3). 215–252. https://doi.org/10.1111/j.1467-9612.2012.00170.x.

Dahl, Östen. 2000. Animacy and the notion of semantic gender: Part I: Approaches to gender. In Barbara Unterbeck, Matti Rissanen, Terttu Nevalainen & Mirja Saari (eds.), *Gender in grammar and cognition*, 99–115. Berlin: De Gruyter.

Dahl, Östen. 2008. Animacy and egophoricity: Grammar, ontology and phylogeny. *Lingua* 118(2). 141–150. https://doi.org/10.1016/j.lingua.2007.02.008.

Dahl, Östen & Kari Fraurud. 1996. Animacy in grammar and discourse. In Thorstein Fretheim & Jeanette K. Gundel (eds.), *Reference and referent accessibility*, 47–64. Amsterdam: John Benjamins. https://doi.org/10.1075/pbns.38.04dah.

Dowty, David. 1991. Thematic proto-roles and argument selection. *Language* 67(3). 547–619.

Erelt, Mati, Tiiu Erelt & Kristiina Ross. 2007. *Eesti keele käsiraamat* [The Handbook of the Estonian Language]. 3rd edn. Tallinn: Eesti Keele Sihtasutus.

Erelt, Mati, Reet Kasik, Helle Metslang, Henno Rajandi, Kristiina Ross, Henn Saari, Kaja Tael & Silvi Vare. 1993. *Eesti keele grammatika II* [The Grammar of the Estonian Language]. Tallinn: Eesti Teaduste Akadeemia Eesti Keele Instituut.

Erelt, Mati & Helle Metslang (eds.). 2017. *Eesti keele süntaks [estonian syntax]*. Tartu: Tartu University Press.

Ferreira, Fernanda. 1994. Choice of passive voice is affected by verb type and animacy. *Journal of Memory and Language* 33(6). 715–736. https://doi.org/10.1006/jmla.1994.1034.

Grewe, Tanja, Ina Bornkessel, Stefan Zysset, Richard Wiese, D. Yves von Cramon & Matthias Schlesewsky. 2006. Linguistic prominence and broca's area: The influence of animacy as a linearization principle. *NeuroImage* 32(3). 1395–1402. https://doi.org/10.1016/j.neuroimage.2006.04.213.

Hakulinen, Auli, Maria Vilkuna, Riitta Korhonen, Vesa Koivisto, Tarja-Riitta Heinonen & Irja Alho. 2004. *Iso suomen kielioppi* [Grammar of Finnish]. Helsinki: Suomalaisen Kirjallisuuden Seura.

Hiietam, Katrin. 2003. *Definiteness and grammatical relations in estonian*. University of Manchester dissertation.

de Hoop, Helen & Andrej L. Malchukov. 2007. On fluid differential case marking. *Lingua* 117(9). 1636–1656. https://doi.org/10.1016/j.lingua.2006.06.010.

Hopper, Paul J. & Sandra A. Thompson. 1980. Transitivity in grammar and discourse. *Language* 56(2). 251–299.

Huumo, Tuomas & Liina Lindström. 2014. Partitives across constructions: On the range of uses of the Finnish and Estonian "partitive subjects". In *Partitive cases and related categories*, 153–176. Berlin: De Gruyter.

Kaiser, Elsi. 2002. *Case alternations and NPIs in questions in Finnish: Proceedings of the 21st West Coast Conference on Formal Linguistics*. Somerville, MA: Cascadilla Proceedings Project. 194–207.

Kaiser, Elsi & John C. Trueswell. 2004. The role of discourse context in the processing of a flexible word-order language. *Cognition* 94(2). 113–147. https://doi.org/10.1016/j.cognition.2004.01.002.

Kamide, Yuki, Gerry T.M. Altmann & Sarah L. Haywood. 2003. The time-course of prediction in incremental sentence processing: Evidence from anticipatory eye movements. *Journal of Memory and Language* 49(1). 133–156. https://doi.org/10.1016/s0749-596x(03)00023-8.

Kiparsky, Paul. 1998. Partitive case and aspect. In William Greuder & Miriam Butt (eds.), *The projection of arguments*, 265–307. Stanford, CA: Centre for the Study of Language & Information.

Kiparsky, Paul. 2001. Structural case in Finnish. *Lingua* 111(4–7). 315–376. https://doi.org/10.1016/S0024-3841(00)00035-8.

Kratzer, Angelika. 2004. Telicity and the meaning of objective case. In Jacqueline Guéron & Alexander Lecarme (eds.), *The syntax of time*, 389–423. Cambridge, MA: MIT Press.

Krifka, Manfred. 1992. Thematic relations as links between nominal reference and temporal constitution. In Ivan A. Sag & Anna Szabolcsi (eds.), *Lexical matters*, 29–53. Stanford, CA: CSLI Publications.

Lago, Sol, Diego E. Shalom, Mariano Sigman, Ellen F. Lau & Colin Phillips. 2015. Agreement attraction in spanish comprehension. *Journal of Memory and Language* 82. 133–149. https://doi.org/10.1016/j.jml.2015.02.002.

Lamers, Monique & Peter de Swart (eds.). 2012. *Case, word order and prominence: Interacting cues in language production and comprehension*. Dordrecht: Springer. https://doi.org/10.1007/978-94-007-1463-2.

Lindström, Liina. 2004. Sõnajärg lause tuumargumentide eristajana eesti keeles [word order distinguishing between core arguments in estonian]. In Liina Lindström (ed.), *Lauseliikmeist eesti keeles* [Grammatical relations in Estonian], 40–49. Tartu: Tartu Ülikooli eesti keele õppetooli preprindid 1.

MacDonald, Maryellen C. 2013. How language production shapes language form and comprehension. *Frontiers in Psychology* 4. 1–16. https://doi.org/10.3389/fpsyg.2013.00226.

Marantz, Alec. 1991. Case and licensing. In *ESCOL '91: Proceedings of the eighth Eastern states conference on linguistics*, 234–253. Ohio State University.

McFadden, Thomas. 2004. *The position of morphological case in the derivation.* University of Pennsylvania dissertation.

Miljan, Merilin & Ronnie Cann. 2013. Rethinking case marking and case alternation in Estonian. *Nordic Journal of Linguistics* 36(3). 333–379. https://doi.org/10.1017/S0332586513000309.

Miljan, Merilin, Elsi Kaiser & Virve-Anneli Vihman. 2017. Interplay between case, animacy and number: Interpretations of grammatical role in Estonian. *Finno-Ugric Languages and Linguistics* 6(1). 55–77.

Nelson, Diane C. 1995. *X⁰ categories and grammatical case assignment in Finnish.* University of Edinburgh dissertation.

Norris, Mark. 2018a. Non-autonomous accusative case in Estonian. *Finno-Ugric Languages and Linguistics* 7(2). 7–38.

Norris, Mark. 2018b. Unmarked case in Estonian nominals. *Natural Language & Linguistic Theory* 2(2). 523–562. https://doi.org/10.1007/s11049-017-9377-9.

Ogren, David. 2015. Prototypes, variation, and construction-specificity. *SKY Journal of Linguistics* 28. 277–312.

Ogren, David. 2018. *Object case variation in estonian da-infinitive constructions.* Tartu: Tartu University Press.

Polinsky, Maria & Omer Preminger. 2014. Case and grammatical relations. In Andrew Carnie, Yosuke Sato & Daniel Siddiqi (eds.), *The Routledge handbook of syntax*, 150–166. London & New York: Routledge.

Poole, Ethan. 2015. A configurational account of Finnish case. *U. Penn Working Papers in Linguistics* 21(1). 1–10.

Prat-Sala, Mercè & Holly P. Branigan. 2000. Discourse constraints on syntactic processing in language production: A cross-linguistic study in English and Spanish. *Journal of Memory and Language* 42(2). 168–182. https://doi.org/10.1006/jmla.1999.2668.

Radford, Andrew. 2004. *English syntax: An introduction.* Cambridge: Cambridge University Press.

Ritter, Elizabeth & Sara Thomas Rosen. 2001. The interpretive value of object splits. *Language Sciences* 23(4–5). 425–451. https://doi.org/10.1016/S0388-0001(00)00032-2.

Rosenbach, Anette. 2017. Constraints in contact: Animacy in English and Afrikaans genitive variation — a cross-linguistic perspective. *Glossa: a journal of general linguistics* 72, 1. https://doi.org/10.5334/gjgl.292.

Schlesewsky, Matthias & Ina Bornkessel. 2004. On incremental interpretation: Degrees of meaning accessed during sentence comprehension. *Lingua* 114(9–10). 1213–1234. https://doi.org/10.1016/j.lingua.2003.07.006.

Snedeker, Jesse & John C. Trueswell. 2004. The developing constraints on parsing decisions: The role of lexical-biases and referential scenes in child and adult sentence processing. *Cognitive Psychology* 49(3). 238–299. https://doi.org/10.1016/j.cogpsych.2004.03.001.

Spoelman, Marianne. 2013. *Prior linguistic knowledge matters: The use of the partitive case in Finnish learner language.* Oulu: University of Oulu dissertation.

Şükrü, Demiral, Matthias Schlesewsky & Ina Bornkessel-Schlesewsky. 2008. On the universality of language comprehension strategies: Evidence from Turkish. *Cognition* 106. 484–500. https://doi.org/10.1016/j.cognition.2007.01.008.

Svenonius, Peter. 2002. Case is uninterpretable aspect. In Henk J. Verkuyl & Henriëtte de Swart (eds.), *Proceedings of the Utrecht Perspectives on Aspect Conference December 2001.* Utrecht: University of Utrecht.

Tael, Kaja. 1988. *Sõnajärjemallid eesti keeles (võrrelduna soome keelega)* [Word order patterns in Estonian (in comparison with Finnish)]. Preprint, KKI-56. Tallinn: Institute of Estonian Language & Literature.

Tanenhaus, Michael K., Michael J. Spivey-Knowlton, Kathleen M. Eberhard & Julie C. Sedivy. 1995. Integration of visual and linguistic information in spoken language comprehension. *Science* 268(5217). 1632–1634. https://doi.org/10.1126/science.7777863.

Trueswell, John C., Michael K. Tanenhaus & Christopher Kello. 1993. Verb-specific constraints in sentence processing: Separating effects of lexical preference from garden-paths. *Journal of Experimental Psychology*: Learning, Memory and Cognition 19(3). 528–553. https://doi.org/10.1037/0278-7393.19.3.528.

Vainikka, Anne. 1993. The three structural cases in Finnish. In *Case and other functional categories in Finnish syntax*, 129–160. Berlin: De Gruyter. https://doi.org/10.1515/9783110902600.129.

Verkuyl, Henk J. 1993. *A theory of aspectuality: The interaction between temporal and atemporal structure*. Cambridge: Cambridge University Press.

Index

absolutive case, 29, 49–54, 177, 253, 254, 314
accusative case, 8, 9, 16, 17, 28, 29, 32, 39, 43–46, 49, 128, 130–134, 141, 143, 147, 148, 151, 153, 154, 156, 158, 160, 162–164, 166–171, 177–179, 184, 186, 187, 189, 190, 192, 193, 195, 196, 198–208, 211, 212, 237, 238, 240–242, 251, 253–255, 258–264, 266, 304, 307, 310–317, 341, 345
affectedness, 2, 5, 12
Agree, *see also* agreement, 16, 131, 135, 136, 146, 147, 164, 259, 261, 264, 265, 304, 306, 317
– and Case assignment, 15–17, 20, 127, 128, 130, 304–306, 309, 311, 312, 314, 316, 317
– dependent Agree, 19, 20, 128, 147, 160, 172
agreement, *see also* Agree
– object agreement, 3, 5, 13, 15–17, 131, 155, 156, 162, 171, 253, 254
– subject agreement, 13, 129–131, 136, 140, 142, 143, 151–153, 156, 160–163, 168–171
Amharic, 3, 17, 237
animacy, 2, 14, 20, 77–81, 83, 90–92, 94, 98, 99, 101, 106, 108, 110, 112, 115, 119, 121, 257, 272–274, 276, 279, 280, 286, 287, 294–299, 305, 306, 318, 322–325, 328, 330–343, 345
Antekerrepenhe, 49
Arabana, 49

BA-construction, 271–274, 276, 280, 281, 283, 285–295, 297
Basque, 237

case, *see also* dependent case
– abstract Case, 8, 15, 16, 185, 191, 194, 204, 211, 212, 304, 306, 311, 342, 343
– case features, 8, 9, 12, 37, 38, 42, 47, 195, 196
– Case Filter, 15, 82
– default case, 149, 317, 343, 345
– lexical Case, 128, 147, 148, 151, 163–166, 242

– morphological case, 8, 10, 15, 21, 49, 138, 141, 142, 212, 304–306, 317, 333, 340, 342, 344
– structural Case, 128–131, 140, 147, 151, 152, 160, 163, 165–171, 196
– syntactic Case, 37, 42, 49, 309, 343
Catalan, 34
clitics, 81, 119, 251, 254, 255, 258–267
– and agreement, 82, 83
– Big DP, 82, 83
– clitic doubling, 3, 20, 81, 83–85, 95, 100, 107, 221, 255–258, 262, 264
comitative case, 344
comparatives, 108–110
concord, *see also* agreement, 49, 104, 189
configurational case, *see* dependent case
constituent order, 272
constraints, *see* Harmonic Grammar, hierarchies, Optimality Theory
coordination, 19, 118
cumulativity, *see also* gang effects, 2, 20, 27–31, 34, 35, 37, 44–46, 48, 54–57, 59, 65, 68–71, 119
Czech, 31

dative case, 2, 9, 20, 78, 109, 119, 130, 168, 169, 196, 306
definiteness, 2, 16, 20, 32, 81, 93, 103, 104, 106, 182, 272, 274, 276, 279, 286, 295, 298, 299
dependent case, *see also* case, 11, 17–20, 127–131, 141, 147, 160, 166–168, 170–172, 196, 212, 304–306, 309, 311, 314, 315, 317
differential absolutive marking, 51, 52
differential argument encoding, *see* differential absolutive marking, differential object marking, differential subject marking
differential argument marking, 3, 12, 27–29, 31–38, 44, 48, 49, 55, 65, 68, 69, 178, 180, 204, 205, 211, 304–306, 308, 309, 311, 314
– and morphology, 36, 37, 42–44, 119

– functional motivation of, 5, 6, 179–182, 184, 186, 189, 192, 193, 196, 197, 200, 201, 204, 211, 212, 265
differential case marking, *see* differential object marking, differential subject marking
differential object marking, 1–16, 19–21, 32, 37, 38, 40–42, 48, 77, 78, 80–84, 86, 87, 90–92, 94–97, 99, 101, 102, 106, 108–111, 114, 120, 121, 131, 138, 141, 146, 152, 155, 162, 170, 171, 181, 182, 192, 198, 200–203, 205–212, 221–223, 225, 226, 228–232, 236–238, 243–245, 248–258, 261–263, 265–267, 271, 272, 274, 286–288, 292–299, 306, 307, 309, 315
– and dative case, 253
– and oblique case, 249
– and dative case, 2, 9, 20, 118, 221, 232, 236, 237, 239–244, 247, 248, 250, 253–255, 257–266
– and information structure, 2, 12, 14, 20, 271, 298, 299
– and morphology, 3, 5, 8–10, 118–120, 324, 333, 339–341, 344
– and movement, 5, 10, 12, 16, 18, 19, 116, 154, 155, 171, 212, 213
– and oblique case, 221, 237–239, 249–251, 253, 265, 266
– prepositional, 3, 78, 80–86, 92, 93, 99–102, 108, 109, 111, 113–118, 120, 121, 237
differential subject marking, 20, 37, 131, 135, 141, 145, 152, 181, 182, 184, 186–194, 197, 198, 203–205, 207–213, 306, 309
Distributed Morphology, *see also* impoverishment, 38, 180
Djapu, 49
Dyirbal, 49

ECM, *see* exceptional case marking
ellipsis, 79, 81, 101–107, 109, 110, 113, 115, 116
English, 15, 56, 62
ergative case, 18, 49–51, 177, 183, 184, 196, 253, 314
Estonian, 21, 37, 303, 305–325, 328, 329, 333, 334, 341–344
exceptional case marking, 160, 162

Finnic languages, *see also* Estonian, Finnish, 237, 306, 309, 342
Finnish, 37, 237, 307, 309, 311–317, 341–343
focus, *see also* information structure, 2, 13, 14, 281, 282
French, 242

gang effects, *see also* cumulativity, 30, 31, 48, 55, 69
gender, *see also* phi-features, 17, 38, 81, 112, 115, 116, 129, 238, 254, 265
– semantic gender, 81, 112, 115
genitive case, 129, 135, 136, 140, 142, 145, 146, 149, 150, 153, 158–160, 166, 169, 196, 239, 307, 309–311, 315, 317–321, 323, 324, 330, 331, 337–345
German, 38, 40, 306
– Mannheim German, 28, 38–41, 43–45, 48, 54, 65
– Palatine German, 38
grammaticalization, 14, 98, 100, 121
Greek
– Asia Minor Greek, 20, 178, 180, 186, 203, 205, 211
– Cappadocian Greek, 178, 179, 199–203, 208, 212, 213
– Livisiot Greek, 178
– Pharasiot Greek, 178
– Pontic Greek, 20, 37, 178, 179, 185–194, 196–198, 201–205, 208, 212, 213
– Silliot Greek, 178
– Standard Modern Greek, 185, 190

harmonic alignment, *see also* Optimality Theory, 33, 35–38, 41, 45, 51, 181
Harmonic Grammar, *see also* Optimality Theory, 20, 27, 30, 31, 45–48, 54, 55, 65–71
Haya, 31
Hayu, 31
Hebrew, 14
hierarchies, 2, 14, 29, 32, 53, 253, 263
– animacy hierarchy, 2, 14, 28, 32, 181, 245, 258, 272
– case hierarchy, 196
– constraint hierarchies, 6–8, 32–35, 37, 51

– definiteness hierarchy, 2, 14, 28, 32, 35, 41, 50, 51, 181, 229, 245, 272
– grammatical function hierarchy, 181
– person hierarchy, 32, 181
Hindi, 1–3, 8, 9, 16, 31, 35, 182, 237
Hungarian, 5, 14, 16

iconicity, 182, 201
impoverishment, 8–10, 37, 38, 44, 53, 179, 180, 197, 198, 202–205, 207, 211, 212
Indo-European languages, *see* Czech, English, French, German, Hindi, Italian, Latvian, Persian, Polish, Romanian, Spanish
information structure, *see also* focus, topic, 12, 14, 110, 298, 299
inherent case, 195
Iranian, 237
islands, 56, 64, 69
Italian, 20, 37, 221, 223, 232, 234, 236, 237, 241, 243, 247, 248, 252–258, 263, 281
– Accettura, 223
– Aidone, 236, 247, 256
– Albidona, 228, 246
– Alimena, 226
– Avigliano Umbro, 235, 236, 247
– Cagnano Amiterno, 222
– Camerota, 228, 246, 259
– Canosa Sannita, 223, 245
– Celle di Bulgheria, 224, 229, 245, 259–261, 265
– Central Italian, 221, 222
– Ciró Marina, 229, 247, 252
– Colledimacine, 222, 256
– Corsican, 221
– Gallo Matese, 225, 230, 254
– Giovinazzo, 226
– Gorgoglione, 227, 261
– Guardia Perticara, 227, 259, 261
– Ittiri, 224, 229, 246
– Làconi, 228, 231, 247, 257, 259–261
– Mercatello sul Metauro, 234, 247
– Mercato Saraceno, 233, 257, 258
– Minervino Murge, 227, 231, 246, 250, 256
– Modena, 257
– Modica, 228, 231, 247
– Montefeltro, 232, 257

– Munacia d'Auddè, 225, 229, 230, 246, 249, 257
– Müstair, 252
– Neapolitan, 84
– Nocara, 224, 227, 231, 259
– Orroli, 226
– Paulilatino, 224, 229, 230, 257
– Romansh, 221
– Rontagnano, 233, 258
– S. Vittore, 225, 246, 259, 260
– Sant'Agata Feltria, 233, 256
– Sardinian, 221, 259
– Scuol, 225
– Sicilian, 236
– Southern Italian, 221, 222, 252
– Tempio Pausania, 224, 246, 260
– Torricella Peligna, 223, 256

Japanese, 14, 240

Kalkatungu, 34
Kayne's Generalization, *see also* clitics, 20, 77, 80, 82–84, 86, 88, 97, 100, 110, 121
Kham, 49, 50, 52
Khanty, 12, 16
Kolyma Yukaghir, 4, 9
Korean, 31

language processing, 304, 305, 319, 320, 342, 345
Latvian, 31
left-branch extraction, 31
Lexical Functional Grammar, 14
leísmo, *see also* loísmo, 262–264, 266, 267
LFG, *see* Lexical Functional Grammar
licensing, 5, 10, 12, 15, 16, 20, 77, 80–82, 84–86, 88, 89, 91–98, 101, 105–107, 109, 110, 112–114, 120, 121, 127–131, 140, 151, 152, 154, 157, 160, 163, 168, 170–172
– secondary licensing, 20, 77, 81, 82, 86, 96–98, 103, 106, 110, 113, 116, 120, 121
local conjunction, *see also* Optimality Theory, 6, 20, 27–29, 31, 33–36, 38, 41–43, 45, 48, 51–56, 58, 59, 61–65, 68, 71
locality, 11, 34, 55, 56, 64, 305, 344
locative cases, 233, 236, 244

long-distance extraction, 27, 28, 31, 55, 65, 68, 70
loísmo, *see also* leísmo, 260–267

Mandarin Chinese, 20, 271–277, 281, 285, 287, 288, 294–299
Mannheim German, *see* German
Mansi, 12
marked nominative languages, 200, 212
Mongolian, 166, 271
morphological structure, 197, 202, 204, 205, 212

Nez Perce, 49
Niger-Congo languages, *see* Haya
nominative case, 38–40, 128–131, 135, 140, 142, 147, 149–151, 166, 168, 170, 171, 177–179, 184–187, 189–200, 202–208, 211, 212, 304, 306–310, 314–316, 318, 319, 321, 323–325, 328–334, 336, 338, 340, 342, 343
number, 238, 306, 308, 309, 318, 319, 322–325, 328, 330–337, 343

object agreement, 160
oblique case, 169, 196, 317, 340, 343
Optimality Theory, *see also* Harmonic Grammar, 6, 8, 20, 27–31, 35, 36, 44, 48, 57–59, 63, 64, 70
Ostyak, *see* Khanty

Pama-Nyungan languages, *see* Antekerrepenhe, Arabana, Djapu, Dyirbal, Kalkatungu, Pitjantjatjara, Warrangu
partitive case, 307–315, 317, 318, 321–326, 328, 329, 331, 332, 334–337, 339, 340, 342, 343, 345
partitives, 79, 81, 95, 101, 106, 107
passive, 118, 245–249, 267, 344
PCC, *see* Person Case Constraint
Persian, 35
Person Case Constraint, 94, 119
phi-features, 13, 15, 80, 81, 84, 85, 94–100, 104–106, 112, 115, 116, 129, 135, 136, 140, 238, 264, 265
Pitjantjatjara, 49

Polish, 71
possession, 238–240, 243, 253, 266

Quechua, 14

Rheinischer Akkusativ, *see* Mannheim German
Romance languages, *see also* French, Italian, Romanian, Spanish, 83, 84, 232, 237, 239, 240, 245, 254, 255
– Ibero-Romance, 254
Romanian, 20, 77, 78, 80–89, 92–99, 103, 107, 109, 114, 117–121, 244, 255, 256
– Aromanian, 84
– Megleno-Romanian, 84
Ruwund, 2

Sakha, 128, 141, 155, 167, 238
Salish, *see* Upriver Halkomelem
scales, *see* hierarchies
scrambling, 31
Semitic languages, *see* Amharic, Senaya, Tigre
Senaya, 3, 85, 86
Sino-Tibetan languages, *see* Hayu, Kham
Slavic languages, *see also* Czech, 31, 237
small clauses, 92, 93
Spanish, 3, 4, 12, 16, 35, 37, 83, 245, 252, 254–256, 258, 260, 262, 263, 266, 271
– Porteño Spanish, 83, 258, 263, 266
– Standard Spanish, 258, 263, 266, 267
specificity, *see also* definiteness, hierarchies, 1, 2, 13, 21, 32, 43, 44, 53, 77, 85, 90, 91, 93, 107, 114, 117, 119, 182, 257, 273
spell-out, 8, 212
stringency, *see also* Optimality Theory, 70, 71
subjunctive, 91
Subset Principle, 198
superiority, 31
syncretism, 9, 237, 240, 243, 317, 345

three-way system, *see* tripartite alignment
Tigre, 271
topic, *see also* information structure, 2, 13, 14, 21, 110, 232, 271, 281–283, 287, 292, 295, 296
– external, 271, 281, 283–285, 292, 293, 295–298

– internal, 271, 274, 281, 283–287, 290–295, 297, 299
transitive V–O compound verb construction, 274, 277–280, 284, 285, 288, 289, 291–296
transitivity, 18, 32, 49, 51, 53–55, 138, 140, 141, 151, 153, 157, 160, 162, 166–169, 242, 259–261, 313, 314
tripartite alignment, 28, 29, 48–50, 55, 65
Trumai, 37
Tundra Nenets, 13, 271
Tundra Yukaghir, 9
Turkic languages, *see also* Sakha, Turkish, 129, 166, 239
Turkish, 3, 20, 37, 127, 129, 131, 132, 135, 141, 142, 147, 149–151, 153, 155, 160–164, 166, 167, 169, 171, 180–183, 200, 204, 205, 209, 211, 237

unaccusativity, 94, 169, 185
Upriver Halkomelem, 49
Uralic languages, *see* Estonian, Finnish, Hungarian, Mansi, Khanty, Tundra Nenets

verb copying construction, 271, 274–276, 286, 288–292, 294–297, 299

Warlpiri, 49
Warrangu, 49
word order, *see* constituent order

www.ingramcontent.com/pod-product-compliance
Lightning Source LLC
Chambersburg PA
CBHW030519230426
43665CB00010B/683